Ireland and Irish Emigration
to the New World
from 1815 to the Famine

Ireland and Irish Emigration
to the New World
from 1815 to the Famine

BY
WILLIAM FORBES ADAMS, Ph.D.

Baltimore
GENEALOGICAL PUBLISHING CO., INC.
1980

Originally published by
Yale University Press
New Haven, 1932
Copyright © 1932
By Yale University Press
Copyright © renewed 1960
By Lucy Wilcox Adams
All Rights Reserved
Reprinted by Genealogical Publishing Co., Inc.
Baltimore, 1980
By arrangement with Lucy Wilcox Adams
Library of Congress Catalogue Card Number 79-90753
International Standard Book Number 0-8063-0868-0
Made in the United States of America

PREFACE

THE peculiar destiny of the Irish race, forever separated from, yet forever circumscribed by its Anglo-Saxon neighbors in two continents, has fascinated authors of many races, but without producing any authoritative studies of the Irish in Europe and America. To trace a portion of this destiny and its place in the history of three nations is the first purpose of this study. The second is to illuminate that transition period in human migrations, largely neglected by its students, from pioneer movements of population to the controlled and regimented emigrant trade of our own day. Minor aims are best explained by the history of the work. It originated in a study of Irish influence on Anglo-American relations, undertaken at Stanford University in 1920. The investigation of Irish economic background, of the emigrant trade, and of British policy occupied a year of residence at Oxford in 1923-1924. The American end was taken up in ensuing years at Yale University. The whole was written and amplified during 1928-1929 in Ireland and London, where I was enabled, by the aid of a grant from the Sterling Memorial Fellowships Fund, to complete the work as a dissertation in partial fulfilment of the requirements of the Graduate School in Yale University for the degree of doctor of philosophy. Since that time it has been entirely rewritten with considerable new material on the American consequences of Irish migration. Obviously a research in such broad and varied fields cannot be wholly definitive, and some of the conclusions are admittedly tentative. The certainty of the judgments given decreases from the chapter on government policy through the story of the immigrant trade and Irish social and economic life to that portion of the last chapter dealing with American effects, a thorough study of which would take me far beyond the scope of the present work.

Acknowledgments of obligations running back over ten years might fill a chapter; I shall mention only the greatest. To three men I can pay tribute only in memory: to my father, who first made history live for me and who aroused my interest in the field of this book; to Sir Charles Lucas, for his friendship and the wealth of his knowledge of colonial affairs, always freely given; and to Mr. Hubert Oldham, late Professor of Statistics at the National University, Dublin, for personal favors and his invaluable guidance through the mazes of Irish economic literature. It is happier to acknowledge the aid of living friends. Professor Charles M. Andrews has given me innumerable suggestions and ideas and the encouragement of his friendship, in addition to such supervision as this work has had. Professor Henry M. Fairchild generously opened to me his bibliography on immigration. Professor Samuel E. Morison while at Oxford gave me valuable introductions to Irish history; and Mr. Hubert Hall, in addition to making me familiar with the facilities of the Public Record Office, has created a personal obligation which I cannot hope to repay. My colleague, Mr. J. W. Olmsted, has read proof for the entire volume. I wish also to thank the librarians and staffs of the Public Record Office, of the National Library, Royal Irish Academy, and Trinity College, Dublin, and of the Linen Hall Library, Belfast; Mr. Leftwich, Librarian of the London Custom House, Mr. Kennedy, Librarian of the Macrae-McGee College, Londonderry, Dr. Farrand, Captain Haselden and others of the Huntington Library; and the officers and staffs of the Los Angeles Public Library and the

University of California Library, who have granted special facilities for the completion of this work. With deepest gratitude I would add that it would never have been completed without the aid of Doctors E. Terry Smith of Hartford, Connecticut, Jerome B. Thomas of Palo Alto, California, and A. Ray Irvine of Los Angeles. Friends will recognize that the greatest obligation of all is omitted, in deference to a wish which I cannot disregard.

WILLIAM FORBES ADAMS.

Los Angeles, California.
  March, 1932.

CONTENTS

MAPS

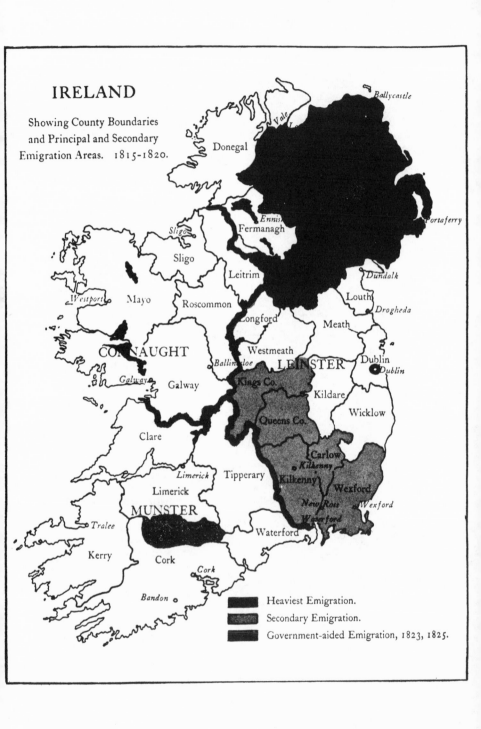

IRELAND

Showing County Boundaries
and Principal and Secondary
Emigration Areas. 1815-1820.

Ballycastle

Vale

Donegal

Portaferry

Sligo

Sligo

Ennis
Fermanagh

Dundalk

Leitrim

Louth

Westport

Mayo

Roscommon

Drogheda

Longford

Meath

CONNAUGHT

Westmeath

Dublin

Ballinasloe

LEINSTER

Dublin

Galway

Kings Co.

Galway

Kildare

Queens Co.

Wicklow

Clare

Carlow

Kilkenny

Limerick

Tipperary

Kilkenny

Wexford

Limerick

New Ross

Wexford

MUNSTER

Tralee

Waterford

Waterford

Kerry

Cork

Cork

Bandon

Heaviest Emigration.

Secondary Emigration.

Government-aided Emigration, 1823, 1825.

CHAPTER I

IRELAND IN 1815

Erin, the tear and the smile in thine eyes,
Blend like the rainbow that hangs in the skies:
Shining through sorrow's stream,
Sad'ning through pleasure's beam,
Thy suns with doubtful gleam,
Weep while they rise.

THOMAS MOORE.

I.

FIFTEEN hundred years ago, the Teutonic tribes poured into the decaying Roman Empire under the pressure of a Mongol horde. Five centuries later Norse pirates, driven from their strongholds by the growing power of monarchy, streamed south from their bays and fjords and set up new kingdoms and dynasties from the Baltic to the Mediterranean. Today, millions of Chinese seek in Manchuria a refuge from the Four Horsemen who ravage the Middle Kingdom. Probably every other great movement of population has had behind it a similar drive. The forces of expulsion have been greater than those of attraction; the emigrants have fled from a known evil to a hoped-for good. The European emigration of the early nineteenth century is no exception to this rule. War, followed by chaos, with its attendant want and misery, was a social solvent no less powerful in 1815 than in 1648 or 1918. The process was nowhere so apparent as in Ireland, where the age-old burden of alien rule inflamed every grievance and retarded every remedy. Ireland, which for centuries had lain outside the main currents of European life, suffered comparatively little during the long campaigns of the Napoleonic Wars, but it caught the full impact of peace-time disorganization and turbulence. The scourges of disease, famine, and civil disorder descended with pitiless regularity upon the land, and in the half century that followed, three million of its citizens left the country. Ireland had already formed ties with the United States only less strong than those of Great Britain, and it was to America that the victims looked as to a promised land.

The compelling motive behind this great shift of population, the most momentous in the first half of the nineteenth century, was distress. Other factors—familiarity with the attractions of America, and an established interest in the carrying of passengers—played their part,[1] but it is in the state of Ireland that we must look first for the causes of emigration, as well as for the background of character and opinion that shaped the destinies of a million emigrants.

It is not easy to reconstruct the Ireland of this period. All observers were struck by the wild squalor and by the savagery of agrarian conflict, but few discerned the currents that were flowing underneath. Her own writers have preferred to dwell on the legendary glories of Cuchulain and Deirdre rather than on the flamboyant vulgarity of O'Connell and his mob. The imaginations of thousands of high spirited young Englishmen were fired

[1] S. von Walterhausen (*Handwörterbuch der Staatswissenschaften*, II, 77) gives first place to the desire for better things rather than the pressure of need in promoting emigration. I agree with Ferenczi (*International migrations*, I, 83) that European conditions came first. Saffell's contention (*Immigration problems*, pp. 148-149) that commissions from transportation interests outweighed all other factors between 1835 and 1860 is tenable for Ireland for those years, but inapplicable to the formative period preceding, and very dubious for the post-famine rush.

by the revolutionary movements on the continent, but they failed to see in the rick burnings and farmhouse attacks in Ireland anything but the festering of old sores. No leader came forward to interpret the conflict. Tom Moore was an expatriate by choice and interest, O'Connell a demagogue. The racy and amusing novels of Lady Morgan and Charles Lever illumine only a small corner of the Irish scene. Among more sober chroniclers, no one equalled the insight of Arthur Young or the accumulated knowledge of Wakefield; but the wars altered Young's Ireland beyond recognition, and the peace soon modified the accuracy of Wakefield's account of 1812. For the next thirty years descriptions of Ireland came mainly from the pens of professional travellers—usually foreigners.[2] It is from such unsatisfactory sources, and from the distorting medium of parliamentary reports and the papers of statesmen, that we have to construct our picture of Ireland in 1815, and discover the causes and facts of emigration.[3]

First among these was pressure of population. Into a country of twenty million acres,[4] of which only thirteen and a half millions were useful land, were crowded over

[2] The best informed of these, Gustave Beaumont, was unfortunately too close to the political leaders of his day to escape their bias. He was aided by Thomas Drummond, Under-Secretary for Ireland, and by prominent Irish Nationalists.

[3] Most modern writers on Ireland follow Lecky in subordinating economic and social history to political. The chief exception is Professor George O'Brien's *Economic history of Ireland from the Union to the Famine* (hereafter cited as O'Brien). My principal objection to this work, aside from its obviously propagandist nature, is to the indiscriminate use of unreliable sources. D. A. Chart, *Ireland from the Union to Catholic Emancipation*, and James O'Connor, *History of Ireland*, are better but too brief.

[4] English or Statute Acres. The Irish acre was larger—121 Irish acres equalled 196 English. Most statements as to rents, size of farms, etc., are in Irish acres, but in some cases it is impossible to tell which are indicated.

six million people.[5] By 1821, the density of population was greater than in any other European country;[6] and by 1845 the numbers had swelled to over eight millions. There had been too many people for the land during the eighteenth century when grazing kept down the numbers who could be employed, but never such congestion as in 1815. We have no accurate statistics for earlier times, but probably there were not more than four and a half million people in Ireland in 1790.[7] The rapid increase which started about 1785 and continued for fifty years, unlike the contemporaneous increase in England, owed little to the Industrial Revolution. It has been attributed to many different causes—to the desire of landlords to increase the number of their tenantry, to the influence of the priests, to the bounties to soldiers during the wars—but the best explanation lies in the rise of small tillage farms, accelerated by the repeal in 1785 of the laws which prevented Roman Catholics from holding land. The new farmers had too little capital to pay money wages and gave land to their laborers, who became property holders for the first time. Periodic higher wages, increased employment, possession of land, and the absence of education to increase their wants encouraged the cotters to marry earlier; while war prices, army employment, and the recklessness common in war periods aided in the spread of improvidence. These conditions ceased in 1815, but peasant habits were already well established.

The six millions of Irish were fairly evenly distributed throughout the good lands of the island. In each of the four provinces there were over a million inhabitants, in

5 Just above that of the Netherlands, *Edinburgh Review*, XLI, 386. (Jan., 1825.)

6 The estimate of the unofficial and incomplete ''census'' of 1813 was 5,937,856. There was no complete census before 1821, and no accurate census before 1841.

7 Bushe's estimate put the number at 4,040,000 in 1788.

none more than two millions. Ulster, with its manufacturing, supported 368 persons per square mile of arable,[8] Munster and Connaught 320, and Leinster 255. In the years that followed, the increase in the western provinces was so rapid that they soon approached the condition of Ulster. In 1841 the figure for Ulster was 434, for Connaught 411, for Munster 396, and for Leinster 281. The low average in Leinster arose from the number of large grazing farms in that province, and remarks about dense and rapidly growing settlement apply to it only in part.[9] Throughout the other three provinces, and to a less extent in Leinster, there existed what Lecky called "a dense improvident, impoverished and anarchical population,"[10] and Halévy, "a vast proletariat, ignorant, miserably poor, superstitious and disorderly."[11] Even in 1815 it could be called redundant, surpassing the numbers which Ireland with the best application of its resources could then decently support; and it did not cease to be redundant until the great emigrations of the next half century brought it once more below the level of 1815.[12]

[8] In Ireland "arable" meant land fit for either tillage or grazing.

[9] I have constructed these tables from various census returns of population and the table of arable, by counties, in the census of 1841. The extent of arable would have been slightly less in 1821, but the reclamation of waste was not sufficient to cause any appreciable change. There are no accurate returns of arable before 1841. The Census Commissioners in that year compiled a table of density of rural population, excluding towns of more than two thousand. I exclude only Dublin and Belfast, since with these exceptions the towns and cities of Ireland, even the ports, were absolutely dependent on agriculture, and their inhabitants a part of the one dominant industry, the raising and marketing of agricultural produce. See *Parl. Pap.* 1843, No. 504, p. xiii.

[10] *History of Ireland in the eighteenth century,* V, 426.

[11] *History of the English people in 1815,* p. 409.

[12] This doctrine is unpalatable to Irish patriots, and has been denounced by Professor O'Brien, whose opinion has recently been accepted by W. A. Carrothers (*Emigration from the British Isles,* p. 41); but it has overwhelming support, *inter alia* from Horace Plunkett (quoted in *Edinburgh Re-*

The dominant industry, supporting directly or indirectly no less than ninety per cent of the population, was agriculture. From 1815 to 1845 there was no fundamental change in its character, or in the social organization of the rural population. The gradual improvement in farming methods, copied tardily from England, did not reach the great body of small occupiers, whose prosperity and quality declined as their numbers increased. The census of 1841 showed sixty-six per cent of the people employed primarily in agriculture, twenty-four per cent in other activities, of which trade (largely concerned with farm products) accounted for the greatest number. In 1815 there were fewer manufactures, and most of those engaged in spinning and weaving were farmers as well. At least seven-eighths of the inhabitants lived in the country itself. A few lived in villages on the great estates, after the English style, but the great bulk in cabins or houses on their own holdings.[13]

All the land was owned by a superior class, and almost all of it was leased or rented to the lower orders of farmer and cotter, very little being kept in demesne. The typical landlord was an owner of large estates—a gentleman, ill-educated, but generally honorable and respected, fond of the pleasures of the turf and the table, and intensely jealous of his own position. The squireen of Maria Edgeworth's *Castle Rackrent* was a more common figure, but he did not control any large proportion of the land, and small holdings owned by the occupier were almost unknown outside the county of Wexford. The island was the preserve of a landed aristocracy, most of whom were members of the Irish peerage, led as of old by the Fitzgeralds (Dukes of Leinster). A considerable

view, CCXXXVI, p. 122), and the scholarly study of G. T. Griffith, *Population problems of the age of Malthus*, pp. 45-88.

13 Census of 1841, *Parl. Pap.* 1843, No. 504, pp. xvii-xviii.

number were absentees who owned large estates in Great
Britain and rarely if ever visited their Irish holdings,
while another and equally important class, among whom
were the great families of Lansdowne and Devonshire,
held estates in both countries and visited their Irish lands
for perhaps three months in the year.

The absentee landlord has long been the villain of the
Irish piece. He has been blamed for much that was worst
in Irish conditions, including some things for which he
was not responsible. The mismanagement of estates was
generally laid at his door, though the weight of testimony
suggests that the character of the agent was more important than the residence of the owner,[14] and residents and
non-residents alike were too often exacting and arbitrary.
The drain from the country of three or four million
pounds a year, spent largely in London, was a real loss;
but the failure to invest any surplus in Ireland, which has
been charged to absenteeism, was largely the result of
insecurity.[15] Its most serious aspect was not economic but
social; the lack of authority and leadership in a country
aristocratic by tradition and in the form of its government.[16] "Such is the dearth of nobility and gentry in Ireland at present," wrote one Irishman in 1818, "that they
are obliged to admit the wives and daughters of the merchants to the Castle, which never was done before."[17] By
failing at his petty court to tickle the vanity of a people
peculiarly susceptible to flattery, and above all, by running away from his duties as grandjuryman and local

14 Wakefield, *An Account of Ireland, statistical and political* (hereafter
cited as Wakefield), I, 259-260, 269, 297-299; H. D. Inglis, *Journey throughout Ireland during the spring, summer, and autumn of 1834*, II, 295-296.

15 *Infra*, pp. 44-46.

16 Wakefield, I, 290; J. Pim, *Conditions and prospects of Ireland*, pp.
148-149; G. Beaumont, *Ireland: social, political and religious*, I, 312; see
also section on Absenteeism in O'Brien, pp. 514-525.

17 Henry McDermott to Charles O'Conor, Apr. 30, 1818. *O'Conor Papers*,
in the Huntington Library.

magistrate as well as landlord, the absentee owner contributed to the decay of Ireland, and deserves some measure at least of the opprobrium heaped upon him.

Most estates were managed by an agent, or agents, and the actual business dealings between lord and tenant were few. Even resident landlords were to a great extent cut off from those who held under them. The more popular of them were accustomed to give an annual dinner to their important tenantry, partly as a show of generosity, partly no doubt to promote good feeling, but of ordinary social intercourse there was none. Thackeray's account of an agricultural society dinner at Cork may be taken as a fair picture of relations between the two classes:

To have heard a nobleman, however, who discoursed the meeting, you would have fancied that we were the luckiest mortals under the broiling July sun. He said he could conceive nothing more delightful than to see, "on proper occasions"—"*mind on proper occasions*"—"the landlord mixing with his tenantry; and to look round him at a scene like this, and see *the condescension* with which the gentry mingled with the farmers." Prodigious condescension truly! This neat speech seemed to me an oratoric slap in the face to about nine hundred and seventy persons present; and being one of the latter, I began to hiss by way of acknowledgement of the compliment, and hoped that a strong party would have destroyed the harmony of the evening and done likewise. But not one hereditary bondsman would join in the compliment—and they were quite right too. The old lord who talked about condescension is one of the greatest and kindest landlords in Ireland. If he thinks he condescends by doing his duty and mixing with men as good as himself, the fault lies with the latter. Why are they so ready to go down on their knees to my lord? A man can't help "condescending" to another who will persist in kissing his shoe strings. They respect rank in England—the people seem almost to adore it here.[18]

18 *The Irish sketch book*, p. 65.

The landlords have been almost universally blamed for the continuance of evil conditions in Ireland; but one reason for their inertia must have been the practical impossibility of getting a true picture of conditions on the land. The reports of agents were strongly colored by their own interests, and direct complaints from the farmers were so interlarded by servile expressions of loyalty and gratitude, especially during the years immediately after 1815, that the landlord might well have doubted the seriousness of the difficulties to which his attention was called, or the existence of any strong temper among his tenants to take vigorous action to bring about changes. Even when they realized, as the most active resident landlords did, the evils which existed, they were often so hampered by local and other restrictions that it was almost impossible to bring about improvements.

Over half the landlords held their estates in entail and were no more than tenants for life. They could not sell without the consent of the eldest son after he had reached his majority, and in most cases could not raise money on the land for purposes of improvement, nor guarantee to a tenant the fruits of his improvements.[19] The holdings themselves were often badly divided and in many cases subject to long-term agreements which could not be changed. Typical holdings throughout a large part of Ireland were for a period of 21 years, or three lives.[20] The

[19] *Transaction of the Central Relief Committee of the Society of Friends during the Famine in Ireland*, p. 112; *Digest of Evidence taken before Her Majesty's Commissioners of inquiry into the state of the law and practice in respect to the occupation in Ireland*, I, 231-232. (Hereafter cited as *Digest of Evidence, Devon Commission.*)

[20] Professor O'Brien and most other writers speak of the one year tenancy as the rule, but this can only be by including the great horde of subtenants over whom the landlords had no control. The great bulk of the land was held in the first place on long leases, until the forties when the annual lease became more common. The accounts of the Buckingham estates in four counties for 1819 show most of the tenants holding on leases to 1829 and

change in the whole agricultural situation brought about
by the fall in the price of grain after 1815 caused these
long leases and other restrictions to bear heavily on landlord as well as farmer. It is not surprising therefore that
when opportunity presented itself at the expiration of a
lease, the proprietor usually took advantage of it to consolidate his holdings and evict non-paying tenants. This
was made comparatively easy by reason of the fact that
rents were normally in arrears at least six months, and
in many places two years. This custom, known as the
"hanging gale," existed through most of Ireland, and
was common among many of the better class farmers as
well as the poorer tenants.[21] The desire to consolidate
later brought many landlords to look favorably on emigration,[22] but in 1815 when war psychology dominated the
minds of the upper classes this was not true. They wanted
the pauper tenant off their lands but not out of the
country.[23]

During the wars the demand for grain, particularly
wheat, had brought about a considerable increase in the
total acreage under grain, and the rent of all lands that
could be used for such purposes jumped to unprecedented
figures. With the drop in prices after the war, when wheat
fell from ninety shillings gold in 1813 to sixty-three shillings in 1815, tenants were incapable of paying these
increased amounts, and many landlords were forced to
make reductions of from twenty-five to fifty per cent, and
even then found it necessary to forego overdue payments

1840; the 1827 and 1832 accounts are much the same, whereas in 1848 all
but one tenant in Clare and Longford were renting from year to year.—
O'Conor Papers.

21 Wakefield, I, 244; O'Brien, pp. 108-109.

22 *Parl. Pap.* 1836, IV, Poor Inquiry (Ireland) Part II, 39-40.

23 *Report of the association for promoting the employment of the poor in
the county of Kilkenny,* p. 3.

from earlier years. This brought about a serious diminution in income, and some of the largest proprietors found
it difficult if not impossible to maintain the luxurious
style of living to which the prosperous years of the war
had accustomed them. The Duke of Devonshire, whose
war-time income had been £12,000 a year, found himself
considerably distressed; while a young man who had been
receiving £8,000 from his lands collected only £200 for
the latter half of 1815, and was forced to flee to France
to escape the debtors prison.[24] Some landlords—a sufficient number of them to bring odium upon the whole class
—preferred to retain the high rentals and resorted to
extreme exactions in an effort to collect them. In 1816 and
1819, they secured new acts to facilitate evictions, and
increase their powers to distrain, the usual methods of
forcing the payment of rent. Under these acts the legal
cost of an eviction was reduced to forty-five shillings, or
about one-quarter of the cost in England.[25]

Meanwhile, the decline in grain prices was much more
rapid than in provisions or Irish meat. Lands which during the wars had been converted from pasture to tillage,
now became more profitable as pasture, and canny proprietors soon realized that they would have a surer, and
in the end a greater, income from lands let out for grazing purposes. Such farms were of course much larger
than tillage farms and reduced the number of tenants
upon a property. This change, stimulated by a number of
improvements in stock breeding,[26] was particularly evident in Limerick, Tipperary, and the border counties between Leinster and Ulster which before the war had been
the great grazing centers of Ireland.

[24] Lady Arundell (Mary Grenville) to Charles O'Conor, Feb. 16, 1816.—
O'Conor Papers.

[25] Digest of Evidence, Devon Commission, II, 828.

[26] O'Brien, pp. 34, 52-54.

The natural result of this effort to wring from the land
a greater income than it was capable of yielding was
extreme hardship for all agricultural classes. The man
who evicted a good tenant for failure to continue paying
a high rent often accepted in his place a poorer type who
was willing to promise more than he could pay,[27] and thus
contributed to the progressive degradation of the Irish
farming classes so often commented on between 1815 and
1845.

The Irish gentleman derived a considerable part of his
income from the land, but he was not altogether dependent upon it, nor were his interests wholly confined to it.
Politics engaged his attention almost equally with his
duties as a proprietor, and in many cases he was a share-
holder in the British government.[28] Most of the Irish
peers had been deprived by the Act of Union of any
hereditary seat in parliament, but all the principal families had some weight in the choice of the representative
Irish peers, and exercised paramount influence in elections to the House of Commons. Interest in elections was
a vital financial concern. A family which was losing
money on lands held by poor tenants could often, through
the votes of those same tenants, exert such influence as to
recompense them for losses on their estates. The Government paid £15,000 a seat to the owners of boroughs
disfranchised at the Union, when seats sold for £2,000 for
the duration of a parliament; and the value of those that
remained increased considerably. County seats had an
even higher value, since official patronage was usually
distributed by county members.[29] The decline after 1815

27 P. Ryan, *Prize essay of the Royal Irish Academy*, 1822, p. 61; O'Brien,
pp. 89-90.
28 The Irish invested £2,000,000 a year in government securities. W. N.
Hancock, *Is there really want of capital in Ireland?* pp. 9-10.
29 E. Porritt, *The unreformed House of Commons*, I, 341; II, 296-298,
315, 361-366, 481-492. It was not unusual to see in Irish papers advertise-

in the number of official positions in the gift of the great political families, especially the decline in the number of army and navy commissions, was a grievance of many Irish landlords.

This valuable political influence had two important effects on the landlord. In the first place, since it could best be exerted in London, it caused many of the important proprietors to become absentees. In the second place, it rendered them more willing to retain unprofitable tenants, and thereby hindered the most economical use of the land.[30] So long as the forty shilling freeholder remained an important political figure, that is until 1829, this interest acted as a check upon the tendency to evict. After the abolition of the forty shilling franchise, as a part of the measures which are generally grouped and called Catholic Emancipation, evictions in this class became distinctly more numerous.

While political influence at Westminster belonged only to the greater landlords, all the gentry of Ireland shared in very extensive political power at home. It might almost be said that they were the political power. The Lord Lieutenant and his court in Dublin represented the wishes of the British cabinet, but for the carrying out of their schemes as well as the information upon which their plans were based, they were almost entirely dependent upon the Irish gentry. The whole enforcement of law rested in their hands. In 1815 there was no Irish police establishment outside of Dublin, and the militia or yeomanry who were scattered throughout the country in

ments begging aid from important families in securing government offices. One such plea promised ''three hundred thanks'' to the lady or gentleman securing the advertiser a prominent government post.

[30] Wakefield, I, 302. A table of forty shilling freehold voters shows that this tendency was most marked in Connaught. Munster and Ulster have about an equal proportion, while in Leinster this class was comparatively small.

fairly large numbers could only act when called out by the Justice of the Peace or Resident Magistrate. The Resident Magistrates were the landlords, and where there was no resident landholder there was no government official. There are instances of districts sometimes eighty square miles in extent which were without an administrative officer.[31]

As members of the grand jury, which levied all local assessments, the large landholders controlled local financial affairs. They had, moreover, almost complete control of justice, since only landholders served on the grand jury, through which all county presentments passed. This control was checked in some degree by the influence of the presiding judge who rode circuit from Dublin, and whose point of view represented the administration. The great defect in the judicial system, from the standpoint of the gentry, lay in the fact that the petty juries were largely composed of members of the lower classes. While the grand jury could often protect members of its own class by failing to bring an indictment against them, it could not always secure the punishment of agrarian disturbers, who were quite as frequently protected by their friends on the petty juries. This, in a country where there was continuous agrarian friction, too often brought about the complete failure of the judicial system.[32] Only in time of serious disturbance of the peace, when the terms of the Insurrection Act were put into force, did the central government interfere directly in the control of local affairs. There was no year between 1815 and 1823 when this act was not in operation in some part of Ireland, but the

31 See the complaint from Banbridge in the *Belfast News Letter*, June 12, 1818.

32 Jurors were not, like prosecutors and informers, in danger of mob intimidation, but they frequently sympathized with the accused. Unanimity in trials for religious rioting was secured, up to 1835, by the simple practice of ruling out Catholic jurors as fast as their names were drawn.

greater part of the country was under the normal jurisdiction of the gentry.

Before 1826 landlords as a class had little direct effect
upon emigration, though their opinions were not without
weight. They determined to some extent the government
policy, and at home they could encourage or discourage
the emigrating spirit among their superabundant tenantry. There came a time when many of them were glad
to pay the passage to America for dispossessed tenants
who had otherwise not sufficient means of emigrating. But
in 1815 the war was still uppermost in their minds. Tenants, however poor and miserable, were a source of
strength to the country, and to encourage emigration was
treason. The United States—the customary goal of emigrants—was by tradition and interest the natural enemy,
the last great exponent of Jacobinical democracy and
mob rule, and destined to renewed conflict with Great
Britain in the near future. The London *Times* in 1815
spoke of the encouragement of Irish emigration as ". . .
a plot of a most treasonable kind," while the *Sun* expressed this vivid opinion:

The minds of the ignorant are acted on by every means which
treachery and falsehood can invent; the disaffected part of the
Press is zealously at work; every disloyal engine is employed
which can delude the mistaken population of the Sister Island
into a persuasion, that an earthly Paradise exists on the other
side of the Atlantic.

We know not what measures Government have taken, or may
take, to counteract this conspiracy. Something, and something
effective, must be done; for the mischief is great; and the evil
hideous. Were it only the Catholic Agitators—the now idle Board
—the Spouters at Public meetings—and the secret organizers of
Caravats, Carders, and other midnight Assassins, who desired to
enter into nearer fellowship with kindred spirits elsewhere—
with the semi-savages of Kentucky, and the scalping Heroes of

the United States, we should advise our rulers to provide them food, clothing, ships, and a premium on exportation; but we should lament for the sake of individuals who might be misled by these tempters, were any considerable number of the People to be deceived into this fatal experiment.[33]

Irishmen did not often go as far as this, but several of the Irish papers quoted these extracts with approval, and except in parts of Ulster, where emigration was an old and accepted habit, the landlord who looked on it favorably was a marked exception.

II.

BENEATH the proprietary class, and almost wholly cut off from it by economic and social barriers, lived the great mass of the rural population, the farmers and agricultural laborers. The prevalence of very small holdings made the farmers the more numerous group, but the greater uniformity in character of the laborers, and the far-reaching effects of their competition and their habits upon all other classes, give to their condition of life first place in a description of the background of Irish immigration.

In 1815 the laborers formed a vast coherent mass of from two to three million people. All of them, if we except servants living in the houses of the farmers or gentry, were cotters holding a cabin and little or no land. This cotter peasantry, though legally on a par with the British, actually occupied an intermediate position between the peasants of England and the semi-servile laborers of Prussia and Russia. In England the Poor Law, while it tied the laborer to his parish, secured him subsistence even though he had no land and no employment. Ireland had no Poor Law, and the landless man, outside the cities,

[33] *Dublin Evening Post*, January 9, 1815.

was forced to beg, steal or starve. The beginnings of the Industrial Revolution, which offered new employment to English and Scottish agricultural laborers, exerted little influence in Ireland in 1815.

Agricultural employment, which was scarce enough everywhere in 1815, was particularly bad in Ireland. This was not a new feature of Irish history. Even during the prosperous years of the Napoleonic Wars there had been an over-supply of labor, and wages had remained low. The normal day's wage throughout most of the island was sixpence, together usually with one meal, or eightpence without. In northeastern Ulster the rate was higher, but except during harvest time, when wages rose as high as a shilling a day, the laborer could not expect more than tenpence anywhere.[34] Cotter tenants frequently paid a part of their rent in labor, and in that case often received less than the standard rate of pay.[35] This would have been sufficient to provide a fair subsistence if they had been able to count on continuous employment. As it was, most laborers were unemployed for half the year,[36] and not more than one out of three had steady work.[37] Low wages, lack of legal provision for the poor, and the uncertainty of any monetary income at all made the Irish peasant absolutely dependent upon such food supply as he could raise for himself, and do much to account for the traditional tenacity with which he clung to his tiny holding.[38]

[34] Wakefield, I, 379-420 passim, 511; Parl. Pap. 1826-1827, No. 550, Evidence Select Committee on Emigration, pp. 267-271; Parl. Pap. 1836, No. 43, Third Report Poor Inquiry Commission, p. 3; Digest of Evidence, Devon Commission, I, 475-476.

[35] S. Nicholson, Report on the general state of agriculture in the district of country adjoining the Middle Shannon, p. 59.

[36] Parl. Pap. 1826-27, No. 550, pp. 267, 440; Parl. Pap. 1836, No. 43, pp. 5, 12.

[37] G. C. Lewis, On local disturbances in Ireland, p. 312.

[38] "The land in the country resembles a fortress eternally besieged and

From 1815 to 1845 the cotter relied almost wholly upon his potato patch for subsistence,[39] and his holding was rarely used for any other purpose than the raising of potatoes for himself, his family, and his pig. The pig was his one regular source of income, and as such an important figure in Irish economy. The old saying "the pig pays the rent" was an exaggeration however. The price of pork on the hoof remained fairly low throughout most of the period after 1815, and though the animal usually paid a part of the rent he could not pay it all,[40] and in lean years did so only at the expense of hunger and almost starvation for his owner.

An estimate of a cotter's annual budget made in 1814 shows earnings of £13 over and above rent and the cost of a young pig.[41] This estimate assumes the unheard of blessing of labor at a shilling a day throughout the year. Taking wages at eightpence and the selling price of a pig at the usual thirty shillings, the surplus earnings are reduced to £8, with which to pay for clothing, food (herrings and perhaps salt), whisky, tobacco and religious dues. Another estimate, in 1834, allowing for average employment (half the year) gives earnings of £6.1.4., a part of which would have to go towards paying the rent.[42] There were, of course, vast numbers who made much less.[43] As the normal rate of passage to North America

defended with indefatigable ardour; there is no safety unless within its precincts." Beaumont, *Ireland*, I, 299. There is an excellent discussion of the evil effects of this absolute dependence on land in G. C. Lewis, *On local disturbances in Ireland*, pp. 78-85, 308.

[39] The spectacle of six or seven millions of people sustained by a potato diet is more easily understood in the light of Wakefield's estimates that the average yield was over ten tons per acre. Tables in Wakefield, I, 370-406.

[40] In many cases the rent was paid in labor. Then the pig bought the clothing, or perhaps tobacco and whisky. *Parl. Pap.* 1826, No. 404, Evidence, Committee on Emigration, p. 128.

[41] *The interests of Ireland*, p. 41.

[42] Inglis, *Journey throughout Ireland*, II, 300.   [43] O'Brien, pp. 19-20.

shortly after 1815 was from six guineas up, emigration was almost impossible for this class.

The average rental of fair or good potato land in all parts of Ireland except the extreme west fluctuated between £6 and £10 an acre.[44] In the west, where rents were usually somewhat lower, this advantage was offset by the greater scarcity of employment, and the distance of any market to which the family rent provider could be taken. Everywhere the cotter paid in exorbitant rental for the necessity of holding some land. In bad years, and indeed during most of the period following 1815, large numbers of laborers failed to pay the rent to which they had agreed. In such cases, those who held from the proprietors or larger farmers were likely to receive more consideration than those who held from the petty farmers.[45] Cottage tenures were only let from year to year and tenants had no legal claim to retain their holdings for more than the twelvemonth even if they paid the rent. Competition for land continually pushed the rent to the maximum figure, and kept even the best of the laborers on the verge of ruin. Farm consolidation after 1815 increased the pressure, though some of the evicted settled on waste lands and others went into the towns.[46] Under such conditions there was no incentive to improve the small holding

[44] *Parl. Pap.* 1826, No. 404, pp. 128-208.

In Connaught and Munster, and to a less extent elsewhere, potato ground was frequently let under the conacre system, where the lessor supplied the fertilizer or manure and prepared the ground, while the tenant supplied the seed and all subsequent labor and took the crop. Conacre rents rose as high as £14 to the acre, but the average was £10. Many writers have dwelt on the viciousness of this system, asserting that it bore heavily upon the poor tenant, but it is difficult to see how tenure of this type was more burdensome to the peasant than other cottage tenure. It was simply a bigger gamble. The conacre holder paid more on the chance of a better crop, and if the season was good he got it.

[45] *Digest of Evidence, Devon Commission,* I, 475.

[46] O'Brien, pp. 52-56.

for the future, and every reason for taking out of the ground all that it would yield in a single year. This was one of the causes for the decreasing productivity of all land held under small tenure during the first half of the nineteenth century.[47]

Neither hope for the future nor memories of the past encouraged the cotter to improve his lot. Even if he were able through good fortune to save a little, there were almost insuperable obstacles to his rising into the farmer class. The progressive increase of rents, which accompanied a steadily and rapidly growing population, in most cases wiped out the savings of any one year in the years following. Laborers and small farmers could not get money from the banks and were forced when they needed it to borrow from local usurers at rates up to 100 per cent per annum.[48] Every circumstance conspired to defeat industry and thrift, and to reduce the level of cotter subsistence to the barest minimum of food, shelter, and clothing. Even in the best of times their food had been potatoes, a little milk, and occasional herrings. Some few enjoyed meat at Christmas time, but the majority never tasted it from one year's end to another. As times grew worse after 1815 and fewer cotters could afford to keep a cow, milk too disappeared as a regular part of the diet.[49] In the north oatmeal usually supplemented potatoes, but misery was as prevalent there as elsewhere, and bad harvests frequently brought the people to the verge of starvation.[50] Herrings were easily obtainable off almost all

[47] Most writers agree on this. Lord Ennismore thought this class of tenant not harmful, but the small farmer of five to ten acres ruinous to the land. Evidence before Emigration Commission, *Parl. Pap.* 1826, IV, No. 404, p. 201.

[48] *Digest of Evidence, Devon Commission*, I, 194-196.

[49] Nicholson, *Agriculture of the Middle Shannon*, p. 57.

[50] *Edinburgh Review*, XXXVII, 105 (June 1822); P. Ryan, *Prize essay of the Royal Irish Academy*, 1822, p. 81.

parts of the Irish coast and from Donegal to Kerry were an essential part of the food of the cotters. They did not, however, improve the standard of life, and those who held tiny tracts along the seacoasts were amongst the poorest of the Irish peasants, and remain so to this day. When fishing is bad, the potato supply is rarely sufficient to maintain them, and the cry of famine which has arisen almost annually in Ireland has usually come first from these poor fishermen.

The peasant's hut has been described so often that it is hardly necessary to add to the number of pictures. Without windows, and in many cases without a chimney, its ventilation was always bad, and not improved by the fact that the whole family, including the pig, generally slept in its one room. Except among the Scots of Ulster it was usually filthy.[51] Sunk low against a damp hillside or a bog which grew up around it,[52] it could neither be dried nor heated by the fire of wet peat, which was all the peasant could afford. Even this poor fuel was not always obtainable. Leaseholdings normally included rights of turbary, but the cotter in many districts had to pay for the turf which he cut himself, and in bad times he did without.[53] Dirt, cold, and bad air made the cabin a breeding ground for disease, and facilitated the spread of epidemics,[54]

[51] J. G. Kohl, *Ireland*, p. 194.

[52] Dr. Sigerson of Dublin, who was on fever relief work in Connemara in the '80's, tells of mounting a little hump in the bog to look for such a hut, when he was startled by a voice beneath his feet crying, ''Arrah, doctor, come down off the roof; the patient's inside.''

[53] Clavering, *Letter to the Duke of Leinster*, p. 14. ''Dry turf makes an excellent fire, but the cottage turf stack is always exposed to the weather and never really dry.''

[54] See W. Harty, *Historic sketch of the contagious fever epidemic in Ireland (1817-19)*, especially p. 187. The principal items of advice to peasants on the prevention of fever are: Remove offal from your cabin; fill up holes in the floor; wash out with soap, water, and lime; get fresh air by breaking down the cabin walls, if necessary; keep out officious neighbors; above all,

which from 1817 on played an important part in promoting emigration.

Education was practically unknown among the cotters. The schools subsidized by the Kildare Street Society of Dublin served only a small part of Ireland, and were under suspicion as agencies for proselytizing to the Protestant church. Roman Catholic hedge schools, taught by the priests, had a spasmodic existence throughout a large part of the country, but their teaching was confined to arithmetic, a few simple matters of religious faith, and legends of the country. These schools were no longer illegal and frequently had school rooms, but they were more remarkable for the extraordinary character of their texts than for the quality of the teachers.[55] In 1821, out of 1,700,000 persons between the ages of six and fifteen, there were only 394,000 school children in all Ireland.[56] Illiteracy was widespread, and in the wilder portions of the country almost universal. The writing of Irish had almost died out, though in Connaught, Longford, and the mountainous parts of Ulster and Munster Irish was the common tongue, and English known only by the gentry. Even after the beginnings of national education in 1831 nearly half the Ulster Protestants could not write their own names.[57]

In manners and customs the Irish peasant was somewhat more backward than his English kinsman. Unchecked by law or by the example of a superior society, his passions had free rein, and the proverbial Irish love of fighting found frequent opportunities for expression,

no wakes. *Londonderry Journal*, Oct. 21, 1817. This last piece of advice was useless. Wakes were amongst the favorite diversions of the peasantry.

[55] Thackeray, *Irish sketch book*, pp. 163-179; *Edinburgh Review*, XXXVII, 87-90 (June 1822); Chart, *Ireland from the Union to Catholic Emancipation*, p. 148.

[56] Census of 1821, *Parl. Pap.* 1824, No. 577, p. 379.

[57] J. Pim, *Journal* of the Dublin Statistical Society, 8th Session, p. 21.

notably at fairs, which were the great gathering places
for clan or faction. Sometimes the ostensible cause was
religious difference,[58] sometimes a family or tribal quarrel,[59] sometimes the local pride of Kerrymen or Limerick-
men,[60] but these were merely the excuses to satisfy an
innate love of fighting. Unfortunately, the brutal instincts
also took a more unpleasant form, and violence to women
was only too frequent in the backward parts of the community.[61] Quarrels in many cases terminated fatally with
the blow of a spade or any handy weapon. More serious
affrays with muskets and swords usually arose out of the
work of secret societies in agitating over religious, and
especially over agrarian, disputes. Prior to the Young
Ireland movement in 1848, however, there was no connection between these disturbances and political treason.

The tendency to passionate crime was aggravated by
the almost universal prevalence of drunkenness in all
parts of.the country. Legally distilled liquor was beyond
the means of the cotters, but poteen, the produce of the
illicit stills, was cheap, and obtainable everywhere. The
Poor Inquiry Commission, after long study, stated:
"Among the many causes of Irish misery which have
been brought under our notice, one of the most prolific,

[58] These were of course most numerous in the counties where Catholics
and Protestants of the poorest class were closely mingled, such as Londonderry, Tyrone, Monaghan and Cavan. See the Address of Judge Day at the
Monaghan Assizes, *Belfast News Letter*, August 9, 1816.

[59] E.g. at Emly in Tipperary the Hogans and the Fitzgeralds arranged a
faction fight. The result was a battle in which over a hundred participated.
Belfast News Letter, Oct. 3, 1820.

[60] "The quarrel is frequently about the merits of their respective counties." Poor Inquiry Commission Report; Section on Crimes. *Parl. Pap.* 1836,
No. 40, p. xx.

[61] There were 159 cases before the police in 1844, over half of them in
the six counties of Mayo, Galway, Tipperary, Kerry, Cork, and Waterford.
Digest of Evidence, Devon Commission, I, 324. Generally such cases did not
reach the police.

assuredly the most pernicious, and, we fear, the most difficult to be reached by any direct legislation, *is the inordinate use of ardent spirits*—its baneful effects are felt by every class.'[62]

Disturbances, organized and unorganized, but particularly the former, had a most disastrous effect upon the prosperity of Ireland. They poisoned the relationship between landlord and peasant, and still more between both these classes and the greater farmer, to whose ranks belonged the loathed middlemen, who took large leases and sublet them at extravagant rents. Landlords protested with justice that they could not give out land at a reasonable rental without these middlemen immediately reletting it at a great advance, and encumbering it with a multitude of pauper tenants. Attempts were made to prevent the practice, but before 1826 clauses in leases forbidding subletting, like those against subdivision, proved unenforceable in the Courts.[63] The break-up of grazing lands into small tillage farms during the war had greatly increased the number of middlemen, and the peasants had come to regard them as necessary, if undesirable, landlords.[64] A man ejected for non-payment was quite likely to take his own land back again from the middleman at an advanced rent.[65] The necessity of leasing from him did not make the middleman more popular, and he was frequently blamed for the whole system of high rents.[66] The

---

[62] *Parl. Pap.* 1836, No. 43, p. 30. There is a full discussion of drunkenness in C. Haliday, *Observations on the habits of the labouring classes in Ireland.*

[63] G. C. Lewis, *On local disturbances in Ireland*, p. 313, note. A farmer took 100 acres, letting out 25 or 30 of it at £4, payable in labor at 6½d. a day. In two years the subtenants would be broken and turned off. Evidence of Odell of Limerick, *Parl. Pap.* 1826, No. 404, pp. 209-210. An effective Act against subletting was passed in 1826, but repealed in 1832 in favor of a less powerful measure.

[64] O'Brien, pp. 43-45.   [65] Wakefield, I, 287-288.

[66] O'Brien, pp. 91-94. He has accepted the accusation as true. There is,

cotter made no distinction between the honest, non-profiteering farmer who took over the land of an evicted tenant, and the middleman whose sole object it was to make a living out of small leases; and the whole farming class shared the hatred incurred by a part.

In its mildest form this hatred showed itself in the form of threats or attacks upon the farmer by the dispossessed or their friends. Such attacks were common to all parts of Ireland with the exception of the extreme western districts already mentioned, and the singularly peaceful county of Wexford.[67] Elsewhere, threatening notices, followed by violence, were frequent after 1815. The usual procedure was first to post a notice warning the new tenant to abandon the farm and remove his animals and other goods within forty-eight hours. If this was not done, and it usually was not, a band of peasants armed with pitchforks and knives, and sometimes with muskets, would appear at the farmer's door on a conveniently dark night. The attackers generally took the precaution of blacking their faces, but the evidence in the trials shows that some of them were usually recognized by the farmer. If the attacking party were simply intent on removing the new occupant, they put coals to the thatch and withdrew to a short distance to await results. But where bad blood had been roused, the attackers stationed themselves outside the house and attempted to pre-

however, much evidence that middlemen were no worse landlords than others. As usual, they suffered from the misdeeds of a few. One of their worst practices was to turn off all subtenants shortly before their own leases expired, lest the proprietor relet direct to the occupiers, thus eliminating the middleman. *Digest of Evidence, Devon Commission;* Wakefield, I, 286 ff.

[67] Wexford was a county of large farms and little excess population, except in the towns, and the seat of a profitable tobacco culture. Its best district, the Barony of Forth, was the home of Welsh farmers who owned their land. J. Pim, *Conditions and Prospects of Ireland,* p. 282, note; O'Brien, pp. 35-36; Kohl, *Ireland,* pp. 120-121.

vent any escape after it had been set on fire. A simpler method was to break down the door and massacre the inhabitants within; but as almost all farmhouses were armed and kept ready for defence, burning was much preferred.

The ejected tenant had no real hope of reoccupying the land, and the purpose of the demonstration was often to prevent the reletting of lands from which evictions had taken place.[68] No such rational explanation was necessary, however. The ejected man had lost his only source of livelihood and instinctively struck back. This type of vindictive crime might be directed against any class of tenant, but the improving farmer suffered most severely. It does not seem to have been effective in preventing the reletting of land, but the frequency of such occurrences unquestionably disturbed the more peaceful farmers, and provided a powerful incentive to emigration. Although in every county sessions, examples were made of offenders, evidence for conviction was difficult to procure in such cases, and the law was powerless to prevent a repetition. The day of the public prosecutor had not yet arrived, and the injured party, if he survived, often dared not prosecute; while the feeling of the peasantry was such that they refused to coöperate in any attempt to bring the criminals to justice.[69]

This was the state of agricultural society in compara-

[68] Prof. O'Brien (pp. 110-111) explains "the so-called agrarian outrages" as attempts to force the incoming tenant to compensate his predecessor for improvements. He is supported by a generalization in the *Digest of Evidence, Devon Commission*, pp. 3-4, but the selection of evidence (pp. 322-362) does not support the assertion. I have examined some 200 cases of agrarian outrage between 1815 and 1825 without finding one in which tenant-right was involved.

[69] E.g. The case of Edward Cassidy at the Monaghan Assizes. Cassidy had been evicted for two years' back rent. The new tenant was burned out. The evidence against Cassidy was clear, but the peasant jury returned a verdict of *Not Guilty*. *Belfast News Letter*, July 21, 1818; *Digest of Evidence, Devon Commission*, I, 320.

tively peaceful periods. At intervals throughout most of Ireland, and almost continuously from 1815 to 1823 in the counties of Limerick, Tipperary, and Clare, there was a condition approaching civil war. Insurrection was not merely the action of a few unfortunate individuals. It was an organized concerted movement in opposition to high rents, to tithes, and especially to evictions, on the part of the whole agricultural population.

It was impossible to do much against the landlord directly. The estates of the gentry were large and usually well protected, and gentlemen travelled armed and with armed retainers. Furthermore, it is doubtful whether in a country with the aristocratic tradition of Ireland, the great mass of peasantry could have been brought to any direct attack upon their lords. Some few attempts on gentlemen's houses did take place, but they were exceptional, and their object was frequently to obtain arms, and not to do any direct damage either to the person or the property of the landlord.

The feelings of the peasantry were inconsistent, after the fashion among ignorant and passionate men. They acknowledged the leadership of the gentry and looked to them for help in time of distress, yet they could be swayed to commit outrages disastrous to the welfare of their lords. Probably the mob never examined beyond the immediate cause of its anger, and struck blindly, not at the proprietor who was responsible, but at the agent who carried out an eviction or levied distress, or at the tenant who replaced an evicted family, choosing rather to attack the farmer against whom their grievances were more direct. Yet the leaders in such organizations as the Whiteboys and the Rockites were themselves substantial farmers.[70] These men doubtless hoped to secure protection for themselves by belonging to the strongest organized power

[70] "Not the lowest"—G. C. Lewis, *On Local Disturbances*, p. 88. See the troubles in County Down, *Belfast News Letter*, Nov. 19, 1816.

in the community, but their avowed objects, the enforced
non-payment of rents and tithes, show that they hoped
for a general agrarian reform.[71] The immediate grievances of the dispossessed were the banners under which
warfare of wider significance was carried on.

The methods of secret societies were much the same as
those practised by individuals. A hundred local Captain
Rocks would post notices threatening destruction to those
who did not quit farms, or who persisted in paying a rent
higher than that agreed upon by the association. Where
these bodies were powerful notices were usually obeyed;
for in cases of opposition violence was sure to follow.
Occasionally they succeeded in getting the landlord's consent to a maximum rent,[72] but such agreements did not
last. The local courts were powerless to deal with this
organized crime, and the activities of the agitators continued unchecked until the gentry of the district found
it necessary, by application to Dublin Castle, to call into
operation the Insurrection Act. A period of violent military repression, and trials by extraordinary tribunal,
would then follow. Sometimes the act was kept in operation for as much as two years at a time, but for the most
part after about six months the district was declared to
be tranquilized, and the normal condition of agrarian
unrest gradually reasserted itself.

Those organizations usually had a religious character,
since it was only by means of religious oaths that the
more ignorant peasantry could be bound to complete

[71] H. Pollard, *Secret Societies of Ireland*, p. 34. Reports of County Assizes in newspapers. It might seem that vindictive attacks on new tenants
differ essentially from general conflicts in the interest of the whole community, but in practice no such distinction is possible. Almost invariably the
new tenant was transgressing some rule of the secret organizations, and vin-
dictiveness found an easy cloak in the necessity of common action against
high rents.

[72] Harty, *Contagious fever epidemic in Ireland*, p. 206, note.

secrecy. The most widespread secret society in Ireland at this time, that of the Ribbonmen, a Roman Catholic group, was strictly religious, with no agrarian purposes,[73] but it was undoubtedly used at times for agrarian ends. The gentry often chose to regard outrages as evidence of religious warfare, and attempted to disguise as protection of the church their efforts to save their incomes.[74] Even in defending tithes they were protecting themselves; for nearly one-third of the value of the tithes claimed by the owners in 1834, when the system was altered, was the property of laymen, and of the remaining parishes, another third was in benefices in the gift of laymen. In Munster and Connaught the proportion was still higher.[75] Religious opposition to tithes was a minor factor,[76] and if they played a small part in Ulster, it was not because Presbyterians objected to them any less than Catholics, but because in most parts of Ulster potatoes were not tithable, whereas in the south the potato tithe was customary.[77] One of the worst features of the tithes was that it varied in character from parish to parish, and the injustice was patent to everyone. Tithes did not become a major issue until 1831, but they shared in the popular hatred, and were usually coupled with rents in any statement of grievances or of causes of emigration.

In general, religious differences had nothing to do with

[73] There are various "secret rituals" to the contrary, all palpably "faked" by government witnesses.

[74] Doubtless many were sincere. It is still easy to stir up a panic over a "Popish Plot" in Ulster.

[75] *Parl. Pap.* 1834, No. 382, *Applications for Relief by Tithe owners, 1831-33; Parl. Pap.* 1824, No. 438, *Benefices and Patronage in Ireland.*

[76] In 1831, the Terry Alts, at war against tithes, ordered the Protestant clergy to increase the pay of their curates. *Belfast News Letter*, May 6, 1831.

[77] Also because tithes fell most heavily on the cotter where grazing and tillage were mixed, pasture being exempt from tithe. Wakefield estimated the value of the potato tithe at six to ten shillings an acre for poor land, and 12 to 14 shillings elsewhere, I, 449. But the tithe was usually paid in kind.

agrarian crime. Catholic farmers were attacked by Catholic peasants, and Presbyterian farmers by Presbyterians. Continuous disturbances of this character slowly drove out of the country, not only the immediate victims, but all who hoped by industry to amass a competence. There were those who chose to fight, and those who preferred to emigrate. During periods of suppression, however, many who had chosen to fight also found it wiser to emigrate. Pacification was usually accomplished only after a few of the leaders, against whom evidence was particularly strong, had turned informers. These then had a choice of shipping to America or awaiting annihilation at home. More hardy spirits emigrated to escape prosecution.[78] Both types came from the better class farmers. Contrary to popular belief,[79] Ulster was not exempt from this sort of agrarian unrest. Though suffering less from organized disturbances than the extreme southwest, the northern counties were as hard hit as most of Leinster, and very much worse than Connaught.[80] Even

[78] See the dispatch, Whitworth to Sidmouth, June 5, 1816, printed in the *Belfast News Letter*, July 5, 1816; also the illuminating chapters, 19 and 20 in Lever's *Harry Lorrequer*.

[79] E.g., Beaumont, II, 14-19. Often repeated by later writers.

[80] A summary of serious agrarian crime, drawn from newspaper accounts, for the years 1815-1822, illustrates very clearly the state of the country. Two counties only, Cavan and Leitrim, had a clean bill for the whole period. Four other counties in the same region of the northwest (Sligo, Fermanagh, Tyrone, and Longford), and four in the south (Cork, Kerry, Wexford, and Wicklow) had no serious outrage before the beginning of general insurrection 1821-22. (Galway would also have belonged to this list had it not been for the folly of magistrates who fired on Ribbonmen merely because the latter were administering oaths.) *Belfast News Letter*, Feb. 11, 1820.

There were two especially disturbed areas: (1) The northern counties of Munster, with Kings County; (2) the five northeastern counties of Leinster. All of these nine counties were under the Insurrection Act at least four of the six years before 1821. These are the two regions in which most tillage land was returning to pasture after the war.

The significance of particular outbreaks will be discussed in the account of emigration.

the County Down, which had long been famous for its industry and comparative prosperity, was the scene of
many agricultural attacks during the years after 1815.[81]

Disturbances were not, as in England during the same
period, confined to mere rick burnings. Irish agrarian
outrage was always characterized by a greater recklessness of life and property and more thorough organization. It would be difficult to overestimate its evil effect. At
its worst it kept society in a state in which improvement was well nigh impossible. Even when there were no
more than two or three outrages in a county in any given
year, the feeling of insecurity induced by them was a serious deterrent to the investment of capital in agriculture.
To the better type of farmer, who had practically no other
field for investment, this was ruinous.

Throughout this period the peasant, who suffered least
from the continuous disturbances, had little opportunity
or incentive to prove his ability as a workman. Long
periods of enforced idleness, a soil which normally secured him sufficient subsistence without strenuous effort,
and the lack of markets for any surplus, doubtless had an
unfortunate effect on his character as a laborer, as contemporary observers frequently pointed out. The following quotations are characteristic:

Another consequence from some of the causes we have stated
is the extreme idleness of the Irish labourer. There is nothing of
the value of which the Irish seem to have so little notion as that
of time. They scratch, pick, dandle, stare, gape, and do anything
but strive and wrestle with the task before them. The most ludi-
crous of all human objects is an Irishman ploughing. . . . The
whole is a scene of idleness, laziness, and poverty, of which it is
impossible in this active and enterprising country, to form the
most distant conception; but strongly indicative of habits,

[81] Report of Down Assizes, *Belfast News Letter*, Aug. 12, 1817. Down also
had serious agrarian troubles in 1816 and 1822.

whether secondary or original, which will long present a powerful impediment to the improvement of Ireland.[82]

Although they (tenants) are idle during the whole winter, and
a great part of spring, the cultivation of their land is generally
late. This leads to late sowing and late reaping, and hence a very
great loss is sustained. One-half of the potato crop is often
planted so late, that sometimes the crop is scarcely worth gathering; and I have often seen part of a good crop ungathered in the
middle of January.[83]

The apologists of the peasant do not deny his idleness,
but attribute it to the evils of a land system which gave
him no hope of improvement,[84] and in truth the record of
the Irish workingman when he went to England or the
United States shows not so much a lack of energy or willingness, as lack of training, sobriety, and persistence.[85]
The natural concomitant of hopeless idleness was improvidence of the type common among the very poor—
early marriages and large families. Most women were
married before they were twenty, men a year or two later.
The priests were said to have encouraged it as a deterrent to immorality,[86] and because they depended for their
living on marriage, baptismal, and other fees;[87] but the
best testimony is that poverty and ignorance were the
real causes.[88] The same factors explain the unusual extent
of mendicancy and petty pilfering. Professional beggars

[82] *Edinburgh Review*, XXXIV, 333-335 (November, 1820).

[83] Nicholson, *Agriculture of the Middle Shannon*, p. 58.

[84] Hancock, W. N., *On laissez faire and the economic resources of Ireland*,
p. 3; O'Brien, pp. 71-74.

[85] G. C. Lewis, Report on the Irish poor in Great Britain, in *Parl. Pap.*
1836, No. 40, pp. xx-xxxii.

[86] E.g. Harty, *Historical sketch of the contagious fever epidemic in Ireland (1817-1819)*, pp. 195-198.

[87] O'Connor, *History of Ireland, 1798-1924*, I, 210.

[88] Bicheno, *Ireland and its economy*, pp. 160-161; Evidence of the Rev.
James Doyle and John Bodkin before the Committees on Emigration, *Parl.
Pap.* 1826, No. 404, p. 347; 1826-27, No. 550, p. 274.

were a distinct class, wandering from place to place, spreading disease and trouble for magistrates.[89] There were few able-bodied men among them, for begging was a disgrace. But every spring and summer cotters' wives and children, and in bad years the cotters themselves, took to the roads to beg enough potatoes to keep them until the new crop was ready. This casual mendicancy was a recognized part of Irish life, and a regular drain upon the charitable portion of the community. Probably it did less harm than the accompanying petty theft which effectually discouraged the growth of root crops, fruit, or anything easily carried away.[90]

Another type of roving has some bearing on the growth of emigration. Since the eighteenth century some of the cotters had been in the habit of going to England for the harvest. At times whole families left their land, but the women and children were usually left at home to look after the potatoes, while the men went in search of employment across the Irish Channel. This seasonal migration was the one influence tending to weaken the connection between the peasant and his land, and therefore an important agency in promoting emigration. In 1815 when facilities for crossing the Irish Sea were undeveloped and transportation was by means of small vessels, whose sailings might be delayed a week or more by adverse winds, and whose fares were a serious obstacle, the movement was not very important. The rush of Irish labor to England, which began in the twenties, was a result of the

[89] Harty, *Historical sketch of the contagious fever epidemic in Ireland*, p. 5.

[90] I have seen trees in Connemara hacked to stumps by peasants who wanted wood. The gentleman who owned them had tried in vain to raise both timber and fruit. On the whole subject see G. C. Lewis, *On local disturbances in Ireland*, p. 311; and his report in *Parl. Pap.* 1836, No. 40, pp. xxi-xxii.

development of steam communication between the two kingdoms.

One group of cottagers stood apart from the rest. These were the farm servants of the landlords. Their small garden plots were usually held in return for service, although sometimes there was a money rent as well. Their wages were as low or lower than the standard of the district, but thanks to continuity of employment their condition was never so desperate as that of the other laborers, and they were generally looked upon as a fortunate class. Occasional gratuities from their employers, and the practice of paying them annually or semi-annually—one of the payments falling in May during the height of the emigrant season when sailings were cheap—put them in a better position than most cotters for emigration. In general, however, the laborers of this period were too apathetic, too ignorant, too poor, and too home-loving to seek escape from their conditions.

III.

THROUGHOUT most of Ireland there existed between the ranks of the gentry and this lowest type of peasantry a populous farming class, the source of almost all the emigrants to America before 1815, and of a majority of them until 1830. A few, including the yeoman graziers of Kildare and the hated middlemen of the south, approached the lesser gentry in wealth, though not in rank or public esteem. These did not number ten per cent of the whole, and the great mass of the farmers were holders of thirty acres or less, often indistinguishable from the laborers either in welfare or housing. They were set apart, nevertheless, both in the minds of the people and in their legal condition. While some held for one, three, or seven years, normal farm tenure was for a period of twenty-one years or longer, and this in itself secured them a more certain place in the community than that held by the cotter. A lease for twenty-one or thirty-one years and three lives, which was the commonest form, created a freehold, giving the occupier a vote and increasing his social importance. It is true that at the end of a long lease this holding had often become so subdivided among members of the family, or even sublet in part to others, that the individual plot of each man was no larger than a cottage garden, and his condition little better than that of the laborer.

In most parts of Ireland subdivision was made worse by the prevalence of the rundale system, under which subtenants held scattered patches or strips after the mediaeval plan of sharing good and bad land. Landlords often refused to recognize subdivision, and treated such lands as though they were partnership leases (which also existed independently), holding each tenant responsible for the rent of all, and so forcing the industrious to support the idle. The results were disastrous. Crops deteriorated twenty-five per cent,[91] the value of the land declined in like proportion,[92] and ultimately the soil was ruined. The Hon. E. G. Stanley told the Emigration Committee in 1827 that he found 600 people on 400 acres of poor land in Limerick. He "cleared" almost half of them, but still got no rents from the remainder, and had to distribute food among them to prevent starvation in 1826, though that was not a famine year.[93] After 1826 proprietors succeeded in decreasing the amount of subletting, but

[91] Evidence of Lord Henry Carbery, *Parl. Pap.* 1826, No. 404, p. 345.

[92] R. Murray, *Ireland, its present condition and future prospects*, p. 20; Nicholson, *Agriculture of the Middle Shannon*, p. 34.

[93] Evidence Committee on Emigration. *Parl. Pap.* 1826-27, No. 550, p. 460. On the whole subject, see *Digest of Evidence, Devon Commission*, I, 418-420; and O'Brien, pp. 48-51.

their efforts to prevent subdivision among the heirs or in dowries were vain.

The custom of the country thus favored deterioration; and the state of the law did nothing to check it. The farmer had no legal security for improvements he might make. They belonged to the soil—that is, to the landlord. The right implied the English practice that the landlord should make the improvements, but outside Ulster there was no recognized custom on this point. The proprietor might make arrangements to compensate for improvements,[94] but he could not bind his successor to keep such agreements. The incentive to improve depended largely on the value of the improvement to the tenant while his lease lasted. The fact that many tenures were for lives introduced an uncertainty as to the length of leases which was an obstacle to improvement, though this aspect has

[94] The unsatisfactory state of the law on this subject has given rise to some extremely biassed generalizations on the callousness and cruelty of landlords, which are still current among Irish writers. That the practice was superior to the rule is proven by the animadversions of the witnesses before the Devon Commission on the management of estates under the courts, which were said to be much worse than other proprietors. Their explanation is as follows:

"The principal causes of the evil influence of the courts on estates committed to their charge seem to be the following: first, the absence of any fund from which the cost of improvements may be defrayed, or of any security to the tenant of remuneration for improvements effected by him, as the court is not affected even by *that moral obligation which in most cases prevents proprietors from taking any undue advantage of their tenants improvements;* and the short term of seven years granted by the courts, and their system of letting to the highest bidder, render it unsafe for the tenant to make any considerable outlay upon his farm."

I take this as evidence that on other estates some or all of these conditions existed:

(1) There was a proprietor's fund for making or aiding improvements.

(2) Tenants were not ejected, or their rents raised, on account of their improvements.

(3) Leases for more than seven years were the rule.

been overemphasized.[95] In 1829, out of 216,000 forty
shilling freehold tenures, 191,600 were for a term of years
(usually twenty-one), and three lives.[96] Most landlords
would not grant longer leases because they could not
prevent tenants from subletting or subdividing and eventually ruining the land; and twenty-one years was long
enough for improvements to compensate the farmer if
only he could have counted on peace and his ability to
escape eviction. The "hanging gale" added an artificial
uncertainty to the length of tenure, which was unfortunately encouraged by benevolent landlords who forgave
back rents.[97]

Fortunately for Ulster, the custom of that province
gave its farmers a better chance of return on their investments. Though by law all improvements belonged to the
landlord, and the farmer had no legal claim to recompense for anything he did, the tenant was traditionally
expected to make the improvements, and custom allowed
him a return on them. This Ulster tenant right was later
declared by Professor Hancock to be the single difference
which accounted for the superior condition of Ulster
farmers, in comparison with those of other parts of Ireland.[98] Hancock was writing with the intention of securing
a change in the land laws in the interests of the farmer,
but subsequent history has done much to prove the truth
of his contention. Tenant right did not make the holding

[95] By Prof. O'Brien, pp. 105-107. Wakefield found the legal security of
tenure better in Ireland than in England, I, 578-579. See also *Digest of Evidence, Devon Commission*, I, 14-16.

[96] Porritt, E., *The unreformed House of Commons*, II, 294.

[97] *Digest of Evidence, Devon Commission*, II, 757-758.

[98] W. N. Hancock, *Impediments to the prosperity of Ireland*, p. 98; and
especially "*The tenant right of Ulster considered economically.*" He was
supported by Sharman Crawford, M.P. (*Depopulation not necessary*, pp.
10-12), whose overenthusiastic claims as to the beneficial results of the
"Ulster custom" are quoted with approval by Prof. O'Brien, pp. 112-114.

itself any more profitable; for the incoming tenant, who had at the start to pay for improvements, often found himself heavily burdened in taking up his land. On this ground landlords frequently denounced it as an evil.[99] It did not reduce rents,[100] but it did give the farmer an incentive to improve his land, and by decreasing the bad feeling on the transfer of farms from one family to another, it worked beneficially for Ulster agriculture[101] and industry.[102]

Another feature of the same custom tended to check subdivision. According to Professor Hancock, "If a tenant dies, the landlord or his agents decide which member of the family is to get the farm; it cannot be divided without his assent. The common practice is for some one member of the family to get it, the others being paid a small sum of money as provision."[103] In addition, it provided leaseholders, even of the smallest class, with a capital on which they could fall back in case of emergency,[104]

[99] John Henchy, *Observations on the state of Ireland*, p. 22. Dufferin, *Emigration and the tenure of land in Ireland*, pp. 122-126. The Devon Commission, while approving of compensation, *by the landlord*, for improvements, objected to the sale of good will, with or without improvements, to the incoming tenant. *Digest of Evidence*, I, pp. 2-5.

[100] In 1841, when cottage manufacture was ceasing to aid the Ulster farmer, rents were still 25-30 per cent lower in the south. Nicholson, *Agriculture of the Middle Shannon*, p. 54, note.

[101] M. J. Bonn, *Modern Ireland and her agrarian problem*, p. 70.

[102] Gill attributes the superior development of the linen industry in the north in part to the settlement there of the Scots and most of the Huguenots, who taught the trade to Ireland, but primarily to the possession of tenant right. (*Irish Linen Industry*, pp. 22-29, 146.) As the great class of journeymen in the north enjoyed no tenant right, while southern enterprise failed even with security of tenure in some places, I am inclined to lay more stress on the first cause. Professor Alison Phillips attributes the decay of southern industry to "ignorance and inertness" caused primarily by religion—*Edinburgh Review*, CCXXXVI, 126-129.

[103] Hancock, *Landlord and Tenant*, Appendix, pp. 41-42.

[104] Year to year tenants had no right in their improvements, even in Ulster. Hancock, *Landlord and tenant question*, Appendix, p. 30.

and it was this capital which frequently supplied the means of transporting the unsuccessful farmer and his family to America. These advantages were unfortunately diminished by legal uncertainties, and the greedy and unscrupulous were too often the only gainers.[105] It would be a mistake to think of Ulster farming as in any sense progressive,—Young had found conditions very bad, and attributed the poverty to the division of interest between agriculture and manufacturing,—but it was probably a little less backward than in the south.

The hovel of the small farmer was frequently no better than the cotter's, and he was nearly as dependent upon the potato for food, and on outside employment to enable him to pay his rent, in which respect he was no freer than the laborer.[106] He too, thanks to high rents and small holdings, which prevented any proper rotation of crops or pasture, lived practically on the margin of subsistence. This poverty-stricken and turbulent class formed the most numerous group in Ireland. In the more thickly settled counties such as Monaghan and Armagh it constituted the common basis of society. There the average farm was less than ten acres in size, and the majority were less than five acres. This condition had spread to the whole of Ireland by 1841 when there were 440,000 holdings of less than five acres, and 380,000 of about that size. The proportion of small holdings was highest in the nongrazing provinces of Ulster and Connaught.[107] Farmers in these districts usually raised grain as well as potatoes.[108] They might have some land in pasture, and in normal years keep a little grain and wheat for their own con-

105 *Ibid.*, pp. 46-47.

106 Evidence before Committee on Emigration, e.g. Strickland; *Parl. Pap.* 1826-27, No. 550, p. 336.

107 Tables from the Census of 1841 and Poor Law Reports, in *Digest of Evidence, Devon Commission,* I, 393-396. These include cotter holdings.

108 *Ibid.*, I, 14.

sumption, but even the holders of ten acres were subject to famine. The future held out little promise for them, but they had behind them a tradition of independence, and in 1815 the memory of better times, which made them less content than the cotter to sit quietly under their difficulties, and more ready when opportunity presented itself either to fight or to emigrate.

Between the small farmer and the large, or substantial farmer, there was no recognized line. The peasants called the man with thirty acres a large farmer, and the gentry were glad enough to have such tenants in preference to the rabble,[109] declaring that the latter would be better off if they gave up their holdings and took employment as laborers.[110] In 1841 there were 330,000 holders of from five to thirty acres.[111] Their lives were by no means comfortable,[112] for they did not as a rule accumulate any capital,[113] and a single bad year was enough to wipe out their little stock. Land agents were ruthless in distraining for rent, and after 1816 everything from growing crops to the family clothing were objects for seizure. Even where they could acquire a small surplus, there were no proper facilities for investment or safekeeping. Savings banks were started in several Irish towns immediately after 1815, but they were too distant for most farmers, and their facilities appear to have aided only town workingmen and servants.[114] The usual place for savings was a hidden

109 Evidence of J. S. Vandeleur, *Parl. Pap.* 1826-27, III, p. 301. By 1843 landlords were pleased if they could clear enough tenants to let farms of 15 acres or more. Evidence before Devon Commission, *Parl. Pap.* 1845, XIX, 45, 329; XX, 559; XXI, 394, etc.

110 Evidence of Maj. Genl. Richard Bourke of Limerick, *Parl. Pap.* 1826, LV, No. 404, p. 341.

111 *Digest of Evidence, Devon Commission*, I, 396.

112 Nicholson, *Agriculture of the Middle Shannon*, pp. 56-57.

113 Wakefield, I, 427.

114 Of several such banks in Antrim, only that of Belfast acquired more than a few subscribers. *Belfast News Letter*, Feb. 20, March 5, 1815, etc.

cupboard or tile in which gold and notes were deposited,[115] and many of the attacks upon farmhouses and cottages made under cover of agrarian agitation were in reality disguised robbery. This was particularly true following the peace, when bands of marauders, many of them ex-soldiers, roamed almost unchecked over a large part of the Irish kingdom. These bands were well armed and did not hesitate to destroy houses and barns if they were baulked in their search.

Above this group of intermediate farmers were 48,000 greater tenants or large farmers, and it was to them that the landlords looked for the agricultural salvation of Ireland. When occasion demanded that they should evict paupers, or attempt to clear part of their estates, they usually sought to regrant the land to their more prosperous tenants, upon whose fortunes their own so largely depended. Such men might come from the ranks of the smaller holders; for owners were glad to combine small farms for the best of their lesser tenantry. Despite the efforts of landlords, however, subdivision went on faster than consolidation, and there were probably more of the substantial farmer class in 1815 than in 1841. They and their children provided most of that superior emigration with capital which disturbed the Irish press at intervals between those years. They alone of the Irish had the ability and enterprise to push into the new lands of the Ohio and Mississippi valleys, and they took their place with American, English, Scottish and German settlers in building the new agricultural west. Most of them, however, had too much at stake in Ireland, and too little knowledge of America to abandon a country in which the mirage of better times was always on the horizon.

Unfortunately, conditions combined to defeat the hopes

[115] Wakefield, I, 593. This was still true in 1837. Speech of Thomas Wyse in Commons, May 1, 1837; *3 Hansard*, XXXVIII, 435.

of farmer and landlord alike. Ireland, contrary to the opinion of most of its patriots, was not ideally suited for grain. The climate was too variable and much too wet, and the crops suffered from mildew. Fluctuations in prices, occasioned in part by the terms of the Corn Laws and by the manipulation of speculators, induced farmers to attempt higher rents than they could afford, and to neglect other crops in favor of wheat. From 1815 to 1825, and from 1828 to 1833, the price of wheat never varied less than twelve shillings a quarter annually, and sometimes rose or fell as much as six shillings in a single week. In 1816 it went from 53/1 to 103/11;[116] but despite the Corn Laws, the increase of British and foreign competition after 1815 more than offset the increased market offered by the growth of British manufactures.[117]

All crops suffered from backward farming methods. The usual practice was a seven years' rotation: one year manured for potatoes, two years of grain, three in grass, then another year of grain before the ground was manured again. Scientific rotation was almost unknown.[118] Some few tried to raise root crops, but the peasants stole them.[119] The agricultural societies founded by the gentry accomplished little. Their interest was mainly in the breeding of stock, and the greater part of their prizes went to gentlemen members, not to farmers.[120] Yet despite all the evidence of bad farming, there is proof that after 1820, and still more after 1825, some of the Irish, proba-

---

[116] Tables of weekly prices, 1815-1826, and 1828-1840 in *Parl. Pap.* 1826-27, No. 25; and *Parl. Pap.* 1842, No. 18, Part I, pp. 18-31.

[117] Foreign wheat was legally excluded from 1819 to 1825, but during this period the British production was very greatly increased through enclosures and improved farming. Porter, *Progress of the Nation*, I, 159.

[118] *Digest of Evidence, Devon Commission*, I, 14; Wakefield, I, 360-420, a general description of tillage farming.

[119] O'Brien, p. 35.

[120] *Ibid.*, pp. 38-40; *Londonderry Journal*, Oct. 15, 1822.

bly the larger farmers, were increasing the yield of their acres. The export of grain of all kinds rose three and four hundred per cent without any noticeable increase in land under' tillage.[121] Some of this was grain formerly used in distilling, and now drawn out by the improvement in communications to a better market; but the home consumption for other purposes was already so little in 1815 that no great increase in export was possible from that source. The story of these improvements and their effects belongs to another chapter; it is enough here to point out that the average tillage farmer did not share in them, though he was primarily dependent on grain. When it was scarce he had little surplus to sell. When it was abundant, prices were sometimes so low that he cleared his rent with difficulty.[122]

No general estimate of rents is possible, but there is overwhelming testimony from all classes that they were too high, and they are among the grievances most frequently cited as a cause of emigration. Compared with the rent of similar land in Great Britain, they were indeed low, but in the light of the general ignorance and insecurity in Ireland, they were exorbitant. Proprietors as a rule favored large farmers by letting to them at reduced rates, though this was less frequent in Munster and Connaught where much land was let to the highest bidder.[123] Unfortunately, the pressure of cotter competition forced up all land prices just when the evils of wartime leases were declining. The practice of distraining for rent reconciled many landlords to a cotter tenantry, guaranteeing them even against paupers. According to the

[121] Porter, *Progress of the nation*, II, 84.

[122] In 1820, when crops were excellent, prices were so low, and pigs so cheap that neither the farmers nor cotters could pay their rents. But money was scarce that year on account of bank failures. Report of the Kilkenny Agricultural Society, in *Belfast News Letter*, Sept. 29, 1820.

[123] *Digest of Evidence, Devon Commission*, II, 753-756.

report of the Central Relief Committee of the Society of Friends:

This practise had a serious effect in deteriorating the character of the tenantry in Ireland. It has subjected the farmer possessed of capital to an unfair competition, by admitting the offers of persons who, having nothing to lose, were willing to offer any rent in order to obtain possession of land. . . . The law of distress enabled the middleman to raise the rent of land by the competition of paupers.[124]

The most profitable rural industry, the raising of cattle for provisions or butter, did not form a sufficiently large part of the business of an ordinary farmer to save him from losses on poor crops or from low prices. After 1815, with the fall in the price of butter, this too was depressed, thereby causing distress in Limerick,[125] the center of the butter trade. The greater part of the business was in the hands of farmer-graziers who formed a distinct class and did not share in the economic fortunes of the ordinary farmer. Altogether, they held more land than the tillage farmers, and in some counties they were the only large-scale tenants. They raised cattle or sheep, primarily for the meat trade, selling to packers at Limerick and Cork, to English buyers in their home markets, or shipping their animals to Liverpool.[126]

Despite all these evidences of desire for improvement, —a desire blocked by insecurity, ignorance, evil land laws and customs, and many other factors—attempts have been made to prove that Ireland lacked the capital for its own improvement, and that absenteeism was the primary

[124] *Transactions of the Central Relief Committee of the Society of Friends*, p. 123.

[125] Earl of Limerick in the House of Lords, Feb. 19, 1816, 1 *Hansard*, XXXII, 632.

[126] Wakefield, I, 308-321, especially 311.

cause of this evil. Doubtless the preponderance of interest in affairs outside Ireland on the part of many landlords did lead them to neglect their Irish estates, but the majority had capital and interest enough to lay out considerable wealth in draining, fencing, buildings, and implements, had they not been deterred by the uncertainty of any return on their investment.[127] Pamphleteers wrangled continuously on this subject, but the first real students of the question agreed that in a country where investors put two million pounds a year into British government securities at low rates of interest, while Irish interest rates remained consistently high, lack of capital was not the difficulty.[128]

The prohibition of joint stock or note-issuing banks outside Dublin prior to 1824, and the frequent failures of the little rural private banks, did much to prevent the existing capital from becoming available; but the later extension of credit facilities and the success of Montgomery's Bank in Belfast, even before it became a joint-stock concern, suggest that where enterprise and security existed capital was not lacking.[129]

As Cunningham concluded, however, "the land never had such rest that a sense of security could grow up, or that the country could become an attractive field for the investment of capital by moneyed men, either as pro-

[127] Prof. O'Brien claims that the custom of the country, recognized by all except the landlords, was for the tenants to make all improvements, hence the landlord would not have improved in any case (p. 110). This "Ulster custom" had been general, but was no longer recognized in the south. G. Sigerson, *History of the land tenures and land classes of Ireland*, pp. 281-282.

[128] M. Longford, *Report of an address before the second session of the Dublin Statistical Society;* Hancock, *Is there really want of capital in Ireland?* pp. 9-14.

[129] Dillon, *History and development of banking in Ireland*, pp. 4-7, 33-36, 49.

prietors or tenants.'"[130] There was no incentive to make improvements. Farm buildings were allowed to decay, and antiquated implements continued in use long after better ones were known. The unwillingness of the more ignorant farmers to use new tools had something to do with this, but in general, insecurity was responsible, and it was insecurity which deterred British capitalists from investing in Irish ventures. At times there seemed to be a promise of extensive operations in Ireland in such industries as the fisheries, railways, and manufactures; but the promise was never fulfilled, and one reason was the greater danger of loss in Ireland from internal disorder.[131] The capitalist had a safer and more promising field for investment in England, or in the development of industry overseas, which absorbed so much British capital.

The worst feature of uncertainty was that it bred suspicion and prevented agreements between those classes which had most to gain by peace and order, thus destroying the only barrier to the spread of agrarian warfare.[132] What poor rates did to the yeoman farmers of England, insecurity did to men of the same class in Ireland. Hence, numbers of them were always ready to emigrate, and they formed a continuous stream, and at times the majority of the emigrants leaving the country.[133]

[130] *Growth of English industry and commerce*, p. 894; also W. Blacker, *Prize essay on the management of land in Ireland*, p. 32.

[131] Speech of the Earl of Carrick before the Kilkenny Association, *Belfast News Letter*, Nov. 20, 1818; *Third report of the Poor Inquiry Commission*, Parl. Pap. 1836, No. 43, p. 25; *Digest of Evidence, Devon Commission*, I, 321.

[132] *Letters from an Irish proprietor to the ministers of Religion in his District*, pp. 7-18; Hancock, *Report on the landlord and tenant question in Ireland*, Appendix, pp. 30, 37; Nicholson, *Agriculture of the Middle Shannon*, pp. 52-53 (and see above p. 2); *Digest of Evidence, Devon Commission*, I, 234-235, 321.

[133] "Do you think that the disturbances which occur so frequently in that

In this detailed account of Irish agricultural life, the existence of a score of causes for emigration is only too apparent. But throughout the period there was an underlying cause which both in Ireland and in England yearly drove thousands of the rural population to America. The Napoleonic Wars and the high prices which accompanied them made the small, unscientific farm profitable for the last time.[134] The five years that followed, years of wretched harvests and a depressed market, were a nightmare to all classes. When they had passed, the poor cultivator fought a slow but losing battle against better methods, larger capital, and in time against fresh soils and superior climate. That battle never ceased in Ireland from 1815 to 1845. In truth, it is still going on; for Ireland has stubbornly refused to recognize the agricultural revolution, and is seeking today to find the salvation of the small farm in rural coöperation. For over a century this economic pressure has continued, and millions, yielding to some one or all of the conditions just described, or to attractions from across the Atlantic, have detached themselves and gone to America. There were periods of greater or less distress, but there was never a year in

country form a great inducement for the Protestants to emigrate?'' *Answer,* ''I am satisfied that is the only cause, generally speaking, of the emigration of the Protestants I have referred to; they have taken alarm.'' Evidence of Major George Warburton of County Clare, May 26, 1824, before the Lords Committee on Disturbances in Ireland, *Parl. Pap.* 1825, No. 200, p. 92. Similar evidence is contained in the petition of John Lawson of Athlone to Bathurst, May 7, 1820; C.O. 384/6, p. 859.

[134] See Cunningham, *The growth of English industry and commerce,* p. 845. This is a favorite controversial topic, but the advocates of the small farm admit that it produces less surplus wealth, and therefore yields less profit. Their claim is that it sustains more people, and must therefore be maintained by the State—what may be called the Socialist attitude. Naturally the landlords, who controlled the land, did not take this point of view. Nineteenth century writers on Ireland fall into two distinct groups; the economist, and the socialist. It is only in recent times that writers try to hold both points of view at the same time.

which the Irish farmer had not sufficient economic motive for leaving his own country and taking his chance in a new land.

IV.

WHILE the agricultural revolution was somewhat belatedly increasing the gross produce of Ireland and simultaneously degrading the peasantry, its younger sister, the industrial revolution, was making a slow and hesitant entry into the island. Ireland was badly placed to take advantage of the new movement. It possessed no good coal of its own, and except in the remoter parts of the island where communications were poor and disturbances frequent, no available water power. Coal had to be imported from Wales and southern Scotland, and to transportation costs was added a duty of ninepence per ton, which had been perpetuated by the Act of Union, and could only be repealed by the British parliament.[135] In Dublin the duty was 1/9, and there was an additional fee of 5½d. charged by the Merchants Guild for measuring.[136] This naturally proved a severe handicap in competing with English manufacturing towns. The lack of iron, as indeed of practically all metals, was a further hindrance to the growth of any machine industry, and the cost of importing machinery and parts from Great Britain in many cases proved the deciding factor in killing attempts to foster manufacture in Ireland.[137] Cheap labor usually seeks the raw materials, and is not in itself a sufficient cause for the development of manufactures. Advantages as to raw

[135] Murray, *Commercial relations of England and Ireland*, p. 334.

[136] *Parl. Pap.* 1836, XXIV, Commissioners on Municipal Corporations in Ireland. Report on the City of Dublin, p. 154.

[137] Of course the unions fought the introduction of machinery. See the evidence of James Fagan, who for two years went armed because he had dared to erect a new mill in Dublin. *Parl. Pap.* 1837-38, VIII, No. 646. Second Report, Committee on Combinations of Workmen, p. 3.

material existed only in the linen industry, to which the climate of Ireland was peculiarly suited, and it survived in spite of many drawbacks. Except in the north there was no upper class prepared to lend its capital or initiative in establishing new industries, and no population accustomed to manufacturing except the highly organized and reactionary trades unionists of the south—the "dawdling drinking workmen"[138] of Dublin, who have changed little in the last hundred years. As time went on and England became the great clearing house for the trade of all parts of the world, the disadvantages of manufacturing in Ireland, from which all goods would have to be shipped by way of England, became more apparent.

The old manual industries of the country survived under protection until 1830; and the census of 1831 showed that one-fourth of the people were still engaged, if only a part of the time, in manufacture. But even without the sweeping away of the duties on British goods in that year they were doomed by the machine-made products of British mills. The displaced artisan and the displaced farmer could not find in Ireland the new employment in factory, warehouse, and rough construction which absorbed their prototypes in Great Britain; and their emigration to Great Britain or America was in many ways merely an extension of the nineteenth century drift to the cities taking place across international boundaries. Artisans had in some respects even more incentive to leave Ireland than the agricultural classes. Even when times were bad and work failed, the farmer or cotter had his own produce and a roof over his head, but the artisan had

[138] Lady Morgan's *Memoirs*, II, 402, J. D. Clarkson (*Labour and Nationalism in Ireland*, pp. 26-29) makes a very bitter attack on O'Connell, Sidney and Beatrice Webb, et al., for criticizing the unions. His work is violently propagandist.

nothing on which to fall back. Hence, as the factory displaced the domestic worker, and as new inventions in turn displaced many of the factory hands, another stream of emigrants swelled the currents already going to America. It rose and fell in volume, for the pressure of distress was less steady among the manufacturing classes, but it did not cease.

The most important Irish manufacture in 1815 as in 1931 was linen, which was largely concentrated then as now in Ulster. There was some weaving, chiefly of linen, in thirteen of the twenty-three southern counties, but a survey made in 1816 showed that in almost every case this was on the decline. The only important southern linen district, the South Cork sailcloth and canvas area, was ruined by the cessation of wartime demand in 1815, though like other southern linen manufactures, it struggled along for some time with the aid of premiums from the Irish Linen Board and export bounties from Parliament.[189]

The true linen area of Ireland included all of Ulster and parts of the counties of Louth, Sligo, and Mayo. Within this region almost every large farmer was a master weaver and employed journeymen weavers, usually cotters, but sometimes artisans living in the house of the master. In 1815 many of the small farmers were also master weavers, but as times grew worse and the majority of them lacked capital to purchase their own yarn and bring their webs to market, they fell gradually into the class of employees, and were in practically the same position as the journeymen. Spinning was performed by women of all classes from the farmer's wife down.

The close relation between agriculture, the linen trade, and emigration makes it necessary to examine the situation in Ulster with some care, for the "old emigration"

[189] Gill, *Rise of the Irish linen industry*, pp. 126-129, 296.

from Ireland, which was also the main emigration for at least 15 years after 1815, came almost entirely from that region. The machine revolution had as yet made little headway in the Irish linen industry, but another revolution—the rise of capitalism—was already well begun. Capital came from two sources: from the successful farmer employing more and more journeymen, and from the bleacher-merchant (the two trades were united in 1815) hiring weavers to prepare cloth for him.[140] These latter were the princes of the trade, the founders of the great linen houses which in time absorbed most of the industry. In 1815, the whole industry was in a state of transition. Three main areas, each producing about one-third of the total output of cloth, were distinguishable.[141] The river banks of the Lagan, the Bann, and the Foyle, in the four northeastern counties, were the seats of all the great bleach-greens and also of the finest weaving, which required more expensive looms and brought slower returns than the ordinary farmer could afford. This was the region of the greater capitalists, who let out work and provided yarn and looms to their employees, and in 1815 were just beginning to bring their workmen into factories,[142] although power-looms were as yet unknown in Ireland. The second area, dominated by the farmer-master weaver, or lesser capitalist, included the southern part of Armagh, Louth, and Monaghan. Its product was coarse cloth, manufactured with cheap coarse yarn, either imported or made by the new spinning machines, which were driving out of the market the homespun with which the poor cottage weaver supplied himself.[143] Only in the intermediate grades of weaving was the independent weaver holding his own; but where communications were

140 *Ibid.*, pp. 145-146.
142 *Ibid.*, p. 268.

141 *Ibid.*, pp. 271-275.
143 *Ibid.*, pp. 145-146, 153-154.

bad and the home supply of yarn essential, where bleachers had not stepped in to control the market, and sales
were still made to travelling drapers, men continued to
weave what their wives and daughters spun, and sold
their pieces every fortnight at the local market or fair.
This was true in the north of Antrim, western Londonderry, Tyrone, Cavan, and the most distant regions,
though these outlying parts—Donegal and the counties
of Connaught—had very little weaving, their product
being largely confined to yarn.[144]

Spinning was the first process to come under the influence of mechanical power, but it had not fallen into the
control of capitalists to the same extent as weaving. The
water-power loom had been introduced in 1808, and by
1817 there were fifteen spinning mills in Ulster,[145] yet in
1821 there were few spinners, except in the counties producing yarn only, who were not working at home as members of a weaver's family.[146] The spread of machine spinning was retarded by the inability to produce any but the
coarsest yarn by this method. Even this manufacture had
an unfortunate effect on the hand spinners forced to compete with the machine and with the rising cotton trade,
and they found their earnings reduced to twopence a
day.[147]

The competition of cotton cloth likewise decreased the
earnings of the independent linen weavers, except in the
northeast region of fine and coarse weaving, with which
cotton did not compete.[148] In that area the establishment of cotton factories raised the wages of weavers,
who could easily transfer from one trade to another, and
they made from six to nine shillings a week at linen.
Women in the spinning mills were equally fortunate, and

---

144 Gill, *Irish linen industry*, p. 38.   145 *Ibid.*, p. 266.
146 *Ibid.*, p. 38.   147 *Ibid.*
148 *Ibid.*, pp. 241-243.

earned four shillings a week. Improvement, however, was confined to a small district around Belfast;[149] and despite higher wages, weavers who gave up farming to work in factories gained little in permanent saving.[150]

The linen trade, which had been checked in its main branches by the wars, was in 1815 expanding rapidly, and was well calculated to improve the condition of master weavers and other manufacturing employers. Unfortunately, the small farmers and cotters did not share in the improvement.[151] Rents were increased on the understanding that the income from the linen trade would help to pay them, and as trade declined the artisan was faced with one more difficulty.[152] Except for a brief revival caused by American demand immediately after 1815, this home industry was in a continuous though fluctuating state of decline throughout the next twenty years. It survived only because the independent weaver was able to work at less than subsistence returns, eking out his earnings with the spinning of the women and the produce of the farm.[153] Landlords considered it a blessing, for it gave the poor something to do during periods of agricultural idleness and so helped to check disturbances. To the artisan himself, the chief importance of his skill seems to have been that it made him somewhat less dependent on the soil, giving him an alternative employment in case he should remove elsewhere. Linen weavers as a body were nearly if not quite as poor as other laborers, but they were more likely to emigrate if opportunity offered. The only exceptions to this rule were the skilled weavers of cambric and

[149] *Ibid.*, pp. 237-238.   [150] *Ibid.*, p. 269.

[151] *Ibid.*, p. 160.

[152] Ordnance Survey of the Counties of Antrim and Londonderry, and parts of other counties, made in 1834-40, under the direction of Jeremiah O'Donovan (MS in Royal Irish Academy, Dublin. Hereafter cited as *O'Donovan Survey*).

[153] Gill, *Irish linen industry,* pp. 224, 327.

damask, who seldom combined their occupation with farming.[154]

Meanwhile, other aspects of capitalistic production hastened the displacement of home industry. Imported flax and yarn from Holland and Russia took the place of some of the Irish product, which was too often dirty; and the gradual introduction after 1808 of scutching mills, which cleaned the stalks much more effectively than the old hand method, aided the capitalist but not the small manufacturer. Scientific bleaching with chemicals was a monopoly of the great bleachers, and brought about the destruction of the small bleach green. In this case the only sufferers were the poor who had carried turf to the old greens. The whole industry was going through a period of relocation rather than decline, but the effect upon hundreds of thousands of independent workers was disastrous, and their old refuge of emigration received a new and powerful impetus.

Linen was the only great cottage industry, and almost the only manufacture in Ireland which did not depend directly for its prosperity on agriculture. There were the usual local trades catering to the needs of the farmers in small towns and villages, which in 1815 were more populous than they are today. Smiths, carpenters, tailors and shoemakers were the most numerous, and were the only trades, weavers excepted, with more than 15,000 members in 1831—and none of them numbered more than 30,000. The only other trades with over 10,000 members were the masons and keepers of public houses.[155] The six groups contained 116,000 men, not quite one in seventy of the population of Ireland at that time. Their importance was, however, out of proportion to their numbers.

154 Gill, *Irish linen industry*, p. 46.

155 *Parl. Pap.* 1833, XXXIX, No. 634, Abstract of Returns. Census of 1831, pp. 345-351.

They catered to the four great needs of the farming population: implements, buildings, clothing and drink; and to
the trading classes in the small towns and cities. With
the cotters, who were practically self-sufficient, they had
little to do.[156] Their fortunes rose and fell with the state
of agriculture. Difficulties of communication protected
local manufacture and the domestic artisan long after
1815, but the condition of the small towns was not encouraging. Although increasing in population, most of them
were decreasing in wealth, and employment must always
have been uncertain.

The drink trade was intimately bound up with agriculture. Illicit distilling, most prevalent in the northwest,
but not confined to any region, occupied the attention of
considerable numbers of the poorer farmers and laborers.
Sometimes this was on no larger scale than a similar
industry for home consumption now carried on in the
United States, but the local still often supplied a small
neighborhood, and the proprietor made a considerable
part of his income in this way. Not until many years after
1815, when the excise was much reduced, did the large
licensed distilleries which employed several hundred
hands apiece, compete on equal terms with these local
manufactures. Meanwhile, the distilling interest was always a source of profit as well as trouble. Brewing was
almost entirely in the hands of licensed traders and was
confined to the towns. It did not employ directly any large
number of persons, but it gave work to a considerable
class of coopers (over 7,000 in all), and to some subsidiary trades. The coopers worked both for the brewers and
the provision merchants, their headquarters in the pro-

---

[156] When the cotter did not make his clothes, he bought cast-off clothing
which was imported from England in large quantities. Bicheno, *Ireland and
its economy*, p. 37.

vision trade being in Cork and Limerick, and in brewing in Dublin.

Other skilled city trades were insignificant in numbers. Dublin alone had employed a considerable number of workers to cater to various luxuries associated with a capital, but in 1815 these craftsmen were still suffering from the decline which followed the Act of Union. The Dublin artisans were more thoroughly organized than any others in the United Kingdom, and the efforts of the unions were frequently blamed by the upper classes for the decay of industry, which was in truth probably doomed by the condition of the city. Like inhabitants of an invested fortress, the unions fought desperately and in the main successfully, to maintain the rate of wages, to exclude non-union labor, and to limit the number of apprentices. Labor disputes were the source of innumerable assaults and beatings, often resulting in death, and were on the whole thoroughly effective in maintaining control of industry.[157] Wage disputes were the least important causes of friction, the unions finding little difficulty in enforcing scales of pay higher than those in Great Britain, and from three to seven times as high as the pay of common labor.[158] Assessments for strikes and unemployed members often took as much as a sixth of their wages, but so long as there was any industry left they kept themselves economically superior to those around them. Unions existed outside Dublin, but never attained to the

[157] See the table of assaults in 9 months of 1824-25 in *Parl. Pap.* 1825, IV, No. 437. Report from the Select Committee on Combination Laws, pp. 15-23. The list shows over 40 cases, arising from disputes of carpenters (10), sawyers (6), slaters (5) and various others. The actual beating was done by members of a different union, so that no one should be recognized by the victim.

[158] *Parl. Pap.* 1824, V, No. 51. Reports from the Select Committee on Artisans and Machinery, pp. 283, 421-423, 444.

same strength, and country wages were on a much lower level.[159]

In general, employment in the manual trades grew worse after 1815, though wherever power could be utilized there was an increase in labor, if not in wages. This was true in the three textile industries, linen, wool, and cotton. Reference has already been made to the changes in the linen manufacture; and a similar metamorphosis was taking place in wool, with less prospect, however, of ultimate success. The continuance of domestic wool manufacturing after the suppression of the export trade by the British Government in the seventeenth century is well known. Throughout Connaught, and in general in all the less developed parts of Ireland, the making of homespun for the use of the cottagers' or farmers' families was customary. But the day of the hand-loom weavers was passing, and manufacture for sale was limited. Between 1800 and 1820, over nine thousand broadcloth weavers in and near Cork went out of work.[160] Weaving in mills on a commercial scale was still carried on, and was even increasing in Dublin, Kildare, and Kilkenny counties,[161] but it was to fight a losing battle against the cheaper wool, more scientific methods,[162] and lower wages of England. For a time, the continuance of the duties on English woolens, regulated by the Act of Union, enabled them to compete in the home market, but even here they were losing ground. Wages were cut temporarily in 1815, but were still above English wages, and from three to four times as high as those of ordinary laborers—a phenomenon arising from the extraordinary strength of the weavers' union.[163]

159 *Ibid.*, p. 72.
160 *Niles' Register*, Oct. 7, 1820, quoting Cork Chamber of Commerce.
161 *Parl. Pap.* 1824, V, No. 51, p. 296. Evidence of Mr. Farrell.
162 Murray, *Commercial relations of England and Ireland*, p. 275.
163 *Parl. Pap.* 1824, V, No. 51, pp. 286, 290. Evidence of J. Houghton.

The most promising of the factory industries was the cotton manufacture of the Belfast area. The increased use of cotton during the wars and the improvements in machinery had already created a prosperous new industry by 1815. The coming of the employers to Belfast was directly caused by troubles with their workingmen in Scotland, but Belfast had some natural advantages for the cotton trade. The labor supply was cheap and unorganized,[164] and the workers were not too ignorant. Linen weavers found the transfer to cotton weaving comparatively easy, while for the spinning processes skilled hands were unnecessary. The cheapness of cotton also gave it importance in the Irish market, and as communications between Great Britain and Ireland were still undeveloped, there was some advantage in having factories on the Irish side.[165] An estimate of 1811 placed the number of cotton operatives in the Belfast district at 22,000.[166] This is probably an exaggeration, but it is true that cotton was the main cause for the rise of Belfast during this period from an insignificant country town to an important city. By 1821 it had a population of 37,000. The cotton trade was on the whole improving, and even during times of temporary slackness the workers were saved from absolute distress by their ability to return to the linen trade. These cotton workers were the best paid and least distressed of the poor of Ireland. Weavers could make from nine to twenty-one shillings a week, and the spinners, who were usually young girls, earned from five to sixteen shillings.[167] Yet even this relatively prosperous group

164 They had been organized by delegates from Glasgow, and were shortly after reorganized, but in 1815 their association had gone to pieces. *Belfast News Letter*, May 5, 1815.

165 There was also a ten per cent duty on British cottons and an export duty on Irish (as well as British), but these were abolished in 1816.

166 Gill, *Irish linen industry*, p. 233.

167 *Ibid.*, pp. 237-238. During a slump the weavers were making eight to

could find higher wages and better times in America, and artisans were, second only to the small farmers, the most consistent of the emigrating classes.

V.

THE census of 1831 showed that nine-tenths of the people of Ireland were primarily engaged in agriculture and trade or manufacture, which were practically synonymous terms. Among the remaining tenth two groups, domestic servants and fishermen, played a part in the furthering of emigration. Domestic servants constituted a large and important body. Unlike the farm servants, they lived in the houses of the gentry or substantial farmers, and worked entirely for money wages. Recruited from the families of laborers or smaller farmers, they were, as far as mode of living was concerned, distinctly better off than the classes from which they came, but the lack of opportunity for advancement spread discontent among the more ambitious, and a considerable number were to be found amongst the emigrants. Their movement was facilitated for many of them by the custom of paying wages annually in the spring, when emigrant ships were most easily available.

Fishermen were of two distinct classes: the local or coast fishermen and the deep-sea fishermen. The local herring fisheries of the western and southern bays have already been mentioned, as this occupation was combined with agriculture and carried on by the poorest class. At Ardglass in County Down, and off the banks of Wicklow, there were larger fisheries where the fishermen, unlike most of those in the west, had sailing vessels and large nets, and competed fairly successfully with the English

twelve shillings. *Belfast News Letter*, May 2, 1815. Much of the spinning and some of the weaving was still done at home.

and Scottish fishers. Their occupation was altogether seasonal, usually covering the months from August to November. During the rest of the year some few found employment as sailors, but the majority lived in small cottages and gardens, and raised their own food. Despite the numbers of fish found off the north coast of Ireland there were no large fishing companies in that part of the country. The only group to play an important part in the development of emigration was the deep-sea fishing fleet which centered at Waterford. The century old connection between Waterford and Newfoundland continued after 1815. In the eighteenth century it had taken many boys as apprentices to Newfoundland, whence they made their way in hundreds to the New England fishing fleets, and such a route to America would not be neglected when emigration recommenced on a larger scale. Fishing also aided emigration to some extent by encouraging Irish shipbuilding, and in the early nineteenth century it enabled Waterford to advance with Belfast, where commercial enterprise was laying the foundations of one of the two great industries of the Ulster city. But for a long time after 1815 the total output from Ireland was very small. No other cities engaged extensively in the trade, and the shipyards of Dublin fell into permanent decline.[168] The cause was rather the advance of shipbuilding on the Clyde and Mersey, and the excess of available vessels in all parts of the world between 1815 and 1825, than any weakness in Irish commerce or the demand for ships.

A survey of the commercial and urban situation reflects the decline which is apparent in agriculture and to a less extent in manufacturing. As a city and mercantile center, Dublin, the second largest city in the United Kingdom,

[168] Evidence of James Fagan, Dublin timber-merchant, in *Parl. Pap.* 1837-38, VIII, No. 646; Second Report, Committee on Combinations, pp. 1-20.

with a population of over 175,000, was preëminent. Its imports and exports, though less in proportion to its size than those of British mercantile cities, were still over five times as great as those of any other Irish city. All the trades and professions usually attaching to a political capital were found there, and the dissolution of the Irish parliament had only diminished, without destroying, its political importance. It was, however, declining in wealth, and many thousands of its poor could find little or no employment. Even in 1815 the slums of Dublin were notorious for their poverty and disease. The loss of commercial importance brought hardship to the mercantile workers and gave to the emigration from Dublin a more urban character than that from any other port.

Cork, the second city in the kingdom, with nearly a hundred thousand inhabitants, specialized in the provision trade, particularly that to the West Indies, and had a further importance as a provisioning base for the British navy. But its commercial importance in 1815 was only slightly greater than that of Belfast, a much smaller town, and it had desperately poor districts which fell into worse plight with the decline in weaving. The only other city of any size was Limerick, the port for an exceptionally rich agricultural area. Waterford and Galway, towns of about twenty-five thousand, both had a considerable provision and grain trade in addition to fishing interests. Of the numerous small ports of Ireland, Drogheda, Londonderry and Newry had an importance rather out of proportion to their size, arising from their connection with the linen trade, while Newry and Drogheda exported grain as well. It is significant of the purely trading character of Irish cities that all the larger ones were seaports. The only inland town of more than fifteen thousand was Kilkenny, which, like all inland settlements, derived its importance from the agricultural districts surrounding it.

Towns and cities alike were increasing in population, though probably at a somewhat slower rate than rural areas; but outside the factory districts of Ulster, population had no relation to employment or wealth. As commercial centers their fortunes varied with those of the country round them, except that they were less directly injured by scarcity of supply at home, and more affected by the state of the market abroad. Agricultural decline naturally produced urban as well as rural discontent, but as the towns catered to the wants of all classes, they did not necessarily suffer from the degradation of a single group.

In 1815, towns and cities were on the whole poor and mean, unlighted, unswept, unpaved—without public water supply, sanitation, or efficient police. The exceptions were the larger cities where parliament had stepped in to create boards appointed by itself or elected by the taxpayers, to take charge of these functions. In general, governmental duties were in the hands of municipal corporations instituted by the Stuarts, which had become in most cases mere echoes of the wishes of a patron. No more damning indictment of corruption and inefficiency can be found than the report of the parliamentary commissioners who investigated these corporations in 1833.[169] Their monopoly of government which prevented any progressive municipal activity, their control of justice in the interests of a privileged group, their appropriation of what had been public property to the advantage of their members, their complete failure to keep peace, and above all the chafing restrictions and heavy tolls with which they hampered trade and aroused the antipathy of the peasantry, played havoc with the prosperity of town and

169 *Parl. Pap.* 1835, XXVII, pp. 8-39.

country alike. By 1815 the power of the corporations was already waning, and the next twenty years witnessed an increasing warfare against their privileges, conducted in the towns by the peasants with violence and coercion, and in the cities by chambers of commerce through legal proceedings. In the matter of harbor control and shipping the larger ports, with the exception of Galway and Londonderry, which continued under the inefficient though well-meaning management of their corporations,[170] were already free. Belfast and Waterford had useful and efficient harbor boards, Cork obtained one in 1821 and had reasonably good control in the meantime,[171] while in Limerick the chamber of commerce took harbor improvement into its own hands.[172] In Dublin, however, the Ballast Corporation, a body created by parliament to control the harbor, failed in its duties both as to harbor improvement and in securing suitable pilotage and other services.

The combination of a growing population with stagnant or declining trade in most cities, and in others with increases of wealth confined to the hands of a few, exerted a pressure on the more active and ambitious townsman similar to that on his rural neighbor. While the hopeless and the ignorant drifted into the city slums, skilled artisans, shopkeepers and professional men joined the van of the exodus to America, where the first two classes were likely to succeed. The decline of industry in one country and its amazing growth in the other made the shift of the city dwellers even more logical and natural than the movement of farmers, laborers, servants and fishermen.

The overwhelming influence of economic causes promot-

[170] *Parl. Pap.* 1836, XXIV, 1163-1166; Appendix, XXVII, 328.

[171] *Ibid.*, XXVIII, 602-604, 714-717; XXVII, 48. The paging of the Appendix is continuous, pp. 1-446 being in *Parl. Pap.* 1835, XXVII, 447-1002 in XXVIII, and 1003 to the end in *Parl. Pap.* 1836, XXIV.

[172] *Ibid.*, XXVII, 409.

ing emigration throws all other influences into the background, but religious and political factors cannot be ignored. Religious friction was always present in Ireland in some degree, but in 1815 it was at a noticeably low ebb. Newspapers congratulated themselves that the obnoxious terms "Popish" and "heretic" were no longer heard, and anticipated the complete disappearance of religious troubles. The vision was premature, but for the time being religion played a very small part in Irish disturbances, and it cannot be said that it was a determining factor in emigration, even during the early years when most of the emigrants were Protestants. It is quite possible, however, that emigration altered the balance of creeds. Unfortunately this can only be a matter of surmise, since there was no religious census before 1831, when Catholics formed eighty-two per cent of the population. Of the preceding period one can only say that Munster and Connaught were overwhelmingly Roman Catholic, while Ulster, outside the Presbyterian counties of Down and Antrim, contained a strong mixture of Catholic and Presbyterian, with a sprinkling of other Protestants. In Leinster alone were there large numbers under the Established Church, and a considerable variety of sectarians, though here also Catholics were in a majority. The proportion of Protestants was somewhat higher in the cities than in the country or small towns, and of course much greater among the landowning class, although the number of Catholic proprietors was rapidly increasing.

Differences of religion were on the whole less important than differences of race in determining the character of the emigrants, and both were most marked among the lower classes. The Scots-Irish peasants of Ulster, and to a less extent the English and Welsh settlers in Leinster, had retained habits and traits which set them apart from the native Irish, and checked the growth of common sympathies or the realization of common interests. They were energetic, moderately clean, and less volatile and susceptible to mass emotion than their mercurial neighbors. A stern and narrow morality cut them off from a whole range of popular entertainment, from friendly fighting to dancing and the enjoyment of the harpers. But the most vital distinction lay in that indefinite quality called morale. The Ulster peasant inherited something of the dour pride and stoicism of his ancestors. The native Irish had developed no such armor, and the self pity, the unending note of sorrow which has sounded in their literature from its earliest days, deepened and strengthened after 1815. Yet all these differences were less than the essential similarities of a common poverty, general insobriety, and a national consciousness which made native Irish, Scots-Irish, and Anglo-Irish call themselves Irish, and resent in common all interferences from across the Irish Sea.

This ardent nationalism extended to the priests and dissenting ministers, who were forced to take their politics very largely from their parishioners; and the fact that the clergymen of the Church of Ireland strove to maintain the English connection heightened their general unpopularity. In 1815, however, clergymen of all denominations united in opposing emigration.

Politics, like religion, played its part in promoting emigration rather by increasing disturbances than by any direct influence. Irish politics, even when elections were controlled by the gentry, were proverbially turbulent, and conducted with mobs as a part of the setting. Election riots were the rule rather than the exception. In a day when voting was still oral and public, control by violence was a comparatively easy matter, and the mob spirit thus engendered amongst the peasantry gave to party quarrels and strife an undue importance in the minds of the people. The influence of this spirit was perhaps most unfortunate among the upper classes, and as time went on the tendency to see all things through political glasses increased, and undoubtedly hindered reform.

The one political topic on which Irishmen of all classes and parties were agreed was taxation. They complained then as they have ever since that Ireland's share of the imperial burden was too great, and that taxes were ruining the country. But twenty years of wars were still to be paid for, and taxpayers all over the United Kingdom suffered in common. The growing manufactures of Great Britain enabled the British to pay their share, though at a terrible cost in poverty and physical deterioration. In Ireland no such expansion of industry occurred to offset the drain of war taxes. In truth, the difficulty was not so much heavy taxation, which was inevitable under the circumstances, but a general economic decline which made any extra burden seem excessive. This fact was not at the time apparent, and taxes ranked as a psychological cause of emigration second only to rents and tithes.

This description of conditions in 1815 may give a gloomy impression of the state of Ireland. To the great mass of the people there was nothing alarming in the situation; farmers always hoped for better crops and better prices, and weavers for an improvement in the market. No such general air of hopelessness and helplessness as followed 1847 was present now; but even in years of comparative prosperity there was always sufficient discontent to account for a considerable emigration. The evils bore with exceptional severity on enterprising spirits who attempted to improve their lot, and thus drove out of Ireland many of its best citizens. The impulse toward emigration—already present amongst farmers, weavers, servants and city workers generally—which had been temporarily checked by the difficulties of transportation during the Napoleonic Wars and almost completely stopped by the American War of 1812, now reasserted itself and inaugurated an important chapter in Irish and American history.

CHAPTER II

THE EMIGRANT TRADE

Modern emigration is not due to governmental policy and is not a national undertaking, but results from the spontaneous decision of individuals on the ground of personal motives.

FERENCZI, *International Migrations,* I, 81.

The amount of immigration which was really spontaneous during the first half of the nineteenth century was small in comparison to the total. The proportion of emigrants who possessed the initiative to migrate without being induced to do so, rounded up, led and directed, was relatively small, just as it was before and has been since.

V. SAFFELL, *Immigration Problems,* p. 147.

IMMIGRATION to the United States, to which until later years the newer movement to British America was largely subsidiary, falls into three main periods—colonial, early nineteenth century, and recent. The enormous development of emigration from southern and eastern Europe after 1870, and the existence of reliable census figures, including those of foreign born, which begin in Canada in 1842 and in the United States in 1850, have made the last period the field of careful and thorough study; while patriotic, religious and genealogical workers have thrown some light upon colonial times. Between these two periods lies a third, cursorily dismissed in the textbooks on immigration, but nevertheless constituting an important chapter in American and Irish history.

Among the thousands who set sail for America in the troubled decades following the Napoleonic Wars, none present a more fascinating study than the Irish, who for more than half a century formed the largest element. They had no connection with continental emigration,[1] and very little with British, except as they competed for the use of passenger vessels or as laborers in the new world, but they illustrate perfectly among their own numbers the change from the old to the new immigrant—the one essentially British or Scottish in blood, Protestant, accustomed to some degree of self government and to the English language, and easily absorbed into American life; the other a foreigner in race, language, religion and habits. A million Irishmen in thirty years came to swell the numbers of a people aggregating less than nine millions in 1815, and added in three decades almost ten per cent to the other increase of population.[2] Their influence on labor conditions, on city politics and social problems, on the growth of the Roman Catholic church, receive illumination from contemporary comments, but can be determined only in respect to the greater migration which followed 1845.

A glance at the statistics of Irish emigration before 1815 and after 1845 will emphasize the significance of these three decades. Patriotic Scots-Irish histories have served to obscure the fact that the emigration of colonial days was very slight. Three thousand emigrants in one year was unique during the early eighteenth century. The numbers rose to six thousand or more before 1774, but the average was only four thousand,[3] and when the census

[1] The common features of all modern European migrations, discussed in *Handwörterbuch der Staatswissenschaften*, II, 61, are the outgrowth of conditions arising after 1850; the Irish emigrant of the earlier period may be compared to the later Italian or Slav, but not to the German or Swiss of his own day.

[2] These figures include Upper and Lower Canada. The increase in population in the United States was about 11,000,000; in Canada 800,000.

[3] C. A. Hanna, *The Scotch Irish*, I, 621-622, estimated them at 5,000 a

of 1790 was taken there were only 44,000 Irish-born in the United States.[4] These, and the emigrants during the French Revolutionary and Napoleonic Wars, were almost all Scots-Irish. Six thousand a year left during the hard times of 1800-1802, but this figure was far above normal.[5] Then for three years, 1812-1814, emigration practically ceased. When in 1816 the number again reached 6,000, it was considered extraordinary, and the 20,000 who followed in 1818 inaugurated a new era. Clearly, the old Scots-Irish movement, steady though it was from 1725 to 1812, cannot explain the great exodus of the nineteenth century, though it provided an invaluable example for those whose history we are about to relate.

The first issues of the Irish newspapers in 1815 brought news of the signing of peace between England and the United States, and on January 5th the Dublin *Evening Post* in an editorial on the probable effects, pointed out the likelihood of an extensive emigration of farmers to the United States. Three months later the final news of ratification by the American government reached Ireland. This was a signal for the appearance in the Belfast and Londonderry papers of advertisements for passengers to America.[6]

No heavy exodus to the United States was possible in 1815. The American flaxseed ships, which had formerly carried the bulk of the emigrant trade, were late in reach-

year from 1725 to 1768, but he allows too many to the earlier years. See Archbishop Hugh Boulter, *Letters*, I, 209.

    [4] *A century of population growth*, p. 117.

    [5] Friedrich Kapp, the first scientific student of American immigration, who used the papers of the New York Emigration Commissioners, gave 6,000 as the maximum estimate of annual Irish immigration at this time. He took this figure from the reports of 1800-1802, not allowing for the unusual pressure of want in the Irish linen industry during those years. See his *Immigration*, in Journal of Social Science, No. 2 (1870), pp. 1-30.

    [6] March 21, 1815.

ing Ireland, thus missing the usual emigrant season; and the demand for tonnage for freight purposes was so great that it was difficult to obtain ships to carry passengers in any numbers. Cargo vessels sometimes took a few, but interest was concentrated in loading goods as promptly as possible, and merchants or shipbrokers were not disposed to trouble themselves with human freight. It is probable that the total emigration from Ireland to the North American mainland in 1815 did not exceed 1500 persons.[7] This was accompanied, however, by an extraordinary movement to Newfoundland, and some 5000 persons left Ireland for St. Johns.

The true emigrant trade was established in the years 1816 to 1818. During 1816 and 1817, from six to nine thousand Irishmen sailed for America in each year, and in 1818 the number was more than doubled. From the beginning the trade was closely linked with the ordinary commercial intercourse between America and the United Kingdom, though commencing in 1816, ships[8] were chartered especially to convey emigrants. This was true even of vessels sailing to New York, to which there was a considerable exportation of Irish goods. But it was the shipping requirements of the American exporters which more than anything else except the passenger acts determined the course of the emigrant trade. Merchants who intended to bring a cargo of Canadian timber or of American staves, ashes, and flaxseed into Irish ports found it profitable to send the vessel back with a freight of emigrants, the return destination being determined to a considerable extent by the likelihood of picking up another eastbound

[7] There are no statistics for this period. For a discussion of this and succeeding figures see Appendix A.

[8] "Ships" in the modern sense; i.e. vessels. Every type from a ship to a schooner was employed. Brigs predominated at first, but later gave way to ships.

cargo. These cargoes need not be for Ireland, since approximately half the ships in the emigrant trade belonged to the coast towns of western England, Wales, and Scotland, and were glad to take goods for any port between Lands End and the Clyde. On the western voyage their ballast or cargo of coal or salt was loaded in England or Wales, and the ships stopped in Irish ports only long enough to embark passengers.

The American commodities which affected the course of trade came from four main areas. Newfoundland shipped fish and oil in large quantities to Waterford, and on a much smaller scale to Belfast, Dublin, and Cork. The fishing vessels in which this trade was carried on were ill adapted for the passenger trade and in most years played a minor part in emigration, but in 1815 when shipping was in such demand they provided an important means of leaving Ireland. The rest of British America, from Quebec to St. Andrews in New Brunswick, had one great staple export, timber and timber products. This required a large tonnage in ships easily convertible into passenger vessels, and the timber ships, for which there were almost no westbound cargoes, became the greatest single medium of transportation. In 1815, the timber trade was practically at a standstill, because the Canadians, who had not expected peace so soon, failed to cut their trees.[9] But from 1816 on, an increasing number of these ships sailed from Irish ports for Quebec, Miramichi, Pictou, Prince Edward Island, Halifax, St. John,[10] and St. Andrews. Generally speaking, about half the trade was to and from Quebec, with rather more than two-thirds of the remainder going to the New Brunswick ports. The demand for timber was common to all Ireland, and timber ships were to be found in every port.

9 *Belfast News Letter,* Sept. 1, 1815.
10 The modern spelling, to distinguish it from St. Johns, Newfoundland.

Cargoes from the United States were more varied. New York and Philadelphia continued, as in colonial days, to send shipments of flaxseed every spring. Other valuable imports were pot and pearl ashes, tobacco, and occasionally flour, cotton, turpentine and other naval stores. Cotton and naval stores were usually shipped direct from the southern ports to Belfast, the only Irish city with any extensive communication with the southern states. Other commodities were shipped from New York, Philadelphia, and Baltimore to all parts of Ireland, but particularly to Belfast and Dublin, which together possessed well over half the entire American trade. Londonderry and Newry imported flaxseed only, and were dependent upon it for their emigrant vessels, when special ships from other ports were not obtainable. New York, the clearing house for American goods of all kinds, had a greater connection with every port in Ireland than had any other American city. Along with more valuable imports, every vessel from the United States carried a large quantity of staves. These, though frequently forming the bulk of the cargo, were not of sufficient value to be shipped for their own sake. Their place on the westbound voyage was taken by coal, salt, or ballast, while emigrants replaced the more valuable goods which made the trade profitable. It is therefore correct to speak of the westbound traffic simply as an emigrant trade; but only in exceptional years were its rewards so great that it paid to send a vessel with passengers regardless of the profit on a return cargo. Such a year was 1818, when the *Nikolai Pawlowitsch* took a load of emigrants from Belfast to Baltimore and returned immediately in ballast to pick up a second group.[11]

One feature of the American trade particularly favorable to emigration was the fact that with the exception of

11 *Belfast News Letter*, Oct. 23, 1818.

the New York packets it was wholly seasonal, and that the seasons were in most cases those best suited to emigrants. Prospective settlers were cautioned again and again to arrive in America as early in the year as possible, so that the earnings and experience of the summer could help to tide over the winter when employment was often bad and the pioneer was dependent on the crops of the preceding seasons. This warning was already pretty generally known in Ireland, and especially in Ulster, before 1815, and it was early confirmed by the misfortunes of those who emigrated late in the seasons of 1816 and 1817. April, May, and June were the recognized emigrant months, and after June few ships carried a full quota of passengers. This was practically the only period at which emigration was possible to Quebec and Newfoundland. Vessels did not leave Ireland before April, in time to reach Quebec at the opening of the St. Lawrence. Those which sailed after June were likely to arrive too late to obtain a return cargo of timber, and if they were delayed, might find themselves ice-bound for the winter. The danger of contrary winds in July and August, in contrast to the generally favorable winds of the spring season, also tended to prevent late sailings. In the case of Newfoundland, the fleet with provisions and other supplies from Waterford regularly set sail every April, returning in October and November, and there was no extensive shipping at any other time of the year.

Similar commercial advantages facilitated the spring trade with the United States. The flaxseed ships tried to reach Ireland in time for the spring planting, and became available for emigration as soon as they were unloaded. Other commodities might be shipped at any time of the year, but it was profitable to ship them with flaxseed in mixed cargoes. Even the Mediterranean trade of Ireland aided this seasonal migration. The southern ports sent

cargoes of provisions to Spain, Portugal, and their Atlantic possessions every winter, and these vessels often
returned in time to take part in the carrying of emigrants.
Only the timber trade of Nova Scotia and New Brunswick
remained entirely independent of seasonal interests, and
ships were as likely to sail in the fall as at any other time.
In fact, the Quebec ships, after returning in the summer
to Ireland, frequently made a second journey to New
Brunswick for timber, thus keeping busy through part of
the winter. This feature of the trade to the Maritime
Provinces gives to them a peculiar interest in the study
of the course of emigration, because it aids in determining the demand for emigrant ships. In rush years, even
the autumn sailings to St. John and St. Andrews carried
large numbers of emigrants, while at other times the same
ships made the voyage in ballast without passengers.

Both American and British ships participated in the
emigrant traffic. Shipping to British possessions was
limited by the Navigation Acts to British bottoms, but
the bulk of the trade between Great Britain and the
United States was carried in American vessels, and the
majority of those which advertised for passengers in
1815 were American. For a short period in 1816 British
ships threatened to supplant American even in this trade;
but from 1817 on the greater part of the traffic to the
United States remained in American hands. Wherever
there was competition American ships were preferred by
merchants and passengers for their superior officers and
crews, an advantage in part offset by the stronger organization of British shipping interests in Ireland. In
1817 the American tonnage in the trade from Ireland to
the United States was 21,894, as against 13,472 tons British. In 1820-1822 Americans had seventy-five per cent of
the trade.[12] The practice of obtaining vessels from the

12 *American State Papers*, Commerce and Navigation, II, 114, 606, 733.

west coast of Great Britain has been mentioned, but with the development of a more regular trade between Ireland and America, numbers of emigrant ships were bought by the Irish merchants, and others were built in Ireland. Emigration was thus one factor in a material increase in Irish-owned shipping which took place in the years after 1815.

The control of the Irish emigrant trade was almost wholly in the hands of Irish merchants, who found that in addition to linens, salt, provisions, glass, etc., they could make room for a considerable body of emigrants and so increase the profits of their voyage. In the numerous instances where vessels which had brought in loads of timber or American goods could find no outward cargo the sale of passages proved a blessing. It was a short step from this to the chartering of ships especially for the purpose of emigration. That step was taken early in 1816, but the business still remained in the hands of the regular merchants, who probably expected to pick up a return cargo by the same vessel. Not until 1817 are there evidences of the existence of offices, subsidiary as a rule to some commercial house, which made a specialty of selling passages and did not engage in general business.[13] Ship captains shared regularly in the profits of the passenger trade. They sometimes took cargoes and passengers as a private venture, but as a rule worked in conjunction with a mercantile firm.

The emigrant offices, whatever their character, depended upon advertising to secure passengers. In the north this was customarily carried on through the newspapers, where practically all ships from Londonderry,

[13] Old firms such as John Shaw and Co. of Belfast put their emigrant business into the hands of younger members of the family. The first independent passenger broker may have been Francis Taggart of Dublin and Belfast, who commenced business on June 1, 1818.

Belfast, and Newry advertised from a month to three months before sailing. Once the trade was well established advertisements appeared regularly every February or even earlier, and often ceased long before the vessels sailed,—a probable indication that the passenger list was already filled. Some ships, presumably because of uncertainty as to the date of arrival and availability for emigration purposes, were advertised spasmodically. Advertisements also appeared in the southern papers, but they seem to have been rather the exception than the rule. This was certainly true in Dublin, where the Dublin *Evening Post,* although a popular paper favourable to emigration, carried advertisements for less than half the ships which sailed. *Saunders News Letter,* a somewhat aristocratic sheet, carried still fewer; *Ramsay's Waterford Chronicle* advertised only a small number of the emigrant vessels from that port, and the *Limerick General Advertiser* almost none. This is in part a reflection of the slight extent of emigration from the south, but it also implies the existence of some other means of publicity. We know that the publication of handbills for all sorts of purposes was general in Ireland, and it is probable that these were used for advertising emigrant ships. Unfortunately none of them seem to have been preserved.

We have newspaper advertisements for ships from all the leading ports, and for Belfast and Londonderry for at least four-fifths of those that actually sailed. The *Belfast News Letter* and *Londonderry Journal* not only contain preliminary advertisements for ships expected to sail, but also carry final notices and warnings to passengers telling them when they must be on board, in a form which implies that this was the only official communication between the shipping agent and his passengers. These shipping notices supply an interesting and varied picture of the emigrant trade of the time, and their steady

increase is a valuable indication of its growing importance. Early in 1816 the *Belfast News Letter* began print-
ing a special section devoted to notices of ships for
America, a feature which did not appear in the Dublin
papers until 1818, and not elsewhere until much later. The
rise and spread of rural emigration agencies, subordinate
to the central agencies at the ports, must have done much
to supplant other methods of advertising. The first of
these were branches of the house of Robinson and Buchanan of Londonderry, the oldest emigration port in
Ireland, which had for over a century kept in close communication with its American colonists. In years to come,
the Buchanan family, with members in Omagh, County
Tyrone, and Londonderry, in St. John, Quebec, New
York, and Louisville, became an outstanding factor in
the continuous contact between the Ulster emigrants and
their home country. No other port had rural agencies before 1818, when numerous branch houses were established
by firms in Belfast, Newry, and Dublin.

The advertisements furnish a key to the things which
the emigrant thought important in the matter of transportation. At first it had been sufficient to give the name
of the ship and its master, the tonnage, destination, and
probable date of sailing. Later, a standard type of advertisement appeared during normal seasons of which the
following may serve as a sample:

NOW IN THIS PORT—FOR PHILADELPHIA. The beautiful
coppered ship HIPPOCAMPI, 350 tons burden. Captain TI-
PIER will sail for the above port first fair wind after the 16th
June. This ship sails remarkably fast, has the very best accommodation for Passengers, and, as a number have already engaged,
speedy application will be necessary to prevent disappointment.

A SURGEON will be shipped and every care and attention
paid by the Subscribers to have an abundance of water and Fire
laid in for use of those who wish to embrace so favourable an op-

portunity. For Freight or Passage please apply to the Captain on Board, at Donegal quay, or to J. SHAW and CO, 47 Princes Street.

Belfast, May 31, 1816.[14]

The most important item was a quick voyage, not only because the vessels were small and most passengers poor sailors, but because short rations and even starvation might overtake those who were too long on the ocean. In 1815 provisions were furnished by the shipping company in accordance with the requirements of the British passenger act of 1803, and included meat and molasses as well as the standard Irish foods. This proved too expensive a method of provisioning. It was moreover unsuited to the habits of most Irish emigrants, and a cheaper trade in ships supplying only water and fuel soon replaced most of the more expensive passages.[15] Licenses from the Treasury to dispense with those terms in the passenger acts requiring captains to give out meat and provisions regularly during the voyage made this practice possible, and a change of language in the act of 1817,[16] which governed the trade to British America, may have allowed masters to carry provisions without issuing them.[17] The same act dispensed with the presence of a surgeon, formerly required on all vessels carrying fifty or more persons, and vessels to the United States made the most of

[14] *Belfast News Letter*, June 11, 1816. The same advertisement appeared in the Dublin *Evening Post*.

[15] This practice seems to have continued longest where it was an established feature of transportation to America, that is Londonderry; whereas from Belfast and the southern ports passages without provisions became the rule in 1816.

[16] *57 Geo. III, c. 10.*

[17] S. C. Johnson, who gives a chapter to conditions of transport in his *Emigration from the United Kingdom to North America*, overlooks this act, and assumes (p. 104) that ships sailing openly and legally did issue provisions. The most honest and unquestionably legal ships, even to the United States, only advertised fuel and water.

their superiority in this respect. The advertisement of a surgeon in 1816, therefore, could only have been directed against illegal competitors, or those carrying few passengers. As emigrants were usually crowded either in narrow between-decks, or in one-deck ships on top of the cargo, where the only requirement was five clear vertical feet below the deck, unhealthy conditions were unavoidable, even when contagious disease did not break out, and a surgeon was a valuable addition.

Students of emigration have written lengthy descriptions of the evils of this "new slave trade," as it was sometimes called, comparing them to the horrors of the Middle Passage.[18] A close examination of conditions on a large number of ships seems to indicate that the abuses have been exaggerated. Most of the descriptions have come from years such as 1817, 1831 and 1832, and 1847, when the trade was altogether abnormal, and the chance that some passenger would bring fever or cholera on board overwhelming. In the period we are describing, even including 1817, outbreaks of contagious disease on emigrant ships were rare, and deaths on board infrequent considering the poverty of the voyagers and the numbers of small children, for whom the trip was always most difficult. Probably two-thirds of the deaths were those of children. For our purpose the chief importance of bad conditions was in their effect upon the trade, or the general current of emigration, and it is safe to say that at this time they had none. Many slow voyages and wrecks in 1815, due to exceptionally unfavorable weather, did not in the least deter the emigrants of 1816; while unhealthy

18 See Johnson, *Emigration from the United Kingdom to North America*, pp. 101-122; and Cowan, *British emigration to British North America, 1783-1837*, pp. 205-226. These interesting descriptions, correct for the years of extraordinary traffic or disease, give a very misleading impression if applied to a longer period.

conditions and reports of abuses in the next two years were entirely unavailing to check the emigration of 1818.

The abuses which most seriously affected the emigrants took place before the ship sailed. Agents and captains were artists in misrepresentation.[19] The most obvious item of falsification was the tonnage of the vessel, which largely determined the speed and comfort of the voyage. The advertised tonnage of the *Hippocampi* was 350; its

[19] Their tricks were not confined to hoodwinking emigrants. In 1816 the British brig *Fame* for St. John (Francis Taggart & Co.) and the American ship *Lucy* (Thos. Folingsbye), engaged in a duel for passengers. The *Fame* opened fire with advertisements of cheap passage, including food, and as an extra bait: ''Persons can, for one dollar, be landed on the most populous part of the state of Massachusetts'' (i.e., the Maine coast!). This was answered by an anonymous advertisement denying the truth of the distance from New Brunswick as given by the *Fame*, while the *Lucy* advertisement warned against the disease, overcrowding and long voyages of vessels to British America. The *Fame* then resorted to veiled warnings: ''the capture of Pensacola by storm is substantially a declaration of war on the part of the United States against Spain; and the strongest proof of the anxiety of the Public for *British* Vessels, is, that a schooner, 72 tons burthen per register, is now on the berth in the port of Belfast, for passengers to the Continent of America.—Wonders will never cease! . . . An advertisement having appeared relative to an old British transport . . . which vessel was captured during the American war, and now sails under the U.S. flag, as the American ship *Lucy*, the public are warned against engaging their passage on board said vessel, before making due inquiries from those on whose information they can rely.''

Six days later things were going badly, for Taggart, a Dublin man, wrote: ''The port of Belfast is a wonderful place. The ship *Lucy* has jumped from 700 to 900 tons burthen since she arrived here. These up country folks are strange animals—how easy it is to gull the Northerns.'' Next week he felt confident enough to double his rates of passage, while saying nothing new against the *Lucy*. The climax came on August 28th. The *Lucy*, ready to sail, was held up and her captain put in prison on charges by a certain disreputable character, who was supposed but never proved to have been employed by Taggart. The outcome of this little comedy was that the *Lucy* sailed, her captain restored, but the *Fame* did not. Taggart, an upstart agent, went out of business. Probably the northern emigrants were not so gullible as he thought! *Belfast News Letter*, July 10, 14, 21, 28; August 3, 7, 11, 27; September 1, 1816.

tonnage per register, 162. This is a very modest exaggeration, and the average claim of the Belfast agents was about three times the actual registered tonnage. Southern agents, who were newer to the trade, did not at first follow this practice, but they soon caught on, and exaggerations became as common in Dublin as they were farther north. Only in Waterford, where a large section of the community was well acquainted with ships and shipping, were the actual registered tonnages given, and the emigration from Waterford was too insignificant to excite the competitive imaginations of its agents.

A much more serious abuse was the misrepresentation of dates of sailing. Here again writers have over-stated the facts. It is true that the first advertised sailing date of a vessel was usually a month or more in advance of the actual clearance date; but emigrants, at least in districts from which emigration was common, did not pay undue attention to these first notices. In all northern ports the agents inserted a final notice of clearance to warn passengers of the day when they must be on board. In most cases these appeared about a week beforehand, allowing ample time for the emigrant to come to port and make his final preparation. Only in a few cases of obviously poor class ships out of Londonderry did the final notice appear only a day or two before the vessel cleared, implying that the passenger would be in town ready to go whenever word came. Vessels did, however, delay their clearing, and an analysis of the Belfast trade for 1816 shows that this came on the average eight days later than the notified date.[20] The average in itself is misleading, because it includes one ship which gave four successive final notices, and actually cleared over two months after the first one. In general, during the regular emigrant season clearances were reasonably prompt, and delay is a sign of slack trade

[20] Compiled from advertisements and ship news, *Belfast News Letter.*

or over-competition, whereas during the autumn and winter no great reliance could be placed on the announcements.

The principal effect of delay upon the poor emigrant family was to diminish, sometimes even to exhaust, its store of provisions. In cases where the ship found the supplies, there was some question as to the master's responsibility for giving out rations before the ship actually sailed. From the existence of advertisements stating that food would be given out from the date set for clearance, whether the ship sailed or not, I assume that this was not the universal practice. In any case, the greatest hardship fell upon those passengers who "found themselves"; and in some instances appeals were made to public charity to enable emigrants to renew their supplies after they had been defrauded by unscrupulous agents.

The chief safeguards of the emigrant were the passenger acts, the first of which was passed in 1803,[21] as a result of exceptionally hard times and extensive emigration in the preceding two years. Before taking up the history of these Acts, so intimately connected with the direction and character of emigration, it may be well to say a word as to their operation. Writers on emigration have been prone to assume that the early acts were largely ineffective, although examples of violation have come mostly from later years. The enforcement of the Act of 1803, the principal law governing ocean transportation until its repeal in 1823, was in the hands of the customs officials. As originally passed, it required a resident magistrate to supervise with the collector of customs the passenger list of an outgoing vessel, but this provision was found burdensome, and repealed by a special amending Act in 1818.[22] Masters and owners of vessels were required to give bond not to exceed the legal number of passengers, to carry out the other terms of the acts, and to keep and report at the end of the voyage a full log showing that the provisions had been complied with. The efforts of government were largely concerned with keeping numbers within the law. Collectors were expected to muster passengers before giving final clearance papers to the master, and severe penalties were prescribed for taking any others on board after the muster had been held. Final notices of ships from Dublin and Waterford always stated that the muster was to take place on a particular day; but advertisements and emigrant news of Belfast and Londonderry omit all mention of it, a circumstance which may well have been due to the fact that the practice was too well known to need comment.

The most frequent violations of this provision are said to have been amongst small vessels sailing illegally from obscure bays or harbors where no Customs official would be present,[23] but a check of arrivals from Ireland in Canada and the United States shows that the proportion of ships coming from such minor harbors was insignificant. The law could be evaded by collusion between shipper, master, and collector; and it is perhaps a curious coincidence that one of the most successful emigrant ships from Londonderry, the *Marcus Hill,* which as a rule made no public advertisement—in the north an indication of a somewhat shady trade—was named after the collector of the port,[24] a close friend of the leading merchants.

Revenue cruisers, whose main duty was the prevention of smuggling into Ireland, and between Ireland and Great

[23] Johnson speaks of such sailings as "a daily occurrence"—*Emigration from the United Kingdom to North America,* p. 103. From Ireland, there was not one in a month unless the vessels were so successful that they escaped all notice on both sides of the Atlantic. The exaggerated statements of passenger act reformers were drawn from rush years.

[24] Not Lord Marcus Hill, chief patron of the city of Londonderry, but presumably a relative.

Britain, served as a final government check upon emigrant vessels. The only example of the seizure of an emigrant ship during this period which has come under my notice was that of the *Hippocampi,* whose advertisement has been cited above. It had sailed from Belfast with about twenty-five more passengers than its tonnage permitted, and was forced to return to port and disembark some of them, and a fine was laid upon the master and owner.[25] The total penalty was not severe, and other vessels may have chosen to take the risk. The absence of seizures might indicate either that the revenue cruisers were not attempting to enforce the law, or that the trade was on the whole legal. The best evidence of a general compliance with the terms of the act comes from the lists of passengers regularly printed in the *Quebec Mercury,* and occasionally in various American papers. Such lists in almost all cases show a total immigration well within the legal capacity of the ships involved. Exceptions appear only in 1818 and 1819, and are indications of a poor class of emigrant traffic which was springing up at that time.

The passenger act of 1803 allowed one person, including passengers and crew, for every two tons unladen in a British ship going from the British Isles to any part of America, except Newfoundland and Labrador. Foreign ships were restricted to one passenger to every five tons, regardless of the number of the crew or weight of cargo. This obviously gave a great advantage to the British shipowner; but so extensive was the demand for passages in 1815, and so high were the fares, that American and British ships participated equally in the emigrant trade of that year, which went almost wholly to New York and Newfoundland. In neither case can we say that the destination truly indicates the goal of the emigrants; for all the available ships returned to New York, and passen-

[25] *Belfast News Letter,* July 2, 1816.

gers, who were then merely a sideline, had perforce to go there too. Even Londonderry, which had much stronger historical connections with Philadelphia than with New York, sent its flaxseed ships back to the northern port. Londonderry, Belfast, and Dublin sent at least thirty vessels with passengers to New York in 1815, and to judge from occasional references in the newspapers, a number of others must have gone from Newry. We have no means of knowing how many emigrants were carried in these ships, but if they were in the same proportion as in succeeding years there were probably between one and two thousand.

The influence of the passenger acts is illustrated by the singular popularity of the Newfoundland route in 1815. Ships could go to Newfoundland without restriction, and passages were therefore cheap.[26] Over thirty-six hundred persons, almost all of them from Ireland and very poor, are said to have gone there in 1815.[27] The majority seem to have sailed from Waterford, but some ships were advertised from Belfast, and possibly from other ports as well. Many of these people undoubtedly went on to the United States or to Canada in the same year;[28] others remained through the winter, causing more acute distress than had ever before been known in St. Johns. During 1816 small parties of the emigrants went to Quebec, while

[26] Newfoundland and Labrador were exempted from the terms of the Act by *44 Geo. III*, c. 44. Miss Cowan says the fare from Ireland to Newfoundland was ten shillings. *British emigration to British North America*, p. 131. *Note.*

[27] Actually 3,026 men and 373 women officially reported, but six ships make no report. *Belfast News Letter*, Sept. 12, 1815. This report appeared in all the Irish papers and was the basis of a paragraph in the *Annual Register* for 1815.

[28] The first accounts assumed they were all bound for the United States. Miss Cowan says many reshipped to Nova Scotia and Prince Edward Island. *British emigration to British North America*, p. 131. *Note.* I think rather more went to Quebec. *The Mercury* notes a number of arrivals.

even greater numbers returned to Waterford. It may have been the reports of hardship, which were known in Waterford early in 1816, or it may have been a new Passenger Act in that year regulating the Newfoundland and Labrador trades,[29] but whatever the cause, emigration to Newfoundland practically ceased in 1816 and never revived as an important part of the Irish movement to America.

The emigration of 1816 indicates clearly the course which would have been pursued had the passenger acts remained unaltered. The year opened with the Act of 1803 in full force, but a series of diplomatic exchanges between John Quincy Adams and the British government resulted early in the emigrant season in an order giving American as well as British vessels permission to carry one passenger for every two tons.[30] Parliament soon altered the arrangement, but for over two months, at the height of the season, restriction was at a minimum and conditions for carrying passengers to the United States and British North America were identical. It speaks conclusively for the preferences of the Irish that the exodus in this year was almost wholly to the United States. Over two thousand emigrants left Belfast for New York alone. Very nearly as many went from Londonderry, and probably a thousand from Dublin. Philadelphia received at least a thousand, and Baltimore many hundreds.[31] In addition, there were a few emigrant ships to Boston, Norfolk, and Charleston. Canada, on the other hand, got almost no Irish. Less than two hundred were noted in the arrivals at Quebec. This was not for lack of shipping facilities, for at least a dozen vessels arrived from Irish

[29] *56 Geo. III*, c. 83. This is interesting as the first attempt to limit passengers in accordance with space. Each was to have twelve square feet of deck.

[30] For a full discussion of the politics of emigration, see *infra* Chapter VI.

[31] All estimated. See Appendix.

ports. With a single exception they brought no more than half a dozen passengers each. At the same time hundreds were arriving weekly from Scotland. It seems certain that the new emigration from the south of Ireland, like the older movement from Ulster, was setting definitely towards the United States. Occasional attempts were made in advertisements to spread information about Canada, and to emphasize the advantages of free grants of land and government aid. Similar attempts, often untruthful as regards the assistance provided by government, were made to popularize the Maritime Provinces, but the shipping thither was even less than that to Quebec, and emigration negligible.

It was the passenger acts of July 1, 1816, and March 17, 1817, which changed the course of Irish emigration, and gave to it the character which it retained until 1827. The first act, which limited all vessels to the United States to one passenger for five tons, had immediate effects. Vessels about to leave Ireland found themselves required to return some of the passages already paid, and very naturally raised the fare on those which remained.[32] So great was the demand, however, that even as late as September, 1816, ships were able to get a full quota of passengers under the new restrictions. The act of March 17, 1817, which superseded all earlier legislation for ships to Canada, Nova Scotia, and New Brunswick, permitted vessels to carry one adult, or three children under fourteen years of age, for every one and a half tons unladen. The usual minimum provision requirement for twelve weeks was included, but so worded that the master need not give out provisions if the passengers had already supplied their own, and the presence of a surgeon was no longer obligatory. The means of enforcement were practically unchanged, but as an additional check, collectors,

[32] Advertisement of the *Hercules* in *Londonderry Journal*, July 30, 1816.

after mustering the passengers, were required to give a certified list to the master to be inspected by an official in the colonies before any passengers were allowed to land.[33]

The advantage of the British America ships came too late in 1816 to affect the emigrants of that year, but at the opening of the 1817 season when they were able to carry ten passengers for every three taken to the United States, they were assured of all but the wealthiest emigrants. Canada and New Brunswick rapidly absorbed the bulk of the emigrant traffic and became the accepted routes to New York and Philadelphia as well as to the west. Most of the change came immediately. Instead of the thirty-one ships which had gone from Londonderry to New York and Philadelphia in 1816, there were now six. The falling off from Belfast was less marked, and from Dublin there was no decrease; but in these two cases the continuance of regular trade, and indeed the revived demand in America for British and Irish goods which had been at a low ebb in 1816, accounts for the maintenance of considerable shipping. The reverse side of the picture is the appearance of an important trade to Canada and the Maritime Provinces from all the emigrant ports. Londonderry sent ten ships to Halifax, St. John and St. Andrews; Belfast and Dublin each sent five, but their principal trade was with Quebec, to which between them they sent over thirteen hundred emigrants.

A number of factors undoubtedly contributed to this change in the course of trade. The flood of emigrants in 1816 had produced a surplus of labor in the American ports and led to hard times, reports of which were not slow in reaching Ireland. James Buchanan, the British Consul at New York, took advantage of the situation to urge all settlers to go to Canada, and succeeded in securing from the British government authority to spend up to ten dol-

33 57 Geo. III, c. 10.

lars per head in forwarding distressed emigrants to Upper Canada. Under this authority he sent over 3500 people, mostly from Ireland, to the Peterborough district.[34] He did not wait until the distressed came to him for aid, but sent his agents aboard incoming vessels offering free transportation to all who would accept.[35] The government at home made the most of these facts and increased for the time being its offers of assistance to emigrants to British America.[36] This was the work of the Colonial Office; but independently and perhaps unintentionally parliament aided the change in another way. The Canada timber trade would in any case have picked up rapidly after 1815, but the government as one of its measures to strengthen Canada and secure its allegiance after the war of 1812, had put into effect a new scale of timber duties, under which Canadian timber was admitted free, while foreign timber paid 65 shillings a load.[37] The result was a sharp decline in the Irish Baltic trade, particularly noticeable in the northern emigration ports, and a very rapid expansion in their trade with the American colo-

[34] He had sent 3,566 by May 1, 1819, nearly half of them in 1816— *Revised return of emigrants assisted to Canada.* C.O. 384/4, p. 299.

[35] Letter of a County Down farmer who emigrated in the spring of 1816: ''When we arrived at New York, we were greatly embarrassed by the intrigues of the British Consul. He sent his emissaries among the passengers of our ship as he did the passengers of other ships, intimating that there was no employment for emigrants, and all here was in starvation, but that he would send them free to Canada, and give them lands and livings, on swearing they would never enter the United States as citizens. Some were so weak as to be deluded, but the passengers in our ship being mostly republicans, went on cheerily to look for employment.'' Dublin *Evening Post*, Oct. 16, 1817.

[36] *Infra*, Chapter VI.

[37] Porter, *Progress of the Nation*, II, 122. The timber duties were instituted as a reprisal against the closing of the Baltic ports in 1807, but the Act of. 1815 was to foster colonial shipping. There were similar duties on deals, headings, etc.

nies. The new duties may not have helped the Canadian timbermen in any great degree. Indeed it was alleged that a large part of the so-called Canadian timber came from the United States; but it did secure the conveyance of the timber to British ships sailing from colonial ports, and undoubtedly stimulated emigration to British North America. While other branches of the British carrying trade were declining under a variety of difficulties, the timber ships, taking the only bulk product which would repay a long voyage, absorbed more than a third of British tonnage.[38] The worst vessels, rated C3 at Lloyds, were good enough for timber, and they needed only a few extra deals hastily put up for berths in any Irish port, to be ready for emigrants.

A second stimulus to the Canadian trade was furnished by the conflict over West Indian Trade, and secondarily over the New Brunswick plaster of Paris trade, which reached a head in 1817. Early in the year Congress had passed a law forbidding the importation of plaster of Paris after July 4,[39] with the result that in the summer of 1817 there was a rush of ships from all the ports in New Brunswick and Nova Scotia, providing a regular service to United States ports as far south as Norfolk.[40] The trade continued to be carried on illegally, or by license of the colonial governors, and may have brought some passengers to the United States, but after the first year it was no longer essential to emigration by that route. Even in 1817 one vessel carrying only passengers sailed from Halifax to New York, and from 1818 on such trips were frequent. The importance of the plaster of Paris trade was in providing easy facilities for emigrants at a time when

---

[38] There is a masterly review of the shipping situation, 1815-1826, in *Huskisson's Speeches*, pp. 488 ff.

[39] "The Plaster of Paris Act."

[40] Reports of British Consuls, B.T. 6/23.

the route to the United States by way of the Maritime Provinces was first becoming generally known.

It seems obvious from the course of trade that a change in conditions of transportation, rather than any disinclination of passengers to go to the United States, was creating a new direction of emigrant traffic. This is clearly true of Londonderry, which even in 1817 had no Quebec trade and sent all its vessels to the ports most convenient for the United States. Up to 1817 ships advertised for the British Colonies had laid emphasis upon climate, soil, conditions for granting land, and other advantages, but in 1817 and 1818 ships for Halifax, St. John and St. Andrews were advertised as "for the United States." This route was first used in 1816 when two ships from Waterford, advertised as clearing for Halifax and St. John, touched there, and then brought their passengers to New York,[41] but no general appreciation of its advantages existed before 1817—and indeed throughout most of 1816 they were non-existent. It is impossible to say what proportion of the Irish passengers to Nova Scotia and New Brunswick went on to the United States, but ninety per cent is a reasonable estimate. The capacity of the provinces to absorb settlers was very limited in 1817, and probably only those Irish stayed who had not the means to go on to New England, which was already turning from agriculture and commerce to manufacture and needed cheap labor.

It is likewise difficult to determine to what extent Quebec emigrants went on to the United States. Obviously Quebec could only be used as an entrance to the western country, including upper New York, although it was advertised as the "cheapest route to Charleston."[42] The

---

[41] *Waterford Chronicle,* May, 1816; Consular Return, New York for July-December, 1816, B.T. 6/23.

[42] The *Economy* from Dublin advertised: "such as intend to visit New

emphasis on pioneer emigration, that is, on routes to the trans-Alleghany districts of the United States, first appeared in 1816 in the advertisement of a ship from Belfast to Baltimore.[43] In 1817 it became common, and stress was laid repeatedly on the cheapest and most direct route to the Pittsburgh district. Quebec ships soon dropped their references to government land grants, or subordinated them to a recital of the advantages of Quebec as a gateway to the West; and it is safe to say that the majority of the emigrants went there in the hope of going on to the United States, though it is not so certain that all or nearly all reached their destination. At a much later date it was estimated that two-thirds of the Quebec emigrants left the colony, and this is perhaps as good a guess as any.[44]

The decisive factor in the new course of emigration was cheapness. Fares always varied a great deal according to the time of year and the demand for passages. In 1816 we find a minimum passage rate of £6 from Belfast to Quebec,[45] a fare of £7 from the same port to Baltimore,[46] while another ship earlier in the year charged seven guineas to St. Andrews.[47] In other words, there was

York, Philadelphia, Baltimore, or Charleston, will find this vessel by far the cheapest conveyance, she being the only vessel for Upper Canada, which is so convenient to the above places." Dublin *Evening Post*, Mar. 25, 1819.

[43] The *William; Belfast News Letter*, Feb. 9, 1816; "for Kentucky and the West."

[44] A. C. Buchanan (emigration agent at Quebec from 1828) wrote opposite his table of immigration: "It is calculated that an average of 2/3 of all the emigrants arriving in these years (1815-1828) passed into the United States." Buchanan to Aylmer, May 7, 1831; C.O. 42/223. But Buchanan had not been in Quebec before 1828, and there was no source from which accurate information could be obtained; furthermore, he made no effort to distinguish between different years, though the reasons for going *via* Quebec varied.

[45] By the *Dart; Belfast News Letter*, June 25, 1816.

[46] By the *Nancy; Belfast News Letter*, July 2, 1816.

[47] The *Thomas Gelston*. But this was a superior ship which sailed regu-

no distinct advantage in the Canadian route in 1816. In
1817, the standard rate from Ireland to the United States
was ten guineas.[48] This fare was quoted from Belfast to
New York in June.[49] On the same day a ship from Londonderry to St. Andrews offered to take passengers for
five guineas.[50] As the Canada ships also took three children for one full fare, the advantages for poor families
are obvious.

The year 1817 was one of transition. The full effect of
the factors which were bringing about the transference
of the major part of the emigrant traffic to Canadian
ports was not apparent until 1818. There was no actual
drop in the number of passengers to the United States.
Pressure throughout the year was so heavy that most
ships were able to take full quotas for any port, but the
enormous increase in the total emigration, which probably
reached twenty thousand in 1818, was largely absorbed
by the Canadian ships. It is unusual to see the price of
passages falling during a rush year, but the numbers of
ships available brought them to a new low level. While
direct fares to the United States remained at ten guineas,
indirect passage by way of New Brunswick, which was
now regularly quoted, could be had for £5.[51] The regular
rate to St. John, and also to Quebec, was three and a half
guineas,[52] and one advertisement offered passages at two

larly each spring, and could doubtless afford to charge more than others.
Its cabin fare was 12 guineas. *Belfast News Letter,* Feb. 9, 1816.

[48] So quoted for Belfast-New York, Belfast-Baltimore and Dublin-
Philadelphia, May to July, 1817.

[49] By the *John M'Cammon; Belfast News Letter.*

[50] The *Jane.* It had been trying vainly to get passengers for Halifax.
Londonderry Journal.

[51] E.g. The *Ganges* for St. John. In this case the master guaranteed to
supply conveyance from St. John to the United States; in others the original
ship went on. *Belfast News Letter,* July 31, 1818.

[52] From Londonderry, Belfast and Dublin. From lesser ports it was whatever the ship could get. The *Harp* from Limerick wanted five guineas to St.

and a half guineas. This last is untrustworthy, however, as it came from an agent of shady reputation, whose quoted fares altered from week to week.[53]

The tide of emigration was now at its flood. Quebec on the north drew something over five thousand emigrants, of whom probably eighty per cent came from Belfast and Dublin. The Nova Scotian ports to the east received only a trickle. Halifax practically dropped from the picture in 1818, and never reappeared as an important destination. This was due partly to the hostile policy of the Nova Scotian government, which discouraged settlers, especially the Irish,[54] and partly to the inconvenience of Halifax as a stopping place for the United States. The New Brunswick ports were much better situated for emigrant traffic, and St. John took the lion's share, a share which must have approached that of Quebec. Ships came from all the Irish ports, but especially from Londonderry, from which there were nineteen vessels in this one year, the largest number between any Irish port and any port in North America. It is curious that Londonderry did not discover the Quebec route until 1818, when it sent a single ship, whose advertisements found it necessary to describe the location of Quebec.[55] South of St. John, and until 1823

John. *Limerick General Advertiser*, July 28, 1818. The same thing happened in the larger ports where it seemed profitable. Thus the *Fame* (*supra*, p. 81, *note*) put up its prices at one time to £4.11.0 "hold" (steerage), £6.2.9. "steerage" (second cabin?), and £25 cabin—these to St. John. *Belfast News Letter*, Aug. 11, 1818.

[53] William Marquis of Dublin, in Dublin *Evening Post*, July 18, 1818.

[54] Nova Scotia and Cape Breton were already "full," hence the antipathy to new settlers. *Historical geography of the British colonies*, V, Canada, Part III, by John D. Rogers, p. 67. (Hereafter cited as Rogers, *Canada*.) The evidence of governmental opposition to immigration is from the twenties, but it applies to the earlier period.

[55] The *Columbus*. "For Quebec in Canada . . . perhaps no colony in the British Empire holds out such real advantages to emigrants from the extent of its trade and commerce, and the facility and cheap conveyance to all parts

technically an outport of it, lay St. Andrews. To it came occasional ships from various Irish ports; but practically all its emigrants, amounting to two thousand in 1818, were from Belfast. They came very largely from County Down, a great number of the ships sailing from Porta-ferry within the Belfast customs district, and a few from Strangford Loch in the same area.[56]

We should not be far wrong in estimating the whole emigration to the British American ports for this period at between thirteen and fifteen thousand, and may assign another seven thousand to the United States.[57] There was little change in 1818 in the distribution among the United States ports. Under the peculiar circumstances of 1815, and again later when emigration was slack and most passengers went in the ordinary packet ships, New York absorbed an exceptional share of the trade. A year such as 1818, when destination was largely determined by the emigrant demand, gives a better idea of the real aims of the emigrating classes. In that year Philadelphia became almost as important as New York, and Baltimore was not far behind Philadelphia. Between them the three ports received most of the newcomers. Ships bound for Boston appeared first at Dublin in 1816, and occasionally in later years from southern ports, but with the exception of a single vessel from Belfast, for which two-thirds of the passages had been prepaid in America,[58] none of them

of the Continent by means of its inland navigation laying it open to every part of the United States, to which the most easy excess (sic) can be had at all times.'' *Londonderry Journal*, July 21, 1818. This was the first Quebec advertisement in Derry.

56 Ship news in *Belfast News Letter*, J. M. Spearman, Collector at St. Andrews, to W. F. Odell, Esq., May 19, 1831 in C.O. 188/41. Spearman's list of arrivals begins with 1823 but it indicates that St. Andrews never drew largely from any port but Belfast. See also Appendix.

57 See Appendix.

58 The *Mexico; Belfast News Letter*, April 24, 1818.

sailed from Ulster. In this case the prepayment was presumably by Ulstermen settled in New England. At first sight it seems an anomaly, but it is to be explained by the large share held by Boston in the New Brunswick and Nova Scotian trade. Practically the whole of the emigration to New England must have come by that route. South of Baltimore there were emigrant ships to Norfolk, Charleston, and New Orleans, which did not as a rule bring large numbers of passengers. It may be interesting to note the distribution of emigrants from Belfast in this year, 1818:[59]

Quebec	2268	St. Andrews	1939	New York	522
Pictou	246	St. John	43	Philadelphia	448
Prince Edward			——	Baltimore	364
Island	22		1982	Charleston	223
	——			New Orleans	61
	2536			Boston	29
					——
					1647

The general trade of Belfast, which facilitated a greater choice of ports for emigrants than existed elsewhere in Ireland, gives peculiar interest to this table. Except for the unusual number to St. Andrews and to the southern ports, the proportions might be typical of any of the main Irish cities. The numbers in the first column give some indication of the strength of the movement toward the western country. To them should be added the few to New Orleans, which, like Baltimore and Quebec, was advertised as the best route to the Mississippi.[60] Practically all the rest, excepting a few to Baltimore and

[59] *Limerick General Advertiser*, Jan. 8, 1819. From Belfast Custom House returns; therefore "official," counting children to British America as fractions. The actual number would be greater.

[60] E.g. The *Edward Downes* advertised that river steamers made New Orleans the best port for Kentucky. *Belfast News Letter*, Sept. 16, 1817.

possibly to Philadelphia, were seeking the east coast of the United States.[61] As yet the numbers wishing to stay in Canada were but a small fraction of the whole.[62]

The advantages of the United States were many and well known. Insofar as the emigration came from old districts where it had been long established—and the greater part did originate in such districts—there was a natural tendency to follow relatives and friends. Furthermore, to the emigrant seeking work, an old and established society was preferred to a pioneer and on the whole poor community. The arrival at times of fifteen hundred emigrants in a single day[63] in a town of fifteen thousand, the population of Quebec at this time, could only create a surplus of labor, of which the inhabitants would try to rid themselves as quickly as possible. The small group of British merchants there and at Montreal could not employ the emigrants, and the French Canadians did not want them. Except for the beginning, in 1816, of an Irish fringe round the city of Quebec, the immigrants of 1816-22 all went on to the upper province.[64] But facilities for travel up the St. Lawrence were poor, even after the establishment in 1817 of Quebec-Montreal steamers, and the expenses often too great for the new arrivals,[65] so that it became necessary to assist many on their way. In Upper Canada the situation was somewhat better; for the large farms in the older districts, the numerous growing towns, and the gov-

[61] New York was an excellent starting point, but, unlike other ports, it was never advertised ''for the west.'' Possibly New York ships needed no special advertising.

[62] Miss Cowan (*British emigration to British North America*, p. 124) has mistaken the change in route for a change in destination—a natural error until one has studied actual shipping conditions.

[63] There were 1,337 arrivals, including 1,082 Irish, on Aug. 2, 1818. *Quebec Mercury.*

[64] Rogers, *Canada*, pp. 139, 147.

[65] For details see Cowan, *British emigration to British North America*, pp. 137-140.

ernment work on roads provided occupation for many.[66] At the same time, its capacity to absorb laborers was still limited to a few thousand a year. In the United States, on the other hand, except for a short period of commercial distress in 1816, the laborer had no difficulty in getting a job in the ports, and if he were willing to go inland he could be almost sure of securing permanent employment. The older communities also offered opportunities for a large number of specialized trades, particularly for artisans and manufacturing hands.

It was the pioneer farmer whom Canada really wanted, and for him were written the advertisements setting forth the advantages of free grants of land and government aid. Unfortunately, the inducements sounded better on paper than the facts warranted. In order to obtain any grant, the emigrant needed the recommendation and testimonial of a resident magistrate and his local clergyman, and these were not easy to get in Ireland where the resident gentry were few and far between, and most of the emigrants worshipped at a church whose ministers were not recognized by the authorities. Moreover, the so-called free grants required the payment of large fees, quite beyond the means of any but the wealthiest emigrants, and so much of the most available Canadian land was either granted to non-residents or held in crown and clergy reserves that settlers often found themselves forced some distance into the wilderness.

In contrast with these conditions, the easy terms of the American government grants and the long periods allowed for payment, with the advantage of settling on the edge of already established communities, seemed far more attractive, and if the minimum claim—320 acres before 1820—was too large, the emigrant could always join the

[66] "The whole history of this period was a history of roads." Rogers, *Canada*, p. 85.

numerous squatters in the justifiable hope that he could secure right of preëmption later. The mere fact that thousands every year were pushing into the American west was an irresistible magnet for people as gregarious as the Irish. Doubtless the custom of going to the United States, together with unfamiliarity with Canada, would, in the beginning, have taken most of the emigrants to the American west in contrast to the Canadian, but this preference continued after Canada was well and favorably known.

The Irish conception of American conditions, which largely determined the direction of emigration, was on the whole accurate. Amongst the abuses of the emigrant trade, misrepresentations regarding America have been frequently cited. They appear often enough in shipping advertisements, but it is unlikely that they could have had any serious effect upon the bulk of the emigrants.[67] Many of the Irish newspapers made a feature of American news, and there is ample evidence of close and constant communication across the Atlantic. Throughout 1816 the Dublin newspapers carried on a violent controversy regarding emigration and the advantage of the United States;[68] while all over the country papers gave publicity

[67] This statement is open to contradiction. Miss Cowan says: ''But in spite of the attempts of the *Times* and the Scottish newspapers to publish reliable reports of the hardships to be met in the new world, the great majority in this early period went aboard ship deluded and inspired by glowing accounts of a land where wealth was easily won, certain of nothing except that the future abroad could scarce be worse than that at home.''—*British emigration to British North America*, p. 118. A study of the Irish newspapers leads me to the opposite conclusion (especially as regards Ulster, which supplied the bulk of the emigration), despite the evidence of Thomas Addis Emmet, who wrote: ''Most of those who come out are grievously disappointed, because they set out with false notions, and very small, if any, means.'' Dublin *Evening Post*, Sept. 17, 1818. One man ''grievously disappointed'' attracts more attention than ninety-nine who are satisfied.

[68] Principally the Dublin *Evening Post* vs. the *Correspondent*.

to government offers of land and aid to settlers in Canada. The newspapers in important emigration ports printed a number of letters from settlers describing conditions, wages, cost of living, and other facts of interest. Some papers, such as the Dublin *Evening Post,* made a point of publishing these facts at the beginning of each emigrant season. The published letters were only a few of the many hundreds that came back from America advising or warning friends of the conditions to be met with. Insofar as the state of America affected Irish emigration these letters were the greatest single agency.[69]

With them must be classed prepaid passages. Successful emigrants were not satisfied to send good advice. They made every effort to bring over families and friends, who in turn brought others, and so kept up a continuous and expanding stream. Sometimes the money for passage was sent back, but as safe and easy means of transferring money did not then exist, and Irish exchange was at times almost unobtainable,[70] it was far simpler to pay the passage to the master or his agent in the American port, and warn the friend or family when to be on the lookout for the ship. The initiative of Irish merchants, who early established branches in the American ports, or at least had correspondents there, aided this practice.[71] We are able to follow its extension through the advertisements which were customarily inserted in the papers notifying

[69] The Irish papers also published large extracts from Cobbett, Birkbeck, Bradbury, and others; but these were far less valuable to emigrants, and much more given to propaganda.

[70] "The hardest matter to be obtained here is Bank of England or Bank of Ireland notes, and therefore I find it the more difficult to send you £24 to pay for your passage and the three children"—letter of an emigrant glass-blower to his wife in Dublin. Boston, May 4, 1816, Dublin *Evening Post,* July 25, 1816.

[71] Some firms such as Malcolmson and Bell of Belfast, were already connected with New York firms before 1815. Most of the leading merchants in the transatlantic trade on both sides of the water were Quakers.

passengers whose fares were paid to come into port and secure their berths, which they would otherwise lose. Such notices appeared first in the Londonderry-Philadelphia trade, probably the oldest regular emigrant trade in Ireland.[72] This was in the spring of 1816. In the autumn, similar notices from New York ships were printed in Londonderry, Belfast and Dublin—though this last is an isolated example where the notices seem to have been a new thing. By 1818 fares from Belfast were paid in Philadelphia, Baltimore and Boston, and from Newry in New York and Philadelphia. Evidently the custom was not yet generally known farther south. The absence of this practice among ships sailing to British America was due to the dispersion of the emigrants into districts from which communication with Quebec or New Brunswick was difficult. Prepaid passages appeared in Quebec in 1819, probably as a result of the establishment there of Campbell Sweeny, a Belfast merchant.

With the end of 1818, the chief American inducements to emigration came to an abrupt halt. Some few passages were still prepaid, but there were no more encouraging letters, and in general the reports were a severe check to emigration. The obvious cause was the panic of 1819 in the United States, which was nearly as ruinous to the western farmer as to the merchant and laborer of the eastern cities.[73] The effect upon emigration had apparently not

[72] E.g. The *Active*, a flaxseed ship, advertised long before its arrival that a majority of the berths had been secured in Philadelphia. *Londonderry Journal*, Jan. 23, 1816. The practice must have been familiar before 1815, but I have found no evidence of it before 1776.

[73] The earliest *printed* notice of hard times which I have found is in the *Belfast News Letter*, May 18, i.e., in the middle of the emigrant season; but this is a letter from Danville, Kentucky to Lifford, Donegal. If we allow for the delays in transit of this letter, and its news to Belfast it seems certain that private advices from the Atlantic states reached Ireland much earlier.

been foreseen by the Irish shippers. Encouraged by the great outflow of 1818, they provided even more liberal accommodation the following spring. Never had competition been so keen; but as the season advanced ship after ship withdrew its advertisement and sought a cargo in some other branch of trade. Despite these facts, the numbers actually sailing to British America did not decrease, and from the northern ports, as well as from Munster, there was a slight gain over 1818. This apparent contradiction is explained by the larger proportion of unadvertised vessels in what may be called the poorer emigrant trade. The better class emigration, which had given character to the movement of the four years following the peace, now came to an end. Never in any sense a panic exodus, it reacted immediately to American conditions; hence the almost complete falling off of passengers to the United States, to which, because of the restrictions of the passenger acts, only the wealthier emigrants could afford to go.

There can be no doubt of the superior quality of the emigrants of this period. The fares which we have quoted were in themselves sufficient to prevent the poorest from going.[74] Rates of passage fluctuated enormously, and for that reason fares were seldom mentioned in advertisements. When they do appear it is obviously because they are considered low and meant to give additional attractiveness to the vessel. A somewhat startling picture of conditions in 1815 is disclosed by the notice on September 26 of the *Emperor Alexander* from Londonderry to New York: "For the encouragement of passengers, the first forty who enter after this date will be charged only

[74] To the quoted fare must be added from one to two pounds for provisions. Evidence of John Astle and A. C. Buchanan, *Parl. Pap.* 1826, No. 404, pp. 172, 336.

Twelve Guineas each.'"[75] This rate was again mentioned from Belfast in 1817,[76] and it is noteworthy that the cheaper fares quoted earlier in this chapter never appeared before late June, when the greatest demand for ships was over. Many advertisements were especially directed to the attention of farmers and sometimes mechanics, but not to the lower classes. In April, 1818, the Dublin *Evening Post* wrote: "It is a melancholy thing that emigration is necessarily restricted to the class immediately above the labouring order, who cannot raise the money to pay their passage.'"[77] This does not sound like very high class emigration, but a month later the same paper said: "Along with the strong and active farmers of which these exportations chiefly consist, many to whom the times have still left a hundred or two, are going to embark it in the purchase of land, and are taking their former labourers with them.'"[78] In the same year the Cork *Southern Reporter* said of a vessel for Philadelphia: "She has been advertised but a few days, yet the numbers who are applying for passages is almost incredible. Persons from the neighbouring towns—tradesmen, shopkeepers, and even professional men who had realised some little property while there was any business doing, or any money stirring, are crowding to another country, where, whatever the produce of their industry may be, it will not be broken in upon by enormous taxation.'"[79]

Not the laborer, nor, as has been claimed, the evicted small farmer who was almost as poor, made up the bulk of the emigration in this, the year of cheapest passage since the war.[80] As the quotations indicate, farmers—

[75] *Londonderry Journal.*
[76] See the advertisement of the *Jessie, Belfast News Letter,* May 23, 1817.
[77] April 30, 1818.   [78] May 21, 1818.
[79] Quoted in the Dublin *Evening Post,* April 13, 1818.
[80] Politicians in search of a grievance connected two independent facts—

amongst whom should be included the small farmer-weavers of the north—city shopkeepers and artisans were the first to seek in America the opportunities which they could not find at home. The artisan movement appears to have been particularly strong in the first two years. Over half the letters from America which appeared in the Irish papers came from men who had been engaged in some trade in Ireland.[81] The year 1816 was particularly bad for Irish manufactures, and it may be that the revival in linen and cotton, which followed it, served as a check upon this class of emigration.[82] The condition of the towns throughout Ireland was, however, such as to warrant some continuation. The English laws against the emigration of artisans in any branch of manufacture applied to Ireland, but they were almost wholly inoperative,[83] and

eviction and emigration—and the ''poor ejected tenant forced to abandon his native land'' became a stock figure of Irish oratory. He will be found in dozens of pamphlets. Unfortunately, he has been allowed to creep into history without proper credentials. Miss Cowan says: ''From the south of Ireland, where the change to large farms was already causing the eviction of the forty-shilling free-holders and the numerous population of small cottages . . . the emigration was quickly outstripping that of the north.'' *British Emigration to British North America*, p. 125. The implication as to cause is as erroneous as the statement of fact as to origin. Miss Cowan distinguishes too sharply the emigrants of the South and the North; the latter, she thinks, were ''men of some means, who accomplished their settlement in the colonies with comparative ease''—*ibid.*, p. 124. To my mind one of the greatest proofs of the quality of the emigration is that the Dublin *Evening Post*, after three years advocacy of it as a relief for the poor and oppressed, finally described the movement as a drain on the country's wealth and a curse to Ireland.—April 30, 1818.

[81] Including linen and cotton weaver, carpenter, sawyer, printer, glass-blower, smith, millwright, etc. The poorer emigrants probably could not write, but there are a number of letters from farmers.

[82] For the revival in the linen industry see *Belfast News Letter*, Jan. 30, 1818—Letter of R. Williamson; for wage fluctuations in other trades see *Parl. Pap.* 1837-38, No. 646—*Second Report, Select Committee on Combinations of Workmen, passim,* and *Parl. Pap.* 1824, No. 51, pp. 434, 440, 447.

[83] Evidence of Charles Boyd, General Surveyor of Customs, *Parl. Pap.* 1824, No. 51, p. 57.

so far as we know, passengers from the north were never asked to take the required oath. It was apparently administered in Dublin, however, and the Dublin *Evening Post* in an effort to aid emigrants pointed out, probably incorrectly, that magistrates had no right to enforce the taking of such oaths.[84] In any case, the Irish artisan was not likely to get into difficulties for swearing falsely. If his conscience were tender he could take advantage of such a ship as that for St. Andrews which advertised itself "For tradesmen and others, who cannot go to the States, as St. Andrews is within a mile of them";[85] since the law did not apply to artisans emigrating to British possessions. The only sign of a serious effort to enforce it appears in the case of a vessel sailing from Liverpool, which required a legal certificate to the effect that the passenger was not an artisan.[86]

The number of artisans helps to explain the complaint often made by the Irish in America that their countrymen would not go west, but insisted on staying in the seaports.[87] This habit has always been common among Irish emigrants, even when they came from the land, but it is quite possible that the earlier settlement in the ports by men who would naturally find their best employment

[84] July 30, 1816.

[85] The *Harp; Limerick General Advertiser*, June 30, 1818.

[86] The *Master* for Philadelphia; Dublin *Evening Post*, May 30, 1818. There was one attempt to enforce the act in Ireland against five glass blowers who had left their employers in Liverpool and were suspected of having gone to Ireland, *en route* for America. In order to stop these men, their employers informed the local customs, which reported to the Lords Commissioners of the Treasury. They transmitted the papers to Dublin Castle, which sent them on to the Irish Commissioners of Customs, who in their turn sent warning to officials in the four leading emigrant ports. By this time the glass blowers were doubtless safe in America. Customs 1/348, Minutes of the Irish Commissioners of Customs, Leinster and Ulster, Nov. 20, 1815.

[87] See especially *Hints to Irishmen who intend with their families to make a permanent residence in America* by the Shamrock Society of New York.

there served to draw to the same districts later emigrants who might better have gone on the soil. The motives which kept the artisans in the eastern seaports also influenced the small farmer-weavers of Ulster, whose farming at home had only been for the purpose of raising their own food. When they reached America they turned naturally to the occupation which promised the largest immediate return. The infant textile industry of the United States, first nourished by the cutting off of supplies during the Napoleonic Wars, was fighting a desperate battle for existence in 1816 and ensuing years. Nevertheless, the wages of weavers were from two to four times the earnings of a handloom worker in Ireland, and employment except in 1816 and 1819 was good.[88] America had few skilled weavers of a quality equal to many of these Irish emigrants, who taught their trades to the American workmen, and exerted an influence on the industry out of proportion to their numbers.[89] The reorganization of the Irish linen industry described in the preceding chapter, was a constant cause for the emigration of this class. While we do not know the exact numbers, it is significant that the greatest emigrant counties in Ireland were those largely inhabited by the small independent weaver. Neither of the preceding classes played any large part in the pioneer emigration which became important in 1817, and it is from amongst the true farming population that we must look for this type. Continuous agricultural depression was a sufficient motive, and the wealthier farm-

[88] A letter from Louisville, July 25, 1818, said weavers would do particularly well. *Belfast News Letter*, July 13, 1819; but near Washington blanket weavers were making only ''five shillings a day and grog,'' or about half the earnings of many other tradesmen. Dublin *Evening Post*, Oct. 16, 1817.

[89] There were never more than a sprinkling of Irish in the woolen mills before 1830, and no great number in cotton; but the skilled weaver was always at a premium. Cole, *American wool manufacture*, I, 368; Clark, *History of manufactures in the United States*, I, 400.

ers went in greater or less numbers in all years. The movement became more pronounced in 1817. In that year the richest western lands of the United States, which had been held back from settlement by Indian disputes and quarrels over frontier posts following the Treaty of Ghent, became available.[90] This undoubtedly drew some settlers, but conditions in Ireland were quite sufficient to account for the increase. The harvest of 1816 was below average; that of 1817 was ruinous, the export of wheat and barley being lower than at any other time since the beginning of the century.[91] Hard times had brought on an increase of agrarian unrest, and disturbances were more frequent in 1817 and 1818 than in the two years preceding or following.

The manner of emigration throws some light on the character of those who were leaving the country. It has been said that the Irish, unlike other emigrating peoples, normally go by individuals rather than by families, and that a much larger proportion, therefore, are between the ages of fifteen and forty—that is, are capable of supporting themselves.[92] These characteristics are the marks of poverty. The Irish preferred to emigrate in families when they could, and in this first post-war period a large proportion were able to do so. Statistics of the passengers from Belfast for three years indicate that from one-half to two-thirds went in families,[93] while a list of prospective

[90] I.e., the old Northwest territory. Of course there had been settlement earlier, but it is noteworthy that the few emigrant notices of the West before 1817 were all of Kentucky, whereas later advertisements stressed the Pittsburgh districts and Ohio. Knight's *The emigrant's best instructor*, published in 1818 was largely devoted to a description of Ohio, Indiana, and Illinois.

[91] Porter, *Progress of the nation*, II, 84.

[92] A standard observation, first made, I think, by Mayo-Smith.

[93] Returns for 1816-1818 give 10,555 individuals and 1,276 families. (Contemporary Irish writers estimated the population at 5 or 6 to the family.

emigrants from the counties of Wexford and Carlow shows a still higher ratio.[94] Nine-tenths of these latter emigrants were farmers, the remainder mechanics. It is the artisans who seem pretty regularly to have gone individually or in parts of families. A Dublin shipper, John Astle, testified: "The general custom is, that when a family is about to emigrate, two or three of the youngest and strongest go on first, and then, when they obtain a footing, they send for the rest of the family."[95] This procedure might apply to any type of emigrant, but the Dublin merchants were most familiar with the city artisan class. We have further testimony of the same character from the Dublin *Evening Post:* "There are many tradesmen go out, and leave their families; but it is only until they can earn in another land the means of transporting them."[96] The passenger lists of half a dozen ships from Dublin, Cork, and Sligo show less than one-fourth of the passengers to be related to one another.[97] They also show that not one passenger in five was a woman—a marked contrast to the later Irish emigration in which women were as numerous as men. As most of the women who did go were members of families, we may assume that the extensive emigration of Irish servant girls had not yet begun.

This may be only another way of saying that emigration of the poor was not important. Doubtless lack of ability and not of inclination was the primary cause. We have noticed the three thousand and more who went to Newfoundland in 1815 at a fare said to be only ten shil-

From examples in passenger lists I think 5 is a fair average.) *Limerick General Advertiser,* May 18, 1819.

[94] There are 5,502 individuals, 991 families, the ratio being the same in the Protestant and Catholic lists.—Samuel Elly to Bathurst, Dec. 4, 1817 in C.O. 384/1.

[95] *Parl. Pap.* 1826, IV, No. 404, p. 337.

[96] July 20, 1816.   [97] From the Dublin *Evening Post.*

lings.[98] Most of them were supposed to be bound for the
United States, though many went on to Quebec the next
year. Actually, destination did not matter a great deal.
The dominating idea was to get out of Ireland. As Samuel
Chearnley wrote to Bathurst:

> The Irishman will sail for Canada! Yes my Lord! Even though
> the printed circular from our Castle of Dublin stares him in the
> face, in dreadful sentence, admonishing and cautioning in dread-
> fully forewarning words that the cold Canadian blast must be his
> doom to stiffen, and bleach his corse before the wintry storm, to-
> tally unaided by Government, and only as to a few trifles sup-
> plied—if he sails not before the first of June—if this is meant as
> a warning to Irishmen going to Canada, let me tell your Lord-
> ship, it's nugatory, and worse than useless, it won't operate
> against his going out, be assured my Lord—for the Irishman sails
> to Canada because he will not remain in Ireland; it's overstocked.
> Grounds too high accordingly—scarce room.
>
> But I can vouch for a fact, what you may not know my Lord—
> three fourths of those I saw sail from this port will land at
> Quebec with four, or five dollars in their or families possession.[99]

Chearnley did not add that the total emigration from
Cork to Quebec in this year was only 155.[100]

Opportunities for large scale emigration of the poor
were not ripe. During the period of 1816, when it was
easy to take numbers to the United States, vessels sailed
to Amboy from Belfast, Londonderry, Newry, Dublin and
Limerick. There was no regular trade to Amboy, and
ships only went there to avoid the restrictions and supervision of the customs officials at New York, usually because they were infringing the passenger acts. These Amboy ships never advertised their rates of passage, but
they probably made a specialty of cheap fares, though the

98 Cowan, *British emigration to British North America*, p. 131. *Note.*
99 Cork, June 18, 1817, in C.O. 384/1.
100 From shipping returns in the *Quebec Mercury*.

demand for passage by better class emigrants was so great, and fares to legitimate ports so high, it is unlikely that even they catered to the lowest class. The same situation would have kept such emigrants out of the Canada traffic in 1817, especially as potatoes were extremely scarce that year, and the cost of provisioning therefore unusually heavy.

The real beginnings of poor emigration must be dated from 1818, the year which brought to a close the better class movement. Everything conspired to make it a record year. The example of others going in ever increasing numbers could not but tell upon the poorer people. There was a real fever for emigration. Possibly it drew much of its strength from another and more dangerous fever which had spread over Ireland in 1817. The defective potato crop of the preceding autumn produced a condition approaching famine throughout practically the whole island, and as always happened in Ireland the weakened resistance of the people brought on a violent outbreak of the typhus which was endemic there. The worst of the disease was over by the end of 1817, but it hung on in many communities, and the fear inspired by it aided that unsettlement of mind which often precedes emigration.[101] Where thousands of poor had wished to leave Ireland before, tens of thousands now sought an escape.

The only question was one of means. For a few there were "fairy godmothers" to smooth the way. The first to play this beneficent role was the much-censured government. In 1815 it had begun to settle ex-soldiers in Canada, giving them free transportation, small grants of land, and free implements. The original beneficiaries of the scheme were Highlanders, but in 1816, and on a larger scale in 1817, the plan was extended to Ireland. Not more than

[101] See Harty, *Historical sketch of the contagious fever epidemic in Ireland, 1817-1819.*

a few hundreds in all actually went under government supervision, but the publicity thus given to emigration was enormous, and requests for aid poured into the Colonial Office. Direct help was abandoned in 1818, but a scheme was still open by which landlords or other men of capital could secure large grants of land and free transportation, by taking out a number of settlers and paying a considerable deposit as a guarantee that they would not leave the colony.[102] Under this arrangement the more enlightened landlords were able to get rid of some of their surplus tenants without causing hardship. The most famous enterprise of the kind was that of Richard Talbot, who went to join Sir Thomas Talbot's settlement near London in Upper Canada, taking with him over two hundred of his tenants from Kings County.[103] Other landlords, who themselves remained in Ireland, paid the deposit to obtain land and passage for their tenants. Among these was W. K. Newenham of Tipperary, one of the greatest authorities on the condition of Ireland at the time.[104] Unfortunately such men were exceptions, and the majority of landlords still looked upon emigration with suspicion, seeing in it an attempt on the part of tenants who were in arrears—as indeed most of them were—to escape without payment.[105]

[102] On Government colonization see *infra*, Chap. VI. I mention it here as one stimulus to the general interest in emigration.

[103] Talbot to Bathurst, Dec. 29, 1817 (C.O. 384/1), gives interesting details of the composition of his group. Among 72 families there were two gentlemen, 48 farmers, 6 shoemakers, 3 smiths, 3 carpenters, and weavers, tailors, painters and a bricklayer. This Talbot Settlement is described in Cowan, *British emigration to British North America*, pp. 79-81, and very fully in E. A. Talbot, *Five years residence in the Canadas*.

[104] Mentioned in a letter from Burrisokane, Tipperary, Oct., 1818; C.O. 384/3.

[105] Sometimes applications for government aid were followed by letters such as the following: Sir John Read to Bathurst, Scariff, Clare, March 17, 1819:—''My Lord, I have just learned that an application has or is in-

For those who could not get aid from above, there was still coöperation. Emigration societies, especially among union tradesmen, which have played an important part in Great Britain, and were doing so during these years, were slow to start in Ireland, and never became very important, though there is evidence that one was being formed in the southeastern counties in 1818, not among tradesmen, but in the farming communities.[106] No effective work seems to have been done before 1819, however.

The unaided poor had one familiar method of reaching the promised land. Throughout the eighteenth century this class had gone to America by working out passages as indentured servants. The practice appears to have been in abeyance immediately after 1815; for shipowners would not bother with it when they had plenty of cash passengers. But in the vastly increased traffic of 1818 it was resumed, and the Cork *Southern Reporter* says, "Hundreds of tradesmen, who have not the means of paying their passage, are offering to bind themselves for any term of years that may be required, in order to reimburse the owners of the vessel. The same scene we are given to understand, is taking place in every part of the country."[107] In August of the same year, the *Halifax Packet,* bound from Londonderry to St. John, advertised, "A few stout laborers, or mechanics, will be taken out by the ship at a very reduced rate, and immediate employment secured them at St. John's to enable them to pay the

tended shortly to be made by several persons tenants to my property for permission to obtain a passage to Canada to become settlers there or in some other of His Majesty's Colonies. As they are endeavouring to quit this country defrauding me of my rent I trust your Lordship will discountenance their application and prevent them the opportunity of robbing me. . . ." C.O. 384/5. See also *infra*, p. 117.

[106] Peter Roe to Bathurst, New Ross, Nov. 26, 1818, enclosing the prospectus of such a society. C.O. 384/3.

[107] Quoted in the Dublin *Evening Post*, April 13, 1818.

balance of their passages.'"[108] Pennsylvania, which received both Irish and German redemptioners in larger numbers than all the rest of America, was forced in 1818 to pass new legislation to protect them from fraud. Thereafter, the increasing stream of immigrants soon flooded the country with a cheaper labor than that of the indentured servant, and although the practice lasted in Philadelphia as late as 1831, it had ceased to be significant by 1820.[109]

All this was normal and legal, but at the same time a new illegal traffic of the poorest sort was springing up, and small vessels, usually of less than 150 tons and carrying at times more than one passenger per ton, made their way from Sligo, Waterford, and Cork, to Portland, Salem and New Bedford, choosing ports to which emigration was uncommon, and where no British consul was on hand to report infractions of the laws.[110] Another practice was to drop a part of the passengers at some unfrequented spot before proceeding to the advertised destination. Thus, one ship, ostensibly under stress of weather, put into Lubec, Maine, before proceeding to Philadelphia, while another dropped two-thirds of its passengers at Newport and then went on to Norfolk.[111] As the United

[108] *Londonderry Journal*, August 18, 1818.

[109] Herrick, *White servitude in Pennsylvania*, pp. 263-266.

[110] E.g. The *Maria*, Waterford to Salem, had 126 passengers, tonnage 186; the *Catherine*, Waterford to Boston, had 67 passengers, tonnage 64; the *Ann*, Cork to Boston, had 60 passengers, tonnage 76. All but one of these illegal vessels came within the Boston Consular district, which extended from Rhode Island to New Brunswick. Consular Returns, Jan., 1818-Jan., 1819. B.T. 6/24-26. The absence of such ships from earlier reports seems rather strong proof that this type of trade had just arisen.

[111] The first may have been a genuine case of distress. The second, the *Chesterfield* of 75 tons, had 53 passengers. The notation opposite her entry at Newport is "She had cleared from Cork for St. John, N.B., but was in fact bound to Norfolk, Virginia, with her passengers. She left some here and started for Norfolk with the rest." Newport Return, July-Dec., 1819; B.T. 6/27.

States had as yet no passenger act, American officials merely reported these facts, and the offenders went unpunished. Their only real danger was in getting clear of the Irish coast.

The profits on this trade were enormous. The charterers of one miserable little vessel with a legal capacity of 107 passengers, which brought 160 people from Cork to Philadelphia, paid £450 to the owners and themselves took over the fitting with berths, water casks, fuel and provision, besides depositing £50 to cover damages by the passengers. The owners, with almost no expense to themselves, cleared nearly as much as the new fast Liverpool-New York packets, established in 1817, could make from their cabin.[112] The charterers in their turn, with the connivance of the captain, fleeced the passengers for supplies, sequestered part of their baggage, and must even at the lowest rate of passage have made one hundred per cent on their investment.[113] The whole extent of this illegal emigration was probably not more than one or two thousand a year, and its importance lay mainly in the encouragement which it gave to the emigration of the poor.

One extraordinary emigration route deserves mention for the light it throws upon the readiness of the poor to embrace any opportunity of reaching the New World. In 1818 and 1819 small and overcrowded ships of the type just described were sailing from the Channel Islands to America, eight going from Guernsey to Baltimore in the

[112] The Black Ball line, later joined by two others. They were too expensive for emigrants until the development of steerage passage about 1827. J. R. Spears, *Story of the American merchant marine*, p. 224.

[113] A long account of this vessel, with a copy of its "charter-party of affreightment" is in Anthony Baker to Castlereagh, Dec. 22, 1818; F.O. 5/133. A similar vessel in 1819 charged its passengers £7 apiece. Gilbert Robertson to Planta, July 29, 1819; F.O. 5/144.

two years.[114] This was not an illegal trade, since the acts of 1803 and 1816 had neglected to include the Islands, an omission repaired, so far as British America was concerned, by the act of 1817. It might be supposed that the passengers would have come either from the south of England or from France, but we have to account for the rise of an unprecedented passenger traffic from Waterford to Guernsey during these years.[115] This traffic can only have been bound for America. Distress and yellow fever in 1819, even more than the American passenger act of that year, put an end to it, and to most of the poor emigration.

It has not been difficult to trace two parallel but distinct economic types in the emigration of this period. We are on more debatable ground in attempting to draw religious lines. At the beginning it was assumed that the emigration would be primarily Protestant. The Dublin *Evening Post* said: "One of the peculiarities which distinguish the character of the native Irish, is a vehement and, in many instances, an absurd attachment to the soil on which they were born. . . . This applies more particularly to the Catholics, for the principal emigrants of Ireland are the Presbyterians of the North.'"[116] A year later the same journal pointed out as a curious fact that Dissenting ministers were going to New York at the rate of one a week, while so far as it could learn no Roman Catholic priests had emigrated.[117] We should be wrong in assuming that all Ulster emigrants were Dissenters, but undoubtedly a large proportion of them were. There can also be no doubt that a very considerable number of

[114] B.T. 6/24-27. Their total tonnage was 1180, their passengers 781.

[115] Shipping News, *Waterford Chronicle*.

[116] March 2, 1815.

[117] June 22, 1816. Actually some priests were emigrating, but not at the rate of one per week.

Protestants were going from the south. Most of the petitioners to the Colonial Office were of that persuasion. Talbot stated that all his emigrants were Protestants; and the list of 5,502 prospective emigrants from Wexford and Carlow shows 4,027 Protestants and 1,475 Catholics.[118] One cannot place much reliance upon the evidence of the petitions, however, since many petitioners must have thought their chances would be better if they claimed to be Protestants. Perhaps the best evidence on the situation in the south is supplied by a letter from Charles Rolleston, a landlord of Kings and Tipperary counties to Bathurst, May 8, 1819:

My anxiety for the welfare of this part of the Empire urges me to force myself upon your notice, and particularly from the view I have of the very general emigration of the Protestants from this country, which I as well as many of the most considerable part of the gentry of this country look on with the greatest regret, as we are convinced the day is not far off, when they will be wanting in this country more than in Canada, and if free ships are granted any more, it will be of serious injury. I am myself acquainted with those who went in a free ship last year from Cork, they were from my neighbourhood, and some of them went to get rid of their debts and though able to pay them were induced to take advantage of the free ship to cheat their creditors. There are now many of them expecting to get off in the next free ship of the same description, and some of the party who are ready to go are Roman Catholics and are intent on passing as Protestants, this to my own knowledge.[119]

All that can be said definitely of the southern emigration is that much of the better class was Protestant, while practically the whole of the poor emigration must have been Catholic.[120]

118 R. Elly to Bathurst, Dec. 4, 1817; in C.O. 384/1.
119 C.O. 384/5; and see the letter of Sir Robert Peel, *infra*, p. 262.
120 Because practically the whole of the poorest class was Catholic.

Geographical distribution was more important than religious affiliation in determining the direction of emigration. Catholics tended to go where other Catholics had gone before, and laborers to follow laborers; but far more influential than either were the geographical ties which sent the inhabitants of an Irish village to a single community in America, even over many generations. The pioneer character of much of the post-war emigration is shown by the tendency to settle in shiploads in new communities rather than to follow old channels.[121] Though the bulk of the emigration was from Ulster, the south was most affected by these new settlements; for the main currents of northern emigration were already set.

The most important evidence of the sources of emigration is furnished by the ports of embarkation. The average emigrant not only had to carry his provisions, but also took with him a considerable amount of household goods. As practically all of them reached the ports by road, and most of the poorer sort, including the small farmers, on foot, distance was a primary consideration. There are instances of passengers from such distant counties as Queens and Wexford sailing from Belfast,[122] but these are exceptions to a general rule. For emigration purposes all northern and central Ireland was a country in which the road systems, like river systems, rose in a central plateau, diverging from it to carry their streams of emigrants to the sea. This plateau, a region in which the springs of emigration never ran dry, occupied the southwestern counties of Ulster, above all Cavan and Monaghan. Their inhabitants swelled the numbers of those sailing from Sligo, Londonderry, Belfast, Newry, and Dublin; and when merchants first began to establish

121 Various reports from emigrant ships. Dublin *Evening Post*.

122 See for examples the signatures to the letter of thanks by passengers on the *Suffolk*, Belfast-Quebec, *Belfast News Letter*, July 14, 1818.

branch agencies in inland towns, it was in these counties that competition was most severe.[123] Though it is impossible to estimate the numbers going by such diverse routes, we must concede to this area of farmer-weavers preëminence amongst the sources of Irish emigration.[124]

The rest of Ulster emigration is easier to distinguish. Londonderry served the people of Tyrone, western Derry, and that broad lowland section of Donegal known as the Laggan Vale which stretches along the eastern edge of the county from Strabane to the sea. The characteristic emigrant of this region was the Presbyterian small farmer, but there were some of the better class, and tradesmen from the city of Londonderry. On an average, the Derry emigration may be estimated at about one-fifth of that of all Ireland, although at first it may have been somewhat larger.[125] Eastern Londonderry, Antrim, most of Down and northeastern Armagh found it more convenient to emigrate by way of Belfast. This local restriction would apply to most of the poorer emigrants, but Belfast on account of its better ships and more general service attracted high class emigration from a wide area; and through its virtual monopoly of the southern and St. Andrews trade, of nearly half the Quebec trade, and a very large proportion of all the rest, must have sent at least a third of the total emigration. Newry, wedged in between Belfast and Dublin, drew almost wholly from the counties lying due west of it, that is, the southern counties of Ulster—recruiting few passengers from the districts of Leinster immediately to the south. We have not the figures from which to estimate its numbers, but it was

[123] Bailieborough and Belturbet, Cavan; Monaghan and Ballybay, Monaghan, and Enniskillen appeared most frequently among the branch agencies.

[124] See map opposite p. 1.

[125] Estimated from shipping and contemporary references. See Appendix for the share of all the ports.

considered at the time to rank just below Londonderry as the fourth greatest emigrant port. Taking together these three ports, the majority of whose passengers came from Ulster, and adding those who went from there by way of Dublin and Sligo, we may say that Ulster was supplying two-thirds of the emigrants at this time.

The only other outstanding emigrant port was Dublin. It ranked second to Belfast, and the sources of its emigration are therefore of exceptional interest. Sample passenger lists of four vessels to New York, though not in themselves sufficient to give certain information on this point, are at least suggestive. The greatest single source, including over a third of the passengers, was Dublin itself, second to it the Ulster "plateau," third, southeastern Leinster, especially Wexford, and lastly Kings, Queens, and Carlow, the counties adjoining the Munster border.[126] The nearer counties of central and northern Leinster took almost no part.[127] The importance of the two southern districts is attested by the fact that Wexford itself sent out several ships to Quebec,[128] and that numbers who sailed from Waterford came from Wexford county and from Queens and Carlow, while Kings and Queens also found an outlet through Limerick.[129] Half the

126 Dublin *Evening Post,* Nov. 11, 1815; June 21, 1816.

127 The one exception to this in the evidence is a note in the Dublin *Evening Post* of Aug. 20, 1816; the *Adams* advertised in a Thursday's paper, reaching the country on Friday; by Tuesday it was completely booked by farmers from Kildare, Meath and Wicklow. I do not put much trust in such statements where no real evidence of origin is given.

128 Wexford got an early start in the Quebec trade, ranking next to Belfast and Dublin in 1816 and 1817, but thereafter its importance declined. Ross (included in the Waterford returns) was better suited to most emigrants, besides being a better port.

129 The Dublin *Evening Post,* May 21, 1818, gives reports of emigration from Carlow, Limerick, Waterford, and Castlecomer (Kilkenny). The last is illuminating for the new exodus of the poor. "Last Saturday, about 70 labourers, who had resided in Kilkenny and Queens County Collieries, passed

petitions for aid to emigrate in 1817 and 1818 came from
Leinster, and of these two-thirds were from Dublin and
Wexford alone.[130] Estimating the Dublin emigration at
about twenty-five per cent of the total Irish, or about ten
thousand for the period, we may assign to these districts
of Leinster some six or seven thousand emigrants.

There remains for Munster and Connaught only a small
fraction of the total migration. This seems at first sight
surprising; for Cork had at all times a large American
trade, not far below that of Belfast itself. In this case the
extent of shipping is deceptive. In 1815 Cork sent more
ships to Quebec than any other Irish port, and in 1818
and 1819 was still third in the Quebec trade, but its ships
carried not more than 350 emigrants in any one year.
Even Waterford and Limerick had more passengers to
Quebec, probably because they drew upon the Leinster
emigration districts. There are no such conclusive figures
for the United States ports, but newspaper references to
emigrant ships from Cork are very infrequent. An analysis of the direction of shipping, discloses the significant
fact that during the three years, 1816 to 1818, the clearances of ships from Cork, Waterford and Limerick to the
United States were less by 6,700 tons than the arrivals,
while during the same period clearances to the United
States from Ulster ports exceeded arrivals by 14,700 tons,
of which 9,100 were in vessels carrying no freight other
than passengers.[131]

It is necessary to dwell upon the slight extent of this

through the town of Castlecomer on their way to embark for America; they
had previously disposed of their cattle, furniture, etc., to provide for their
expenses and equip themselves for the voyage; they were attended by a
numerous collection of their friends and acquaintances, who travelled several miles with them, regretting at every step, that they had not the means
of proceeding with them.''

[130] Compiled from C.O. 384/1-3.

[131] *Parl. Pap.* 1822, No. 523, Ireland. Trade with the United States.

Munster emigration, because the movement, being new, excited attention at the time and was much exaggerated. The quotations from Samuel Chearnley and the *Southern Reporter* are typical.[132] Another example of the same sort may be taken from an editorial in the *Limerick General Advertiser:* "The desire for emigration, had, we imagined, nearly arrived at its acme, but we find that it still continues unabated. On Wednesday the *William* dropped down the river with a full cargo of passengers, and another vessel, the *Union,* shortly follows with a similar freightage."[133] The actual emigration by these two ships was 180,[134] and only four other vessels, all of them with smaller passenger lists, sailed from Limerick to America that year.[135] Its total emigration could not have been over four hundred. As regards the county of Limerick, its lack of emigration is illustrated by its ignorance of all things American displayed in the touching postscript of W. H. Ryan of Pallasgreane in his petition for aid to emigrate in July, 1819: "P.S. It is reported here that Canada belongs to the French, and is given to the soldiers to protect it, but for my part, I don't heed that. I may as well die in battle, as die out of it."[136] Two months later he had changed his mind; for he wrote on September 17th: "Your Memorialist is determined to settle in Charles Town, in South Carolina, British America, and to purchase a settlement there, for which he troubles Your Highness for a passport to that province."[137] We might perhaps apply to Munster the remark made by the Earl of Carrick in reference to Kilkenny: ". . . The demand for labour has never been equal to the supply furnished

132 *Supra*, pp. 104, 110.   133 May 8, 1818.
134 Given in Dublin *Evening Post*, May 21, 1818.
135 Ship News, *Limerick General Advertiser*.
136 C.O. 384/5. Ryan to Bathurst, July 1, 1819.
137 *Ibid*. Ryan to Bathurst.

by a population feelingly attached to their native soil, and therefore reluctant to emigrate. . . .'"[138] We should however qualify his statement, remembering that the fever of 1817 had done much to break down this reluctance; hence the rise of the very poor emigration in the next two years, almost all of which came from the south of Ireland. Evidently there was a demand for passage provided it was not too expensive. The number of petitions for aid to emigrate from Munster, a quarter of the total from Ireland and only slightly less than the number from Ulster, bears out this conclusion.

There is ample evidence that the Munster men were not stuck in their native mud. During these years many thousands of weavers and others, particularly from south Cork, left their homes for England, swelling the laboring population of the great industrial towns of the north.[139] The movement was not confined to Munster. In the same period other thousands from Connaught and Ulster were starting Irish quarters in British cities from Glasgow to London. The exodus from Ulster to Great Britain did not equal the emigration to America, but in Munster and Connaught it made up almost the whole of the migration from those provinces. During these first post-war years,

[138] *Belfast News Letter*, November 17, 1818. Speech at a meeting of the Kilkenny Association.

[139] A. Redford, *Labour migration in England, 1800 to 1850*, pp. 119, 130-133, and Map G. They settled particularly in Lancashire.

Irish emigration to America *via* Liverpool, the most difficult of all movements to trace, had already begun in this period. In 1817, the *Catherine*, Liverpool-Philadelphia, advertised in Dublin, and in 1819 the *Regent*, Liverpool-St. Andrews, advertised in Belfast. In both cases the agents offered to pay the fare to Liverpool of all steerage passengers. This route would therefore be only a trifle more expensive, but rather inconvenient, as the Irish sea crossings were in small sailing vessels. These two advertisements are isolated instances, the first beginnings of a practice which became important ten years later. Dublin *Evening Post*, May 12, 1817; *Belfast News Letter*, Feb. 26, 1819.

however, conditions of British labor were too unfavorable to attract any Irishman who could possibly hope to reach America, and only the poorest settled across the Irish Channel.[140]

Connaught's share in the emigration to Great Britain was considerably less than that of Munster, and its part in the American trade almost negligible. The infrequency of petitions for aid to emigrate—there were only four in two years[141]—seems to betoken almost complete lack of interest. The numbers from Sligo are not indicative, since they came either from the linen district of that county, or from the Ulster counties of Cavan, Fermanagh and Donegal. What may be called typical Connaught emigration went in a few ships each year from Galway, Newport and Westport, mainly to New Brunswick. I am inclined to believe that town workers from Galway, with artisans from the inland towns, and occasional farmers, made up the bulk of this emigration. It is improbable that many emigrants came from the small holdings characteristic of this region, most of which reported fifteen years later that emigration was almost unknown there.

Certain features appear to be common to the districts of extensive emigration, and probably played a considerable part in promoting it. The first of these was an economic condition somewhat superior to that of Ireland as a whole. The possession of property and the fear of losing it may well have provided a greater incentive to emigration than desire to retrieve a status already lost. In any case it provided the means. A second feature was the presence of settlers of other than Irish origin—Scots in

140 There are no statistics for this movement, but emigration to Great Britain did not attract attention until the twenties, whereas that to America became a matter of national concern in 1816. A very extensive emigration of British workers took place during these years, especially in 1819.

141 1817-1818; C.O. 384/1-3.

Ulster, English and Welsh in Dublin and southern Leinster. Possibly there was more initiative in these than in the
native Irish districts; possibly also the transplanted settlers were less attached to their homes, although most of
their ancestors had been there for a hundred and fifty
years or more. The common use of the English language
was apparently the most decisive factor. The importance
of language was clearly shown by the mountain regions
of Cavan, Tyrone, Derry and Antrim. These districts,
whose inhabitants were cut off by the barrier of language
from those about them, stood out like little islands in the
sea of Ulster emigration.[142] To those who spoke only
Irish, America might well have seemed, as the anti-
emigrant pamphleteers described it, "a vast snowy
desert."

The importance of this first rush of emigration was
little understood at the time. The revival of a movement
which had practically ceased, a movement of citizens to a
country with which Great Britain had recently been at
war, naturally roused hard feelings, and accounts for the
somewhat hysterical outbursts of 1816.[143] By 1819 this
antipathy had largely died out, and the subject no longer
excited general interest. Its opponents had ceased to fear
it, and its friends no longer hoped from it any real improvement in the state of Ireland.[144] The transfer of forty
thousand Irishmen to America appeared to have no effect
whatsoever, except upon the emigrants themselves. Agricultural and labor conditions continued unchanged. The
effect upon the United States was no more perceptible.
The few thousand farmers, the gangs of road and canal

---

[142] See below, Chapter IV. A detailed study of the sources of emigration
is made possible by the Poor Inquiry Commission Report of 1836, and the
O'Donovan Survey of 1833-40. Although these belong to a later period much
of their evidence is applicable to the whole movement after 1815.

[143] *Supra*, p. 15.   [144] Dublin *Evening Post*, April 30, 1818.

laborers,[145] the factory operatives, might all have been obtained without it. The Irish were as yet too few to count politically, and one must take with a grain of salt the claim that the Irish ward of New York, led by Emmett, swung the gubernatorial election against Rufus King.[146] The Irish vote may not have been the deciding factor, but their attitude at this time helps to explain their later political allegiance. They hated the Federalists, particularly King and John Randolph, because they were pro-British—an echo of the Hartford Convention—and anti-Irish. In Congress, Randolph denounced the Irish Republicans, many of whom were still coming to the United States after 1815.[147] Thus from the beginning, the Irish aligned themselves with one party, and developed an organization into which later emigrants were naturally drawn.

The real importance of the emigration of this period could scarcely have been foreseen at the time. Exaggerated and contradictory statements concealed the fact that the habit of emigration was slowly but irresistibly spreading from Ulster into the other provinces as direct contact with America increased. The desire to emigrate increased faster than the means, and created in many districts discontented groups who looked to America for the ultimate solution of their difficulties. Meanwhile, the creation of recognized emigrant routes, some of them from ports which had hitherto had no connection with the trade, provided the means for a steadier and more continuous outflow. These routes determined the currents

[145] The Erie Canal was started in 1817, and from the first employed a large number of Irish, as did the Pennsylvania road-builders during this period. See Dublin *Evening Post*, July 22, 1817, quoting the New York *Shamrock* on opportunities for emigrants.

[146] Dublin *Evening Post*, June 22, 1816.

[147] *Ibid.* Randolph was speaking on the Bank Bill.

and to some extent the destinations of the emigrants. Increased business developed a class of brokers who made a specialty of passenger traffic, and kept the advantages and possibilities of emigration constantly before the people. Their competition helped to break down the barrier of expense, and their activities, together with those of the Irish in America, were the leading factors in keeping the movement alive until the second and greater rush of the late twenties, to which this period was only a prelude.

CHAPTER III

THE SEVEN LEAN YEARS, 1819-1826

My name is Paddy Leary,
From a spot called Tipperary,
The hearts of all the girls I am a'thornin';
But before the break of morn,
Faith! 'tis they'll be all forlorn,
For I'm off to Philadelphia in the mornin'.

Chorus.

Wid my bundle on my shoulder,
Faith! there's no man could be boulder;
I'm lavin' dear old Ireland without warnin'
For I lately took the notion,
For to cross the briny ocean,
And I shtart for Philadelphia in the mornin'.

Irish ballad.

FOR three centuries the twenties have been a decade of awkward and critical adjustment after war. Speculative and radical leaders, alert to the waning force of post-war conservatism, have seized their opportunity, and new powers have arisen to disturb the weary rest of princes and statesmen. Ireland, preparing the ground in 1821 for a peaceful political revolution at home, had no wish yet to follow the example of Spain, of Naples, or of Greece; but Irishmen, inflamed by the heroics of Byron, crossed the sea to fight under the standards of Bolivar and San Martin. Admiral Cochrane of Chile and General Devereux of Venezuela became popular heroes, and government hesitated to recognize Colombia for fear of the too obvious parallel between Bolivar and O'Connell. Beneath the political and religious turmoil in Ireland raged a far more desperate agrarian strife, which opened the way for a trans-oceanic migration such as neither Ireland nor any other European people had ever known before. For the moment, the high cost of transportation kept emigration below the 1818 level; but the Irish pot seethed all the more for its heavy lid, and when that was removed in 1827 the overflow was spectacular.

The four years ending in 1823 constitute one of the blackest periods in the social history of Ireland. Agrarian outrage, which had become somewhat less frequent after the famine conditions of 1817-18, reappeared with increased bitterness late in 1820. The chief center of trouble was the grazing area of Galway and Roscommon, where the stupidity of the magistrates in breaking up by force peaceable gatherings of Ribbonmen, created a state of war amongst a peasantry hitherto notable for its tranquillity.[1] At the same time, southwest Munster, always a hotbed of trouble, was achieving something like united rebellion against tithes and rents under the Whiteboys. The turmoil in these provinces overshadowed disturbances in Ulster and Leinster, though the latter were well above normal. By the spring of 1822, in spite of constant applications of the Insurrection Act and numerous shipments of convicts to New South Wales, government by terror—in which the Whiteboys slightly surpassed the gentry and the crown—was still the order of the day.

The reign of anarchy was brought to an abrupt halt by famine. G. C. Lewis, who studied Irish conditions for the

[1] *Belfast News Letter*, Feb. 11, 1820. Many of the gentry made the mistake of confusing agrarian and religious activities; hence their oppression of the most active Roman Catholic organization. H. C. Pollard (*Secret societies of Ireland*, pp. 32-33) has made the same mistake.

Poor Inquiry Commission after the famine of 1831, remarked their quiet acceptance of want:

To the mere passive state of suffering produced by the scantiness of food, or the failure of the potato crop, the Irish peasants, a class remarkable for their patient endurance, are willing to submit; and hence we find, that, at times, when a large part of the population are hanging over the verge of starvation (a state in which the English peasantry would infallibly break out into disturbance), the country is nevertheless for the most part tranquil.[2]

The potato crop of 1821 had been short, and by the following March peasant supplies in the West were exhausted. The situation differed from that of 1818 in that it was local, only Munster, Connaught, and the county of Donegal being affected; but in this case the failure was far more complete and the consequent famine more disastrous, accompanied as it was by such heavy rains that mud cabins were "melted down like sugar."[3] Government and charitable aid were set in motion in May, and hundreds of thousands of pounds spent on food and employment for the poor. It could not prevent a considerable death roll, but probably did much to minimize the after effects. The famine itself ended with a fair crop in July and August, but as usual the accompanying fever continued, though with less virulence than between 1818 and 1822, and physically, the peasants were well on the road to normal by the spring of 1823.

The revival of agrarian agitation, which accompanied improved conditions, lacked much of its former violence. The most immediate reason for the change was the new direction given by O'Connell to the activities of the secret societies. All of them were in name religious, and it was

2 *On local disturbances in Ireland*, p. 91.
3 Lord Cloncurry, *Letter to the Duke of Leinster*, p. 14. *Note*.

by uniting them through the priests that he created the tremendous force of the reorganized Catholic Association, whose real effectiveness commenced in 1823. Henceforth the members of the societies directed their main energies toward Catholic Emancipation.[4] It is difficult to determine which was cause and which effect; whether the decline of agrarian agitation made possible the rise of a united movement for Emancipation, or whether the Catholic cause, by eclipsing the agrarian, diminished unrest; but one cannot accept the claim of O'Connell's admirers that his rule ended agrarian crime. It is clear, however, that from 1823 to 1829 disturbances took on a more religious and less economic character. In consequence, Munster, where a considerable proportion of the landlords were Catholic, suffered less, while the border counties of Ulster became the scene of frequent and serious riots.[5]

All classes were hard hit by the famine and continued unrest. The farmer did not starve for want of potatoes, but his misfortunes were heavy. The failure in May of 1820 of two Cork banking establishments, whose notes amounted to £350,000, or four-fifths of the circulating medium of Cork and Kerry,[6] was followed by the collapse of nine of the remaining twelve in Munster; and by the end of 1821 there were only six counties in Ireland still containing a solvent bank.[7] Trade came to a standstill, factories were closed, and the farmers, who had a superabundance of grain, found it useless to carry their prod-

[4] Lecky speaks of the Catholic Association as being formed in 1825, but a body of that name had existed as early as 1816. O'Connell's central organization, begun in 1823, was constantly changing its name in order to escape the penalties of the laws against secret societies.

[5] The religious friction was much worse after the rejection by the Lords of the Catholic Relief Bill in 1825.

[6] *Belfast News Letter,* May 30, June 2, 1820.

[7] "Hibernicus"; *Practical views and suggestions on the pre-conditions and permanent improvement of Ireland,* p. 34.

uce to market. Unfortunately for them England was also well supplied during these years, and grain prices fell steadily through 1822.[8] In 1820 only flax is said to have yielded a profit.[9] Many rents were still at war levels, and landlords found it impossible to collect them. Under such conditions the outlook in 1823 seemed dismal indeed.[10]

For once, however, the prophets of gloom were mistaken, and there followed two years of marked improvement—the first since the war. For this the famine was in some degree responsible. Neither Parliament nor the London Tavern Committee, which administered the greater part of the charitable subscriptions, put the majority of their funds into food.[11] A large amount was spent on the building of roads, which were badly needed in the wilder parts of Cork and Kerry, and on improving harbors for the sake of the fishermen. The immediate effect was the introduction of capital where there had hitherto been little or none. New lands were developed, and the fishing industry, which had been subsidized by act of Parliament in 1820, revived temporarily. The new roads opened up regions which had been centers of lawlessness, and aided in the destruction of the retreats of bandits and other professional criminals.[12] The better feeling engendered during the famine by charity, in which the southern gentlemen took a considerable part, furthered social amelio-

[8] Wheat and oats were cheaper in 1822 than in any other year before 1835. Wheat prices in Porter, *Progress of the nation*, I, 156; oats in *Parl. Pap.* 1842, No. 18, Part I, p. 17.

[9] *Londonderry Journal*, Oct. 31, 1820.

[10] Farmers could not pay sixpence in the pound on their rents. See the account of Ballinasloe Fair in *Belfast News Letter*, Oct. 15, 1822.

[11] *Report of the committee for the relief of the distressed districts in Ireland;* especially pp. 20-21, 195, 347.

[12] Porter, *Progress of the nation*, II, 11-12, contrasting two reports of Richard Griffith before and after the famine; *Parl. Pap.* 1830, No. 667: Report of the Select Committee on the State of the Poor in Ireland, p. 40.

ration; while a new police system, superseding the wholly
obnoxious Insurrection Act, which was applied to Munster in 1822, and later to all Ireland, gave somewhat
better security against depredations.[13]

The return of comparative peace aided in, and was
aided by, general economic revival. The next two years
brought excellent crops of grain, for which the prosperous British manufactures provided a constantly rising
market. The advance was greatest in oats, and Ulster
farmers benefited particularly.[14] Farming prosperity
gave good employment to other classes as well, and by the
end of 1825 the outlook for Ireland was better than at
any time since the peace. Capital, prompt to take advantage of the new situation, was assisted by a change in the
banking laws. The monopoly of general banking, held by
the Bank of Ireland, had been abolished in 1821, but it
was not until a new act in 1824 legalized joint stock banks
of issue in Ireland that any practical competition was
possible. The result was the transformation of Montgomery's Private Bank at Belfast into a joint stock institution, and the establishment of the Provincial and Hibernian banks. The Provincial, with headquarters in London
and English capital behind it, obtained the widest influence in Irish banking, while the Hibernian, a Roman
Catholic institution, united the interests of many who
found themselves excluded from power in other financial
and commercial concerns. By the end of 1825 these banks
had offices in Belfast, Cork, Limerick, and Clonmel, and

[13] *Belfast News Letter,* April 8, 1823; citing a letter from Wellesley to
Peel, Sept., 1822. The government was wise enough to make forty per cent
of its constables in Munster Catholic. *Parl. Pap.* 1824, No. 257.

[14] The export of oats to England rose from 569,000 quarters in 1822 to
1,729,000 in 1825, that of barley in even greater proportion. Wheat decreased
slightly in quantity, but its value was greater. Porter, *Progress of the nation,* II, 84.

in the succeeding years branches were established in all the important towns in Ireland.[15]

The banks, besides rendering British and Irish capital available, provided credit facilities for a number of new companies formed to exploit Irish resources. In addition to the large scale fishing companies already in operation, societies were created for the promotion of Irish mines, manufactures, and transportation. It is true that the Ulster Canal Co., organized in 1824, made little headway during these years, and that the mining schemes were largely visionary; but the readiness of capital to embark on such ventures clearly illustrates the prevailing faith in the future of Ireland.

In this prosperity the textile trades, the only important industries outside agriculture, shared to some extent. An attempt made during the famine of 1822 to aid cottage production in linen and wool manufacture, although it was not in line with the economic developments of the time, gave employment and temporary benefit to a number of peasants. Cotton however was in a position for rapid expansion. The abolition in 1823 of the duties on almost all goods between England and Ireland enabled Irish cottons to compete in the British market, and there followed a phenomenal growth of Irish production, aided not a little by a strike of Glasgow cotton spinners in 1823 which drove Peter Hutchison, one of the largest manufacturers, to Belfast. Hutchison not only greatly increased employment, but paid his workmen at a higher rate, with the result that in the winter of 1824 all cotton wages in Belfast were raised.[16] Other trades shared in the

15 M. Dillon, *History and development of banking in Ireland*, pp. 6-7, 49-53, 61.

16 *Belfast News Letter*, Mar. 30; Sept. 17, 24; Dec. 21, 1824. For the value of cotton imports and exports see *Statistical illustrations of the territorial extent and population of the British Empire*, pp. 50-51. Manchester

general activity of that year, and artisans of all sorts found employment good and wages steady.[17] The cotters, too numerous even in the best of times to find regular employment, alone gained little or nothing from the revival.

With the British financial crisis of 1826 the wave of prosperity came to an end.[18] Capital, so abundant before, was withdrawn from all but the most certain investments.

and Glasgow were sending yarn to Ireland to be woven.—Henry Parnell in the House of Commons, May 11, 1824. 2 Hansard, XI, 672-674.

[17] See the evidence of R. Hutton and others, *Parl. Pap.* 1825, No. 417; Minutes of Evidence, Select Committee on Combination Laws. It has been necessary to emphasize this point because Prof. O'Brien, an ardent protectionist and nationalist, has stated that ''. . . the growth of industry in Ireland was hindered by the impediments which were placed in the way of accumulating capital in Ireland, and of utilizing it if accumulated; and that this deficiency was in no way compensated for by any readiness on the part of British capitalists to invest money in Irish enterprises,'' and also that ''. . . one of the results of the repeal of the Union duties was to discourage British manufacturers from investing capital in Ireland.'' (*Economic history of Ireland from the Union to the famine*, pp. 442, 440.) It is remarkable that one of the political tracts quoted by O'Brien (*ibid.*, p. 441) to show the hostility of British capital, goes on to say: ''The present system of excluding the goods of English manufacturers, by the imposition of protecting duties, is unjust towards England, and injurious to ourselves, as *we must get them,* and we are compelled to pay ten percent for this protection, as it is called. . . . The consequence (of retaining the duties) has been that in the struggle, the few manufacturers that were in this country have failed for want of a market and a sufficient capital to enable them to bear losses, and we are compelled to pay, between protecting duties, Customs House charges, etc. etc. nearly twelve percent more for English goods than any other country in Europe. It is impossible that anyone can successfully defend this exclusionary system.'' (*Impartial review of the true causes of existing misery in Ireland*, pp. 15-16.) The great defect of the repeal of the duties in 1823 was that it left intact the duties on coal; and in this Parliament was acting in accordance with the wishes of protectionists who wanted still greater public aid for Irish coal. See *The case of Ireland in 1815*, p. 41. The true causes of the decline of Irish manufactures under British competition—the greater natural resources—are discussed in W. N. Hancock, *Report on the alleged violence of the working classes in Irish towns*, pp. 10-13.

[18] *Belfast News Letter*, June 6, 1826.

Speculative concerns, like the Irish Mining Co., disappeared entirely, and the Irish Company for Promoting Manufactures, which had intended to erect mills for grain, flax, etc., was forced to suspend operations. Agriculture suffered more directly in the falling off of British demand, and the failure of private banks, particularly in Cork.[19] All classes were hard hit, the artisans feeling the change most acutely. The wool trade which had been kept going only by temporary demands or by public aids, collapsed.[20] The abolition of the Union duties and the paralysis of the English market caused Leeds manufacturers to dump large quantities of cloth in Ireland. This proved the death blow of the domestic industry. The factories near Dublin continued to wage an unequal struggle for existence, but any hope of expansion was lost.[21]

The linen industry was at the same time going through the first stages of a general reorganization. Bounties granted by the Linen Board on machine spinning and on coarse weaving were withdrawn in 1823. The same year saw the end of regulation in England, greatly to the embarrassment of the Linen Board which was stripped of practically all power in 1825. Bounties on the export of various types of linen from Ireland were reduced by ten per cent, and further reductions made each year to 1830 when all subsidies ceased. The bleachers and great manufacturers were on the whole well pleased, for the cessation of regulation paved the way for further improvements and aided later expansion.[22] At the time, however, there was some dislocation of trade, and a good deal of discon-

19 Dillon, *History of banking in Ireland*, p. 56.

20 Earl of Blessington, *Observations addressed to the Marquis Wellesley*, p. 69; and see Murray, *Commercial relations of England and Ireland*, pp. 346-347.

21 *Parl. Pap.* 1837-38, No. 145, Second Report, Railway Commissioners (Ireland), Appendix III, p. 75. Letter of O. Willans on Wool Manufacture.

22 Gill, *Irish linen industry*, pp. 294-307.

tent amongst the factory operatives. The old handloom industry, already doomed by factory competition, was little affected by these changes. Coarse weaving declined somewhat in the northeast and in Munster, but it seems to have increased in Connaught, where the lower standard of living made it practicable.[23] The earnings of a handloom weaver had already sunk below six shillings a week early in the twenties,[24] and by 1823 women spinners found it impossible to make twopence for a full day's work.[25]

It was the cotton operatives who felt the crisis most severely. Late in 1825 they struck in order to maintain their union, and in 1826 further strikes ended disastrously. The employers, with the new combination laws behind them, set out to break the union. They were partially successful, though a weak organization continued.[26] Wages were cut, and by the summer over ten thousand operatives were unemployed in the Belfast district.[27] Similar struggles in other trades resulted in weakened unions, lower wages, or such a disruption of industry as to drive the particular manufacture to some other locality. The greatest sufferer from these disputes was Dublin; but artisans all over Ireland felt the loss of organized power, and the year 1826 was the beginning of a period of depression for craftsmen of all sorts.[28]

The distress of 1826, which was general throughout the United Kingdom, enabled the advocates of emigration as a means of relief to bring their ideas to the attention of the country for the first time. The appointment of two

23 *Belfast News Letter,* Jan. 6, 1826.

24 *Belfast News Letter,* April 4, 1826; this was the maximum, and many did not make over sixpence a day.

25 *Belfast News Letter,* March 21, 1826.

26 *Parl. Pap.* 1837-38, No. 488, p. 229.

27 *Belfast News Letter,* May 5, 1826.

28 See evidence of wages, etc., in *Parl. Pap.* 1827-38, Nos. 488 and 646: First and second Reports, Committee on Combinations.

parliamentary committees on emigration indicated a change in the attitude of the upper classes. Nowhere was this more marked than in Ireland. The desperate years of the early twenties, and the less tragic, but startling depression of 1826, brought home to landlords the necessity for some far more general remedy than had yet been attempted. Many were still skeptical of the effectiveness of emigration, but almost all were friendly to it as a palliative. Suspicion of the emigrant, so evident during the first years after the war, and the desire to keep tenants, however unprofitable, while there remained any arrears of rent to be paid, are no longer dominant.[29] At the same time, the belief that man power should be conserved for the sake of military strength, although maintained in theory, ceased to enter actively into considerations of public policy. If many landlords still objected on general principles to seeing their peasantry depart, they were thankful enough when practical opportunities arose to get rid of bad tenants or negligent farmers.[30] Political motives doubtless increased their willingness. The revolt of the freeholders had already begun, and Lecky's description of the Catholic Relief Bill of 1829, as marking "a great social revolution in Ireland—the substitution of the priests for the landlords as the leaders of the people,"[31] might more properly be applied to the organization of the Catholic Association. Like most Englishmen, Lecky first noticed the change in the Clare election of 1828, but the Irish newspapers had begun to comment on it two years earlier, and it was mentioned by one observer

29 Evidence of numerous landlords before the Committees on Irish disturbances and on emigration. *Parl. Pap.* 1825, No. 200; 1826, No. 404; 1826-27, No. 550. The Committees were not packed, and witnesses' opinions vary considerably.

30 See the evidence of A. R. Blake, *Parl. Pap.* 1826-27, No. 550, p. 458.

31 *Leaders of public opinion in Ireland*, p. 249.

in the summer of 1824.[32] Whatever the cause, landlords appearing before the Emigration Committee, expressed their willingness to support any scheme of emigration for their tenants, and offered to contribute as much as twenty pounds for a family of four;[33] while others, without waiting for parliamentary action, were yearly sending out small groups, and in this way at least retained some influence in emigration.[34]

It is difficult to determine to what extent the increase of politico-religious excitement affected emigration. Few Irishmen are averse to political conflict, and the political activity up to 1829, as well as the delusive hopes of improvement from the Reform may have operated as a slight check.[35] The Catholic clergy have been said to have discouraged the movement, their enemies claiming that they did not want to lose the various fees which were their only income, their friends that they were trying to protect their flocks from the drift towards Protestantism, which was then believed to be the fate of most settlers in the United States. The general character of the priests seems to belie this first argument, but there may have been some truth in the second. The Catholic church in America was at that time very largely French, and its great offices in the hands of Frenchmen under the superior jurisdiction of Quebec. The Irish emigrants found themselves out of

32 Mr. Nimmo, engineer and land agent, before the Committee (Lords) on Disturbances in Ireland; *Parl. Pap.* 1825, No. 200, p. 162.

33 Gabbet of Limerick, *Parl. Pap.* 1826, No. 404, p. 129; Lord Ennismore, *ibid.*, p. 198; and J. M. Marshall of Kerry, *Parl. Pap.* 1826-27, No. 550, p. 409.

34 The practice was already familiar when Buchanan went to Quebec in 1828; and see evidence of J. L. Foster, *Parl. Pap.* 1826-27, No. 550, p. 337.

35 Wilmot Horton claimed that the Catholic Association was opposing emigration, but this may only have been his way of recommending his favorite cause—government aid to emigrants—to the House of Commons, *2 Hansard* 19, p. 1504.

sympathy with this French Catholicism, which was more advanced than their own, and there were numerous quarrels. In many emigrant districts, however, there was no Catholic church at all. One step towards remedying this state of affairs was taken in 1820 when John England, a popular and able priest of Cork, was sent to Charleston as its first bishop. His work and that of other Irish prelates for the next thirty years was the organization and unification of what may be called the Irish Catholic church in America. But all this was scarcely begun in the twenties, and churchmen were as a rule very uncomfortable as to the fate of their emigrating parishioners.[36]

Emigration is primarily an economic matter, and other factors were more important than priestly influence in keeping down the Catholic exodus. Throughout these years, as in the preceding period, over half the emigrants sailed from Ulster ports, and according to the testimony of A. C. Buchanan, who knew that trade well, the northern Catholics were too poor to go.[37] In the west, landlords, while denying that poverty was the cause, testified that the Catholics were still too much attached to the soil to emigrate.[38] The exceptions to this were in parts of Munster which had suffered most severely during the famine, and from them even the poorest were eager to escape.[39] The only notice of a large Catholic emigration comes from Dublin, where John Astle, a considerable shipowner, stated that three-fourths of his emigrants were of that

[36] Guilday, *Life and times of John England*, esp. Chap. I. In 1820, the French attributed troubles in the church to ". . . the influx to our shores of a number of unworthy priests from Ireland, especially in recent years" (*ibid.*, p. 12).

[37] *Parl. Pap.* 1826, No. 404, p. 175.

[38] Evidence of Col. John Irwin of Sligo, and John Godley of Lietrim; *Parl. Pap.* 1825, No. 129. Committee on the State of Ireland, pp. 694, 737.

[39] I.e., Clare and southwest Cork; *Parl. Pap.* 1825, No. 200, p. 91; *Parl. Pap.* 1826, No. 404, p. 317.

church.[40] It is clear that from Ireland, as a whole, Protestants were still in a large majority.

The small amount of emigration among all creeds and classes is more difficult to account for. The numbers, which had begun to decline in 1819, fell in 1820 to 9,869, of whom 5,580 went to Quebec, 2,975 to the Maritime Provinces, and 1,314 to the United States.[41] The next year Quebec received only 4,041, and the United States, including those who came via New Brunswick, about 1,500.[42] This is the lowest point in the whole history of emigration after 1815, and it is not easy to explain why it should have come at this time. The effects of the American panic of 1819 were certainly not lasting. By autumn passages were again being prepaid to the United States, and the numbers going to the southern ports were not far below normal. Yet despite improved accounts from America there was a distinct falling off in the next year. The American passenger act of 1819 could not have been responsible, as its legal requirement of five tons for every two passengers was only half as strict as the British law already in force. Its only possible effect would have been in providing a second check upon the overcrowded illegal vessels which occasionally sailed from southern Irish ports, but there is no evidence of these in 1820.[43]

Probably the best explanation of the falling off in the American trade is improved conditions in Great Britain, where manufactures were expanding and trade booming from 1820 to 1825, and laborer's wages were three shillings a day, which was as much as most Irishmen could make in the United States.[44] Steam communication with

40 *Parl. Pap.* 1826, No. 404, p. 337.

41 British American and U.S. figures from *Parl. Pap.* 1822, No. 425; Ships and Passengers, Ireland, Quebec figures from *Quebec Mercury.*

42 *Quebec Mercury* and Young's Estimate; see Appendix.

43 B.T. 6/27; Consular Returns, America, 1820.

44 V. S. Clark, *History of manufactures in the United States,* I, 391-392.

Great Britain, established by 1825 from Cork, Waterford, Dublin, Drogheda, Belfast, and Londonderry, reduced the cost of passage at times to fourpence.[45] Aberdeen and Dundee manufacturers advertised for weavers, and particularly for spinners, in their new factories,[46] and the Irish Catholic population of London, which ranked next to Lancashire and Glasgow, increased by more than 46,000 between 1819 and 1826.[47] Even a special depression in the linen industry of Ulster in 1820, while it caused a few weavers to go to America,[48] had little effect in increasing the proportion of emigrants of that class. The United States immigration return for 1820 gives the occupations of 678 Irish emigrants, of whom 250 were farmers, 141 laborers, 70 weavers and spinsters, 81 other artisans, 52 merchants, and 84 clerks, professional men, servant girls, et al.[49] A return of Irish arriving at Passamaquoddy three years later shows corresponding proportions, except as to merchants, of whom there were but two out of 240.[50]

[45] Evidence of Henry H. Drummond, M.P., for Stirling, *Parl. Pap.* 1826-27, No. 850, p. 64. But the ordinary deck passage from Belfast to Glasgow was one shilling, and rates to Liverpool were somewhat higher.

[46] *Londonderry Journal*, May and June, 1825.

[47] *Parl. Pap.* 1826-27, No. 550, p. 591.

[48] *Causes of the discontents in Ireland and remedies proposed*, p. 46.

[49] *U.S. Doc.* 45, No. 118. This was the only year in which nationality, occupation, etc., were entered opposite each individual, making possible an analysis of Irish immigration. Information of this sort for later years is obtainable only when the arrivals at any port were exclusively Irish. The line between farmer and laborer is very indefinite; in several cases when the father of a family was a laborer, the children are classed as farmers. Among Ulster emigrants, farmers may usually be assumed to be weavers, and *vice versa*. The term *spinster* was used equally of men and women, but there were few men among them—doubtless because flax spinning was wholly a woman's occupation, and the cotton spinners were not emigrating at this time.

[50] *U.S. Doc.* 118, No. 108, p. 5. There would naturally be few merchants or professional men, as Passamaquoddy received only the poorer emigrants who came *via* New Brunswick.

With the coming of acute distress in 1822, a revival of American emigration appeared likely, and for two years Irish arrivals at Quebec exceeded eight thousand a year. This was a new record. It is notable, however, that the augmentation came from Ulster and Munster, whereas Dublin, the source of the greatest artisan emigration, experienced a falling off.[51] Belfast gained less than Newry and Derry, whose trade to St. John was also enlarged. Trade to the United States showed only a small increase. From every indication—offers of employment for emigrants, greater abuses by agents, cheap fares—this was a movement of the poor, which might soon have attained such numbers as it finally reached ten years later, had not the British passenger act of 1823 intervened.

The new act[52] repealed all preceding passenger acts and nominally equalized conditions of passage to British America and to the United States. Vessels on transatlantic voyages were limited to one passenger to five tons, but Customs licences might be issued enabling them to carry one passenger to every two tons unladen. Such licences were apparently habitually issued to Quebec; for statistics of ship arrivals in 1824 show that the numbers arriving on the various ships were no fewer than in preceding years, and far in excess of the ordinary provisions of the law.[53] The act permitted the granting of similar licences to British or American vessels for the United States, and no doubt they were issued in many instances; but the terms of the United States passenger act would

[51] Some of the Munster increase is attributable to the government aided movement from Cork in 1823, but even without it there was a distinct rise, beginning in the preceding year, from Cork, Waterford, and Limerick.

[52] *4 Geo. IV*, c. 84.

[53] *Quebec Mercury*, 1824. There were fifteen arrivals with over 150 passengers each, although the only one of over 750 tons register was the *Harrisons*, which brought 409 passengers from Derry. It was the largest ship in the emigrant trade at the time.

have prevented shippers from taking full advantage of the concession, and the apparent equalization of conditions of passage to Canada and the United States was deceptive. As the tonnage requirements of licensed ships under the new Act were the same as those already in existence to British America, and licensed ships to the United States were less strictly limited than before, this obviously would not explain changes in the amount of emigration; but the act was more severe in other respects, notably in requiring a space of fifteen square feet per person, and the presence of a surgeon on all vessels carrying more than fifty people. The last requirement was particularly awkward; there were not enough doctors in all Ireland to satisfy it, and in 1825 vessels from Belfast were advertising frantically for surgeons.

The effect of the act was to increase the cost of passage to a point beyond the reach of the poor. Fares from Londonderry and Dublin to St. John and Quebec had been as low as £2,[54] but after 1823 the cheapest rate quoted to British America was £3.10.[55] The almost unanimous testimony of Irish witnesses before the Emigration Committee of 1826 was that the Act had raised the class of emigrants, and the course of trade seems to bear this out. The numbers from Munster, always the source of a very poor type, declined markedly.[56] Of those who did go, the greater part were said to be mechanics, cotters being unable to afford the expense.[57] In the north, shipping advertisements ceased to offer employment to emigrants to America, and land became the main inducement. There

[54] *Londonderry Journal*, April 11, 1820. The *Jess and Flora* for St. John; June 18, 1822, the *Janet Dunlop* for Quebec. Evidence of John Astle, *Parl. Pap.* 1826, No. 404, p. 336.

[55] Evidence of A. C. Buchanan, *Parl. Pap.* 1826, No. 404, p. 173.

[56] Those to Quebec fell from 1,845 in 1822 and 1,806 in 1823, to 966 in 1824. *Quebec Mercury.*

[57] Evidence of Gabbett, *Parl. Pap.* 1826, No. 404, p. 126.

was some falling off among the better classes as well, and the increase (caused by the relaxation of tonnage requirements) of one or two thousand in those going direct to the United States was more than offset by the decline between 1823 and 1824 from 3224 to 1175 at St. John,[58] 1095 to 272 at St. Andrews,[59] and 8413 to 5168 at Quebec.[60] The change is therefore in part a redirection of emigration caused by the approach towards equalization of rates to British America and the United States, but it is also a reflection of the temporary improvement in the state of Ireland. That check ceased to operate in 1826, when over thirteen thousand emigrants sailed for British America, and five thousand for the United States. In this exodus even the poor participated to some extent,[61] financed possibly by contributions from America which were by now extensive.

A new act passed in 1825,[62] to go into effect in the following year, replaced the law of 1823, though its terms were in general the same. A special clause permitted the commissioners of the Treasury to exempt from its regulations ships from Ireland to British America. It appears that in practice such exemptions were only granted in respect of the requirements for carrying provisions, which had already been allowed under the preceding act.[63] At the end of 1826, therefore, emigration to America, while much more popular, especially in Munster, than it had been seven years earlier, was not yet possible on an extensive scale.

[58] C.O. 188/41, St. John Customs to W. F. Odell, May 18, 1831. These are for all arrivals but practically the whole were Irish.

[59] C.O. 188/41. St. Andrews Customs to W. F. Odell, May 19, 1831.

[60] *Quebec Mercury.*

[61] They were pouring into Albany from New York and Quebec in September, 1826. *Parl. Pap.* 1826-27, No. 550, p. 36, quoting the *Albany Advertiser.* These were not all Irish.

[62] 6 *Geo. IV*, c. 116.

[63] *Parl. Pap.* 1826-27, No. 550, p. 107. Evidence of A. C. Buchanan.

Changes on the other side of the Atlantic had contributed to this popularity, and were to some extent affecting the course of the movement. Both Quebec and St. John had emigrant societies by 1820, designed in part to aid the new arrival, but primarily to protect the colony from disease and a pauper population. The rise of a poor class trade in 1818-19 created problems in all the ports, particularly those of British North America, which were far too small to handle such an influx. In 1819 the Quebec Society embodied in its annual report some paragraphs of warning and advice to emigrants, which were widely copied in Ireland. Instead of discouraging prospective settlers, as was doubtless intended,[64] it proved an encouragement, for agents used the existence of the societies as inducements to the poor to go to those ports.[65]

Settlers of a somewhat more energetic but equally poverty-stricken class were provided for by two experiments in assisted emigration under Colonial Office control in 1823 and 1825. The 2,591 farmers and laborers from the North Riding of Cork taken out to Ontario by Peter Robinson were hardy and turbulent spirits, whose arrival caused considerable protest. Many of their neighbors took alarm, and were only slowly reconciled as the settlements progressed. Mismanagement in 1825 caused real hardship among them and numbers ran off to the United States, but the majority stayed and throve far better than they could

[64] E.g., in the *Belfast News Letter*, Jan. 14, 1820, the report is copied, with emphasis on all the evil aspects of emigration.

[65] *Londonderry Journal*, Jan. 18, 1820. Advertisement of the *Dominica Packet:* ". . . besides a society has recently been formed at Quebec for the purpose of affording assistance to poor emigrants who may be without means to support themselves should they not fall into work immediately on landing, or require to go into the interior to meet their friends." The Society was aware of both uses of its work, and argued from them that it could not properly be accused of either aiding or preventing emigration. *Quebec Mercury*, Nov. 16, 1821.

have done in Ireland.[66] Extravagant claims have been made as to the significance of this experiment. Rogers, in his historical geography of Canada, wrote: "No Celtic Roman Catholic Irishmen ever emigrated to the new world except to Newfoundland before the War of Independence, and after the war, hardly any went to Canada until Robinson created in them the taste to go."[67] The refutation of that statement lies in the Quebec emigrant returns, which show a greater influx from Cork and from Munster generally in 1822 than in either 1823 or 1825;[68] and famine, not government assistance, was the motivating force. Furthermore, the district of north Cork from which these emigrants were drawn, did not, as did some neighboring districts, become a center of extensive emigration until the great famine stimulated the exodus from all Ireland.[69] The experiment was equally unimportant from a Canadian standpoint. The assisted Irish, even with government aid, did not prosper like the independent settlers,[70] but they fared better than their poorer countrymen who followed later, and they became a useful section of the community.

Inducements to wealthier emigrants had begun to appear in the schemes of land speculators, and the first British American land scheme to be advertised in Ireland was promoted by the owners of one half of Prince Edward Island in 1817, with William Marquis, the Dublin ship agent, as their representative.[71] It does not seem to have

[66] There is a full account of this in Cowan, pp. 96-116.

[67] *Canada: Geographical*, p. 165.

[68] *Quebec Mercury;* see Appendix.   [69] See Map opposite page 1.

[70] *Parl. Pap.* 1845, No. 657, p. 920; Evidence of John Godley; and see *Parl. Pap.* 1826, No. 404, pp. 292, 338; and *Parl. Pap.* 1826-27, p. 31. The unassisted settler was expected to build a house, make a road, and clear five acres in the first year. Robinson's men (those of them who didn't decamp), averaged 6½ acres each after three years.

[71] See his *Short description of Prince Edward Island,* and advertisement of the *John, Belfast News Letter,* March 19, 1819.

attracted much attention, but three years later James For-
rest of York in Upper Canada managed a successful venture in selling land to emigrants. He came to Belfast,
chartered a ship there, and then went the rounds of the
leading market towns of Armagh, Monaghan and Tyrone,
engaging passengers, who were also to be purchasers of
his land.[72] A similar trade in New Brunswick lands was
carried on by A. Campbell at Londonderry.[73] The most
ambitious scheme of this period was that of N. Ward of
Marietta, Ohio, who travelled about Ireland selling his
land, and engaging passages through various regular
agents. Ward shipped his clients to Baltimore, offered
them transportation facilities from there to Wheeling,
West Virginia, and free passage down the Ohio to Marietta, but he refused to negotiate with any purchaser with
less than £25 capital.[74]

The American land act of 1820 reduced the price of government land to $1.25 per acre, and the minimum sale to
eighty acres; but the abolition of the credit system,. the
control of many land auctions by speculators, and continued hard times from 1820-1829, brought sales to a low
level. The practical recognition of squatter rights also decreased sales while at the same time it increased population. Squatting was not a practice likely to appeal to the
Irish farmer, however, accustomed as he was to seeing
men turned off their lands for the slightest defect of
title.[75] The Irish gained more from the New England migration of the twenties, and in the long period of social
unrest which followed Irish labor came in to supplant
American.[76]

[72] *Belfast News Letter*, April 14, 1820. Advertisement of the *Active*.

[73] *Londonderry Journal*, March 7, 1820.

[74] *Belfast News Letter*, Jan. 7, 1823.

[75] P. J. Treat, *The national land system*, 382-383; B. H. Hibberd, *History of the public land policies*, 101.

[76] J. T. Adams, *New England in the Republic*, 314, 328.

Meanwhile, timber merchants were also taking a hand in the promotion of emigration. At their offices in Quebec and St. John passages were paid for friends in Ireland, and the practice became almost as common there as in the United States. They were particularly active between 1820 and 1822, when threats of a change in the duties on timber, and even of a possible abolition of the preference given to Canada in 1809, greatly increased shipments, and the tonnage available for emigrant traffic was far beyond the demand. This may have been partly responsible for the very cheap fares then prevailing.[77] At the same time, the rapid fall in timber freights was an added inducement to make some profit on the westbound voyage.[78] This exceptional activity was ended by the new duties of 1822, which proved to be harmless to the Canadian trade. The reductions on Baltic timber were somewhat greater than on Canadian, but an effective preference still remained. The one important clause in the new schedule was one requiring Canadian timber to be accompanied by a certificate of Canadian growth. Quebec merchants frankly admitted that most of their export came from the United States, and for a time there was something like a panic in the trade,[79] until legal ingenuity came to the rescue and the Quebec customs decided that United States timber might be admitted to Canada and shipped to Great Britain under the lower schedule.[80] The timber vessels continued to carry the great bulk of the emigrants, and their

[77] *Reply to the observations of a British merchant on the report of the select committee of the House of Lords relative to the timber trade*, p. xix.

[78] Freights from Quebec to England fell steadily from £2.16.3 a ton in 1817-1820 to £1.18.9 in 1830-1833. *U.S. Doc.* 590, No. 23. Report on the trade and commerce of the British American colonies.

[79] See *Quebec Mercury*, May 26, 1821, and Sept. 6, 1822.

[80] This is open to question, but it seems to be the purpose of the decision recorded in the *Quebec Mercury*, Oct. 25, 1822. The officers at Halifax disagreed.

importance to the emigration trade was used as an argument for the maintenance of preferential treatment.[81]

Canadian merchants, thanks in part to the development
of canals and roads at this time,[82] were able to offer employment to the poor emigrating in their vessels,[83] and
offers were even made to forward passengers to Pitts-
burg, Illinois, etc.,[84] for the majority of the emigrants
were still going to the United States. W. B. Felton of
Quebec put the proportion as high as eighty per cent,[85] and
his evidence was later corroborated by A. C. Buchanan.
After the depression of 1819, shipping advertisements
generally referred to British American ports as best for
particular parts of the United States,[86] and New Brunswick continued until 1822 to be the recognized route to
New York and other coast cities.[87] In 1824, Buchanan objected to suggested changes in the passenger act because,
he said: "By placing the emigration and expense on the
same footing to the United States as to the British Colonies, the whole would be turned to the former."[88] There
was, however, considerable opposition in the Colonies to

[81] *Speech of Joseph Marryat, Esq., in the House of Commons on Monday,
June 5, 1820, upon the petition of the ship owners of the Port of London
against any alteration in the duties on timber,* p. 24.

[82] Notably the Lachine Canal, 1821-25; the Welland Canal, 1824-29; and
the Fredericton-St. John road, 1826. Rogers, *Canada: Geographical,* pp. 83,
167.

[83] See the *Isabella* and *Jess and Flora* for St. John; *Londonderry Journal,* Feb. 1, April 11, 1820; the *Janet Dunlop* for Quebec, June 4, 1822.
One offer was to procure places as servants.

[84] E.g., the *Active,* Belfast-Quebec; *Belfast News Letter,* Mar. 17, 1820.

[85] *Parl. Pap.* 1826, No. 404, p. 48.

[86] This was in some degree due to the end of government offers of aid in
obtaining land, but primarily to the revival of trade in the United States.

[87] *Niles Register,* Aug. 3, 1822: quoted in Chickering, *Immigration into
the United States,* p. 85.

[88] Buchanan to Dublin Chamber of Commerce, March 9, 1824. Cited in
Parl. Pap. 1825, No. 129, p. 26.

the poorer emigrants, especially the Irish, an opposition
caused to some extent by their disease and intemperance,
but chiefly by the inability of the country to absorb so
large an influx. "The lower Irish," said Buchanan, "on
first coming into the country are such, that they think
they are doing you a great service by working for you. I
would rather pay higher wages to Canadians, or those
emigrants who have been some time in the country, than
those just arrived."[89]

American urban employers were likewise unfriendly to
the Irish, who introduced rioting into industrial disputes;
and the great majority of the dollar-a-day unskilled
workers of 1825 were native born. Down at the docks,
however, and wherever crude labor at 75 cents a day was
wanted, the Irish held sway.[90] The canal mania proved
their boon. The Erie had employed 3000 as early as 1818,
and thenceforth the Irish were indispensable, building
every canal in the North until the Civil War. By 1826, five
thousand were working on four canals, while a dozen other
waterways from Maine to Toledo and Louisville were under construction.[91] Road work, also under public grants,
raised employment in the Northwest, and helped to maintain the incentive for poor emigration *via* the St. Lawrence route.[92] Political conditions also favored the growth
of emigration at this period. Massachusetts and Connecticut abandoned their religious qualifications for voting,
formerly maintained against the Irish, and their property

[89] *Parl. Pap.* 1826, No. 404, p. 175, and see the evidence of W. B. Felton
and Bliss of New Brunswick, *ibid.*, pp. 48, 101, 112. Bliss said in part: "The
Scotch never fail; they are industrious, thrifty, sober and obedient to the
laws—qualities in which the Irish are often deficient. As it seems by Mr.
Uniacke's evidence that the Irish do so well in Nova Scotia, I should hope
the Scotch might be sent to us" (p. 112).

[90] Clark, *History of manufactures in the United States*, I, 391-392.

[91] A. F. Harlow, *Old tow paths*, 53-55, 72-73.

[92] Hibberd, *Public land policies*, pp. 234-235.

qualification became a dead letter.[93] Robert Gourlay's *Statistical Account of Upper Canada,* published in 1822, acquainted many prospective emigrants with the success of Irish settlers in that area.[94]

In 1823, the thriving New Brunswick emigrant trade suddenly collapsed. Higher fares may have been one cause, but there were other factors involved, notably the decrease of timber cutting above the Atlantic ports, and the development of a new timber area round Bay Chaleur and the south shores of the Gulf of St. Lawrence.[95] The experience of earlier years suggests that timber ships might profitably have taken emigrants to St. John and then gone into the Gulf for their return cargo, and the decline in shipping indicates a decreased emigration by the New Brunswick route. At the same time the West Indian trade dispute entered a new phase with the opening of specified ports to direct trade with the United States in American vessels, and most of the former trade by way of the Maritime Provinces was killed. Between 1822 and 1825 American shipping entering British America fell from 92,000 to 48,000 tons.[96] It is improbable that this decline in any way affected the passenger trade, which did not use the West India ships, but the general shrinkage of New Brunswick trade may have injured the popularity of that route. Attempts in 1825 to revive the St. Andrews trade from Belfast, where emigration was beginning to increase again, were a failure, and the ships finally

93 J. T. Adams, *New England in the Republic,* pp. 321-323; McMaster, *History of the United States,* III, 192.

94 I, 233-234, 306-307, 352-353.

95 Even in 1826 when there was some revival in the passenger trade, Belfast, Dublin and Cork sent 17 vessels to Miramichi, St. Peters and other ports in the gulf, and only 14 to St. John—a most unusual proportion. From *Belfast News Letter,* Dublin *Morning Register,* and Cork *Southern Reporter.*

96 *A. St. J. Baker to Canning,* May 30, 1825; F.O. 5/204.

changed their destinations to other ports. The renewed activity of 1826 caused some improvement, but Munster took no part in it. Apparently passage *via* St. John had become too expensive for the poorer peasants, and was no longer sufficiently cheaper than the direct route to the United States to attract many small farmers and artisans.[97] One outlet, however, still remained open to the very poor. Servants for the Newfoundland fisheries were exempted from the provisions of the Act of 1823, and a considerable emigrant traffic was carried on under cover of this ruling. The Act of 1826 freed the Newfoundland trade altogether, and for three years there was a revival of emigration by way of St. Johns. It differed from the rush of 1815 in that the vessels did not as a rule drop all their passengers in Newfoundland, but cleared again from there to Quebec.[98] The trade was really a branch of the Quebec trade, exempted from the provisions of the Passenger Act, and it excited fewer complaints than that of 1815.[99] While the poorer emigrants were transferring from the New Brunswick to the Newfoundland and Quebec routes, those of a better class were discovering the advantages of Liverpool as a port of departure. The development of steam communication made it almost as convenient for passengers as direct sailing, and as the practice increased it gradually deprived the Irish ports of much of their freight trade to

[97] *Parl. Pap.* 1826, No. 404, p. 170. Evidence of A. C. Buchanan.

[98] The emigrant ships for St. Johns, as distinct from the fishing ships, regularly returned to Ireland from Quebec.

[99] Sir Thomas Cochran to Goderich, St. Johns, Sept. 25, 1827; in *Parl. Pap.* 1828, No. 112, p. 11—though he protests strenuously against the lack of all regulation. These ships were sometimes entered at Quebec as ''from Ireland.'' The lack of regulation was even defended on the ground that the required provisions made emigrants ill, while the man to Newfoundland ''. . . gets no more than his breadth and length upon the deck of a ship, and he has no more provisions than a few herrings, and he comes out a hearty man.''—Uniacke, in *Parl. Pap.* 1826, No. 404, p. 46.

the United States, and enhanced Liverpool's advantage of frequent and regular sailings.[100]

Free transportation to the English port gave the emigrant the full benefit of fares which ran from £4.10.0 to £7,[101] and appear to have been on an average lower than those from Ireland.[102] The change involved landing at New York, to which the westbound Liverpool traffic was largely confined, but this was no handicap. After completion of the Erie Canal in 1825 settlers found it a convenient port for the west, and not unsuitable for those parts of the Atlantic seaboard to which the Irish were accustomed to go. From 1823 on it received more than half the total American immigration;[103] and in self-protection the New York legislators passed a series of ordinances, the final effect of which was to require a payment of $3.00 per head for each immigrant.[104] This tax drove a few of the Irish poor to Philadelphia, but the majority of those for New York were landed at Amboy, and the acts did little good. The only other United States port of great interest to the Irish was Baltimore, which after 1823 absorbed an increasing share of the direct emigration from Belfast.

The growth of the Liverpool trade owed something to the reduced importance of the regular Irish merchants in the emigration traffic. They naturally sent emigrants from their own wharves, and whenever possible in their own ships; but the shipbroker, or passenger agent, who

100 Porter, *Progress of the nation*, I, 266. Regular service from Liverpool was new when *Niles Register* commented upon it, Feb. 24, 1821.

101 Table of fares in 1822, in C.O. 384/87; B. Emigration to Canada; and *Parl. Pap.* 1826, No. 404, p. 297.

102 Fares were not often quoted during this period, but the lowest I have found was six guineas.

103 See tables in Bromwell, *History of immigration to the United States.*

104 This was commutation money for a bond to protect the city against paupers. See Hall, *Immigration and its effects upon the United States*, p. 204; for amount of tax, *Parl. Pap.* 1826, No. 404, p. 184.

chartered the middle section of a timber vessel for passengers, and sold passages in advance without reference to particular vessels, had no incentive for favoring one route rather than another. The same men who chartered a Liverpool ship to take on a load of emigrants in an Irish port, also sent other emigrants to Liverpool to take passage there. The advertisements show that by the middle twenties by far the greater part of the trade from Ulster and Dublin had fallen into their hands, the regular merchants taking only a small number in their vessels. The continuous years of low class traffic, 1819-1823, had given undue advantage to the less scrupulous agents, and merchants found it difficult to compete.[105] In Ulster, the organization of emigration had now reached a stage where the would-be emigrant needed only the money to pay his passage; everything else was done for him. The brokers had sub-agents whose business it was to visit the principal towns on market days during the spring, thus reducing to a minimum the inconvenience of securing passage.[106] The movement from the south was not yet sufficient to make profitable such a development, and control of emigration there remained in the hands of merchants, who sometimes sub-let a part of their space to agents in the smaller towns.[107]

[105] How could any ordinary trader compete with the *Hope*, from Dublin to Newfoundland and St. John, which offered: ''In addition to the superior accomodation for passengers in the above vessel, TWO QUARTS OF OLD MALT WHISKEY, AND TWO QUARTS OF VINEGAR will be given to each passenger, as Sea Stores, gratis'' (Dublin *Evening Post*, May 15, 1819). J. H. Shaw of Belfast probably achieved the greatest originality when he requested passengers by the *Caledonia* to come in early ''. . . as the ball intended to be given to the passengers will take place on the evening of the 14th; the ship sails first fair wind after.'' *Belfast News Letter*, Oct. 11, 1822.

[106] See the *James* for Quebec; *Belfast News Letter*, May 12, 1820.

[107] Thus J. and T. Carroll at Cork took part, and an agent at Kinsale

The growth of the New York-Liverpool trade gave to American shipowners, who controlled most of it, some revenge for the loss of the passenger traffic in 1817. Their agents began to supplant the Irish charterers, and while British shipping from Ireland to America remained stationary at about 3000 tons a year, American tonnage rose from 9500 to 18,000. It receded thereafter, but Americans never lost control of the direct route to their country.[108] The emigrant carriers belonged in about equal proportions to the two countries, British ships retaining a fair share in the trade to Philadelphia and ports south, but losing most of the New York business.[109]

The repeal of the Passenger Act early in 1827 brought to a close this period of restricted emigration, and opened the way to a full operation of forces which had been greatly strengthened during these years. At the beginning of the twenties Munster was in no sense an important center of emigration, but by 1827 many, if not most, of its poor and middling inhabitants were ready and eager to seek their fortunes abroad. The dismal years before 1823, and to an even greater extent perhaps the two years of hopeful improvement which intensified the subsequent failure, had done a great deal to foster the emigrating spirit. Long before the government check was removed, the social check in Ireland had largely disappeared and the influence of the upper classes was on the whole favorable. There remained only the inherent attachment to the native soil—an attachment in many cases intensified by ignorance—which formed the principal obstacle to the ex-

took another part, in the *General Elliott* for Prince Edward Island and Quebec; Cork *Southern Reporter*, Mar. 13, 1823.

[108] Watterson and Van Zandt, *Tabular statistical views of the population, commerce . . . of the United States*, pp. 97-103.

[109] From consular returns of arrivals by British vessels in the United States, in F.O. 5/160-204.

tension of emigration. It had been broken down to some extent in Munster and Leinster, and was almost non-existent in Ulster, but in Connaught it was still a formidable barrier. The events of the next ten years were to undermine this influence and introduce Irish emigration on a grand scale.

CHAPTER IV

THE RISE OF LARGE SCALE EMIGRATION

O, the times are hard and the wages low,
O'Melia, whar you bound to?
The rocky mountains are my home,
Across the Western ocean.

That land of promise there you'll see,
O'Melia, whar you bound to?
I'm bound across the western sea
To join the Irish army.

To Liverpool, I'll take my way,
O'Melia, whar you bound to?
To Liverpool that Yankee school,
Across the Western ocean.

There's Liverpool Pat with his tarpaulin hat,
O'Melia, whar you bound to?
And Yankee John the packet rat,
Across the Western ocean.

Beware these packet-ships, I pray,
O'Melia, whar you bound to?
They steal your stores and clothes away,
Across the Western ocean.

Whall's Sea Shanties.

THE years that followed 1826 were crowded with events of momentous importance to the United Kingdom, in that field dearest to the hearts of Irishmen—politics. For

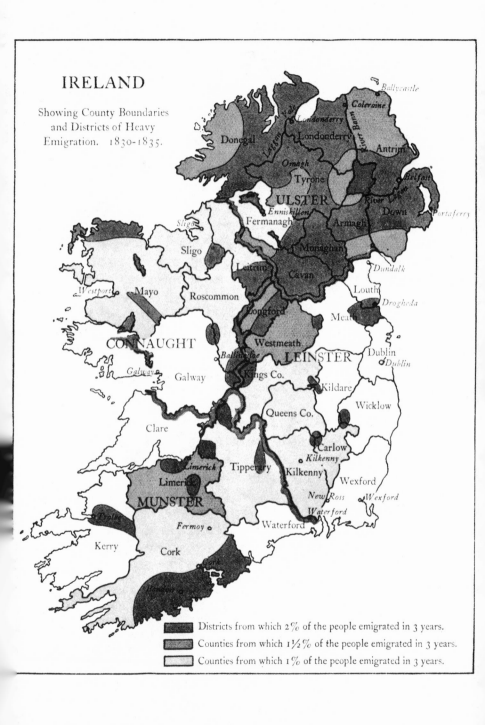

IRELAND

Showing County Boundaries
and Districts of Heavy
Emigration. 1830-1835.

Ballycastle

Coleraine

Donegal

Londonderry
Londonderry

Antrim

Omagh
Tyrone

Belfast

ULSTER

Enniskillen
Fermanagh

Armagh

Down

Portaferry

River Lagan

Sligo

Sligo

Monaghan

Dundalk

Leitrim

Cavan

Westport

Mayo

Roscommon

Longford

Louth

Drogheda

Meath

CONNAUGHT

Ballinasloe

Westmeath

LEINSTER

Dublin
Dublin

Galway

Galway

Kings Co.

Kildare

Queens Co.

Wicklow

Clare

Carlow

Kilkenny

Tipperary

Kilkenny

Wexford

Limerick

Limerick

New Ross

Wexford

MUNSTER

Waterford

Tralee

Fermoy

Waterford

Kerry

Cork

Cork

Bantry

Districts from which 2% of the people emigrated in 3 years.

Counties from which 1½% of the people emigrated in 3 years.

Counties from which 1% of the people emigrated in 3 years.

three years all other topics paled beside the struggle for Catholic Emancipation. No sooner was that won—and lost—than two new issues absorbed the attention of politicians: abolition of tithes, and an Irish Poor Law. Both gave way before the campaign for parliamentary reform, which had the support of practically every faction in Ireland, though it yielded meager benefits there. The death of the king and the fall of the hated Wellington-Peel ministry opened the way for a number of Irish acts: national education in 1831, repeal of the subletting act in 1832, tithe reforms in 1832 and 1834, the creation of the Royal Irish Constabulary in 1835, and the investigation by parliamentary commissions of the state of the poor and of municipal corporations, both of which gave rise to important legislation a few years later. After 1832, tithes and the Poor Law again held the center of the stage, but political activity was for the time more diffused. The alarms and excursions of the earlier six years had concealed from the view of all save those directly interested, a growth in the spirit and practice of emigration of greater significance for the future of Ireland than many of the political questions which were being agitated.

In 1827, the movement of Irish to America for the first time since 1818 reached an official total of at least twenty thousand. There is strong reason to believe that the returns were especially defective in that year,[1] and the actual figure may well have been thirty thousand or over. After a slight setback in 1828 emigration increased annually to the record years of 1831 and 1832, during each

---

[1] There was no return from Newry, although 1341 emigrants had left there by May 25th. The official total from Belfast for the year was 4740, but the agents' books showed that 6442 had sailed before July 10th, and twenty-four passenger ships were advertised to leave after that date. *Belfast News. Letter*, May 25, July 10, 1827. One must add at least 3000 for these two ports alone.

of which over 65,000 passengers left Ireland for America.[2] Such an average could not then be maintained, but after 1835, no year except the wholly unusual 1838 saw less than 30,000 Irish cross the Atlantic. The emigration of the next ten years was peculiarly subject to fluctuations, but its proportions were now so great that nothing short of absolute economic disaster in America could bring it below 30,000. From 1830 onwards the Irish emigrant becomes a recognized and important factor in American economic and social history.

We have described in the preceding chapter the very general desire for emigration amongst the poorer classes in Ulster and large districts of Munster and Leinster, but large scale emigration was impossible without an extension of facilities bringing passage within the reach of thousands who had hitherto been unable to go. For this, a change in the passenger acts was primarily responsible. Early in 1827 the Commissioners of the Treasury, in anticipation of action by parliament, removed some of the restrictions upon passenger vessels.[3] Parliament followed on May 28th with the repeal[4] of the only British passenger act then in force, leaving the traffic, so far as the United Kingdom was concerned, entirely unrestricted, and for a year the only legal check was the American act of 1819. Conditions proved so bad, however, that a new

[2] As the worst reports of overcrowding and other breaches of the law come from these years, it may be that the numbers should be considerably greater. On the other hand, the detailed report from the agents' books of emigration from Belfast for 1832 corresponds very closely to the official returns. *Belfast News Letter*, Dec. 28, 1832. I should not make any large addition.

[3] According to the advertisement of the *James Bailie*, Belfast-St. Andrews, "the delay of the above ship after her appointed time of sailing arose from Mr. Clarke her charterer, having applied for a mitigation of certain restrictions in the Passenger act, which have been now suspended." *Belfast News Letter*, April 27, 1827. See Ch. VI.

[4] By the acts *7 and 8 Geo. IV*, c. 19.

British act was passed in May, 1828,[5] applicable only to vessels to British America. It was far from restoring the stricter regulations of the early twenties, for it revived only the old space requirement of five and a half feet between decks, and permitted the carrying of three passengers to every four tons registered instead of the one passenger to every two tons previously enforced. It eliminated also the detailed specifications regarding provisions, substituting a general order for fifty pounds of breadstuffs (or potatoes from Ireland) to each passenger. This act, which remained in force through the summer of 1835, was in general well enforced in Ireland, except as to provisions,[6] and though it apparently proved less effective at Liverpool where the great quantity of shipping made control difficult,[7] there was little incentive to break a law which imposed so few restrictions.

Relaxed regulations were immediately reflected in cheaper fares. In 1827 when the minimum rate from the north of Ireland to the United States remained at £5, and that from Liverpool at £4, fares to Canada dropped to £2 or at most £3.[8] The act of 1828 apparently made no difference, for the same rates are quoted in 1830. In 1831 the standard fare from Dublin, Belfast, and Londonderry to Quebec was thirty shillings,[9] where it remained during the succeeding years.[10] The passenger act was not altogether

5 9 *Geo. IV*, c. 21.

6 *Parl. Pap.* 1836, No. 35; Report of Poor Inquiry Commissioners, Appendix C. Part I, p. 18: Testimony of Lieut. Miller, Emigrant agent at Belfast; and *Parl. Pap.* 1836, No. 76, p. 5. Annual Report of the Agent at Quebec for 1835.

7 *Parl. Pap.* 1836, No. 40, p. 35: Testimony of Robert Low, emigrant agent at Liverpool.

8 *Parl. Pap.* 1826-27, No. 550, pp. 106, 227: evidence of A. C. Buchanan, W. S. Fitzhugh.

9 M. Doyle, *Hints on emigration to Upper Canada*, p. 83. Competition at Dublin brought the rate down to 25 shillings in 1831.

10 *Parl. Pap.* 1836, No. 35, Part I, pp. 18, 77.

responsible for this continued downward trend, as is shown by the extraordinary drop in fares to the United States which began about 1831, when Liverpool agents offered to take passengers from Newry to Liverpool and thence to New York for £3, children half fare.[11] Three years later the fare from Liverpool to the United States ports was from 50/ to 60/ and passengers were advised to bargain for reductions.[12]

Several factors doubtless contributed to this fall. Bad times in England had caused a surplus of shipping and a decline in the timber rates from British America, which fell to 38/- a ton between 1830 and 1833,[13] their lowest level before 1842. On the other hand, trade to the United States was to some extent picking up, especially after the tariff reductions of 1833, and the settlement in 1830 of the long dispute over West Indian trade, which revived the old three cornered traffic between the United States, the West Indies, and the British Isles. The great majority of emigrants, however, did not travel by ordinary cargo vessels, and the main cause of the reduction in fares lay in the increase of the number of passengers. Emigrant ships during these years could usually count on a full passenger list, and were thus able to operate on a smaller margin of profit for each individual.

This habitual crowding of emigrant ships suggests that the principal check on emigration may have been the amount of space available. During the season of 1832 every one of the twenty-two vessels which left Belfast for Quebec carried its full legal complement of passengers,[14]

[11] *Newry Examiner*, July 1831. The custom of offering free transportation to Liverpool was fully established by this time.

[12] P. O'Kelly, *Advice and guide to emigrants going to the United States of America*, pp. 26, 75.

[13] *U.S. Doc.* 590, No. 23, p. 770.

[14] *Belfast News Letter*, Dec. 28, 1832, which gives the number of passengers by each vessel, and its tonnage.

and the same condition doubtless prevailed at other ports. The total tonnage available in the British American timber trade was set five years earlier at 125,000. Of this 60,000 tons went to Canada and 65,000 tons to the Maritime Provinces.[15] In 1831 it had increased by only 2,000 tons.[16] If we deduct the very considerable amount which left Great Britain before the emigrant season to catch the opening of the St. Lawrence, and the vessels making autumn and winter trips to St. John and Halifax, there remains a tonnage barely sufficient to carry the large emigration of 1831 and 1832. Other merchant ships, unlike timber ships, were not easily convertible for emigration purposes, and it is quite possible that in these years the available tonnage set a definite limit to the amount of emigration.

While cheaper fares made possible this first great emigration of the Irish poor, we must turn to the state of Irish agriculture for its direct cause. The effect of steam communication between Ireland and Great Britain on the course of emigration has already been discussed, but its most significant effect lay in a change in the character of Irish rural economy. Steamers were first used for freight in 1824,[17] and by 1830 twelve companies operating forty-two vessels were carrying animals from Irish ports to Liverpool or Bristol.[18] In the same year the inauguration of steam service on the Shannon, which was connected by canal with Dublin, opened up the western grazing country to easy communication with the English market.[19] The assimilation of the trade between England and Ireland to the coasting trade, accomplished in 1826, reduced many

[15] Parl. Pap. 1826-27, No. 550, p. 455.

[16] Porter, Progress of the Nation (Ed. F. W. Hirst), p. 425.

[17] Marmion, History of the Maritime Ports of Ireland, p. 241.

[18] Belfast News Letter, June 4, 1830.

[19] Parl. Pap. 1837-38, No. 145, Second Report, Railway Commissioners (Ireland), p. 11.

charges on shipping and aided the steamers in drawing
together the two countries. The Irish grazier, formerly
dependent upon buyers at fairs, or on the meat packers
of Limerick, Cork and Waterford, was now able to sell
in a free market, and grazing profits, aided by higher
prices for butter, increased enormously.[20] The result was
a widespread movement for the consolidation of farms,
and increased severity in dealing with under-tenants. The
Whiteboys and the famine of 1822 had shown southern
landlords and farmers the dangers of an abundant population, and the enhanced value of grazing land now gave
them an additional reason for clearing their estates.
To quote one of many similar opinions expressed by
landlords, that of Thomas Spring Rice (later Lord
Monteagle):

I by no means confine the observations I have made with regard
to the general feeling and interest, as against the existence of an
excess of population, to the landlords and inheritors of the soil;
the farmers themselves are becoming just as sensible of the difficulty and the mischief as the landlords. It is the common phrase
among them, ''We now discover that dairy cows are more profitable than cottager tenants.''[21]

The effect of consolidation upon evictions is by no
means clear. The general opinion of the time, endorsed by
Professor O'Brien,[22] held that there was a wholesale
removal of cotter tenants; but the mass of evidence before the Devon Commission, which went into the subject
carefully, showed that consolidation for the purpose of
creating grazing farms was generally accomplished by
transplanting tenants and without eviction, while other

[20] *Parl. Pap.* 1837-38, No. 145, Second Report, Railway Commissioners
(Ireland), p. 9. *Parl. Pap.* 1826, No. 404, p. 127, Evidence of Gabbett.
[21] *Parl. Pap.* 1826-27, No. 550, p. 448.
[22] *Economic history of Ireland from the Union to the Famine*, pp. 52-56.

consolidations caused only a small number of removals.[23] One cannot ignore the mass of contemporary opinion on the other side, but it may be that other causes played a larger part than was then recognized. Ejectment for non-payment of rent as a means of attempting to enforce payment was a recognized proceeding in northeastern Ulster, though not elsewhere. The politico-religious quarrels connected with Catholic Emancipation furnished another motive, and the disfranchisement in 1829 of 200,000 forty shilling freeholders was a signal for further activity on the part of landlords, who wished to create £10 freeholds —then the lowest voting class. Agitation for the passage of an Irish Poor Law, which would have made the gentry largely responsible for the cotters within their district, though not effective until 1838, was preceded by frantic efforts on the part of landlords to remove the pauper population from their lands.[24] These movements for ejectment were greatly facilitated by the act of 1826, which required the landlord's consent to all subleases. The act was considerably modified in 1832, but it proved very effective during its operation.[25]

The necessity of emigration as an accompaniment to eviction was clearly recognized. The Emigration Committee of 1826 said of the Subletting Act: "All the advantages that may be derived from this Act will be diminished, if not rendered nugatory, unless a well organized system of emigration should be established concurrently with the measure itself."[26] A year later the act was declared unenforceable in Cork unless accompanied by

[23] *Digest of Evidence, Devon Commission,* pp. 452-453.

[24] See for example, *Parl. Pap.* 1836, No. 42; Remarks on the evidence . . . by one of the Commissioners. (J. E. Bicheno), p. 24.

[25] O'Brien, p. 160, who follows O'Connell's condemnation of the act; for the landlords' point of view see O'Connor, *Ireland, 1798-1924,* I, 192.

[26] *Parl. Pap.* 1826, No. 404, p. 9.

emigration.[27] The Poor Inquiry Commission of 1833-36, which secured information from every parish in Ireland as to the extent of emigration, how it was aided, and where it went, and on the prevalence of the practice of consolidating farms, and of evictions, supplies positive evidence of the comparatively slight connection between the two. Of the 363 parishes which reported extensive emigration,[28] less than thirty showed a general prevalence of consolidation, and 214 had none at all. The majority of these parishes were in Ulster. In the south, on the other hand, over half the parishes with large emigration reported some consolidation, and over a fifth showed it to be the general practice. It may be said therefore that consolidation was a minor cause of emigration, of chief importance in the south. Eviction was equally effective in all parts except Connaught, and was definitely stated to have brought about emigration in eighty of the 363 parishes.[29]

The emigration of the evicted raises an interesting question—that of the means which enabled them to go. There could be no doubt of their desire. In all the evidence before the Poor Commissioners but two instances occur in which ejected tenants preferred other aid than assistance in emigration,[30] while hundreds expressed a wish to go to America. But there is also much testimony to the

[27] *Parl. Pap.* 1826-27, No. 550, p. 387, Evidence of Dr. Wm. Murphy.

[28] I.e., over 2% of their population in the three years reported.

[29] Compiled from *Parl. Pap.* 1836, No. 38, Poor Inquiry (Ireland), *Appendix F*. Baronial Examinations relative to Con Acre . . . Emigration . . . etc.; and *Supplement:* Answers to Questions (by parishes). The answers were made by the Justice of the Peace and the clergy, including parish priests and dissenting ministers, and represent as accurate a picture of conditions as could be obtained at the time. The landlords frequently went wrong on the amount of emigration (*infra*, p. 188, *note*) but they were quite frank in dealing with consolidation, of which most of them approved.

[30] In Galway and Cork. *Parl. Pap.* 1836, No. 38, p. 133; and Supplement, p. 209.

effect that the evicted were too poor to raise even the small capital necessary for passage at that time. The answer is to be found first in the help of friends, a help so generally extended to Irish emigrants, that in most of the answers to the question: "Have they received any, and what assistance, for the purpose of emigration?"[31] it escaped comment. Others were aided by compensation from their landlords for crops in the ground or for buildings.[32] In addition, there was considerable direct aid from landlords, consisting usually of passage money, sometimes supplemented by a small capital for use on arrival in America. In 1826 landlords had expressed willingness to coöperate in a general scheme, but had given little actual assistance. In 1833 forty-seven parishes reported direct landlord assistance in emigration, and twenty-three others aid by public subscription, presumably from the gentry. These seventy parishes were widely scattered throughout Ireland—only three counties, Cork, Kilkenny, and Queens containing more than five.[33]

Indirectly, evictions added to the causes of emigration by spreading unemployment from districts already overpopulated to others where the pressure had hitherto been less severe. In general, agricultural wages remained the same, ranging from fivepence to tenpence a day for steady labor, or eightpence to a shilling for casual work; but a decrease in the number of working days may well have

[31] Only 39 parishes, of which only one was in Ulster, reported help from friends! The answers show clearly that witnesses were thinking of extraordinary aid, such as that of landlords or public subscription.

[32] *Emigrants Guide* (Westport, 1832), p. 45; quoting the Castlebar *Telegraph*, June 4, 1831.

[33] *Parl. Pap.* 1836, No. 38. Supplement. These returns, which were made largely by the gentry, are probably fairly accurate, but they should be increased in Londonderry, where the London companies, the proprietors of over half the soil, were particularly active in forwarding emigrants.—See Supplement, p. 370: Upper Cumber Parish; and *O'Donovan Survey*, Box 37, Kilrea P.; Box 47, Tamlaght Finlagan P.

made the early thirties especially miserable for the cotter and lowest class of farmer, who was dependent on wages. The distress was perhaps no greater than in 1818 or 1822, but coming after a very general spread of the emigrating spirit, and at a time when fares were only about half as high as in the earlier periods, it became a far more potent cause of emigration than ever before. Its effectiveness may be estimated by the extent of emigration before 1830, when special causes began to operate; but in order to form any just estimate of its share in the whole movement we must glance at conditions among the upper classes of Irish society who had hitherto contributed a considerable percentage of the emigrants.

Tenant farmers of all classes suffered from the increased competition for land, brought about in part by the development of grazing, and in part by the growth of population, which in 1831 exceeded seven and three-quarter millions, an increase of almost a million in ten years. Conditions bore most heavily upon the small farmers, whose earnings had increased little if at all, and who were usually most in arrears. The fate of the larger farmers seems to have varied in different parts of the country. In the west, they too were hard hit by the new competition, and numbers emigrated;[34] but in the eastern counties of Leinster, where landlords were said to have granted more favorable terms to men of this class,[35] many of them, aided by their ability to reap large profits from grazing, found themselves better off than before. In general, however, there is clear evidence of agricultural distress up to 1830, followed by a considerable improvement; an improvement largely confined to those who had some

[34] See statements from Leitrim and Kerry, *Parl. Pap.* 1836, No. 38, pp. 133, 137.

[35] *Ibid.*, pp. 124, 137, 139—reports from Dublin, Wicklow and Waterford.

capital. This distribution shows clearly in the rent-rolls of the landlords. The Buckingham estates in the grazing counties of Westmeath and Longford paid fifty per cent more in 1828 than in 1819, yet left all the small tenants sadly in arrears, while the poorer Clare property had actually decreased in value.[36] The railway commissioners, who reported in 1836 a great increase in the consumption of articles of comfort, concluded with the statement: "The demand seems to proceed almost exclusively from the superior class of landholders, and the inhabitants of the towns."[37]

This quotation illustrates a situation in the towns somewhat similar to that in the country. The commercial classes were quick to respond to the increased prosperity of agriculture, and there are numerous references to improvements in the seaports after 1830. The census of 1830 showed only one port, Drogheda, to be declining in importance; and Henry Inglis in his tour in 1834 reported that all the towns had increased in trade and wealth, with the exception of Kilkenny, Cashel, and Bandon, where special causes operated.[38] Unskilled labor was then earning an average of six shillings a week, and was employed during nine months of the year.[39] This average covers variations from Belfast where wages were seven to eight shillings and employment constant, to Waterford, where the wage was five shillings, and work obtainable only for half the year, and even at the best of times the town laborer led a precarious existence. Skilled labor, on the other hand, came much nearer to earning the same wages which prevailed in Great Britain. Masons and others regularly made 2/6d a day, and after 1830 had fairly good

---

[36] Accounts of the Duke of Buckingham; O'Conor Papers.
[37] *Parl. Pap.* 1837-1838, No. 145, p. 17.
[38] *A Journey throughout Ireland in 1834*, II, 312.
[39] *Ibid.*, II, 313.

employment in most parts of Ireland.[40] Their advantageous position was said to be due to the strength of the
unions in Dublin, Cork, and many of the lesser towns.[41]
The repeal in 1831 of the parliamentary duty on coals
imported into Ireland, and the still more important abolition in the following year of the various local levies on
coal, put Irish manufacturers on an equal footing, as
regards fuel, with their competitors in the south and west
of England, and the erection of mills and installation of
machinery of various sorts proceeded more rapidly after
1832. From ten to fifteen new mills were established each
year,[42] by far the greatest number being flour mills, with
breweries and distilleries taking second place, and paper
factories third. These new factories gave employment to
an increasing number of skilled craftsmen.

Textile workers, the most numerous of Irish artisans,
reaped little benefit from these developments. The depression noted at the close of 1826 continued for four years
more. Belfast cotton workers seem to have become interested in emigration for the first time during this period.
They formed an emigration society in 1826, appealing to
the gentry for aid,[43] and in the following year turned to
the parliamentary committee with a truly pitiful account
of their situation.[44] At that time three-fourths of the
workers earned from two to four shillings a week, and
only a handful of the most skilled were able to make more
than five shillings. Of the 107 petitions received by the
committee, fifty-five were from artisans, and thirty from

[40] Inglis, *A Journey throughout Ireland in 1834, passim;* A. L. Bowley,
Wages in the United Kingdom in the Nineteenth Century, pp. 51-52.

[41] *Parl. Pap.* 1826-27. No. 550, p. 384. This does not apply to the textile
unions, which had been broken in 1825.

[42] *Parl. Pap.* 1837-38. No. 145, pp. 97-113.

[43] *Belfast News Letter,* Sept. 12, 1826.

[44] *Parl. Pap.* 1826-27, No. 550, p. 499.

weavers.[45] Conditions had improved somewhat in 1828, but most of the handloom workers were too poor to purchase their materials, and others were hard hit by the burning of Mulhollands, one of the largest factories in Belfast.[46] Later accounts give no hint of improvement, and the beginning of government regulation in 1831 and 1833 proved a further handicap to the Irish cotton trade, which had thriven partly by reason of the high proportion of children employed at long hours in the mills.[47]

Conditions in the linen industry were less uniform. Ireland had lost much of her spinning to Great Britain during the twenties, and in 1827 imported yarns formerly made at home;[48] but the introduction of power looms in 1826 and of successful power spinning in 1829, marked the beginning of a new era.[49] The small but highly important factory production, largely concentrated in the Belfast area, showed definite signs of prosperity in 1830,[50] and continued to thrive thereafter, aided in part by reductions in the American tariff in 1833.[51] The cottage weaver also gained to some extent from this change, but its advantages did not compensate for the decline in his earnings brought about by the increase of machine manufacture, and by the growing importance of cotton goods. Within a month of the time when Belfast reported a revival of its linen trade, the weavers in the Londonderry

[45] *Ibid.*, pp. 484-499.

[46] *Belfast News Letter*, Feb. 22, July 1, 1828.

[47] The act of 1833, which prescribed a 48 hour week for children under thirteen, interfered with current Irish practice.

[48] There is a good article on this change in the *Londonderry Journal*, Nov. 19, 1833.

[49] Gill, *Irish linen industry*, p. 326; and see W. N. Hancock, *On the compulsory use of native manufactures*, p. 7.

[50] The first notice of change is in the *Belfast News Letter*, May 14, 1830.

[51] *Londonderry Journal*, July 22, 1834.

area were in worse plight than ever before,[52] and the failure of some charities which had kept alive poor spinners both here and in Cork increased their misery.[53] The testimony before the Poor Inquiry Commissioners showed that the weavers were still hanging on, but that cottage spinning had become practically hopeless. From many parishes in the south and west of Ulster spinners were emigrating in large numbers.[54] The extent of the decline is vividly portrayed in parish accounts in the Ordnance Survey. At Dunsfort in County Down in 1834, it was said: "Emigration has been so considerable that the number who have emigrated since 1800 are equal to two-thirds of the present population."[55] In Sligo, we are told: "From many of the villages above described two-thirds of the members of the families have emigrated within the last eight years to the Canadas; in one village containing thirty-five looms, in the townland of Bally-treenan, five only are now remaining."[56]

Social disturbances, punctuating the continuous pressure of economic distress, played an important part in this as in other periods. The religious friction which preceded Catholic Emancipation reached unusual intensity in 1827, and party lines were determined almost wholly by creed.[57] The fall of the Liverpool ministry brought temporary improvement. Catholics were more hopeful and

[52] *Londonderry Journal*, April 20, 1830.

[53] *Ibid.*, Oct. 13, 1829; *Parl. Pap.* 1826-27, No. 550, p. 465. Testimony of John Elmore of Clonakilty. The Londonderry women were being paid 3d a day, or double what they could earn in the open market.

[54] Baronial reports from Armagh, Down, Tyrone and Mayo, *Parl. Pap.* 1836, No. 38.

[55] *O'Donovan Survey*, Box 23.

[56] *Ibid.*, Box 50, Emlafad-Ballymote Parish.

[57] At first many Protestants supported emancipation, but the bitterness after 1825 reduced the number to a handful. Petitions against emancipation in Antrim in 1813, 1823 and 1827 received respectively 13,997, 18,847 and 31,114 signatures. *Belfast News Letter*, March 2, 1827.

the most truculent Protestants a little less provocative, but the fluctuations in the final passage of the bill, and the accompanying disfranchisement of the forty shilling freeholders revived the old bitterness, and conditions after 1829 were worse rather than better. O'Connell, stirred by the success of the revolutions of 1830 on the continent, put new efforts into a campaign for the repeal of the Union, while Protestants, fearing Roman domination, and stimulated by the Tractarian movement, began an active proselytising campaign.[58]

Religion, however, was not the primary cause of the so-called tithe war which followed. Tithes were, as has been pointed out, essentially an economic grievance, accidentally allied with the religious question, and now exploited by politicians. "Later agrarian crime had," as Lecky said,[59] "an organization and a purpose which made it peculiarly easy to give it a political hue." The act of 1832 lifted the direct burden of tithes from year-to-year tenants and tenants at will, but its provisions for commutation of tithes unpaid in preceding years remained a source of irritation.[60] The act of 1834 reduced all tithes by forty per cent, but by making landlords responsible for the collection of the remainder it had a most unfortunate effect in widening the breach between landlord and tenant.[61] Tithe agitation now became openly part of a general campaign against agrarian burdens. How little its real purposes had to do with politics and religion is shown by the action of so-called tithe insurrectionaries in Clare, who turned up 600 acres of land belonging to Daniel

[58] See for example, the *Londonderry Journal*, April 21, 1829.

[59] *History of Ireland in the Eighteenth Century*, V, 483.

[60] Most of the clergy accepted government commutation for these tithes, but the few who did not were of the worst sort. One vicar in Donegal went from cottage to cottage collecting the spare clothing, bedding, working tools etc., of the peasants. *Londonderry Journal*, Dec. 10, 1833.

[61] *Ibid.*, Aug. 12, 1834.

O'Connell, to make it unfit for grazing.[62] Their aims are well illustrated by their demands on a gentleman of Meath whom they required "to agree to an increase of wages, . . . to dismiss his servants, and to dispense with the use of a plough in farming, in order to increase employment for labourers."[63]

These agrarian insurrections, though no more violent than those of the preceding decade, produced a far greater hysteria, partly because they were better known, partly from their more drastic aims. The fearful unanimity of the people, and the revolutionary character of their demands, which amounted to a claim to dictate the use of the soil, roused the gentry to a new pitch of alarm, and brought about the ill-advised coercion of 1833.[64] It is not surprising in such troubled times to find Protestants asserting that insurrection was the primary cause of emigration; but such statements will not stand investigation. Cornewall Lewis, before writing his book on *Local disturbances in Ireland,* obtained full reports from the northwestern area where emigration was heaviest. They ascribed it first to the desire for more land for large families, and second to a wish to escape grand jury cess and tithes. Lewis's conclusion is: "The motive to emigrate with the Protestants is self interest, and a desire to better their condition, and not religious persecution."[65] This is not really inconsistent with the report of the *Londonderry Journal,* which surveyed emigration in 1832:

Most of those who have sailed from this port this season, are, as usual, small farmers who have been in decent circumstances and

[62] *Belfast News Letter,* March 1, 1831.

[63] *Ibid.*

[64] The *Belfast News Letter* gives full vent to the prevailing hysteria. The *Londonderry Journal* (since 1830 a Whig paper), and Dublin and Cork papers make much less of the disturbances.

[65] *On local disturbances in Ireland,* pp. 457-458.

of the Protestant persuasion. Rackrents under Landlords who, could we believe them, are overflowing with zeal for Protestant interests, combined with tithes, are doubtless the chief cause of the melancholy determination which those persons have adopted; but we can well suppose that there are not a few of them who are anxious to find a refuge in the forests of the new world from the feuds and bickerings which prevail to such a deplorable extent in their own country.[66]

Agrarian troubles were worst, however, in the southwest, and it is there that we find them most often cited as the cause of Protestant emigration.[67] The emigration of the insurrectionaries themselves followed the usual course. In 1831, when troubles were at their height, it was reported that "families including 72 persons, who had resolved to emigrate from Clare this Spring have forfeited their passage money to America with the prospect of ameliorating their condition where they are, by awaiting the result of the insurrection which now rages in that county, and the successful issue of which they anticipate will secure them a sufficiency of land to cultivate at home."[68] But with the advent of coercion in 1833, agitators again turned to emigration as an escape from prosecution.[69]

The combination of social and economic evils, with special causes in certain years, produced a total emigration from Ireland in the thirties of about 650,000, of whom roughly two-thirds went to America, and one-third to Great Britain.[70] The influences which sent the great ma-

[66] April 17, 1832.

[67] Notably in the disturbed area of Kings, Queens, Limerick, and Tipperary; and also in Sligo and Wicklow. *Parl. Pap.* 1836, No. 38.

[68] *Belfast News Letter*, April 28, 1831.

[69] Evidence from Clare, Queens, Kilkenny, and Meath; *Parl. Pap.* 1836, No. 38. Supplement.

[70] W. N. Hancock (*On the supposed progressive decline of Irish prosperity*, p. 8) gives 230,000 to Great Britain, and 400,000 to America between

jority across the Atlantic rather than across the Irish Sea were in part economic, in part historical and sentimental. Labor conditions in Great Britain in the late twenties were little better than in Ireland, and in spite of some improvement in 1833 and 1834, wages remained depressed throughout the thirties.[71] This, together with the removal after 1826 of many thousands of Irish paupers annually from British parishes, considerably decreased the numbers going to Great Britain.[72] In spite of these deterrents the movement gained new vigor after 1830, when numerous petitions of complaint against Irish paupers came before Parliament. After 1835 immigration again died down, and most of the 230,000 emigrants to Great Britain must have come in the first five years of the decade, or at the rate of about forty thousand a year.[73] One reason for this unusual influx was the extension of steam navigation, which made it easier for migratory laborers to cross to Glasgow or Liverpool, than to go from the south to the north of Ireland.[74] In time many of them settled in Great Britain, where they continued to do the roughest unskilled labor, especially in the building trade. The only important exceptions were the spinners and weavers of Ulster and Munster, whose wages in Great Britain remained fairly constant throughout the early thirties.[75]

1831 and 1841 but his American figure is too low. I estimate 430,000 for the period.

[71] Tables in Cole, *Working class movement*, I, 182; and see speech of Gladstone, 3 *Hansard*, XXVI, 1236-37.

[72] *Parl. Pap.* 1826-27, No. 550, pp. 69, 283. The poor wardens removed 3660 destitute Irish from Manchester in 1826.

[73] Redford, *Labour migration in England, 1800-1850*, pp. 130-131.

[74] Haliday, *Observations on the habits of the labouring classes*, p. 36. Hancock, *On the condition of the Irish labourer*, pp. 7-8.

[75] Porter, *Progress of the nation*, I, 268 (on wages). On the whole subject see *Parl. Pap.* 1836, No. 40: Poor Inquiry, Appendix G: Report on the State of the Irish Poor in Great Britain, by G. Cornewall Lewis.

It is clear from the character of immigration into Great Britain, as well as from Irish reports, that the better class Irish were turning to America. Even among the weavers, all who could went to America,[76] and we have evidence to the same effect concerning the inclinations of other emigrants.[77] Those who removed to Great Britain were either just able to pay the passage across the Irish Sea, or were sent by public subscription.[78] This movement, therefore, can scarcely have decreased emigration to America, and may ultimately have added to it. Many remained in Lancashire or Scotland only long enough to accumulate the necessary funds for the transatlantic voyage.[79] Conditions in America were far more attractive than in Great Britain, and a Manchester Irishman exclaimed with delight at the prospect of making fifty cents to a dollar a day in New York.[80] To the bulk of the emigrants of this period good wages and steady employment were the chief incentives. Cheap land ceased to be an inducement and almost disappeared from the shipping advertisements, but the great land boom of 1829-1837, by drawing off the discontented poor from the Atlantic coast, left a vacancy to be filled by the emigrants.[81] Most of them were un-

[76] *Parl. Pap.* 1826-27, No. 550, p. 450 (as to Limerick); *Parl. Pap.* 1836, No. 38, Supplement; Ballymooden Parish, Cork. Yet it was the Munster weavers who in the twenties went largely to England; the Scots-Irish had always preferred America.

[77] From all the Ulster counties, and from various districts of Munster and Leinster. *Parl. Pap.* 1836, No. 38 and Supplement.

[78] A frequent practice in the south. The gentry and shopkeepers of Bandon raised £2000 to send weavers to England. *Parl. Pap.* 1836, No. 35, Part I, p. 85. Dublin silk workers were sent in the same way; See Redford, *Labour migration in England*, p. 132.

[79] Of the passages from Liverpool prepaid in America, one-eighth were for Irish resident in England—Evidence of W. S. Fitzhugh, *Parl. Pap.* 1836, No. 40, p. 33.

[80] *Parl. Pap.* 1826-27, No. 550, p. 72. Evidence of Thomas Moody.

[81] Adams, *New England in the Republic*, p. 328.

skilled laborers, and these years when all the states had run wild in canal building, when construction was begun on three great railways, and when road building was continuing apace, offered golden opportunities. Laborers' wages were said to be four times as high as in Ireland, and there was work in plenty.[82] Artisans found fewer opportunities, but the current wages of $4.50 a week for handloom weavers, and of $6 to $9 for cotton spinners and other craftsmen represented wealth to them.[83] Manufacturing distress in 1829 caused some hardship, but two years later conditions had improved sufficiently to create glowing comment in the Irish newspapers.[84] American attractions were kept constantly before the public by means of newspaper articles, as well as by information in the shipping advertisements, especially of ships for Baltimore, the key point for the three biggest construction works in the United States—the Pennsylvania Canal system, with 5,000 jobs in 1828, the Chesapeake and Ohio Canal, with 1,800 jobs, and the Baltimore and Ohio Railroad.[85]

British America was still too sparsely settled to take care of any large number of emigrants, and employment depended primarily upon governmental activities. In New Brunswick, Irishmen worked on the new roads, along which many of them settled.[86] In lower Canada, the long standing dispute between the Governor and Assembly over the control of the purse blocked any heavy appropriations for public works, but the executive contrived to use a portion of the emigrants for road building into the

[82] *Parl. Pap.* 1836, No. 35, Part I, p. 18.

[83] *Belfast News Letter*, July 17, 1827.

[84] E.g., *ibid.*, Oct. 21, 1831; the best weavers were earning thirteen or fourteen shillings a day.

[85] Harlow, *Old towpaths*, p. 73.

[86] Rogers, *Canada: Geographical*, p. 83.

eastern townships, where some Irish settled.[87] Upper
Canada only was in a position to employ large numbers,
and the Rideau and Welland canals absorbed the majority
of the emigrant laborers until 1831, when most of the
work was completed.[88] The Canada company, which took
over the sale of land in an extensive area of western Ontario in 1827, also furnished work for a considerable number, while local works at York, Montreal and Quebec took
care of others.[89] In later years, roads became the main
source of employment here also, though the governor dis-
liked using emigrant labor, which was expensive and inefficient.[90] As long as emigration was restricted, wages for
unskilled labor in Canada were high—four shillings a day
or more in Quebec[91]—but with the coming of large numbers they sank to an average of between 2/6 and 3/6, and
only two shillings on government contracts, which was
somewhat less than the average in the United States.[92]
Artisans earned about the same as in the cities farther
south, but the demand was limited. Canadian attractions
were kept before the public by means of government reports copied in the newspapers, especially after the appointment in 1828 of Mr. Buchanan as emigration agent
at Quebec, and to some extent by shipping advertisements; but for every notice of British America in the
Irish press, there were at least three of the United States.

[87] *Ibid.*, p. 139.

[88] *Ibid.*, p. 167; but there was still work for emigrants on the Welland
Canal in 1834. *Parl. Pap.* 1835, No. 87, p. 17.

[89] A. C. Buchanan, *Emigration practically considered*, p. 52.

[90] Colborne to Goderich, Jan. 10, 1833; in *Parl. Pap.* 1833, No. 141, p.
24. Colborne said the roads cost three times what they should. He wanted to
use the emigrants for agriculture or clearing land.

[91] *Parl. Pap.* 1826, No. 404, p. 174. Evidence of A. C. Buchanan.

[92] Buchanan, *Emigration practically considered*, p. 90 (Copied in several
Irish newspapers); and various reports of the emigration agents, in *Parl.
Pap.* 1831-32, No. 724, p. 12; 1833, No. 141, p. 12; 1835, No. 87, p. 17; and
1836, No. 76, p. 13.

Private letters continued to be of immense importance as sources of information. By the death of Thomas Addis Emmet in 1827, the Irish lost their most respected informant on American conditions, but the loss was more than offset by the increase in the amount of correspondence, which now reached all parts of Ireland. Allowing for inevitable fluctuations and exceptions, the tone of the letters remained remarkably cheerful.[93] Most of the emigrants did well, and many saved money. "As for boarding," wrote one, "I need not insert, for every day here is as Christmas day at home."[94] Many of the Scots-Irish and some others thought of America as their country even before they emigrated.[95] There were, of course, thorns among the roses, and an emigrant of the 1831 rush wrote from Oswego, New York:—"Let no person at home imagine that a person cannot send a bad account home from this place. That is not the case, for they think too many of us are coming here."[96] This is only one of many indications of an American reaction against the new flood of laborers, with their somewhat barbaric customs of drinking and fighting; and the Irish immigration of these years was one of the causes for the formation of the Native American party in 1835.[97]

The importance of American remittances as a factor in this emigration was very considerable. Two of the leading

[93] There are over sixty pages of interesting letters from emigrants in the *Emigrants Guide* (Westport, 1832), pp. 78 ff.

[94] *Ibid.*, p. 133.

[95] *O'Donovan Survey*, Box 34, Clondermot (Londonderry) Parish, "In fact the people especially the Scotch settlers, are beginning to consider America as much 'their own country' as this."

[96] *Emigrants Guide* (Westport, 1832), p. 134.

[97] In 1827 ship captains had difficulty in landing paupers, because of the objections of the American authorities, who had not as yet sufficient legal means to keep them out. Buchanan, *Emigration practically considered*, p. 40. For a typical opinion on the new immigration see H. Duhring, *Immigration*, in the North American Review (1835), Vol. 40, pp. 457-476.

shipping agents at Belfast reported in 1834 that a third of their passages to the United States was paid in America, and added:

> The passages of persons going to British America are also frequently paid there, but not to such an extent as those going to the United States. This tends to show the prosperity of the emigrants in the countries to which they have gone; and there is another great proof of the same in the amount sent to this country by emigrants independently of the money paid for the passages of their friends. Mr. Bell has received remittances to the extent of several thousand pounds from persons in America in favour of their friends at home, generally in small sums of from one pound to ten pounds.[98]

Other agents also were said to have received considerable sums, including over £500 from Baltimore in a single year,[99] and Londonderry agents reported that British American emigrants, though less successful than those to the United States paid half the passages and provided many of the sea stores for their friends in 1834.[100] The largest amounts were naturally sent to Liverpool, where Fitzhugh and Grimshaw, the foremost agents in the emigrant trade, received sums from America for passages ranging from over $12,000 in 1830 to over $19,000 in 1833, seven-eighths of which were for Irish emigrants, and in addition £2500 a year in cash in amounts from £1 to £10. These receipts, if applied wholly to emigration, would have defrayed the expenses of about one-sixth of the Irish sailing from Liverpool.[101]

The obvious importance of such remittances is further confirmed by reports from the parishes, and by shipping accounts. In many villages of Ulster numbers of the poor were only able to emigrate through the aid of friends in

[98] *Parl. Pap.* 1836, No. 35, Part I, p. 18.
[99] *Ibid.*   [100] *Ibid.*, p. 77.
[101] *Parl. Pap.* 1836, No. 40, pp. 32-33.

America,[102] and others were encouraged by this tangible evidence of the success of their former neighbors. At Londonderry, where the practice was oldest and most deeply rooted, ships were chartered for the sole purpose of taking out those whose passages had been prepaid,[103] and tickets for the ships of George Buchanan and Co. were sold in Quebec, Montreal, New York, Philadelphia, and Louisville.[104] This system was largely confined to the districts of extensive emigration. The evidence before the Poor Inquiry Commissioners is far from complete, but it is at least suggestive that of the fifty-seven parishes reported as receiving aid for emigration from America, all but ten were in Ulster and the adjacent counties of Sligo and Longford, and in Cork.[105] Remittances were not always a sign of emigrant prosperity, however, and a good deal of the money sent over was from employers desiring cheap labor.[106] Other employers expected the emigrant to pay his own passage, but allowed him to give security for future payment and procured him a job on landing— the industrial equivalent of the indenture system.[107] The practice seems to have begun in 1827, when Keenan and Cassidy of Pittsburgh took a shipload of laborers for that district and repeated the enterprise the following year.[108]

[102] *Parl. Pap.* 1836, No. 38. Supplement: Glendemot (Derry), etc. *O'Donovan Survey,* Box 16, Skerry (Antrim).

[103] *Londonderry Journal,* Jan. 29, 1833, the *Royal William* for New York, June 17, 1834, the *Ceylon* for Philadelphia.

[104] *Ibid.,* May 1, 1832.

[105] Compiled from *Parl. Pap.* 1836, No. 38. Supplement; and No. 35. Part I. The parish witnesses certainly failed to notice help from America in many parishes of Ulster, and probably elsewhere, but the failure of shipping agents at southern ports to mention the practice speaks strongly against its prevalence there.

[106] *Parl. Pap.* 1836, No. 35. Part I, p. 77, Report of Londonderry agents.

[107] The job procured was of course under their own control, and they maintained their hold over the laborer through his debt to them.

[108] *Belfast News Letter,* June 1, 1827; May 20, 1828.

The largest importers of labor were W. and T. Adair of Baltimore, who sent several shiploads in 1827 and following years from Belfast and Londonderry.[109] Some of these may have been for the Chesapeake and Ohio Canal Co., which imported one shipload of laborers from Liverpool in 1829, and sent for more when many of the first lot deserted.[110]

While American aids and inducements to emigration were increasing steadily throughout the period, the movement itself was subject to distinct fluctuations. These resulted very largely from the necessity on the part of poor emigrants of finding employment as soon as they landed. An unusually heavy season meant hard times for late comers, and bad accounts sent home to Ireland.[111] Such a season was 1827, and in the following year emigration dropped to 17,000. This setback was only temporary, and the next four years showed a continuous increase, far surpassing all previous records. Famine and cholera were the mainsprings. The introduction of inferior qualities of potatoes, together with a succession of wet seasons, and the appearance of a definite blight, had rendered the staple food of the peasantry utterly unreliable, and in thirteen of the seventeen years after 1828 there were partial failures of the potato crop.[112] In some years, including 1830 and 1831, the failure was so bad as to cause famine, which was particularly severe in Connaught. The normal price of potatoes in the country had been 1½d to 2½d a stone according to the season, and a penny higher in Bel-

[109] *Belfast News Letter*, June 1827, June 1828, Oct. 5, 1830, etc. *Londonderry Journal*, June 22, 1830, the *Dumfries*.

[110] J. R. Commons, et al., *History of labor in the United States*, I, 413.

[111] The effect was greatest in Connaught, where the emigrants had few friends in America and must be entirely on their own. Fear of unemployment was given as the sole check on emigration in parts of Mayo and Sligo, *Parl. Pap.* 1836, No. 38, p. 13.

[112] O'Brien, pp. 228-231, quoting Census of 1851.

fast and Dublin, but by June of 1830 the relief committee
was selling them at 5½d in the west, while they brought
7d in Sligo and 10d in Dublin.[113] In the autumn, rain and
wind spoiled not only potatoes but hay and oats throughout the northwestern counties, and by February there was
a general demand for relief, although prices were not so
high as in 1830.[114] The suffering extended to a class somewhat superior to the poorest, and better capable of emigrating, and the appearance of relief ships bearing corn
from the United States added to the amount of shipping
available for passage.[115]

The rush of 1831 was absorbed with some difficulty in
America, and many discouraging reports were sent back
to Ireland. At the instigation of the British Government,
the British American ports levied a tax, similar to the one
in New York, upon all emigrants for the support of hospitals.[116] Though this was known in Ireland before the
season opened,[117] it proved no deterrent to emigration, for
cholera had broken out in the island. Coming from Central Europe by way of Sunderland and Liverpool, it
reached Belfast early in 1832, and by April extended
throughout the east and south with Dublin and Cork as
the worst centers. In May, Drogheda was worst, in June,
Limerick. The disease travelled slowly and did not reach
Londonderry until September. It came over Ireland as a
terrible and incomprehensible curse. The doctors seemed

[113] *Belfast News Letter*, June 22, 29, 1830.

[114] *Statement of proceedings of the western committee for relief of the
Irish poor*, p. 4, etc. *Belfast News Letter*, especially Feb.-June 1831.

[115] *Belfast News Letter*, April 29, 1831.

[116] See *Parl. Pap. 1831-32, No. 730:* ''Copy of Acts passed . . . in British
North America . . . by which a Tax is to be levied on Emigrants.'' The tax
was a dollar a head, or double for those not properly cleared. The Quebec
Assembly restricted their act to two years, and did not renew it; New Brunswick made theirs effective only after it had received the royal signature.

[117] News reached Belfast on April 6, 1832, just as the season was beginning. *Belfast News Letter*.

powerless to check it, and the peasantry resorted to superstitious rites in a vain effort to avert it.[118] The suddenness of attack and the horrible aspect of the victims spread complete terror throughout the country and all who could fled before its ravages. To prevent the worst horrors at sea, the government required emigrant ships to carry surgeons,[119] but the measure had no effect in checking the flood of emigration, and could not prevent some dreadful voyages. The cholera was worst amongst the poorest classes, and provided a more powerful stimulus to emigration than any which had hitherto touched them.

The disease passed from Ireland almost as rapidly as it had come and had practically disappeared by the end of 1832, but the emigrants carried it, as they had carried preceding epidemics, to America. In June, 1832, it broke out in Quebec, where it swept away one-tenth of the population,[120] and it reached the northern ports of the United States about the same time, finding its way south in the autumn and winter, and working its greatest havoc there. The effect upon the emigrants of that year was disastrous. No one would employ them, and many refused even to take their money for fear of contagion. The accounts sent home cut in half the number of emigrants in the following year. That cholera was the only cause of this falling off is shown by the emigration from Londonderry. The Londonderry ships had had clean bills of health in

118 *Londonderry Journal*, especially April 24, May 15, June 19, Oct. 9, 1832. The peasants ran from cottage to cottage with wisps of straw, making an imaginary barrier to keep out the scourge. Doctors were all at variance, the most favored remedy suggested being bleeding and 40 to 60 drops of laudanum. The priests fought to prevent wakes and other sources of contagion, but the people were too ignorant to heed them.

119 By Order in Council, March 17, 1832. *Belfast News Letter*, April 17, 1832.

120 N. Gould, *Sketch of the trade of British America*, p. 5.

the preceding season,[121] and the numbers sailing from the northern port showed no decrease. Even after the first effects had passed away, the memory of this year when thousands of Irish in America, both old settlers and new immigrants, were carried off, remained as a deterrent to many Irish villages. An investigator at Magherafelt, Londonderry, in 1836 reported:—"Emigration varies very much, but certainly is decreasing from many causes—the principal and last of these was the cholera at New Orleans three years ago when so many Irish were swept off—this has since materially damped the taste for emigration, and this in spite of the fact that many who have gone from the neighborhood of Magherafelt have realized large fortunes in New Orleans.'"[122]

On the other hand, cholera strengthened the feeling that Ireland was a doomed country; and the movement of the poor, once started, could not be stopped.[123] In 1834, when accounts from America were good, ships numerous, and cholera had reappeared in the northwest of Ireland,[124] it reached nearly fifty thousand. But once more the rush year was unfortunate. The Quebec Assembly, still at war with the governor, refused to make appropriations for

[121] *Londonderry Journal,* July 10, 1832; June 18, and Sept. 3, 1833, giving an analysis of the emigration of that season. Every vessel to St. John and Quebec was filled to capacity—or more. The official return of emigration from Londonderry for 1833 is more than 1000 below the actual number. See also *Parl. Pap.* 1836, No. 35, Part I, p. 78.

[122] *O'Donovan Survey,* Box 45. Also Box 2, Antrim Parish; Box 32, Bovevagh.

[123] (On aid to emigrants.) "No aid, except from their friends, who frequently distress themselves in order to send off, perhaps the best-conducted son, in the hope that his savings in a strange land may rescue other members of the family from the impending ruin which hangs over this ill-fated country." Matthew Fulham, P.P. of Templepatrick, Longford, in *Parl. Pap.* 1836, No. 38. Supplement, p. 87.

[124] *O'Donovan Survey,* Box 44, Maghera; *Londonderry Journal,* April 8, 1834.

quarantine, and there was a fresh outbreak of cholera at Quebec.[125] Storms also took a heavy toll of ships, and over five hundred Irish emigrants were lost at sea.[126] These factors, together with an improvement in the linen trade, and an increase in the cost of passage, combined to reduce the emigration of 1835 to 25,000.[127] American canal wages, which had sunk to $10 a month, with board, in 1831, went still lower, and by the winter of 1834, when many works were either completed or shut down, men were ready to work for $5 a month, and sometimes for board only.[128] But these drawbacks proved temporary, and Ireland was now ready for a steady emigration of thirty thousand or more a year.

At the beginning of this period two main areas—Ulster, and the more populous parts of Munster—had supplied most of the emigration, though there were not wanting strong expressions of desire in other regions. "Give us but the means," said Spring Rice, "and half the country will go."[129] This statement needs some qualification; for of the 5393 petitioners to the Emigration Committee of 1827 only 114 lived in Connaught,[130] and not until 1831 were emigrants from that province noted as contributing largely to the numbers going to Quebec.[131] Even after the hardships of famine and cholera had aroused the emigrating spirit, J. E. Bicheno said of Connaught:

[125] Roebuck in the House of Commons, Mar. 8, 1835, 3 *Hansard*, XXVI, 680.

[126] *Parl. Pap.* 1836, No. 87, p. 12. The losses were one vessel with 29 passengers from Dublin, one with 250 from Limerick, and one with 271 unknown. This was, I think, the *Lady of the Lake* from Belfast.

[127] *O'Donovan Survey*, Box 44, Maghera Parish; *Parl. Pap.* 1836, No. 38, pp. 134, 138.

[128] Commons, *History of labor in the United States*, I, 415.

[129] *Parl. Pap.* 1826-27, No. 550, p. 450.

[130] *Ibid.*, pp. 484-499.

[131] *Parl. Pap.* 1831-32, No. 724, p. 20.

At the same time, we incline to the opinion that the affection of the inhabitants to their land, and the better understanding that exists between themselves and their superiors, are likely to be impediments in the way of emigration from this province, which will not occur in the same degree in other places.[132]

The rest of Ireland seemed determined to carry out Spring Rice's prophecy. From Tyrone, four men in every hundred emigrated in the course of three years, and the exodus from the rest of the "Ulster plateau" was little less startling. Altogether Ulster accounted for forty-six per cent of Irish emigration in three years, maintaining its numbers more steadily than the other provinces, which were more responsive to American conditions or extraordinary causes at home.[133] The fertile and populous areas of Munster and northern Leinster supplied most of the remaining emigrants, giving to Munster twenty-seven per cent and to Leinster sixteen per cent of the total.[134]

[132] *Parl. Pap.* 1836, No. 42, p. 40.

[133] From port returns; also *Londonderry Journal*, Apr. 8, 1834.

[134] Our best authority for the geographical distribution of emigration in Ireland is to be found in answers to Question No. 45 put by the Poor Inquiry Commissioners: "What number of emigrants, and of what description, have left your parish during each of the last three years?" The replies are in many cases rough estimates or wild guesses, in others such words as "few," "considerable," "a great many," which are meaningless without reference to the prevalence of emigration in other districts known to the witness; but amongst the evidence are many statements of exact numbers, often furnished by the parish priest, or in Ulster by the Presbyterian minister; and where, as in Londonderry, these can be checked against the findings of the Ordnance Survey investigators, they prove to be substantially correct. The Ordnance Survey agents travelled through Londonderry in 1834 and 1835 and made exhaustive reports on the economic and social conditions of each parish, including detailed statements of the emigration of 1833, 1834, and 1835. These constitute the most reliable authority on the origins of emigration which can be obtained.

The evidence before the commissioners, fragmentary, and not covering in all cases the same three years, is valueless as authority for the amount of emigration in any one year, but the number of accurate returns from each county justifies a statement as to the relative prevalence of emigration

The reports in the Poor Inquiry show quite clearly the existence of well defined emigration districts in the south as well as in Ulster (see map opposite p. 158) and there are few evidences of heavy emigration from isolated parishes. Except for the fact that these districts are almost wholly lowland regions,[135] and the common tie of a declining cottage linen industry in the two largest, there are no features which seem to explain their location. An examination of conditions in centers of great and small emigration shows that the state of agriculture, the prosperity or decline of the markets, and other local variations, have no apparent bearing on the movement.[136] The causes of emigration were universal, though doubtless aided by local

among them, and even from districts within the counties. The years covered are 1831-35, and in most cases 1831-33. As the variation in years affects equally the returns from all counties, it does not destroy the validity of this comparison. In all the counties except Down, Antrim, Londonderry, Donegal, and Fermanagh, I have followed the testimony of the priests as being more reliable than others. Their returns run about ten per cent higher than those of the other witnesses.

The percentage of emigrants to total population in these parishes is 1.5 for the whole, whereas in the leading emigrant counties it is as follows: Tyrone, 4.5; Cavan, 2.7; Londonderry, 2.6; Donegal, 2.5; Longford, 2.5; Limerick, 2.3; Monaghan, 2.1; Down, 2.1; Westmeath, 2.0; Armagh, 1.6; Antrim, 1.6. All these figures, computed from *Parl. Pap.* 1836, No. 38, Supplement, are too low for the years 1831-33, but would be approximately correct for 1833-35. They are given here for comparative purposes only.

The only important emigrant counties that fall below the average are Fermanagh, Sligo, and the southern group comprising Cork, Kerry, Tipperary, and Kilkenny, all of which have averages exceeding one per cent.

On account of the unknown origin of the large numbers sailing from Liverpool, the official return of numbers sailing from the different ports gives no check upon the above estimate, but it does indicate that emigration from Ulster varied between thirty-five and fifty per cent of the total.

135 Particularly noticeable in Cavan, Longford, Cork and Kerry, all of which had areas of extensive emigration, bounded by mountains.

136 Local conditions are described in Lewis, *Topographical dictionary of Ireland* (1837). This must be used with great care, as over half the descriptions are taken without revision from the various county agricultural surveys, published between 1800 and 1815.

difficulties such as agrarian friction in parts of the south. The true explanation of the existence of the smaller areas must lie in the continuity of the emigrant movement, and the contagion which makes the success of emigrants from one parish the source of an extended movement from all the neighboring region.

The Poor Inquiry report sheds little light on the religious affiliation of the emigrants, and it is impossible to speak with certainty on this point. The opinion of Henry Inglis after his tour of Ireland in 1834 was that most of the emigrants were Roman Catholics.[137] The geographical distribution would seem to bear this out, although there were still a number of Protestants among the southern emigrants. One return of passengers from Limerick gives 145 Protestants to 573 Catholics, or about a fifth of the total.[138] Since the great majority of the emigrants were by all accounts from the lowest classes, it is unlikely that the proportion of Protestants from the south would be much higher than this; although the fact that the movement to England was almost wholly Catholic[139] may reduce the proportion of Catholics going to America. Meanwhile, however, the Catholic share in the emigration from Ulster was also increasing, and they were supposed to have formed about one-quarter of the numbers sailing from Belfast,[140] and a third of those from Newry.[141] The Presbyterian minister of a Londonderry parish testified:

Since the persecution of Charles II, the Presbyterians, who form two-thirds of the population here, have been accustomed to go to America and are often sent for by friends. Since the diffusion of education, the Roman Catholics have caught the same en-

---

[137] *Journey throughout Ireland in 1834*, II, 310.
[138] *Londonderry Journal*, April 17, 1832.
[139] *Parl. Pap.* 1336, No. 40, p. xiv.
[140] *Belfast News Letter*, April 22, 1831.
[141] *Ibid.*, May 25, 1827.

terprise, and neither class require to be encouraged, as they are going away rapidly.[142]

The detailed reports of the Ordnance Survey make possible a reliable analysis in Londonderry, where of two thousand emigrants from thirty-one parishes, in 1834 and 1835, six-tenths were Presbyterian, three-tenths Catholic, and one-tenth members of the Established Church. As the Catholic population of the parishes was almost equal to the Presbyterian, the proportion of emigrants among the Catholics was little more than half that amongst the Presbyterians, the exact ratios being as follows:[143]

Presbyterians	1.68
Catholic	.89
Established Church	.82

The proportion of Catholics among the total emigration has been estimated as high as eighty-two per cent,[144] but all my information goes to prove that this figure is excessive, and that fifty to sixty per cent is nearer the truth.

Geographic and religious distribution take on greater significance when accompanied by an analysis of the economic status of the emigrants. We have had occasion to mention many signs of increased poverty such as the emphasis of advertisements on opportunities of employment rather than land, the reappearance of various delusive attractions for the ignorant and unwary, very cheap

[142] *Parl. Pap.* 1836, No. 38. p. 356.
[143] *O'Donovan Survey*, Boxes 29-43.
[144] Shaughnessy, *Has the immigrant kept the faith?* pp. 77, 109. This, however, is based on an assumption that the Catholics emigrated in the same ratio to population as did the Presbyterians—the Catholic population of Ireland being in 1831 82% of the total. Professor Shaughnessy has done a valuable work in exposing the impossibility of early estimates of American Catholicism, and the present study would indicate that his revisions, based partly on a study of immigration, can be carried still further.

fares, etc. The newspaper accounts corroborate this impression. "Most of the emigrants were persons in very mean circumstances," said the *Londonderry Journal* in 1834,[145] and four years earlier: "Among those who have foresaken their fatherland are a good number of a station superior to the common run of emigrants, but still we are warranted in reckoning them exceptions from the general mass."[146] The "mass" was itself divided by Buchanan into three groups:

> The description of persons that form the bulk of emigrants we may class under three denominations; first, the small farmer (I allude to Ireland) who has a large family and perhaps an unexpired lease of five or ten years of his farm to run; he disposes of his interest, by which he raises a little money, and added to his little stock of other useful articles, perhaps a web or two of coarse linen, some yarn stockings, and thread of their own make, their feather beds (as hardly a peasant farmer in Ireland but enjoys that comfort), and a supply of provisions of his own raising, off he goes to America. The second class I would call artisans of different grades, and servants. And thirdly, actually labouring paupers.[147]

Buchanan thought this last class the largest, but parish returns, which give the occupations of 36,000 emigrants, show proportions of one-half small farmers, three-eighths laborers and servants, and one-eighth artisans. Two-thirds of the farmers are from Ulster, however, so that outside that province laborers formed practically half. A comparison of these figures with the religious returns suggests that almost all the Presbyterians or Scots-Irish were farmers, and two-thirds of the Roman Catholics laborers. Laborers did not greatly predominate except in Connaught, and in Munster were actually fewer than farmers. The classification also shows about an equal pro-

---

[145] June 17, 1834.   [146] July 6, 1830.
[147] *Parl. Pap.* 1826-27, No. 550, p. 435.

portion of artisans from the three larger provinces, Connaught contributing only a handful.[148] The parish returns are not easily reconcilable with statements from the ports, which agree with Buchanan that laborers predominated in the British-American trade, assigning to farmers only one-third of the emigration from Belfast, and nowhere a majority except from Londonderry to the United States.[149] As the parish estimates of numbers are much too low, and laborers were the class most likely to be overlooked by witnesses, we may correct their returns by assuming a considerably larger number of the latter, thus bringing the figures into comparative agreement with other information.[150]

Observers noted considerable variation amongst the laborers. At their worst they were said to be "of the most useless description, mere beggars, squalid, loathsome, dejected."[151] But this was during the unrestricted rush of 1827, and even New Brunswick, which got the dregs, did not often have such hard things to say of them. Those going to Quebec were acknowledged to be of a superior sort.[152] Buchanan said there were few paupers among them.[153] The majority landed without so much as fifty cents apiece,[154] and could not have raised two pounds per family on their merchantable possessions in Ireland,[155]

---

148 Compiled from *Parl. Pap.* 1836, No. 38. Supplement. The proportion of artisans is to be expected, as they were only ten per cent of the population in Connaught, but 17 to 22 per cent elsewhere. *Parl. Pap.* 1833, No. 634: Abstract of Answers and Returns, Census of 1831.

149 *Parl. Pap.* 1836, No. 35, Part I, pp. 17, 76, 78.

150 I am not inclined to discard the parish evidence, nor to assign to laborers more than a small majority of the total emigration.

151 *Parl. Pap.* 1828, No. 112, p. 34. Report of the St. Andrews Emigrant Society.

152 *Parl. Pap.* 1836, No. 35, Part I, p. 76.

153 *Parl. Pap.* 1826-27, No. 550, p. 112.

154 *Ibid.*, p. 437 (Buchanan).

155 *Ibid.*, p. 298 (James West of Westmeath).

yet it was the general testimony from all parts of Ireland that these emigrants were the best of their class. The city artisans, in spite of higher wages, were little better off; being more intemperate than the laborers and unaccustomed to save. From some cities they were only able to emigrate to England,[156] but from Belfast in bad times they swelled the numbers going to America, being aided by emigrant associations, the larger part of whose funds were raised by charity.[157] It is an unpleasant testimony to the improvidence of the artisans that only three emigrant societies of the mutual assistance type, so common among British workmen, were reported to the Poor Inquiry commissioners.

In spite of their poverty, the laborers were less willing than the small farmers to divide the family for purposes of emigration. The majority of the new settlers in preceding years had gone individually or as parts of families. The parish reports for this period show 11,134 emigrants in families to 8939 individuals. The preponderance of laborers in the emigration from Connaught and in the trade to British America, made emigrants in families decidedly more numerous than from the other provinces,[158] or to the United States,[159] where they were only a small majority. Emigration by families also involved an increase in the number of women, fewer of whom now came independently. Before 1827 they had formed about thirty per cent of the Irish going to the United States, but during

[156] *Parl. Pap.* 1826-27, No. 550, p. 385 (Dr. William Murphy of Cork); *Parl. Pap.* 1836, No. 35, Part I (Limerick).

[157] *Parl. Pap.* 1836, No. 35, Part I, p. 17; *Belfast News Letter*, May 22, 26, 29, 1829. The collections in this year were for the ''Third Belfast Emigration Society,'' composed largely of weavers.

[158] Compiled from *Parl. Pap.* 1836, No. 38. Supplement.

[159] *O'Donovan Survey*, Londonderry County. Families made up 51 per cent of those going to the United States, and 61 per cent to Canada.

this period they averaged about thirty-five per cent, rising as high as forty-eight per cent in 1835.[160] A higher proportion went to Canada, and they were never less than two-fifths of the total Irish emigration during these years.[161] In America this change produced a serious social problem; for instead of an immigration without home ties, easily transferable from place to place, and assimilable through marriage with the native population, solid groups of Irish of the lowest class were thrown as cohesive masses into the melting pot.

Meanwhile, the emigration of small farmers went on as before, the young and healthy going first and sending for the rest of the family the following season. This was usual among the poorer sort, but it included some of greater affluence and better standards. Letters of emigrants show many of them to have been accustomed to a diet that included more than the potatoes, buttermilk and herrings supposed to be typical of this class.[162] According to the Ordnance Survey "they generally go in families and take more or less capital (the price of their farm) with them."[163] Similar notices of emigrants provided with capital from the sale of their farms come from all parts of Ulster, and from Leitrim, Mayo, Roscommon, Carlow, Kings and Meath,[164] and from 1830 on there was a considerable emigration of richer farmers. Some from Derry to the United States took £500 or more, and the capital of whole groups from that port may have averaged £50

160 From statistics in Bromwell, *Immigration to the United States*, derived from the U.S. annual reports.

161 *Census of Ireland, 1841*, Emigration Table No. 5. These figures, like those of the United States, are defective, but should be substantially correct as to the relative number of males and females.

162 *Emigrants Guide* (Westport), pp. 78 ff.

163 Box 11, Glenavy (Antrim) and similar statements in numerous other parishes.

164 *Parl. Pap.* 1836, No. 38. Supplement.

apiece.[165] One farmer from Leitrim emigrated with
£7000,[166] and others on the *James* of Limerick, which was
lost at sea, were carrying £3000 in gold.[167] The parish returns disclose evidence of wealthy emigrants from all
parts of Ireland except Leinster, where the better class
farmers were apparently finding sufficient opportunities
at home.[168] Despite some evidence to the contrary from
agents at the Irish ports, numbers of the well-to-do went
to Quebec,[169] and were said to have formed an important
contribution to the population of Canada between 1832
and 1837.[170]

With the beginning of emigration on a large scale the
ultimate destination of the emigrants becomes a matter
of major importance. The 341,000 who left Ireland for
North America during these nine years fall into three
main groups—160,000 going to Quebec, 114,000 to the
United States, and 65,000 to New Brunswick. This last
figure represents a revival, which affected to a less extent
the traffic to Newfoundland,[171] though not that to Nova
Scotia,[172] and arose primarily from a new movement of

[165] *Parl. Pap.* 1836, No. 35, Part I, p. 77; Bell and Ashe (Shipping
agents) said the average from Belfast to the U.S. was £10. *Ibid.*, p. 17.

[166] *Parl. Pap.* 1836, No. 38, p. 133.

[167] *Londonderry Journal*, July 1, 1834.

[168] *Parl. Pap.* 1836, No. 38. *Belfast News Letter*, June 22, 1830; *Londonderry Journal*, June 18, 1833.

[169] Buchanan said the average for families from Derry was £30 to £50,
some taking £500. *Parl. Pap.* 1826-27, No. 550, p. 113. In 1831 he reported
the arrival of ''very many respectable and wealthy farmers'' from all parts
of Ireland, and especially Armagh, Fermanagh, Cavan, Leitrim, Mayo,
Sligo, Tyrone, Dublin, Limerick and Wexford. *Parl. Pap.* 1831-32, No. 724,
p. 20.

[170] *Parl. Pap.* 1844, No. 181, p. 23; Remarks of A. B. Hawke, Emigration
Agent for Upper Canada.

[171] *Parl. Pap.* 1830, No. 589, p. 76—Evidence of John Musgrove of Waterford.

[172] *Parl. Pap.* 1826-27, No. 550, p. 515. There are no return cargoes from
Halifax.

cotters seeking the cheapest route, and unfamiliar with disadvantages now well known amongst the older emigrant classes. Advertisements indicate a successful traffic by way of New Brunswick from Londonderry in 1829; but an attempt to revive it in Belfast in the same year was unsuccessful, and it was not until 1831 that it again became generally popular.[173] The advertised attractions were as before cheapness and ease of communication with the United States. The shipping agents in Ireland said that all their passengers intended to go to the United States, and almost all succeeded.[174] These were the emigrants who began to do rough work round the Massachusetts mills early in the thirties,[175] and who flocked from their railway construction camps to Boston in 1834 to avenge the burning of the Ursuline Convent.[176] The revival in this trade was only temporary, dying away when the first rush of 1831 and 1832 came to an end. As direct fares to the United States became cheaper, the charge of two dollars from St. John to the American ports[177] left little advantage to the New Brunswick route, and in 1835 the numbers had fallen again to three thousand a year.[178]

Meanwhile conditions at Quebec were also undergoing a change. Fewer advertisements now stressed opportunities of reaching the United States, emphasizing instead wages and employment in Canada. Before 1827, from two-thirds to nine-tenths of the emigrants had been reckoned as going to the United States. This continued to 1830,

173 See *Parl. Pap.* 1831-32, No. 334, pp. 16-19, on the earlier slack period.

174 *Parl. Pap.* 1836, No. 35, Part I, pp. 17, 76.

175 There were 400 at Lowell in 1831—J. G. Shea, *History of the Catholic Church in The United States*, III, 464-465.

176 *Ibid.*, p. 480.

177 *Belfast News Letter*, May 29, 1829; the *Atlantic*.

178 *Parl. Pap.* 1837-38, Vol. XLVII, Part VI, Table of Revenue, Population, etc. Supplement, p. 8.

when two-fifths are said to have stopped in Canada.[179] In
1831 Mr. Buchanan reported that only 6254 out of 50,000
had left the provinces,[180] and his later reports give similar
figures. In 1832, he testified:—"I am warranted in stating
that a very decided turn has taken place in favour of this
Province, and that it is becoming more apparent every
day. Very few Irish or Scotch think of going to the States
now."[181] This evidence, however, was colored by Buchanan's position, which required him to keep as many
emigrants as possible in the colonies. His figures for those
going to each district in Canada are mere estimates in
round numbers, which are subtracted from the total in order to find the number going on to the United States. The
true opinion of the Irish concerning the United States
may be judged from their letters, concerning which
Bishop Doyle said:—"The feeling of comfort, and the
conviction that the family on removing to America would
be happy, has been more strongly expressed in those coming from the United States than in those from our colonies."[182] After the bad times of 1831, this was especially
true, and emigrants in Canada advised their friends to go
if possible to New York.[183] Later parish reports from
various parts of Ulster and from the Queens County exhibit a preference on the part of emigrants for the United
States, Canada being chosen only by those who could not
afford to reach America in any other way.[184]

179 *Parl. Pap.* 1831-32, No. 334, p. 26.
180 *Parl. Pap.* 1831-32, No. 724, p. 24.
181 *Ibid.*, p. 23.
182 *Parl. Pap.* 1830, No. 589, p. 396. Bishop Doyle had been a champion
of Catholic rights before emancipation and was equally popular with the
great mass of Protestants and Catholics. Few men in Ireland knew the
peasants better.
183 *Emigrants Guide* (Westport), especially p. 123.
184 *Parl. Pap.* 1836, No. 38, pp. 136, 140, and Supplement, pp. 269, 356,
etc.

These reports shed no light upon the ultimate destination of the emigrants, the majority giving simply "America," and others referring to the country to which the emigrants sailed. United States returns and Buchanan's reports, even if they were accurate, would not be conclusive as to final residence, since no check was kept upon emigrants after the year of their arrival. The most important evidence as to the settlement of the Irish is to be found in the census of Upper Canada taken in 1842, and that of Lower Canada in 1844, when the Irish-born numbered 122,000. In the eleven years preceding 1842, 253,000 Irish immigrants had entered Canada. Assuming that the great majority of those arriving before 1830 did not remain in Canada, there should still have been enough to balance the deaths during the eleven years,[185] and therefore we may assume that less than half the later immigrants stayed in the provinces. As there is no evidence that the proportion remaining changed after 1835, it should be correct also for the period 1830-35.

It is impossible to say definitely how much of Canada's gain during this period, 1827-1835, was of the better class. Impediments to the acquisition of land were supposed to have kept out wealthy emigrants in earlier years, and these had been only partially remedied after the transfer in 1827 to the Canada Company of large tracts in Upper Canada; its activities were said to have stimulated enterprise in the sale of land in Lower Canada, where the British American Land Co. attempted to colonize the Eastern Townships.[186] Nevertheless, the price was still too high in 1835, when emigrants were attracted from Canada to

[185] The Irish-born in Upper Canada and around Quebec were estimated in 1832 at 43,000. *Parl. Pap.* 1833, No. 141, pp. 19-20.

[186] *Quebec Mercury*, Oct. 26, 1824—an article on the prospectus of the Canada Company; and see Emigration Circulars, Nos. 2, 4, 5 and 6 on the granting of lands in Canada, C.O. 384/87.

Michigan, Illinois and Missouri.[187] Factors other than
land, however, prevented the great majority of the well-to-
do from coming to Canada; for the old superiority of
travel to the United States, attributed to the stricter
provisions of the American passenger acts, became more
marked with the increase of numbers to Canada, and the
attendant over-crowding of vessels and unhealthy conditions.[188] This, and the fact that almost all the farmers had
friends in the United States, were given as reasons for a
growing preference of emigrants from Londonderry for
the latter country.[189] This reason would have had less
weight in other parts of Ireland, but the first was equally
influential everywhere, and some settlers went to Upper
Canada by way of New York. Six thousand were said to
have followed this route in 1833[190] when cholera caused
even laborers to warn their friends against the Quebec
route.[191] The wrecks of 1834 had a similar effect,[192] but it
never became an important alternative because of expense. Occasional ship advertisements did indeed attempt
to prove that it was cheaper, but government reports belied this,[193] and the numbers coming in by way of New

[187] *Parl. Pap.* 1836, No. 76, p. 5.

[188] *Parl. Pap.* 1826-27, No. 550, p. 111; evidence of A. C. Buchanan;
Parl. Pap. 1828, No. 112, p. 10; Report of the Executive Council, Nova
Scotia.

[189] *Parl. Pap.* 1836, No. 35, Part I, p. 77.

[190] *Parl. Pap.* 1834, No. 616, p. 28; Report of emigration agent for Upper
Canada.

[191] *Londonderry Journal*, Sept. 3, 1833.

[192] *Parl. Pap.* 1835, No. 87, p. 6.

[193] Fares for a family from New York to Upper Canada varied from
£3.4.9 to £4.14.3; M. Doyle, *Hints on emigration to Upper Canada* (1831), p.
82; *Parl. Pap.* 1826-27, No. 550, p. 439. The maximum to Quebec was £3.15
to York and £2 to Prescott, in 1827; Buchanan, *Emigration practically considered*, p. 91. This was later much reduced by competition and by activities
of government emigration agents; *Parl. Pap.* 1831-32, No. 724, p. 11; *Parl.
Pap.* 1833, No. 141, p. 18; *Parl. Pap.* 1835, No. 87, p. 20. By 1835 the fare
from Montreal to Kingston had been reduced to 7/6.

York never came near to compensating for those who went from Canada to the United States.

Religion, apparently, exerted no influence on the choice of an immediate destination. Of the emigrants from Londonderry county in 1834 and 1835, both Presbyterians and Catholics sent a small majority to Canada, and only among adherents of the Church of Ireland was there a decided preference—seventy-two per cent going to Canada.[194] Religion did, however, help to determine the residence of those who remained in the provinces. The 44,000 Irish-born in Lower Canada in 1844 were almost all Roman Catholics,[195] and were largely concentrated in the cities of Quebec and Montreal, with a few along the upper St. Lawrence and New York border.[196] Of the 78,000 in Upper Canada, we cannot speak with such certainty, but probably three-fifths of them were Protestants.[197] Though the Catholics in the United States were antagonized by a series of attacks upon their church between 1831 and 1834, the wave of ill feeling had no effect upon the coming of the emigrants, and in many of the attacks the Irish were not directly concerned.[198] Irish Catholic newspapers, of which the Boston *Pilot* was the most famous, appeared in several cities by 1835, becoming the principal champions of

[194] Compiled from the *O'Donovan Survey*.

[195] The census shows 53,000 Roman Catholics other than French Canadians. These would be found almost wholly among the 13,000 Scottish and 44,000 Irish.

[196] Rogers, *Canada, Geographical*, pp. 141, 147.

[197] There were 65,000 Catholics in Upper Canada, of whom 14,000 were French. Most of the remainder would be Irish or Highlanders, and as the Irish were twice as numerous as the Scots, I give them two-thirds of the Catholics, or 33,000.

[198] Shaughnessy, *Has the immigrant kept the faith?* pp. 116, 125. He thinks the anti-Catholic agitation a reaction from Catholic Emancipation. I think it a result of the influx of a large number of Catholics, especially into New England, where they had been practically unknown.

the Church against the denunciations hurled by Lyman
Beecher in 1831.[199]

The Irish suffered more for their love of politics, being
blamed by some Americans for "divisions amongst themselves, chiefly caused by the ignorant and immoral, especially the Irish."[200] But their chief vice was drunkenness:

It is a habit so peculiar to the lower classes of the Irish settled in
the United States, that if a man be seen drunk in that country, it
is immediately inferred he must be an Irishman. The general
opinion of the Americans concerning the Irish character has been
frequently injurious to emigrants, particularly from Ireland, for
in no one instance does it happen that our countrypeople do not
experience diffidence exercised toward them on their arrival in
the United States.[201]

An Irish immigrant reported the same difficulty in Upper
Canada: "Rum is for two shillings per gallon; but my
dear friends, you all know what disgrace it brings on a
man to be counted a sheepstealer, but to be seen drinking
in this country is as disgraceful."[202] Other causes of antagonism were much the same there as in the United
States. The Church party, strongly entrenched in the Legislative Council of Upper Canada under the leadership of
Bishop Strachan, opposed immigration on religious and
social grounds,[203] while their opponents, the radicals, opposed it as the source of cheap labor supply to the
wealthy.[204] The immigrants' only friends, beside such of
their own countrymen as had preceded them, were the
employers, and even they did not always encourage their

199 Adams, *New England in the Republic*, p. 334.

200 Heywood, *A journey to America in 1834*, p. 80.

201 O'Kelly, *Advice and guide to emigrants going to the United States
of America*, p. 20.

202 *Emigrants guide* (Westport), p. 88.

203 See his evidence before the Emigration Committee in *Parl. Pap.* 1826-
27, No. 550, p. 338.

204 A. Dunham, *Political unrest in Upper Canada*, 1815-36, p. 143.

coming. Concerning a group of laborers sent by Lord Portarlington from the Queens county in 1831, Lord Aylmer wrote:

The settlers who were the bearers of your letter arrived some days since at this place, and it so happened that an officer belonging to my permanent staff who is a landed proprietor in Lower Canada was at that moment at Montreal—to him they were referred, but the temper and disposition they evinced were so little satisfactory to him that he would not undertake to receive them on his property.[205]

In the days of the great rush, even the shippers sometimes had too many emigrants. One agent at Belfast found 150 more passengers on his ship than had been paid for, or were legally permitted, and he had to call in the aid of the city authorities to get them off.[206]

The net effect of these antipathies upon the tide of emigration was negligible. Such changes as took place arose from alterations in the normal course of trade. The sudden increases in the number of emigrants had been very largely taken care of by expansion of the trade to British America, and especially to Quebec, in vessels chartered for the purpose. After 1833, when emigration on the larger scale became more regular, the proportion going from Irish ports to the United States increased rapidly, and by 1835 had reached nearly one-half the total. This does not indicate the full extent of the gain, however, since it represents primarily the growth of the trade direct from Ireland to the lesser emigrant ports, such as Philadelphia and Baltimore.[207] The greatest change was the rapid expansion of the Liverpool-New York traffic.

205 C.O. 387/9, Aylmer to Portarlington, June 14, 1831.
206 *Belfast News Letter*, April 8, 1831.
207 The Londonderry-Philadelphia trade was a revival of the old route; the Baltimore sailings from the other ports were a new development. There was no increase to New York from any Irish port.

Advertisements of Liverpool ships now appeared regularly in the Irish newspapers; and in the strenuous competition which developed in Belfast in 1827, and in Londonderry in 1832, the Liverpool ships had the best of it.[208] Instead of adding a small fraction to the emigration from Irish ports as it had done in 1825 and 1826, Liverpool secured fifty per cent of the trade in 1827, seventy-five per cent in 1830, and over eighty per cent after 1834. Belfast agents attributed their loss to the decline of their cargo trade, evidenced by the importation of flaxseed, cotton, and other American products by way of Liverpool.[209] Other Irish ports suffered even more severely. After 1830 Londonderry and Newry received only one flaxseed ship a year from America, and their emigrant vessels took nothing in return but ballast, salt, or a small order of hosiery. Dublin fared a little better with its glass and occasional mixed consignments, but Munster and Connaught shippers did not even try for cargo. Belfast, despite complaints, could still in 1828-29 combine a passenger list of one hundred to one hundred and fifty with a cargo of linen, salt and potatoes worth from one to two hundred thousand dollars in its ships to Baltimore and Philadelphia; it was being beaten only in the New York trade. When the emigrant business picked up again in 1829 all the ports sent vessels to the United States in ballast, which either continued in ballast to British America to get a cargo of timber, or returned in ballast to England —no mean sign of the profits of the emigrant trade.[210] Afterwards, when trade became more settled, Liverpool cargo advantage was more pronounced; but as emigrant ships had usually been chartered from Liverpool, often

208 Liverpool became the standard, and ''as good as Liverpool ships'' a frequent feature of advertisements.

209 *Parl. Pap.* 1836, No. 35, Part I, p. 17.

210 Semi-Annual Consular Returns of trade, 1826-31, in F.O. 5/266-269.

with English cargoes, it seems probable that the activities of agents were a more decisive factor in stimulating passenger traffic from the Mersey port. By 1834, Fitzhugh and Grimshaw had representatives in a number of Irish towns to circulate advertisements and to receive deposits.[211] Their extensive prepaid passages have already been mentioned. The rapid growth of the Liverpool trade brought about a considerable increase of illegal and crooked dealing, which was particularly bad during these years.[212] In one respect however, the emigrants were better off than their predecessors. The average size of the vessels operating from Belfast and Liverpool was now over 300 tons, the smaller ships which had carried emigrants in earlier times now being relegated to the coasting trade.[213] One other change deserves mention in passing. The shift in cotton growing from the east coast to the lower Mississippi, which killed emigration from Belfast to Charleston, substituted in its stead a small but regular movement to New Orleans.

Discussion of the ultimate effects of this emigration belongs to a later chapter, but certain immediate results may be noted in conclusion. The Irish immigration of this period, so much more extensive than anything which had gone before, and containing so much more of the native Irish element, was the first to modify the essentially English and Protestant character of many parts of the United States, especially New York and New England. The problem of assimilation created by their coming was aggravated by the tendency to congregate in cities, and especially in the few cities where numbers of their countrymen

211 *Parl. Pap.* 1836, No. 40, p. 33.

212 *Ibid.*, pp. 34-35; Evidence of Robert Low, Emigration Agent.

213 List of shipping in *Belfast News Letter*, Jan. 8, 1830. Another list of ships and passengers, June, 1827, shows (with one exception) a minimum tonnage to British America of 152, and to the United States of 250.

were already in residence.[214] This tendency has already been noticed as arising from the manufacturing background of many of the earlier emigrants, and the natural gregariousness of the Irish people. It was now increased by the extreme poverty of a large portion of the emigrants, which prevented their easy dispersion from the ports, and by the natural drift of seasonal labor toward hibernation in the cities, a characteristic which had also been marked in Ireland.[215] The primary effect upon Ireland was to increase the attractiveness of America by the addition of some 350,000 to the number of friends and relatives there, thus adding to the desire and the means for emigration in all parts of the country, though to a less degree in Connaught than elsewhere.[216] The very extent of the movement had, however, created conditions in some parts of Ireland which tended to modify the urge for emigration, and so introduced a new phase in the history of the movement.

[214] This habit had already aroused alarm by 1835; see Duhring, *Immigration*, in *North American Review*, XL, 465-469.

[215] Dublin had long suffered from the influx of vagrants and of families of harvest laborers who went to England. The introduction of workhouses under the Irish Poor Law of 1838 did much to break down this habit, as the beggars, both seasonal and professional, kept away from the vicinity of workhouses.

[216] Inglis, *Journey throughout Ireland in 1834*, II, 310; and see the speech of Smith O'Brien, April 28, 1837, in *3 Hansard*, XXVIII, 399.

CHAPTER V

PAVING THE WAY FOR THE GREAT
MIGRATIONS, 1836-1845

Old Dublin City there is no doubtin'
  Bates every city upon the say,
'Tis there you'd hear O'Connell spoutin'
  And Lady Morgan makin' tay.
For 'tis the capital of the finest nation,
  With charmin' pisintry upon a fruitful sod,
Fightin' like devils for conciliation,
  And hatin' each other for the love of God.

    Irish Song quoted in Lady Morgan's Diary

O, in eighteen hundred and forty-one
My corduroy breeches I put on;

Chorus

To work upon the railway, the railway,
I'm weary of the railway.

In eighteen hundred and forty-two,
I did not know what I should do.

In eighteen hundred and forty-three,
I sailed across the sea.

In eighteen hundred and forty-four,
I landed on Columbia's shore,

In eighteen hundred and forty-five,
When Daniel O'Connell he was alive,

> In eighteen hundred and forty-six,
> I changed my trade to carrying bricks.
>
> In eighteen hundred and forty-seven,
> Poor Paddy was thinking of going to Heaven;
>
> *Chorus*
>
> To work upon the railway, the railway,
> I'm weary of the railway.
>
> *Irish ballad*

THE history of Irish emigration from 1835 to the famine forms a continuous story, differing somewhat from that of the hectic years just before, but undergoing no important change in cause or character, despite the three distinct waves in which the emigrants set forth. The first spent itself in two years, in each of which the numbers exceeded forty thousand, and then dropped to eleven thousand in 1838. There followed a steady increase to over 93,000 in 1842 and another drop, this time to 38,000, after which there was an unbroken crescendo that reached 77,000 in 1845, only to be lost in the great flood which followed the famine. These fluctuations were very largely the result of American conditions, but the factors which determined the character of the emigration were to be found in Ireland, and were in part a result of the mass movement we have just described.

Before 1831, the emigrants, if they included many of the poor, also included enough men of capital and enterprise to counterbalance any good which might have arisen from the relief to population. In 1830 a report from Enniskillen stated:

Business in general indicated that, with capital, the spirit of trade and speculation has fled the country. Indeed the number and description of those who have emigrated to America this season contributed greatly to exhaust the capital afloat in the country, as every sovereign which could be scraped together was hoarded up, either for the purchase of land, or to embark in trade on the other side of the Atlantic.[1]

As late as 1833, the editor of the *Londonderry Journal* wrote:

It is remarkable that the great periodical emigrations from this district which take place have had no perceptible influence—indeed we are sure they have had none whatever, on rents or wages. New tenants rapidly fill up the vacancies caused by emigration; and they continue, or at least they make an effort to pay the old rents by living more miserably than their predecessors could well submit to. This deterioration of the quality of the tenantry cannot fail to eventually produce the most bitter fruits.[2]

But within three months the editor had altered his opinion, and on September 3rd wrote: ''Such a great and continuous drain upon the population, has at length had an effect upon wages in some parts of the country, there being now a comparative scarcity of young and able-bodied farm servants and day laborers, who of course insist upon higher terms than they formerly obtained.''

It is vital to an understanding of the results of emigration to know exactly what regions were affected by the change, and on this point the reports of the Poor Commission and of the Ordnance Survey for Londonderry county are conclusive. The following are typical quotations: ''The emigration from this parish is an essential drain to leave any employment for those behind.''[3] ''Emigration has diminished the supply of agricultural laborers and has taken away the best and most well conducted of them.''[4] ''The emigrants consist of the youth

1 *Belfast News Letter*, June 22, 1830.
2 *Londonderry Journal*, June 18, 1833.
3 *Parl. Pap.* 1837, No. 38. Supplement, p. 368; Lower Cumber Parish.
4 *O'Donovan Survey*, Box 43, Macosquin Parish.

of both sexes, farmers and cotters indiscriminately. This drain has increased the wages of labour. It has also to a certain extent relieved the parish by removing numbers who were on the verge of pauperism.'"[5] There are similar though less frequent reports from other counties in Ulster and from south Cork.[6] Some of them claim that rents are kept down, others deny it. The editor of the *Londonderry Journal* evidently thought they were; for he wrote:

> Besides, what check is there on the cupidity of landlords other than the facilities of emigration? But for it, we can suppose that on many estates, the proprietors of which are certainly not rapacious only because they are foreseeing and prudent, the condition of the tenantry would be much worse than it is. The emigration of so many small farmers, with the value of their stock, is an evil, but not an unmixed one.[7]

Inglis thought that emigration provided some check to rents throughout Ulster,[8] and it was stated to have prevented subdivision of farms, and so lightened the burden of the small farmer.[9]

These reports come wholly from districts of extensive emigration. In the rest of Ireland and in those parts of Ulster which were adjacent to non-emigrating regions, the Poor Reports are unanimous in their conclusion that emigration had no effect; that it was, in fact, utterly inadequate to remove any of the evils of the working classes. The commissioners stated that in most counties from one-fourth to nine-tenths of the tenantry would have to be

[5] *O'Donovan Survey*, Box 35. Upper Cumber; also Box 38, Drumachose.

[6] *Parl. Pap.* 1845, No. 616: Evidence before the Devon Commission, Part II, pp. 976, 987; Inglis, *Journey throughout Ireland in 1834*, I, 199.

[7] June 17, 1834.

[8] *Journey throughout Ireland in 1834*, II, 279.

[9] *Parl. Pap.* 1845, No. 606: Evidence before the Devon Commission (Part I), p. 827.

removed in order to secure to the remainder steady employment at tenpence a day.[10] Powerless though it may have been to remove existing evils, emigration was still the only effective check upon a still greater concentration of population, unemployment and distress. In some emigration districts the rural population was stationary,[11] and throughout all Ireland the advance was much less rapid than it would otherwise have been. Between 1821 and 1831, population had increased by fourteen and a quarter per cent. In the next decade the rate of advance was reduced to five and three-quarters per cent.[12] The figures indicate that the normal expansion was somewhat over 100,000 a year, and that after 1831 forty per cent of it was carried off by emigration to America, and another twenty per cent by emigration to Great Britain. If the rate of increase remained the same after 1841, the movement to America removed two-thirds, or 66,000 a year. According to one estimate, the emigration in preceding years of so many of the young of both sexes had already reduced the birthrate in 1841, and prevented any growth of population after that date.[13] In the urban areas an actual decline had already set in. Outside of Ulster, twenty-seven towns showed a normal increase, nineteen were stationary, and thirty-five exhibited losses. The heaviest losers were Cork, which sank from 107,000 to

10 From the baronial reports, *Parl. Pap.* 1836, No. 38.

11 Evidence from South Cork and the linen district of Sligo, in *Parl. Pap.* 1836, No. 38. Supplement, p. 195 ff.; and *Parl. Pap.* 1845, No. 616, p. 190.

12 *Parl. Pap.* 1843, No. 504; Report of the Irish Census Commissioners, p. viii. The census of 1831 was too large, but even allowing for that fact there was a marked change in the rapidity of increase, which the commissioners rightly ascribed to emigration.

13 Hancock, *On the supposed progressive decline of Irish prosperity*, p. 9. The census of 1841 shows a falling off of births in that year—*Parl. Pap.* 1843, No. 504, p. li. As the majority of the emigrants were between 15 and 25 years of age the departure of 630,000 between 1831 and 1841 may well have had serious effects.

80,000, Limerick from 65,000 to 48,000, and Galway from 33,000 to 17,000 between 1831 and 1841. All the southern cities except Dublin declined to some extent.

The decreased pressure of population helps to explain a general improvement in the state of Ireland first observed in 1833 in respect to professions and trade,[14] and extending in 1834 to some of the farmers.[15] Two years later O'Connell found the farmers so prosperous, and even the laborers sufficiently removed from want, that he considered it an ideal time for introducing a Poor Law;[16] and despite three successive years of low prices, the country was considered just before the famine to be in a better position than it had been fifteen years earlier.[17] Property had increased in value, and though rents were higher, they were paid.[18] English capital poured into Ireland in 1836[19] and Irish bank deposits increased by over three millions sterling between 1840 and 1846.[20] Advance was most noticeable in the cities and towns, where trade was booming, and especially in the north.[21] The first railway in northern Ireland was completed in 1839, and the same year saw the beginning of valuable harbor improvements in Belfast.[22] The main factor in the development of the northern cities was the growth of the factory linen indus-

[14] Bicheno, *Ireland and its economy*, p. 159.

[15] Inglis, *Journey throughout Ireland in 1834*, I, 62; II, 167, etc.

[16] *3 Hansard*, XXXI, p. 231.

[17] Various observers; perhaps the best was Jonathan Pim. See his speech in *Journal of the Dublin Statistical Society 8th Session* (1854), p. 10. Even Michael Staunton's *Reply to Mr. Montgomery Martin's "Ireland before and after the Union"* a tract for repeal, admitted the existence of some improvement; *vide* p. 40.

[18] N. W. Senior, *Journals, conversations and essays relating to Ireland*, II, 3, quoting the opinions of W. Steuart Trench.

[19] *Londonderry Journal*, April 26, 1836.

[20] Hancock, *On the supposed progressive decline of Irish prosperity*, p. 50.

[21] Inglis, *Journey throughout Ireland in 1834*, especially I, 61, 190-191; and Kohl, *Ireland*, p. 117.

[22] D. J. Owen, *History of Belfast*, pp. 230, 248-249.

try.[23] Wages, except for the finest weavers, were no higher in 1845 than in 1825,[24] but there was more employment, and the trade absorbed without difficulty the workers of the now declining cotton manufacture.[25] Improvements in the linen market also aided the handloom weavers who were enabled to hang on, and less inclined to emigrate.[26] Mechanics shared in the general revival, aided by an accelerated development of steam power for all purposes, especially in the north and west.[27]

Economic advance in Ireland has always been intimately connected with political and social changes. Thomas Drummond, who took office as Chief Secretary in 1835, bears an enviable reputation among Irish administrators during the first half century. His work was undoubtedly facilitated by O'Connell's coöperation with the Melbourne ministry after 1835, and by the consequent cessation of Repeal agitation. Drummond conciliated Roman Catholic Ireland by giving offices to Catholics, consulting them freely, and breaking the power of the Protestant ascendancy which had hitherto ruled Dublin Castle.[28] The formation of the Royal Irish Constabulary in 1835 was largely his work, and the force, which was to a considerable extent Catholic, constituted the only popular police that Ireland has ever had. Turbulence declined, and agrarian agitation received another blow in the institution of Crown prosecutions, which took the pursuit of

---

[23] *Londonderry Journal*, January 26, Sept. 8, 1836.

[24] Gill, *Irish linen industry*, p. 327; Bowley, *Wages in the United Kingdom in the Nineteenth Century*, p. 53.

[25] E.g., *O'Donovan Survey*, Box 29, Box 10, Duneane Parish; there are similar reports from several Antrim parishes.

[26] *O'Donovan Survey*, Box 29. Artrea Parish, Box 30, Ballyscullion Parish; *Parl. Pap.* 1837-38, No. 145, p. 7; Kohl, *Ireland*, p. 199.

[27] O'Connor, *History of Ireland 1798-1924*, I, 265-267. Details in *Parl. Pap.* 1837-38, No. 145, pp. 99, 112, 113.

[28] O'Connor, *History of Ireland, 1797-1924*, I, 227 ff.

criminals out of the hands of their terrorized victims.[29] The settlement of the tithe question in 1838, when all tithes were replaced by a land tax, the burden of which was in part borne by the landlords, added to the comparative tranquillity.[30]

Improvements were powerless to raise the status of the laborer. The opinion of a German traveller in 1840 was that Ireland had in twenty years improved greatly in transportation, the appearance of its towns, agriculture and schools, that crime and religious and party spirit were decreasing, but not poverty.[31] The evidence before the Devon Commission in 1843 presents the same picture. In some places the small farmer is included in the general distress, but for the most part he was said to be better off.[32] The lot of the laborers, from amongst whom the bulk of the emigrants after 1835 were drawn, was uniformly wretched, excepting always in those districts where extensive emigration had raised wages and curtailed unemployment. In one respect only had their condition improved. The Devon Commission reported that: "Up to this period any improvement that may have taken place is attributable almost entirely to the habits of temperance in which they have so generally persevered, and not, we grieve to say, to any increased demand for their labour."[33] Some increase of temperance may have come from the Spirit Licensing Act of 1836, which made drunkenness punishable for the first time by arrest and fine; but

29 O'Connor, *History of Ireland*, I, p. 231. The change deserves more emphasis than has been given to it.

30 Lecky, *Leaders of public opinion in Ireland*, pp. 270-271.

31 Kohl, *Ireland*, p. 141.

32 On this point the *Digest of Evidence* (I, p. 364) gives a false picture; see the report of the commission, *Parl. Pap.* 1845, No. 605, Nos. 606, 616, 657, 672.

33 *Parl. Pap.* 1845, No. 605, p. 35.

its main development began in 1838 with the work of Father Matthew, a Franciscan friar, whose great emotional crusade, backed by the church and accompanied by tales of miracles, had within two years captured Ireland. The temperance pledge was taken by Catholics everywhere, and in the north by Protestants also.[34] For seven years, until the death of Father Matthew and the miseries of the famine put an end to his crusade, the movement was one of the strongest influences in Irish life. It proved a valuable aid to emigration, both in helping the poor to save, and in increasing their success when they reached America. The Irish Emigrant Society of New York said in an address to the people of Ireland in 1841: "We need not add, that for all persons, in all occupations, temperance, integrity, and the love of peace are indispensable, and that Father Matthew's pledge is as good as the best letter of recommendation."[35] The improved habits of Irish laborers were first noticed in America in 1840, and continued to the famine.[36]

The passage of the Irish Poor Law in 1838 proved to be another stimulus to emigration. It placed a burden, averaging tenpence in the pound before the famine on farmers and landlords, who had to pay the poor rate for their lesser tenants,[37] and both classes were anxious to shift the responsibility. Even before the act came into effect the Emigration commissioners reported: "The desire to emigrate is moreover at the present moment stimulated and encouraged by the proprietors, who are apprehensive of the amount of the charge which may be thrown upon them by the Poor Law, which is now coming into opera-

[34] Kohl, *Ireland*, p. 140.
[35] *Parl. Pap.* 1842, No. 373, p. 27.
[36] Reports of the Emigrant Agent at Quebec; *Parl. Pap.* 1841, No. 298, p. 85, etc.
[37] *Digest of Evidence, Devon Commission*, II, 946.

tion.'"[38] After it became fully effective in 1840 their anxiety was increased. In the testimony before the Devon Commission only one voice, O'Connell's, was raised against landlord aid to emigration, and that on the ground that it was useless as a remedy.[39]

Amongst the landowners and agents who gave evidence, and who were only a fraction of the whole land-holding class, fifteen had given direct financial aid to emigrants, and ten others had given money which had been used for emigrating. Those who aided it directly included Lords Palmerston, Fitzwilliam, Clanricarde, Stanley, and Midleton, such influential landlords as Colonel Wyndham, Judge Pennefather, and Sir Lucius O'Brien, and one land agent of outstanding ability, William Steuart Trench. Some of them had assisted emigration from a number of parishes and even from more than one county. Wyndham filled several ships with tenants from Clare and Galway, and Richard Eaton, an agent in Kilkenny, sent 1,050 in two years. But as a rule the numbers helped were not great, and the main importance of the practice lay in introducing emigration into districts where it was not generally followed, especially in the region extending from Galway to North Cork.[40] To what extent it influenced later emigration it would be hard to say. Agents frankly admitted that many were loath to go, and as the majority were given only their passage,[41]

[38] Colonial Land and Emigration Board to Russell, April 21, 1840, in *Parl. Pap.* 1840, No. 613, p. 55. The proprietors were even petitioning for leave to raise parish emigration funds—*Ibid.*, p. 58.

[39] *Parl. Pap.* 1845, No. 657, p. 940.

[40] Ten of the fifteen landlords who gave direct aid held land in this region.

[41] Clanricarde's tenants received £3.10 in addition to passage; there was conflicting testimony as to Wyndham's practice, but most gave nothing in cash if they could help it. Trench gave his people (in Monaghan) credit on a Liverpool broker. *Parl. Pap.* 1845, No. 606, pp. 554, 997; No. 657, pp. 647-651, 682.

and often arrived in America completely destitute,[42] their experiences may not have encouraged others to follow their example. Almost all the landlord aid was connected with evictions, which were now unusual unless accompanied by some offer of compensation. There is evidence that where eviction without compensation did take place emigration frequently followed.[43]

The unaided laborer found plenty of cause to emigrate after 1839. His earnings had not increased, and his subsistence grew steadily worse. The "curl" which had begun to affect potatoes in 1831 was still prevalent five years later, but it was a season of exceptionally heavy rainfall in 1839 which destroyed a great part of the crop throughout the west, south, and midlands. There were partial failures again in 1841 and 1842, and in 1844 the first traces of the blight which a year later brought on the great famine.[44] The resistance of the people was weakened, and fever increased.[45] Agrarian agitation, often for the purpose of compelling employment, reappeared with considerable violence,[46] and it was strengthened by a revival of the campaign for Repeal, which in 1843 proved a positive check to emigration.[47] At the same time an im-

[42] *Parl. Pap.* 1841, No. 298, p. 89; 1843, No. 291, p. 48; 1844, No. 181, p. 5—Reports of the Quebec agents. Most were sent to Quebec, but Eaton sent some to New York, and Trench allowed them to choose any destination.

[43] All in *Parl. Pap.* 1845, vols. XIX-XXII; see their index under "Emigration" and names of witnesses. The evidence completely disproves Beaumont's statement (*L'Irlande*, p. 137) that the landlords still desired an excessive number of cultivators. Clanricarde and others fought the Irish Poor Law on the specific ground that it would check emigration—*3 Hansard*, XXXVIII, 218-230. For a description of landlord difficulties and attempts at "estate migration" see F. Morehouse, *The Irish migration of the forties*, in Amer. Hist. Review, XXXIII, 582-586.

[44] O'Brien, pp. 230-231.   [45] Kohl, *Ireland*, p. 211.

[46] *Digest of Evidence, Devon Commission*, I, 321.

[47] *Parl. Pap.* 1844, No. 178; General Report of the Colonial Land and Emigration commissioners, p. 11.

proved démand for labor in Great Britain and hopes of
railway construction in Ireland served to keep the laborers from going to America.[48] They were not as a rule
eager emigrants, but hard times drove them forth to the
number of fifty thousand a year and more before the famine; and the evidence before the Devon Commission and
the Ordnance Survey of Antrim both show that they were
emigrating from parishes from which they had never gone
before.[49] For this, education was in some degree responsible. The majority of the laborers in the thirties knew
little or no English, and were under a serious handicap
in America. Some of the New England cities were forced
to make special grants for their education by their own
priests.[50] According to Hancock:

It was not till after 1841 that the education given in the Irish
national schools began to have a considerable effect in diminish-
ing the number of those who could speak only Irish, in increasing
the intelligence of the people, removing their prejudices against
distant countries, and qualifying them to take advantage of the
high wages and facility of acquiring land in the United States
and in the colonies.[51]

The majority of the inhabitants of Ireland were still
illiterate in 1841, but the progress of education was
making rapid inroads on the number.[52]

The emigration report of 1836 commented upon a considerable increase in the number of unskilled laborers,

[48] *Parl. Pap.* 1844, No. 178; General Report of the Colonial Land and
Emigration Commissioners, p. 12.

[49] *O'Donovan Survey*, Box 11, Glynn Parish, Box 15, Baloo Parish.

[50] Lowell was the first—Stewart, *Travels and residence in the free states
of America*, p. 18.

[51] *On the supposed progressive decline of Irish prosperity*, p. 11.

[52] The percentage who could neither read nor write English or Irish in
1841 was for each province: Ulster, 42, Leinster, 48, Munster, 64, and Connaught, 73. In 1851 each province had improved by ten per cent—Census
of 1851, p. xxxvii.

and subsequent reports leave no doubt that they were the predominant class after 1840. The Canadian agents complained continually of this, and Buchanan wrote in 1841:

I quite coincide in the opinion expressed by Mr. Hawke that we receive in Canada quite too large a proportion of mere labourers, that is, persons who can only use the spade and pickaxe. Unless when some extensive public work is in operation, there is much less demand for persons of this class in the province than people at home are generally aware of, and these form the principal mass of emigrants that proceed to the United States.[53]

The emigrants of 1841 were said to be of a better type, though the governor declared that they were only fit to work on roads.[54] In the two years following, one-third of the emigrants arrived destitute,[55] and many of the Irish were only enabled to pay their passage through the help of friends. Dr. Douglas describes a system common among them:

Many of those who did emigrate came out on the credit of friends at home, who made themselves responsible for the payment of the passage money within twelve months after the arrival of the emigrants in this country. On board of one vessel, the bark *Anne* of New Ross, out of 64 passengers, I was assured by the master that only one family had paid their passage money before leaving, all the others having come out in the manner just described.[56]

The poverty of the emigrants again appears in a statement from Cork that they were composed of the laborers at eightpence a day, those who earned sixpence being unable to save enough for their passage.[57] United States

[53] *Parl. Pap.* 1842, No. 373, p. 8.
[54] Sydenham to Russell, June 9, 1841, in *Parl. Pap.* 1841, No. 338, p. 41; Report of Dr. Douglas, *ibid.*, p. 46.
[55] *Parl. Pap.* 1842, No. 373, p. 24.   [56] *Parl. Pap.* 1844, No. 181, p. 25.
[57] *Parl. Pap.* 1845, No. 657, p. 53; Evidence of Samuel Penrose, merchant.

immigration reports indicate that a similar type were coming there. Two returns of Irish arriving at Amboy and Wilmington in 1836 and 1837 give 353 laborers, 160 spinsters, 15 farmers, 6 mechanics, and 1 clerk,[58] and Bagot wrote in 1843: "A large portion, probably the largest of emigrants from the mother country to the United States, has for some years past consisted of this class: of persons unwilling or unable to engage in any permanent occupation, and wandering from place to place, as labour has been in request."[59]

The artisans, who were almost as poor as the laborers, were also said to be coming to Canada in increasing numbers in 1836, and to the United States as well before 1840.[60] Thereafter, improved conditions in Great Britain drew the majority of them to England and Scotland, and a report from Upper Canada in 1841 stated that they formed only one per cent of the immigration.[61] A larger proportion probably went to the United States, but their place in the total exodus from Ireland was considerably less than it had been fifteen years before. Poor though the emigrants might be, the bulk of the testimony before the Devon Commission substantiates the following quotation from Antrim: "In this as in most districts, the industrious and well conducted are almost the only emigrants, while the able bodied idlers and disorderly characters are but rarely known to leave the country."[62] James Tuke, who toured America in 1845 wrote: "They are no doubt as a class, inferior in moral habits and in mental and physical cultivation to most other settlers; but in capability to acquire knowledge, and in a general

[58] From U.S. Doc. 304, No. 163; and U.S. Doc. 331, No. 427.
[59] *Parl. Pap.* 1843, No. 291, p. 68.
[60] Stewart, *Travels and residence in the free states of America*, p. 7.
[61] *Parl. Pap.* 1842, No. 373, p. 24.
[62] *O'Donovan Survey*, Box 10, Drummaul parish.

readiness to labour, everyone to whom I spoke upon the subject bore testimony to their full equality."[63]

The increasing movement of the poor was accompanied by a falling off in the other classes of emigration. Small farmers still set forth from the old districts in Ulster and Cork, and apparently from Tipperary as well, but in many places they were apparently less anxious than before to emigrate.[64] Wealthier farmers went from all parts of Ireland, but were few in number, forming only two per cent of the emigrants to Upper Canada, which took as large a proportion as any other district.[65] The greater part of this superior emigration comes from Ulster, and probably indicates a continuation of the old Presbyterian movement. A Londonderry minister testified in 1844 that: "Emigration is going on with amazing rapidity, and I may add that the most enterprising, industrious, and virtuous part of the people are quitting the country, and leaving us the dregs."[66] At Quebec, the Belfast ships in particular were noted as bringing a superior class,[67] and the returns of the Ordnance Survey for Antrim lend color to these comments. Out of 194 specified occupations of emigrants from that county, 56 were laborers, 55 farmers, 33 textile workers, and 38 other artisans. In many cases the amount of capital taken was mentioned, and the total was not quite £2,000, of which £600 was taken by two bakers, and £500 by farmers.

The preponderant part taken by Ulster in the total emi-

[63] *A visit to Connaught in the autumn of 1847*, p. 47.

[64] Evidence before the Devon Commission. Lord Stanley's agent in Tipperary said that tenants had been glad to go to America in 1834, but that everyone was much more tenacious of land in 1844—a factor which would operate in all parts of Ireland, *Parl. Pap.* 1845, No. 657, p. 277.

[65] *Parl. Pap.* 1842, No. 373, p. 24.

[66] *Parl. Pap.* 1845, No. 657, p. 635.

[67] From the weekly returns of the emigrant ships in Buchanan's annual reports. *Parl. Pap.* 1839, No. 536, p. 36, etc.

gration now came to an end. From some sections there was an actual decrease in the number of emigrants. The Ordnance Survey reports from Antrim, which extend from 1836 to 1840, show that in many parishes which had formerly sent hundreds, emigration had almost ceased, and the reasons usually given were better employment at home as well as bad accounts from America.[68] Only in the northwest was the emigrant spirit as strong as ever, though in part of that district, namely Cavan and Monaghan, increasing poverty and the competition for land held the movement in check.[69] Despite very clear evidence from the Devon Report that emigration was only popular in restricted districts of the south, the great gain during these years came from southern Ireland. Cork supplanted Belfast as the leading emigrant port, and Sligo and Limerick greatly increased their quotas. Of particular significance for the future was the appearance of a little emigration from almost every part of the country.

The shifting of the balance of emigration to the south meant, of course, a corresponding gain in the Roman Catholic element. Reports from Antrim indicate that Presbyterians were still leaving that part of the country more rapidly than members of any other church. Scattered returns from a district of about 100,000 people show that one per cent of the Presbyterians emigrated, and only half as many Roman Catholics.[70] But in the lands just below the Ulster border they were emigrating in large numbers,[71] and at least one part of America, New England, rarely saw a Protestant Irishman.[72] Contemporary Prot-

68 *O'Donovan Survey*, Parishes of Antrim, Carrickfergus, Connor, etc.

69 *Ibid.*, Box 19, Parishes of Drumgoon, Drung, Laragh, etc.

70 Compiled from *O'Donovan Survey*, Antrim County.

71 Evidence from Meath before the Devon Commission, in *Parl. Pap.* 1845, No. 616, p. 91.

72 Edward Everett Hale thought the Protestants all went to Upper Canada. See his *Letters on Irish emigration*, p. 23.

estant opinion that the Catholic church was opposed to this emigration was mistaken. The Rev. Michael Fitzgerald, Archdeacon of Limerick, in his testimony before the Devon Commission echoed the opinion of many other members of the priesthood when he said: "There is one, and in my mind, only one great remedy for agricultural distress in Ireland (postponing the Repeal question for the present), and that is emigration on the largest practicable scale, and on the principle of the emigration to Canada under the sanction of the government in 1822. This is the only effectual remedy in my opinion."[73] In 1843 a Catholic emigration society was started to assist the movement to America under the guidance of the priests.[74]

The increase in the number of women, which had begun in the thirties, continued, and by 1845 they formed almost one-half of the total both to the United States and British North America.[75] This was in part, as has previously been explained, a result of the laborers' habit of going in families,—families now including two-thirds of the emigrants from Antrim and at least as high a proportion elsewhere.[76] The other part of the women's gain was caused by the rising emigration of girls, particularly of servants. They were said in some counties to be more eager to emigrate than the men,[77] and were more certain of obtaining immediate employment in America. They

[73] *Parl. Pap.* 1845, No. 616, p. 792.

[74] *Proposed new plan of a general emigration society* (1842); and *The Catholic emigration society, its necessity, objects, and advantages* (1843). The intention was to buy land and plant colonies in the western United States.

[75] Tables in Bromwell, *History of immigration to the United States*, and annual reports of the Colonial Land and Emigration Commissioners.

[76] *O'Donovan Survey*, Antrim County. One-fourth of the arrivals at Quebec were under 14 years of age and must have come mainly in families—annual reports of the Colonial Land and Emigration Commissioners.

[77] E.g., from Cavan and Meath. *Parl. Pap.* 1845, No. 616, p. 91.

bulked particularly large in the New Brunswick–New England trade, keeping the proportion of women to St. John at over sixty per cent.[78] Most of them went on to the United States, and an Irish traveller in 1840 said that he could not have met less than a thousand Irish servant girls in Boston.[79]

Poverty explains, as it did between 1831 and 1835, the sensitiveness of the emigrant to American conditions. During the first two years of this period reports of employment were good, but the panic of 1837 put a stop to practically every form of public work in the United States, and many in Canada as well. It is true that some work continued on the St. Lawrence improvements, and the few thousand emigrants of 1838 did well;[80] but the news of the Canadian Rebellion was an additional deterrent, and it may have helped to prevent the rapid revival which would otherwise have followed. By 1840, although business in general was still below normal, laborers' wages had picked up, and averaged about seventy-five cents a day at Quebec and a dollar in the United States, which was better than in 1832.[81] Farm labor in Canada was then paying fifteen dollars a month and found.[82] This was the peak, and in the next two years wages and opportunities of employment declined steadily. Artisans' wages which had been running well over a dollar a day were also affected, and in 1842 had fallen as low as seventy-five cents in Canada,[83] while the cheapness of immigrant labor caused some replacement of New England women by

[78] Annual reports of the Colonial Land and Emigration Commissioners.
[79] Stewart, *Travels and residence in the free states of America*, p. 11.
[80] *Parl. Pap.* 1837-38, No. 389, p. 4.
[81] *Parl. Pap.* 1842, No. 301, p. 314; 1841, No. 398, p. 79.
[82] *Parl. Pap.* 1841, No. 333, p. 45.
[83] *Parl. Pap.* 1834, No. 291, p. 42. Normally artisans did better in New Brunswick, though their wages were subject to great fluctuations. *Parl. Pap.* 1842, No. 301, pp. 299-301, 334.

Irishmen in the Lowell mills.[84] This year saw a further stoppage of United States public works, and the laborers, most of whom were Irish, flocked to Canada where they shut out the new emigrants. In February, 1843, Bagot wrote to Stanley:

> The public undertakings in the United States have for the last two years generally ceased, and those who were accustomed to be employed upon them, and who were a constantly accumulating number, have poured into Canada in greater numbers than could be received on the works. They have contended fiercely among themselves for employment, been subject to great distress, and have materially disturbed the peace of the sections of country in the neighbourhood of the public works, having in several instances rendered the presence of a military force necessary to prevent disorder and outrage.[85]

A traveller observed that the three thousand Irish working on the Welland Canal mobbed anyone of another nationality who dared to apply for employment,[86] and in the United States their frequent riots, which were often unorganized strikes, effectively kept others away.[87] As the contractors preferred men who had been some time in the country, the 90,000 immigrants of 1842 found little encouragement anywhere. Some hundreds were sent back to Ireland from Boston through funds raised by an emigrant society,[88] but in New York the calls on their resources had been so heavy that the emigrant societies were bankrupt.[89] Even with the reduced numbers of 1844, there was still unemployment, and canal laborers only earned forty

---

[84] Cole, *American wool manufacture*, I, 371.
[85] *Parl. Pap.* 1843, No. 291, p. 68.
[86] *It Blows, It Snows: A winter's ramble through Canada*, p. 206.
[87] Commons, *History of labor in the United States*, I, 416.
[88] *Parl. Pap.* 1834, No. 291, p. 188.
[89] *Parl. Pap.* 1842, No. 301, p. 315; Consul Buchanan to Colebrook, Sept. 30, 1841.

cents a day.[90] Government emigration agencies in Canada had to close, having exhausted their funds by August,[91] but by this time the effect of the panic of 1837 had largely worn off, and there was some improvement until the excessive emigration of 1846 again made trouble.

The statistics of emigration show that the Irish reaction to these conditions, though just as pronounced as in the preceding period, was slower in taking effect. The principal changes in numbers came as a rule in the second year after the conditions responsible for them. This delay is attributable in part to the new type of emigrants, who, more ignorant than their predecessors, were most of them unable to send back accounts of their experiences; and also in part to the wider distribution of the districts from which the emigrants were drawn, so that news travelled more slowly. Hence in 1844, when American conditions were just changing for the better, we find statements from five districts in Ireland that emigration was being stopped by bad reports, and from three that it was increasing from good reports.[92] Both types of report came from the county Clare from towns not thirty miles apart. It may also be that remittances from America had less effect upon the amount of emigration during these years, although they were still a very important item. They paid for more than half of the ten thousand passages in 1838,[93] and in the following years emigrants going to join friends —most of them presumably on the friends' money—were a majority.[94] The great numbers arriving in 1842 came

[90] *Parl. Pap.* 1844, No. 181, p. 24.   [91] *Ibid.*, p. 8.

[92] Evidence before the Devon Commission; good accounts in Clare, Limerick and Meath, bad in Clare, Cork, Tipperary, Queens, and Mayo. In Galway there was said to be a great desire for emigration, ''but one discouraging letter will discourage them all''—*Parl. Pap.* 1845, No. 616, p. 554.

[93] *Parl. Pap.* 1839, No. 536, p. 31.

[94] Annual reports from Quebec and St. John, *Parl. Pap.* 1842, No. 301, p. 339; No. 373, p. 8; etc.

despite a falling off in the amount of remittances, and it seems probable that during these years the old emigrant classes sent less than formerly.[95] But from 1843 on, the new emigrants were sending back contributions, and we find that three-fourths of the Quebec arrivals were again on their way to friends.[96] There are no figures for the amount of the individual remittances during these years, but those from Canada were as a rule just enough to pay the passages of newcomers, and it was expected that government would then come to their assistance and forward them to their friends.[97]

There was less reason for fluctuation in the emigration of the better class. The bad American harvests of 1835 and 1837 were indeed the cause of reports such as that contained in the following letter from an emigrant schoolmaster in Philadelphia to his friends in Londonderry: "The family that has a good comfortable way of living together or near each other at home, that is in Ireland, have more real heartfelt enjoyment in that home than they ever can have by coming to this country unless they can bring with them strength of sinews, much of determination, and plenty of money to bear them inland and establish them on a farm. . . . Your neighbours round about you enjoy more ease and sleep—and many of them too could command more ready cash than many of the farmers round about there, although these have dwellings like so many villas and eat and drink well.'"[98] The farmers' reverses were only temporary, and the majority prospered, as witness the letter of Dr. Alling of Guelph, Upper Canada in 1840: "We have here a good many of the 'middlemen' of Ireland, who succeed well and make excel-

[95] *Ibid.*, The Antrim Ordnance Survey reports also indicate that fewer contributions were coming from America.

[96] *Parl. Pap.* 1844, No. 181, p. 6.   [97] *Ibid.*, p. 8.

[98] July 9, 1836, in *O'Donovan Survey*, Box 44, Maghera Parish.

lent settlers, adding to the wealth and strength of the province. . . . There is here a very remarkable difference between the educated and uneducated Irish; nearly every man of the former does well for himself and family."[99] Alling stated that the poor also tried to go upon the land, without either the means or the knowledge to make a success, and usually failed; and there is similar testimony from John Godley, an Irish landlord who travelled in Canada a few years later.[100] The land question was still a matter of concern to the colonial and British governments because of its effect upon emigration as well as for other reasons. Canadian reformers fought the land companies, which accused them of trying to prevent emigration,[101] though their primary motive was control of finance. Whatever the reason, difficulties about sales continued, and the price of land remained higher than in the United States, until the Canadian act of 1841 finally settled the disputes by establishing government sale at a fixed price,[102] but the American redemption act of the same year left the advantage still with the United States. Despite the testimony of Alling and Godley this question cannot have affected more than a small minority of the Irish immigrants, for most of them were concerned only with labor.

The real factors determining the destination of emi-

[99] *Statement of satisfactory results which have attended emigration to Upper Canada from the establishment of the Canada Company until the present period*, pp. 65 and 66.

[100] Evidence before the Devon Commission, *Parl. Pap.* 1845, No. 657, p. 921. Godley said: "Every man when he first goes out is anxious to go upon land . . . it is the fever of the country . . . and to that fever, as I may call it, I attribute most of the bad accounts given by emigrants, i.e., to their having yielded to the mania and gone upon land without being qualified."

[101] See the speeches of Roebuck and Robinson on May 16, 1836, 3 *Hansard* XXXIII, pp. 944-945.

[102] Poulett Thomson to Russell, June 22, 1840; in *Parl. Pap.* 1840, No. 613, p. 95.

grants were the amount of employment, wages, and still more the traditional and sentimental attachment to the United States which drew the great majority in that direction. The emigration commissioners wrote to James Stephen in 1841: "It is their land of promise on leaving Ireland, and nothing but actual experience will convince any of them that they might more advantageously settle elsewhere."[103] There was no cause for a change of destination during this period, but there was a gradual shift of route. After 1840 the numbers going direct to the United States were always greater than those going to British America, and by 1845 they had become two-thirds of the total. We have discussed the beginnings of this change in the last chapter, and ascribed it in part to the equalization of fares to the two countries, which continued thereafter to be approximately the same. The rate from Liverpool without provisions was thirty shillings to Quebec, forty shillings to St. John, and to New York seven dollars, or with food ten dollars.[104] Rates from Irish ports were somewhat higher,[105] but it was said that from Sligo it was cheaper to go to the United States than to Canada,[106] and there was no great saving in the Quebec route from any part of Ireland.

The new passenger acts may have been in some degree responsible for keeping up Canadian fares. The act of 1835 limited the number of passengers to three for every five tons, instead of the three to four tons previously enforced, and required ten square feet of deck per person.[107]

---

[103] *Parl. Pap.* 1842, No. 301, p. 318.

[104] Table of steerage rates in January, 1841, in *Parl. Pap.* 1842, No. 301, pp. 206-207.

[105] *Ibid.*

[106] Evidence before the Devon Commission, *Parl. Pap.* 1845, No. 616, p. 193.

[107] *5 and 6 William IV*, c. 53. This and the following act, unlike that of 1828, applied to voyages to the United States as well as to British America.

It also permitted only one-third of the passengers' food to be taken in potatoes—a more serious restriction for the Irish, and one which was most frequently broken. The act of 1842[108] increased the allowance of potatoes to one-half the total provisions, but required a form of contract under which these must be furnished by the ship. It also specified a more substantial ship construction, stipulating that lower decks should be laid upon permanent hold beams, and it increased the count for children by making every two between the ages of one and fourteen equal to one adult passenger. These changes did not add to the cost of passage to Canada, but they may have prevented a decrease, such as had accompanied every preceding augmentation in numbers. Neither did they bring conditions on ships to British America up to the level of those for the United States. The Canadian ships could still carry fifty per cent more passengers,[109] and the wealthier emigrants continued to prefer the United States route for this reason.

A more powerful influence than the passenger acts was largely responsible for the change of route. Liverpool and New York were fast swallowing up the greater part of the transatlantic traffic, and the passenger trade could not hold out alone from the regular course of shipping. Liverpool now employed the British ships which had formerly been chartered for emigrants by Irish merchants, and had practically the whole of the American flaxseed and cotton trade. Canadian timber vessels, the last resort of Irish shippers, came in greater numbers to Liverpool than to all Ireland.[110] The effect of these developments upon Irish

108 *5 and 6 Victoria*, c. 107.

109 The United States rule was two passengers to five tons, the British three to five tons.

110 *U.S. Doc.* 590, No. 23, p. 663. Return of timber vessels from British North America to Liverpool, 1839-1848.

ports may be judged from a letter to the *Londonderry Journal,* in 1836:

Sir, I hear murmurs among the country folks, who are about leaving their native country for a foreign clime, why they are obliged to go from this port to Liverpool before they can get vessels to carry them to their destination. I confess I am greatly astonished how the merchants of Derry can look tamely on, when not a week has elapsed latterly that from fifty to a hundred have not left this city by the Liverpool steam boats to take shipping from thence to America . . .[111]

Contemporary advertisements show that merchants did not "look tamely on," but were using every possible argument to cut out the Liverpool traders. Their efforts were seconded by the editor of the *Journal* with all the arts of insinuation. In reference to the letter quoted above, he said:

We are surprised to learn from our correspondent that there are any persons who labour under such an egregious mistake as to suppose that, in the ordinary season, there is not to be found in this port an abundance of shipping for the accommodation of passengers to America. Not only is there that abundance, but the vessels are more seaworthy and are better provided than the most of those that sail from other ports in the Empire. Of those who leave this for America, by way of Liverpool, some doubtless act upon a sound discretion; but the greater number we are sure are the dupes of imposition; and there are few of them indeed who have not had cause bitterly to repent of having repaired to that port, where they become the easy prey of unprincipled harpies. We do not apply that term to persons in Liverpool who profess to charter vessels for emigration; but we do say that even among them there are some against whom the public cannot be sufficiently put on their guard.[112]

But the contest was an unequal one. Whatever the editor

[111] *Londonderry Journal,* April 4, 1836.
[112] April 5, 1836.

might say, Londonderry could not get ships in 1836,[113] and other ports had the same difficulty. Regularity of service was Liverpool's greatest advantage,[114] and cheaper fares, made possible by larger numbers, were the second. Regularity was also New York's chief asset, and it gained at the expense of every other American port. After 1842 its advantage was temporarily increased by a slump in the timber trade,[115] which had attained unprecedented heights with over 600,000 tons a year, in anticipation of Peel's attack on the colonial timber preference. The duties proved less damaging than expected, and in 1845 the colonial export was nearly 800,000 tons, and the new emigrant route indicates a changed use of timber ships rather than their supersession by other vessels.[116]

It was natural with the change in direction of trade that fewer of the emigrants to Canada should go on to the United States. The Ordnance Survey returns show that it was still a common practice from the north in 1840,[117] and there were public reports in Canada the next year— denied by some authorities,[118] but substantiated by a statement of the emigration agent at Hamilton, Ontario[119] —that great numbers were pouring into the states. On the other hand, the agent at Montreal stated that thousands were too poor to pay the river fare above the city,[120] and as the fare was higher in 1842, it must have been an effec-

113 *Londonderry Journal*, May 3, 1836.

114 So stated by the emigrant agent at Quebec, in *Parl. Pap.* 1844, No. 181, p. 7.

115 It affected Quebec especially; see the report of A. C. Buchanan, Jr., in *Parl. Pap.* 1843, No. 109, p. 7.

116 Porter, *Progress of the nation* (Ed. Hirst), p. 425; *Memoir on the colonial timber trade*, p. 13.

117 *O'Donovan Survey*, Antrim, parishes of Ballycor, Ballynure, Donegore, etc.

118 Sydenham to Russell, 13, July, 1841, in *Parl. Pap.* 1841, No. 338, p. 67.

119 *Parl. Pap.* 1842, No. 373, p. 25.   120 *Ibid.*

tive barrier.[121] This period saw an undoubted increase in the numbers of those coming to Upper Canada from the United States. So annoyed was Governor Colborne with the administration of the emigrant tax and quarantine system at Quebec in 1835 that he threatened to advise all settlers to come by way of New York,[122] and unofficial letters gave similar counsel. A great increase in emigration by this route was reported in 1836.[123] Emigrant tracts, inspired probably by Canadian merchants, tried to put a stop to the practice, but without much success. A considerable proportion of those who came to Canada were not new emigrants, but ones who had been some time in the United States. Of the remainder, many who preferred the New York route split their families in order to take advantage of the cheap fares for children in the Canadian vessels. Dr. Douglas, the medical officer at Quebec, objected strongly to this custom, saying: "It is found therefore to be a great saving for the adults of a family to embark to New York, and to leave the younger members to come out by the St. Lawrence under the charge of some female relative or other friend, trusting in many instances to receive assistance on their arrival here to enable them to proceed to join their parents. The consequence of this is that emigrant vessels coming to this port are too often crowded to excess, though the number actually on board does not exceed that allowed by the Act.' "[124] The emigration agents said that the influx from the United States in 1841 and 1842 was greater than the opposite movement,[125] and the

121 *Parl. Pap.* 1844, No. 181, p. 7.   122 *Parl. Pap.* 1836, No. 76, p. 26.
123 *Parl. Pap.* 1837, No. 132, p. 5.
124 *Parl. Pap.* 1842, No. 373, pp. 29-30. The report from which this is taken was largely responsible for the change in the act of 1842, making children between 1 and 7 years count one-half, instead of one-third, as formerly; the change was not enough to help conditions much.
125 *Parl. Pap.* 1841, No. 338, p. 68; 1842, No. 373, p. 8; 1843, No. 109, p. 5.

large numbers coming for public works support these statements. But in most years the balance seems to have lain in the other direction, although the proportion of Canadian immigrants going to the United States was less than ever before. According to one estimate about half the Irish arrivals left British America, but this figure includes the New Brunswick trade.[126] New Brunswick was still the recognized route to New England,[127] and in several years during this period had an Irish immigration exceeding seven thousand persons. The emigrant agent there claimed that only a small majority left the Provinces, but the letters of Sir William Colebrooke, the governor, show plainly that among the Irish only the destitute families remained.[128] New Brunswick was, however, taking a smaller share of the whole than it had before the thirties. Of the much greater numbers arriving in Quebec, probably from a half to two-thirds now stayed in Canada.

As one might expect, little of the emigration of this period went into the pioneer communities of the west. The Irish Emigrant Society of New York gave the advice which it had given twenty years before: "We would tell all to avoid the Atlantic cities, and to distribute themselves throughout the lands. . . . Thousands continually land entirely penniless and are at once in a state of desti-

126 *Proposed new plan of a general emigration society* (1842), p. 9. The Durham Report (1912 Ed., pp. 217, 256), estimated that 60% of all the immigrants to Canada went to the United States, but this would apply to the years before 1837, not to this period. Leroy-Beaulieu (*De la colonisation chez les peuples modernes*, p. 596) thought that not more than one-third of the immigrants of 1834-1858 stayed in Canada.

127 "It is only from the province of New Brunswick that they come here in any numbers." T. C. Grattan, Consul at Boston, to Colebrooke, Sept. 2, 1841.

128 Colebrooke to Russell, June 9, 1841; to Stanley, Nov. 12, 1841, and May 14, 1842; in *Parl. Pap.* 1842, No. 301, pp. 296, 231, 339. The agents' reports are in *ibid.*, p. 325; *Parl. Pap.* 1846, No. 1706, p. 15, etc.

tution; whereas such person should have at least five pounds on his arrival to enable him to prosecute his journey to the interior.'"[129] Most of the Irish immigrants did not possess this capital, or were too ignorant to make use of it; and the only intimation of a westward migration comes from Massachusetts, where it was said that disappointed laborers were going through New York to the lands beyond the Ohio.[130] This was not a pioneer emigration, however, but a response to the demand for labor in the western states.

These years, when the development of the Liverpool route was preparing the way for the great emigration after 1845, perfected the technique of defrauding emigrants, which was one of the scandals of the famine emigration. The dense ignorance of most of the emigrants and the inability of many to speak English made deception easy, and the passenger acts, though they tried to prevent some of the new abuses, were largely ineffective. The act of 1835 went beyond earlier regulations in giving the customs officials complete discretion as to whether they should hold a ship for unseaworthiness, and it aimed at one serious abuse in requiring a payment by brokers of a shilling a day to each passenger for every day that the ship was detained beyond the date contracted for sailing, unless the weather made delay unavoidable. Through a technicality, this act was found to be unenforceable against foreign ships, but an amending act in 1838 remedied the defect.[181] The act of 1842 was the first to make definite requirements as to ship construction, and to forbid the sale of spirits on board except in certain limited quantities. But its main importance lay in protecting the emigrant in his negotiations before sailing. Licences were

129 Quoted in *Parl. Pap.* 1842, No. 373, p. 27.
130 *Parl. Pap.* 1842, No. 301, p. 314; opinion of Consul Grattan.
181 *1 and 2 Victoria*, c. 113.

required from all passenger brokers, to be forfeit on any proof of fraud, and quicker legal remedies were provided for their victims. Supervision of most terms of the act was transferred from the customs to the emigration agents, whose sole duty it was to look after the emigrant. The regulations regarding shipping conditions seem to have been moderately effective, and the Quebec reports showed regular but not numerous convictions for excess passengers, and especially for insufficient provisions.[182] Despite the fact that neither act required the presence of a surgeon, there was a constant decrease in the proportion of deaths on board or in quarantine.[183] The improvements in health probably owed much more to Father Matthew than to legislation; for the frightful conditions which prevailed after the famine showed the acts to have been quite insufficient.

Unfortunately other forms of malpractice were not preventable by law. The dissemination of false statements about America could scarcely be proven against an agent, since there was only the emigrant's word against his; and Wedderburn, the emigrant officer at St. John complained that: "To add to the emigrants' distress, they have been and are subjected to most gross and reprehensible delusions by the shipping agents throughout Ireland; they not only induce the poor people to believe that they will get lands here for nothing, but that they will also receive provisions for settling on them. The readiness with which the uninstructed receive this flattering, erroneous, and cruel encouragement only augments their subsequent disappointments; and the poor particularly so, as they are fur-

[182] Summaries in Buchanan's report in the Parliamentary Papers; there are more detailed reports in C.O. 384/43 etc. From one-half to four-fifths of the offenders were Irish ships.

[183] Annual reports of the health officer at Quebec, especially *Parl. Pap.* 1844, No. 178, p. 10.

ther assured that there is a government fund provided here to convey them to any part of British North America or elsewhere.''[184] We must remember, however, that the Irish were in the habit of lying to the officials, both as to their expectations and their financial condition, in the hope of getting government aid.

The most serious frauds seem to have arisen from collusion between brokers and boarding-house keepers at Liverpool, whereby emigrants were charged outrageous prices for board and lodging and the handling of luggage, and were frequently sold tickets supposed to be good on American railways, but which subsequently proved to be either worthless or good for about one-third of the amount charged. These practices had begun in earlier years, but were much increased by the expansion of the Liverpool trade, and were now duplicated at New York. They find an echo in the songs and ballads of the period:

> Beware these packet-ships, I pray,
> O'Melia, whar you bound to?
> They steal your stores and clothes away,
> Across the Western Ocean.[185]

The Irish girl in the well-known chantey, "We're all Bound to Go," cries:

> Bad luck unto those say-boys,
> Bad luck to them, I say:
> They broke into my say-chest,
> And they stole me clothes away.[136]

The state committee which examined into abuses in New York found that while native Americans had some share in fleecing the new arrivals, the greater part was the work of older emigrants. Each nationality preyed on

[184] *Parl. Pap.* 1843, No. 391, p. 129.
[185] *Whall's Sea Shanties.*   [186] *Ibid.*

its own countrymen,[137] and even the emigrant societies were not above suspicion. The Committee reported that:

A sense of duty compels them to declare that in their judgment some of these societies do not afford that substantial aid to their brethren upon their arrival in a strange land which they have reason to expect, and your Committee fear that there may be cases where the officers or agents of some of these societies have a more tender regard for the money of the emigrant than for his safety and comfort.[138]

The Irish suffered particularly from boarding-house keepers, but their poverty saved them from the attentions of some other tricksters. The bookkeeper of one irregular establishment stated: "Roach said that he kept the party called *the sixteen* at a great loss for the purpose of controlling the Dutch emigrants; the Irish were worth nothing, the English alone would not pay."[139]

The metamorphosis of Irish emigration was now practically complete. The careful, plodding Ulster farmer had given way to a mercurial creature who was almost as ignorant of the new world into which he had come as an insect released from the chrysalis. The once dominant Protestant blood ran thinly through his veins; but it was not that change which was most marked in his altered character. The typical emigrant up to 1830 and perhaps 1835 was a small farmer, often impoverished and ill versed in his own business, but proud of his independence and determined to improve upon it in the new world. Such men often had to work as unskilled laborers when they arrived in America, but possessing a knowledge of English, and aided frequently by the presence of friends in the country, those with energy had little difficulty in ris-

137 *New York Documents*, 1847, Assembly Doc. No. 46. Report of the Select Committee on Frauds upon Emigrants, p. 5.
138 *Ibid.*, p. 8.
139 *Ibid.*, p. 30.

ing to better jobs. The new emigrant was a laborer, with no background of self-help beyond the indifferent cultivation of his potato patch, hampered by ignorance of the land and of the language, and by a character in which excess of joy and gloom seemed equally unfortunate to the slower tempered Anglo-Saxon. But he too, unlike many of his successors after the famine, was the most vigorous of his kind, and the road to advancement was open to him.

This ends the story of Irish emigration before the great famine, which followed the total destruction of the Irish potato crop in 1845 and 1846. The year 1846 created a new record of 109,000 emigrants. In 1847 the number was doubled, thus inaugurating a decade in which more Irish went to America than had left the island in all its earlier history. The flight after the famine changed the course of Irish development and introduced a new phase of American immigration, but the movement itself, though differing in detail from the exodus of the preceding thirty years, is inextricably bound up with the work of the emigrants whose fortunes we have described.

Before assessing the significance of their progress for themselves, and for Ireland and America, we must attempt some statement of the policy of the British government as it sought to shape the course of emigration and to apply it to the solution of Irish and colonial problems; and of the Canadian and American authorities as they approached the complex questions of large scale immigration.

CHAPTER VI

GOVERNMENT POLICY

. . . in the name of God! what grievance has Ireland, as Ireland, to complain of with regard to Great Britain?—unless the protection of the most powerful country on earth, giving all their privileges without exception, in common to Ireland, and reserving to herself only the painful pre-eminence of tenfold burdens, be a matter of complaint?

—EDMUND BURKE to Dr. HUSSEY, May 18, 1795.

It is vain to expect any relief from England. All parties there concur in hatred to Ireland and Catholicity; and it is also founded in human nature that they should, for they have injured us too much ever to forgive us.

—DANIEL O'CONNELL to Archbishop MACHALE,
July 25, 1840.[1]

THE history of British government policy between 1815 and 1845 falls naturally into two periods. The first fifteen years present a picture of unbroken ascendancy by the Tory party and the aristocracy of land and ships, modified slightly on the one hand by the prejudices of a *gauche* and preposterous court, and on the other by the "mobocracy" of Westminster. In its main outlines, British policy was consistent, whether under Liverpool and Castlereagh, Canning and Huskisson, or Peel and Wellington. It was a policy of strong government tempered with slow reform at home, and of aggressive insistence on national rights abroad. In matters of detail, however, and even on many

---

[1] *Correspondence of Daniel O'Connell*, Vol. II, p. 245.

major issues, few cabinets have been less harmonious than these same Tory groups, or coalitions, cemented together from the fragments of personal influence which composed the unreformed House of Commons. The second period, beginning in 1830, is one of shifting political and personal allegiance, during which prominent men of every rank and opinion sought to adjust themselves to the new world of a reformed parliament, a revivified church, and a reforming crown; and when frequent changes weakened the hold of government upon national life. These moods and changes are reflected in the policy toward emigration, which for thirty years pursued an uncertain course between the indifference of ministers, the assaults of fanatics, and the machinations of interested groups.

To speak of an Irish emigration policy in the days when not one educated Englishman in a thousand had so much as thought of the subject would be absurd. A Peel, concerned for the maintenance of his beloved Protestant ascendancy, or a Wilmot, staking his political future on the championship of emigrant schemes, might give it some attention; but the former soon passed on to greater interests, and the latter was everywhere looked upon as a crank. Insofar as government concerned itself with the question in this early period, it did so through three dissociated and uncorrelated policies, or sets of policies. The origins and causes of emigration fell within the sphere of Irish policy under the Home Office, the Lord Lieutenant, and the Chief Secretary. The emigrant traffic and the destination of the emigrants as it was linked with the traffic, came within the province of the Board of Trade, whose recommendations colored the humanitarian passenger acts, as well as the commercial diplomacy of the Foreign Office. But the growing importance of the colonies, at first strategic and later economic, brought emigration primarily under the consideration of the Secretary for War and the Colonies.

The long and weary tale of British mistakes in Ireland has been told too often to warrant repetition in detail, but its importance for our subject, and the need of subduing the fiery red of Irish propagandist accounts, and the brilliant greens and oranges of partisan English histories, justify a more sober sketch here. The subject lends itself only too readily to extravagant treatment; for the twenty-nine years from the Union to Catholic Emancipation are almost unrelieved by any wise or generous act toward Ireland. Sidney Smith, wittiest champion of the Catholics, might well write in 1807: "The moment the very name of Ireland is mentioned, the English seem to bid adieu to common feeling, common prudence, and common sense, and to act with the barbarity of tyrants and the fatuity of idiots."[2] Smith himself, though neither barbarous nor fatuous, had no real conception of Irish needs, and most Englishmen knew almost nothing of the sister island. They did not read Irish journals, and would have learned little if they had. Sir Charles Morgan and his friends talked of setting up "a good Irish paper" but nothing came of it. Their own press gave almost no Irish news. Travel in Ireland, which later became a favorite holiday ground for English tourists, was prevented by bad roads and frequent disturbances. The bulk of the British gentry, whose prejudices prescribed the limits within which government dared to move prior to 1832, remembered too well the Irish knife in the back in the days of '98 and 1803, and forgot the generous loyalty of the great majority of Irishmen both during the rebellions and the Napoleonic struggle which followed. No people had shown less sympathy for the French Revolution than the Irish Catholics, yet three English gentlemen

2 *Letters of Peter Plymley*, (Ed., 1929), p. 9.

out of five rejected their most reasonable claims in the name of anti-revolutionary security.

Affairs of more immediate domestic concern claimed the attention of government, and Irish grievances found no hearing at Westminster. For five years after the coming of peace, distress and disturbance at home, and security abroad, required the constant attention of the British government and its loyal supporters. In 1820 the queen's trial filled all Britain and Ireland with the stench of dirty royal linen, and parties and families split wide open. Before death had put an end to that tragic farce, European and American revolutions called forth the utmost finesse in English diplomacy to avoid bringing on war while severing old ties and creating new ones beneficial to the rising commercial interests. From 1821 to the end of 1825, no domestic news could compare in interest with foreign news; and just when Ireland seemed to be securing generous consideration, financial panic intervened and centered English attention on their own troubles. Not until 1827 did Irish affairs, in the form of the struggle over Catholic Emancipation, achieve the center of the stage, and action was delayed for another two years by the untimely death of Canning and the political disintegration which followed.

Emancipation was not—if emigration be any clue—the most pressing need of the Irish people, but the unbroken struggle for political equality which raged from 1800 to 1829 served to obscure the more fundamental issues. Personal and party views on all Irish questions were dictated by this one subject. We have seen the attitude of the Tory gentry, guided by a press of which Lady Morgan wrote: "Despotism in politics, corruption in morals, calumny in conversation, degeneracy in taste, bigotry in religion was 'the badge of all their tribe.' "[3] However unfair to the

[3] *Memoirs*, II, 243.

press, it is a fit description of that arch-Tory, the Regent and King, George IV. Unlike his father, George had no special knowledge of or interest in Ireland. The royal visit of 1821, which was the occasion for unprecedented displays of snobbery on the part of the Irish gentry, was politically insignificant. The King saw little of Ireland and learned less; and his Irish pro-Catholic favorite, the Marchioness of Conyngham, was too busy feathering her nest to meddle in the larger issues of politics. His anti-Catholic prejudices, reinforced by the still more obstinate opinions of the heir to the throne, the Duke of York, could not prevent the final passage of Catholic relief, but they were a considerable factor in delaying the measure.

A powerful cabinet might have overridden royal stubbornness, but from 1815 to 1830 there was never a strong cabinet in England. Prior to 1827, it was intentionally divided between "Catholics" and "Protestants"—i.e., supporters and antagonists of emancipation. This one subject was not a cabinet question; each minister took his own line. But the leading "Catholics" refused to push their cause. Castlereagh and Canning were preoccupied with foreign affairs, and Castlereagh, though deeply pledged to it, was afraid of disturbing political arrangements, while Canning was probably tied by a secret promise to the king. Its championship in the cabinet was left to the Grenvillite, Charles W. Wynn, a political pygmy, whose principles, like those of his master the Duke of Buckingham, were universally suspected. The result was a practical victory for the Protestant group, since nothing was done for Catholic relief. The short-lived Canning and Goderich ministries of 1827-1828 might have settled the question, especially as the latter had the support of the Whigs, now thoroughly committed to Emancipation; but dissension over English affairs killed all chance for effective action. It remained for Wellington, Peel and all but the High Tories to be convinced by the fearful unanimity of the Catholic Association before anything was done.

Cabinet opinion on other Irish questions—where there was any opinion at all—was equally unsettled. Attempts at land and tithe reform, introduced by private members, either did not secure the attention of ministers, or were opposed on general conservative principles. The only measures which stirred the government to action were of a coercive nature, or the result of temporary crises, such as the famine of 1822. The blame for this inactivity must rest equally on the government and on the hundred Irish members, whose votes under the system of private and party "arrangement" of majorities, were essential to the ministry, and were potentially as strong as the Nationalist group in 1910-1914. While many of them were English nominees of Irish borough-holders, there were enough Irishmen among them to have exerted a real influence had they so desired.

The Home Office was too deeply engrossed in English affairs to have energy to spare for Irish grievances. Sidmouth, who held office until 1822, knew nothing of Ireland, and was overwhelmed by the tragedy of Peterloo and the Cato Street melodrama, brought on in part by his own incompetence. Sturgis Bourne took office under Canning only as a stop-gap, and Lansdowne, who followed him, had no time for action. The only important Home Secretary during this period was Robert Peel, who served first under Liverpool and later under Wellington; and Peel was principally occupied with his valuable English and police reforms until August of 1828 when he decided on Catholic relief.

The Irish government was thus left in the main to work out its own policies. On one question only were its hands tied. Until 1818, both the Lord Lieutenant and the Chief

Secretary were Protestants. Thereafter, the Irish government, like the British cabinet, was divided, and Protestant and Catholic kept a jealous eye on one another. Fortunately the same jealousy did not extend to other matters. Faced with continuous discontent and frequent crises, "The Castle" groped its way toward reforms, administrative, financial and judicial. They were not always wise and too often unenforceable, but they represent the only systematic attempts at Irish improvement which in any way deserve the name of policy. Here too, as in parliament, the coöperation of the Irish gentry was a *sine qua non*. Divided as to Catholic relief, the gentry were on almost all other questions thoroughly conservative, if not reactionary. They rendered lip homage to *laissez-faire*, which was then striking the shackles from English economic life, but nevertheless maintained in full force the antiquated and deleterious land laws and urban corporation privileges of Ireland; and they lacked the political courage to choose between the stern path of individual self-reliance and the flowery pastures of humanitarian paternalism.

Cut off by pride of rank and wealth from their humbler neighbors, and from the city merchants—"the little haughty shopkeepers of Dublin"—the majority of landlords, Protestant and Catholic alike, either abandoned their estates and duties to overseers in the hard times after 1815, or endeavored to maintain a patriarchal or military despotism outmoded by the events of the preceding twenty years. While the older men, reared in the classic tradition of the eighteenth century, stormed at "the tawdry glitter and the tinsel ornament" with which Grattan and Curran set forth the Irish cause in parliament, all, old and young alike, dreaded popular movements and confounded every attempt at agitation with

incipient revolution.[4] Hence they did nothing, and gave
to a government already dangerously ineffectual a reputation for inaction which has done immeasurable harm
in the last century.

British authority was only too willing to adopt the attitude of the landlords. For six years, from 1812 to 1818,
the Irish Secretaryship was in the hands of Robert Peel,
then a young man in his twenties, who had the misfortune
of entering public life before experience had softened his
youthful prejudices. He was a thorough Tory, holding
that "to keep down the forces of anarchy with a strong
hand was the first duty of government." He wanted "an
honest, despotic government." In this he had the full support of the aged Sidmouth, of the Prime Minister, and of
Wellington, who joined the ministry in 1818 as the king's
servant, and not as a party man. Lord Liverpool made no
pretense of understanding Ireland, and left everything to
his protégé, Peel; while Wellington drew from his own
earlier experiences as Irish Secretary reinforcement for
his naturally militaristic tendencies. Aided in the cabinet
by a narrowly legalistic Lord Chancellor with a morbid
appetite for state prosecutions and measures of coercion,
and by fears developed among the more liberal ministers
by the English riots, Peel and his allies made the use of
the Insurrection Act the backbone of their Irish policy.
When the act was not in force they could rely upon the aid
of the grand juries, which were regarded by the Irish gentry as more important than Parliament. They had the liberty of individuals at their mercy, and could indite for

[4] The expressions are Charles O'Conor's, from a letter written in 1819
and his MS. *History of his own time*, p. 60, in the O'Conor Papers. He was
a distinguished antiquarian and religious controversialist, librarian at Stowe
House, and confidant of all the Grenvilles. A younger brother of the O'Conor
Don, he belonged, like most of the rulers of Europe in 1815, by birth and
temperament to the age of enlightened despotism.

crime without any examination of witnesses and frequently upon mere hearsay.

Within the limits of his understanding of Irish affairs, Peel was a good secretary, and more honest and efficient than most. He has been credited by his biographers with restricting private, though not political corruption, through providing a check on grand jury grants; with initiating a more effective police force; with cutting down illicit distilling by the laying of townland fines; and even with the desire to replace military with civil law, though he sought to make the coercion act permanent. These "reforms" were rather for the sake of government than for the welfare of the people, however, and the same motive governed his desire "to do something with the press." He fought the great step of consolidating the English and Irish exchequers in 1817, which saved the Irish government from virtual bankruptcy, because it meant a loss of his own power. He did nothing to remedy the agrarian problem; certainly he did not realize its importance, though he once hinted at a law against absentees. The post-war economic depression seemed to him temporary and time its only cure, and on that ground he and Lord Liverpool defended their policy of inactivity before parliament.[5] They had given the landed interests the drastic Corn Laws of 1815, after two years of debate in which the needs of Irish agriculture received more consideration than those of England, but there was no one to tell them that the price of grain made little difference to the great body of the Irish poor.

The social question was hidden from Peel, as from most others, by the religious strife. He looked upon the Irish masses as a barbarous people, and attributed their state to the Roman Church. "Papal superstition," he

[5] 1 *Hansard* XXIII, 814; XXXV, 1079; XXXVIII, 290.

wrote to John Wilson Croker in 1816, "is the cause for one half the evils of this country."[6] This accounts for his support of proselytizing educational foundations, which only irritated the Catholics and rendered compromise more difficult, and for his unwavering adherence to the Protestant Ascendancy, the traditional enemy of every Irish reform. Already the recognized champion of the "Protestant" party in the House of Commons in 1813, horror at the atrocities in Ireland and his election for the University of Oxford, the heart of Toryism, made him progressively reactionary. In this policy he had the full concurrence of Whitworth, the Lord Lieutenant. But the center of religious dispute was London, not Dublin, and to London O'Connell transferred the Veto controversy which split the Irish Catholic church until 1820, making it a political issue in spite of the efforts of clergy and gentry for compromise. In London also Grattan hammered at the old issue of Catholic Emancipation. He was supported wholeheartedly by the Radicals and more advanced Whigs, and less enthusiastically by Castlereagh and Canning; but against the combined opposition of the court, the majority of the cabinet, and the great mass of English upper-class prejudice he had small chance of success. Castlereagh perhaps wisely preferred to attack bigotry in the indefensible tithe system, in which he saw "the most comprehensive cause of public discontent in Ireland,'"[7] but he was far too deeply immersed in foreign affairs to do anything effective.

Bigotry and indifference were the two insuperable obstacles to Irish reform. There was little even of effective criticism. Whigs and "Catholic" Tories, English and Irish alike, subordinated all other issues to the religious; and Sir Thomas Morgan went so far as to charge the

6 *Croker Papers*, I, 81.
7 *Memoirs and correspondence of Castlereagh*, II, 139.

government with "scraping up" absenteeism, unemployment, potato diet, the lack of poor laws and of education,
to divert attention from the true grievance of Ireland,
political disability.[8] Such men must share the blame for
the perpetuation of Irish evils. Sir Samuel Romilly complained that he found himself in a minority on Irish questions, which rarely mustered twenty votes,[9] and Sir John
Newport preached land law reform to an empty house.

Good and ill fortune both conspired to bring about a
change in policy after 1818. The addition of Canning to
the ministry in 1816 was offset by that of Wellington in
1818; but the election of that year so weakened the government that some new alliance was sought, and the support of the Grenvillite Whigs was secured in 1819. Lord
Grenville, who had resigned office in 1801, on the failure
to press Catholic Emancipation, had retired from active
politics, but his faction under his nephew, the Marquis
of Buckingham, still maintained the Catholic cause. The
alliance was made possible by the Manchester riots and
the horror of both parties at popular uprisings, and therefore promised little for Irish redress except on the religious question; but the Grenvillites included William
Plunket, an eminent Irish barrister, whose ambition did
not prevent a championship of Irish grievances. Meanwhile, Lord Whitworth had given way to Lord Talbot,
another rabid Protestant, in 1817; and Peel had been
followed in 1818 by Charles Grant, a friend of Canning
and a "Catholic." The alarming spread of famine and
fever in Ireland in 1816-1818 required attention. Peel
had given direct relief and begun considering remedies
before leaving office. Unfortunately, the new secretary
was forgetful and inefficient, and he and the Lord Lieutenant could not work together. The result was three

8 In his preface to Lady Morgan's *Absenteeism* (1825), pp. x-xvi.
9 Romilly, *Memoirs*, III, 189.

years of painful drifting, culminating in a year of outbreaks in 1821, when most of Munster was in arms. Serious consideration of Irish affairs was now unavoidable,
and the cabinet gave itself reluctantly to the task. Long
before this, however, mercantile, colonial, and foreign
interests were taking a hand in Irish affairs and influ-
encing the course of emigration.

The first direct steps in aid of emigration came from
the War and Colonial Office. The War of 1812 had aroused
a demand for the settlement of soldiers in Canada as a
protection against the United States; and the granting of
land to soldiers on discharge, which had begun earlier,
greatly increased during and after the war. The United
States was looked upon for many years as "the natural
enemy" in a future conflict, and the military staff gave
careful consideration to the defense of Canada. Not content with placing on the land ex-soldiers who had been
discharged in Canada, the War Office also offered free
transportation, land, and aid in settlement to others from
the British Isles. The majority of those who took advantage of this offer were Scots, but there were also a number
from Ireland, particularly from the Coal Island station
near Dungannon in Tyrone.[10] The movement was of sufficient volume to interest ship agents, who frequently advertised "for Chelsea pensioners and others." These
military grants, while they took only a few at a time, continued throughout our period, and were one of several
government activities serving to acquaint the Irish people
with the advantages of emigration.[11]

10 Applications for aid from Dungannon in C.O. 384/4.

11 For a detailed study of the emigration policy of the Colonial Office see
Cowan, *British emigration to British North America, 1783-1837*. I have in
several places summarized events described at length by Miss Cowan, my
aim being to concentrate attention on the Irish aspects of policy and to
bring the whole into better perspective with British political history than
can be done in a longer account.

Colonial office aid to civilian emigrants began in 1816 with the dual purpose of strengthening Canada and turning emigration from the United States. The offer of aid was confined to Scotland, but attracted so much attention that in 1817 the office received numerous applications from Ireland asking for assistance. The first experiment had not been successful, however, and all that applicants could get were recommendations for grants of land and for implements. The next year even this help was withdrawn, except as usual from persons with some influence, and applications were regularly answered with the following printed form:

Sir, In reply to your letter dated the —, I am directed by Lord Bathurst to acquaint you that His Majesty's government no longer give encouragement to persons proceeding as settlers to His Majesty's possessions in North America. I am, etc.[12]

The government had in fact determined upon a new plan, and now offered lands and transportation to men with capital who would take at least ten settlers and deposit £10 for each one as security for his remaining. This system was in operation for one year only, and was utilized in Ireland by one group of settlers, Richard Talbot and his 172 tenants from Kings County. The party was almost ruined by a long stay in Cork due to misinformation from the transport agent, and had more troubles in Canada, but was able eventually to join Sir Thomas Talbot's colony near London, Ontario.[13] Unassisted emigration was already swamping the little town of Quebec, and in August of 1818 the Governor General, the Duke of Richmond, wrote to Bathurst: "Pray stop the emigration if possible, unless for those who can bring a little money.

[12] C.O. 384/3.
[13] From the correspondence between Richard Talbot and Bathurst, C.O. 384/3.

I cannot see the unfortunate people starve.'"[14] Thereafter, assistance was only given to the wives and families of settlers already in Canada, who must be recommended by Sir Peregrine Maitland, Lieutenant-Governor of Upper Canada.[15] Colonial and War office activities were valuable chiefly as advertising emigration, but they carried with them the danger of deterring voluntary emigration. News travelled slowly in Ireland, and applications for aid under government schemes continued to reach the Colonial Office two and three years after they had been discontinued; and the fact that government had once offered assistance prompted requests long after any intention of giving aid had been abandoned.

The promotion of emigration, even for purposes of colonial defense, ran directly counter to the prejudices of the ruling class, and twice during 1815 ministers had to defend their conduct in the House of Commons. Vansittart and Goulburn, who were themselves hostile to the loss of citizens and had no great interest in Canada, speaking on behalf of Lord Bathurst, explained his measures of settlement as an attempt to turn emigrants away from the United States.[16] One prejudice was thus invoked to defeat another. The War of 1812 had left behind it the usual dregs of rancor, intensified in this case by what were believed to be fundamental differences of political philosophy. Ministers shared fully the popular bitterness toward the United States. Liverpool and Peel retained unhappy memories of 1810-1812, when as Secretary and Under-Secretary for War and the Colonies they were harassed by the disputes leading up to the American War; and Liverpool pushed the peace negotiations at Ghent in 1814

14 *Bathurst Mss.* (Reports of the Historical Manuscripts Commission, No. 76), p. 451.

15 From C.O. 384/1-7; and see Cowan, pp. 68-95.

16 *1 Hansard* XXX, 53; XXI, 917; March 8 and June 21, 1815.

only in order to have a free hand at Vienna. Canning
wrote to his friend Charles Bagot, when the latter was
appointed first post-war Minister at Washington: ". . .
the hardest lesson which a British Minister has to learn
in America is not what to do, but what to bear";[17] and
Bagot was soon of the same opinion, witness his characterization of Henry Brougham as "American minded"—
"a gin-drinking, straddling, corduroy scoundrel."[18]

In this temper the British government at the beginning
of 1816 faced a question, namely, the destination of British emigrants, which before the year was out excited the
interest of four major departments; and the irascible
American minister in London, John Quincy Adams, re-
sponded in the same vein. Fortunately for their negotiations, Lord Castlereagh, though not less opposed to
democracy and American "Jacobinism" than his colleagues, was determined upon peace and if possible
friendship. He pursued them with the "icy head . . .
that splendid summit of polished frost which, like the
traveller in Switzerland, we all admire; but no one can
hope, and few would wish to reach."[19] The controversy
opened on a simple question of commercial right. The
Treaty of Ghent provided for the conclusion of a commercial convention between Great Britain and the United
States. The Convention, which became effective on ratification in December, 1815, forbade all discriminatory duties against the ships of the respective signatories. In the
succeeding three years charges of violation were common
on both sides. At least one of the violations arose only in
the passenger trade. The New York Port and Health
authorities continued to levy higher dues on British ships,

17 Bagot, *George Canning and his friends*, II, 5.

18 Bagot to Lord Binning, June 1, 1816; *ibid.*, p. 19.

19 Croker's characterization, in a letter to Vesey Fitzgerald; *Croker Papers*, I, 202.

in defiance of national and state laws and court decisions, until in August, 1817, pressure from the British consulate through the district attorney's office put a stop to the practice.[20] The principal dispute, however, arose over the British passenger acts. The practice of mercantile discrimination by means of health regulation had been established in the Act of 1803, which was still in force in 1815. It permitted British ships to carry to America one person for each two tons burthen, but restricted foreign vessels to one passenger for every five tons. As soon as the Commercial Convention came into force, Adams complained of this distinction. Legally he was on uncertain ground, seeking in his argument to identify passengers with goods, and Castlereagh replied on January 3, 1816, that the question of passenger regulation was entirely independent of the Commercial Convention. But the American minister returned to the charge and wrote five days later:

The undersigned is informed that in the commercial intercourse between the United States and Ireland the greatest proportion of the freight of vessels going to America consists of passengers, and that a limitation of the number of them to one person for every five tons is nearly equivalent to an exclusion of the vessels subject to it—while other vessels are not subject to the same limitation. . . . In the trade with America from Ireland, passengers form the principal article of export and to allow them to be exported only in British vessels is in its result the same as if a prohibitory Tonnage duty were laid upon American vessels in the Irish ports.[21]

There the matter rested until a fortnight later Adams raised it orally at the end of a long conference over outstanding disputes, suggesting equalization by an order to

[20] Various letters in F.O. 5/116-124; for the settlement see Sir Charles Bagot to Castlereagh, Sept. 1, 1817, in F.O. 5/123.
[21] All this correspondence, except Adams' original letter of complaint, is in F.O. 5/117.

the port officers. Castlereagh delayed answer, challenging again the legal basis of the American claim, and questioning his ability to stop discrimination except by act of parliament. Both men agreed that emigration was undesirable;[22] but Adams, who knew nothing about the passenger act himself, soon came under pressure from American ship masters at Derry and elsewhere. When, after a month's illness, Castlereagh was again able to see him he raised the issue as the one question urgently requiring a decision. The British minister sought to turn the conversation, but upon being pressed agreed to grant equality in fact, without, however, acknowledging the right to it.[23] In this spirit, a draft answer to Adams' last note completely denying its claim was cancelled, and on its back was written:

It appears to me that if the British Government wishes to discourage emigration by making it burthensome it may so regulate upon a principle of health that a given number of tons shall be required for each passenger, but I agree with Mr. Adams that there should be no distinction taken to the prejudice of American ships.[24]

It still remained to secure action on this decision. Adams, once aroused, was not the man to let a matter slide. Twice during March, on the 11th and on the 18th, he spoke of it to William Hamilton, Under-Secretary at the Foreign Office, only to receive excuses based on the illness of Cooke (the other Under-Secretary), and later on the pressure of parliamentary business.[25] Hamilton must have sent orders to the Irish government immediately after the last conversation, for five days later Mr. Gregory notices having passed on the orders to the Irish

22 J. Q. Adams, *Memoirs*, III, 296; Jan. 25, 1816.
23 *Ibid.*, p. 305; March 1, 1816.
24 Castlereagh to Adams, undated; F.O. 5/117.
25 J. Q. Adams, *Memoirs*, pp. 309, 312.

Commissioners of Customs who would relay them ultimately to the ports.[26] Castlereagh was therefore able to report to Adams at their next interview that equal duties were now in force, but whether by relaxing the regulations on American ships or increasing them on British he did not know. Adams replied that the latter measure would effectually stop all trade from Ireland to the United States, by making it unprofitable.[27] This remark may have given rise to a letter from Hamilton to Stephen Lushington at the Treasury (which supervised customs) explaining the action in Ireland, asking whether a repeal of the Passenger Act of 1803 was necessary, and also whether "for the Public interests" American vessels should be given the slight limitation then applicable to British, or whether the latter should be restricted in the same degree as foreign ships. The Treasury decided on the former course, and by order of April 27, 1816, placed American ships throughout the British Isles on the same footing as British ships, allowing them to carry one person for every two tons unladen. Adams continued to complain as late as October that the administration of the order had been defective in Ireland,[28] but shipping records furnish clear proof that for the emigrant season of 1816 his representations had been successful.

Castlereagh, accustomed to thinking in terms of high imperial policy, had acted thus far from a desire to placate the United States, tempered by anxiety to retain British man power. It was not to be expected that the mercantile interest, deprived after centuries of state aid

26 Gregory to T. R. Lushington (of the Treasury Board); enclosure in Lushington to Hamilton, April 4, 1816; F.O. 5/118. Gregory was Irish under-secretary from 1812 to 1830, and considered by many the presiding genius of ascendancy rule.

27 Adams, *Memoirs*, III, 330; Apr. 9, 1816.

28 Adams to Castlereagh, Aug. 11, 1816, F.O. 5/117; and *Memoirs*, III, *passim*.

of a portion of its privilege, should share his point of view. The Canadian trade owed its initial impetus to the timber duties of 1809, which retaliated against the exclusion of British goods from the Baltic states by giving a considerable preference to colonial timber. It received further stimulus from the War of 1812, when in spite of privateers British America secured much of the triangular trade with the West Indies and British Isles formerly held by the United States. The Corn Laws of 1815 extended the principle of preference to colonial grain, and by 1816 there existed in London and at Westminster a colonial mercantile interest. From some such source emanated a pamphlet published early in 1816. Its title speaks for itself: *The Colonial Policy of Great Britain, considered with relation to her North American Provinces, and West India possessions; wherein the dangerous tendency of American competition is developed, and the necessity of recommencing a colonial system on a vigorous and extensive scale, exhibited and defended; with plans for the promotion of emigration, and strictures on the Treaty of Ghent.* The author combines the usual advocacy of government aid to settlers with insistence on the necessity for turning emigrants from the United States, but he is unique in perceiving the value of the passenger acts for that purpose. "As a measure of precaution to prevent emigration to the United States," he writes, "this act of the British legislature stands unrivalled in political acumen. We must not diminish, but increase the restrictions on that pernicious practice; a practice so fatal to us, so salutary to our enemies. But where the object is bona fide to proceed to the northern provinces, it would be quite fair and expedient to relieve masters of vessels from those heavy bonds. . . ."[29] On this principle government now proceeded to legislate, re-

[29] pp. 146-147.

versing the decision taken in the Treasury Order of April 27th. Adams had perhaps unwisely carried his case in March from Hamilton to the Board of Trade, where he recapitulated to Robinson, the President, the arguments he had used with Castlereagh, adding one new one. Robinson raised the old objections, with amplifications, and promised his consideration.[30] The results appeared in new legislation not at all favorable to American shipping. Mr. Lushington introduced in the Commons on June 10, 1816, a bill for passenger regulation, which passed both houses without discussion in the course of three weeks, and received the royal assent on July 1. The new act, which went into effect immediately, restricted British ships going to the United States to one passenger for every five tons, with other regulations similar to those previously in force for American vessels, thus destroying the old discrimination in law. The Order of April 27th was now unnecessary and was promptly revoked. American ships were restored to their status under the act of 1803, while British ships going to British America (and under the Navigation Laws only British ships could go there from the British Isles) continued under the earlier act to carry one person for every two tons. The effect of this act and of the act of 1817 in turning the course of emigration from Ireland to the United States by way of British America, has already been discussed.

Had the emigration season still been in full swing in July, Adams would undoubtedly have heard from Ireland the results of the change. As it was, he accepted without comment Castlereagh's statement that the act had passed ". . . for allowing American vessels to take as many passengers from Ireland as British vessels,"[31] which implied a statutory continuation of the Order of April 27,

30 Adams, *Memoirs*, III, 313-314.   31 *Ibid.*, p. 386.

though the exact opposite had taken place. Adams continued to find causes for complaint in the execution of the new act, and his suspicions were increased by newspaper reports of a new regulating bill in February, 1817. The papers were mystifying to say the least; the *Times* reporting Goulburn as introducing a bill to amend the act of 1803 so as ". . . to allow the same number of persons to go out to the colonies in foreign ships as would be allowed on board transports";[32] an unbelievable statement, since foreign ships could not proceed to the colonies. Adams suspected a design still further to restrict emigration, and refused to accept Hamilton's explanation given in an interview on March 4, 1817.[33] In this he was wrong, however, for the act relaxed the regulations for British America without affecting those for the United States.

The interview of March 4th marked the close of the controversy over passenger regulation. By the time the emigrant season of 1817 had disclosed the new drift toward British America, Adams was on his way home to take office as Secretary of State; and Richard Rush, his successor, had not the initiative nor the pugnacity of the New Englander. It is doubtful in any case whether he could have done anything, since the colonial passenger acts were no concern of the United States. The revival of industry brought ample employment to American ships, which secured well over half the Liverpool-New York trade through the new packet lines; and the profits of regular and high class passenger service reconciled them to the loss of the greater part of emigrant transportation.

So long as John Quincy Adams maintained a hold on foreign policy—that is, down to 1829—commercial interests were carefully watched and jealously guarded, but in

---

[32] Feb. 20, 1817.   [33] Adams, *Memoirs*, III, 476-477.

respect to the passenger traffic his initial defeat prevented further conflict. The diplomatic victory of Great Britain was the more notable since it left no sense of ill feeling. One cause of the continued friendship was the fact that the Foreign Office had practically nothing to do with the victory. Castlereagh's authority in commercial matters was negligible. His excuses for delay in meeting American claims in 1816 were genuine, and the claims were ultimately met on terms most advantageous to American shippers and in time to give them profitable voyages. His misconstruction of the act of that year was almost certainly due to ignorance. The whole policy of deflecting emigration was worked out by the Board of Trade, the Treasury, and the Colonial Office.

There is no clear proof that the shipping interest was instrumental in securing this change in policy, but it was regularly consulted on all commercial questions, and made its wishes felt through the Board of Trade. Only one section of the trade, the shippers to British America, stood to gain by the new legislation, and their advantage was increased by the simultaneous passage of the act *56 George III*, c. 83, which regulated the carrying trade to Newfoundland and Labrador, and so helped to eliminate another source of competition. Governmental sympathy with this interest was clearly shown in the unsent draft, Castlereagh to Adams, of January, 1816, one portion of which reads:

One of the chief reasons which induced the regulations complained of was to prevent the passing of British subjects into the United States from becoming a systematic traffic, which at no very distant period was attended with serious inconveniences. It must be obvious to Mr. Adams that every government must be naturally interested to prevent the emigration of their subjects from being a lucrative object of commerce to any foreign country whatever, and that it is its duty to frame its commercial regulations upon that principle.[84]

As we have seen, Castlereagh refused to take this ground, preferring to cultivate friendly relations with the United States; but ministerial interest in the question now appeared in an unexpected quarter. On June 24, 1816, the day on which the American passenger bill was introduced in the House of Lords, Peel wrote to Lord Liverpool:

> Irish Office,
> June 24, 1816.
>
> Dear Lord Liverpool,
>
> I think I should be chargeable with a great omission of duty if I did not, previously to my departure from this country to Ireland, call your attention to the great and increasing extent of emigration from Ireland to the United States of America.
>
> If emigration was confined to the south of Ireland where the population is so dense and disproportionate to the means of employing it, I should consider it a benefit to the country. As tending to increase the population of the United States, it might possibly operate to the prejudice of British interests; but, so far as Ireland is concerned, I do not think she would suffer at all by an emigration from the south of ten times the extent of that which is taking place at the present time.
>
> But, unfortunately, the northern inhabitants are the most disposed to emigrate. I had this day a letter from Lord Whitworth, which states that on the last Council day there were upwards of 700 applications from the north of Ireland for permission to leave it, in almost all cases for the United States. At the preceding Council there were, I believe, about 680, and a Council is generally held in Ireland once a week. I think this diminution of the Protestant population of Ireland very unfortunate; but I think it still more unfortunate that not only this country should lose so many industrious and valuable inhabitants, valuable peculiarly as residents in Ireland, but that the United States should reap the advantage from their departure.

[84] F.O. 5/117.

It may be impossible to prevent emigration, but it seems to me to be not impossible to secure to one part of the empire the benefit which is resigned by another, and by holding out ample encouragement to settle in the Canadas, or other parts of our North American possessions, to contribute to their future strength and resources.

How this encouragement can be best afforded I must leave to others to determine. I know it cannot be afforded without considerable expense; but I much doubt whether the saving of that expense at present (necessary as all savings now are) will prove true economy in the end.

Believe me, etc.[35]

As Peel neither before nor after this manifested much interest in emigration or in America, and as he and Liverpool were at this time both in London and in almost daily consultation, this letter can only be regarded as an inspired message; but whether, as it appears, to lend support to the War and Colonial Office settlement plans, or to aid Liverpool, who as First Lord of the Treasury was responsible for the passenger bill in the Lords, is not clear. Apparently Lord Liverpool did not need it for either purpose, and there is no evidence that he made any use of it.

The government was not allowed to rest with legislative measures. An Ulsterman, James Buchanan, who had aided Castlereagh at the time of the Union and had been rewarded by the consulate in New York, brought forward an ingenious plan for turning emigration to His Majesty's possessions. The origin of the scheme is best told in his explanation to Castlereagh:

I fear I am stepping out of my place when I drop an observation on the subject of the Emigration from Great Britain and Ireland, at this Port. A Crisis has arisen well calculated (if seized)

[35] Quoted in Yonge, *Liverpool*, II, 279-280; and Parker, *Peel*, I, 233-234.

to turn the stream from the United States to his Majesty's Colonies in North America. I took the liberty in July last of urging his Excellency, Mr. Bagot, to permit me to send back to Europe a few cargoes of disappointed emigrants that came out here; as great numbers applied to me. I could have done so at the rate of about Three Guineas each, and a few hundreds would have answered the purpose. This Crisis I fear has in a great measure gone by. Since the 19th July I have forwarded to Upper Canada from among the British subjects who arrived here this year, Three hundred and five persons, without expense to government, while I rejected great numbers who have resided here some years, and others of whose loyalty and principles I had some doubt, for tho I deem it an important object to forward to Canada those who had tried the United States and had been disappointed, yet looking forward as I do, that in Canada we may yet have to contend for our preeminence over the world, but particularly for the West Indies, a proper discrimination is important, and such seems to be the feeling of his Majesty's Governors in these provinces. I humbly submit to your Lordship the importance of leading the industrious and comparatively wealthy emigrants from Great Britain and Ireland at once to proceed to the Canadas instead of the United States, but under the present arrangement, tho' expensive, this will not be effected, while did a different arrangement prevail, I am fully persuaded the stream of emigration would tend rapidly to the Canadas and Nova Scotia.[36]

Buchanan began his activities without authorization. Refused funds by Bagot, he wrote on August 17th to Lieutenant Governor Gore of Upper Canada asking for aid in forwarding the poor and suffering. In another letter to Governor Sherbrooke he added the reasons given later to Castlereagh.[37] Gore referred the question to the Colonial Office, to which Buchanan wrote direct on October 3rd, with further arguments based on the importance

[36] Buchanan to Castlereagh, Nov. 12, 1816; F.O. 5/116.
[37] Buchanan to Gore, July 8, 1816; C.O. 42/357; Buchanan to Hamilton, Mar. 15, 1817; F.O. 5/125 (explaining his letter to Sherbrooke).

of stopping Irish Protestants from going to the United States.[38] The rest of the story is a comedy in red tape. Castlereagh was at his home in Ireland, and during his absence Lord Bathurst was acting as Secretary of State for Foreign Affairs as well as for War and Colonies. On November 21 Goulburn (for Bathurst) wrote to Hamilton (for Bathurst) requesting authorization for Mr. Buchanan to spend up to ten dollars apiece in forwarding emigrants to Canada. Foreign office authority was necessary for this, as Buchanan was their servant; and the request was granted and notice sent Buchanan in a letter from Hamilton on December 4th, 1816, the day before Castlereagh returned to London. The first draft of this letter curtailed expenditure to six or seven dollars a person, but this was struck out and ten dollars inserted —possibly by Bathurst himself.[39]

It is by no means certain that Castlereagh would have approved of activities by a quasi-diplomatic agent which approached perilously close to direct attacks upon the country in which he was stationed. Bagot certainly did not, for in 1818 he refused aid to Buchanan for a trip to Upper Canada to arrange about settlers, and warned the consul that this was no part of his public service.[40] Probably Castlereagh never saw Buchanan's letter of November 12th and he may have been unaware of the whole arrangement. Buchanan continued his operations until 1819, opening a special office with additional clerks, and making two trips to Canada for the purpose.[41] His authority was withdrawn in that year, possibly for fear of excessive expenditure resulting from the panic of 1819 which affected many of the emigrants, and possibly also

---

[38] Enclosure in Goulburn's letter, *infra;* in F.O. 5/119.
[39] F.O. 5/116.
[40] Bagot to Planta, Sept. 2, 1818; F.O. 5/133.
[41] Buchanan to Planta, Nov. 5, 1817; F.O. 5/125; and see Cowan, p. 125.

because of his own overzealousness. In February he informed Joseph Planta, the new Under Secretary for Foreign Affairs, that he had ready a volume on the United States calculated to turn emigrants, and particularly the Irish, away from that country, and proposed to dedicate it to Planta.[42] Planta promptly refused the dedication and suggested to Buchanan ". . . the inexpediency of such a publication on your part as connected with your official situation in America."[43] The persistent Irishman made one more attempt in 1822 with a plan for a tract, ostensibly on penitentiaries, but really on pauper emigration. All he received for his pains was a reprimand for not attending to his official duties. The correspondence ends on a plaintive note after seven years' fruitless attempt to collect £696 spent in forwarding 3,600 emigrants, mainly Irish, to Upper Canada, and an equally unsuccessful one to obtain a grant of land in Canada promised for the same services.[44] Perhaps Mr. Buchanan was consoled by his interest in Buchanan and Robinson, the most successful emigrant traders between Londonderry and Quebec, for whom two of his sons were agents, and whose cause he himself had done so much to serve.

The United States government also played a part, though an unintentional one, in changing the course of emigration when it closed its ports to plaster of Paris from the Maritime Provinces after July 4, 1817. The edict caused a rush of ships prior to that date which carried in addition to plaster, the newly arrived Irish emigrants. Short as the rush period was, it was sufficient to establish a new emigrant route, which continued either in smuggling vessels or in steamships practically unhindered by the retaliatory measures of the next years.

[42] Feb. 1, 1819; F.O. 5/144.   [43] Mar. 9, 1819; F.O. 5/144.
[44] Buchanan to Planta, Jan. 21, 1822; Sept. 2, 1822; Planta to Buchanan, July 6, 1822; F.O. 5/172. Buchanan to Bidwell, Jan. 20, 1829; F.O. 5/250.

Two years later the United States government contributed still further toward turning the course of emigration. Hostility to immigration as a menace to American institutions had been the common attitude of the founders of the republic, and its increase after the Napoleonic Wars intensified the distrust. As shipload after shipload of diseased and famished emigrants were dumped upon the wharves of the port cities, sentiment and the instinct of self-preservation combined to demand some check. The result was the first American passenger act in 1819, limiting incoming vessels to two passengers to five tons. The Irish were not the principal cause for the act. The bill was brought into the House Committee on Commerce and Manufactures at the end of the 1817 season, after the wretched Waterford–Channel Island–Baltimore route had ceased to operate, and before the development of a large illegal traffic direct from Munster. It was advocated before the House in 1818 as a means to check the equally vicious and wholly unregulated traffic from the Netherlands, and passed the Senate early in 1819 without discussion.[45] By that time conditions on the Irish emigrant vessels may have increased the desire for regulation, but there is no evidence of it. The American government, unlike the British, apparently did not consult maritime interests in framing its legislation. The act had no immediate effect on the trade with the British Isles, where the regulations were more strict; and after 1823, when British regulations were relaxed, American authorities habitually remitted the fines for overloading, except for vessels caught in gross violation of the law.[46]

[45] Annals of Congress, 15th Congress, 1st and Second Session; especially Second Session, p. 414; Dec. 16, 1818.

[46] A. St. J. Baker (Consul-General at Washington) to John Bidwell, June 23, 1827; F.O. 5/227. The exceptional cases, when vessels were condemned, appear mainly in 1827 and 1828.

Until the great migrations of the thirties again aroused public apprehension, the United States was content to give the utmost freedom to immigrants. By that time the manufacturing interest was powerful enough to prevent legislation, and the law of 1819 remained the only federal act controlling immigration before the famine of 1846. State and local authorities however, having the poor on their hands, were less friendly. The larger ports, by means of quarantine and other regulations, kept away the worst vessels, which landed passengers bound for Philadelphia at Newcastle; those for New York at Amboy, and those for Boston at any one of a dozen New England ports. It was partly to check this practice that the Massachusetts and New York legislatures, in 1820 and 1824 respectively, passed acts enabling local authorities to require bonds for all immigrants, whether from abroad or from other states, who might become public charges.[47] Both these measures were prompted by the influx of Irish poor, and a strict application of the laws would effectually have stopped immigration. It soon became the custom, however, to commute the bond for a small landing fee or head-money, and it was merely a slight addition to the immigrant's expenses.

The same growth of hostility appears in the treatment of petitions from Irish patriotic societies asking for western lands on easy terms for Irish immigrants to prevent their burdening the cities and to encourage others. The New York petition, drawn up by T. A. Emmet, William Sampson, and the most distinguished Democrats of the city, caused a hot debate of four hours in the House of Representatives and was eventually beaten by the narrow margin of 83 to 71. The contest was almost wholly between Democrats—the South opposing, and rural New

---

[47] These acts are reprinted in Abbott, *Immigration*, pp. 106-108. The landing fee varied from $1 to $2.50.

York, with the West, upholding the petition. The force of talent was all on its side, including among future worthies a speaker, a vice president, a justice of the Supreme Court and two cabinet officers, but the growing discontent with the credit system in land sales and the precedent of a rejected petition from a Swiss emigration society were fatal to it. By the time similar petitions from Philadelphia and Baltimore came up for consideration, the immigration of 1818 had aroused uneasiness, and they found no support. After 1820 the change to land sales on a cash basis, made this form of encouragement to immigrants impossible.[48]

Meanwhile, the same conditions which were arousing hostility toward emigration in the United States were undermining it in Great Britain. The lean years after 1815 worked a gradual change in governmental attitude. Density of population ceased to be a virtue, and Malthusian doctrines, which were generally accepted by the ruling classes, came to the fore. Peel, a convinced individualist, was converted by the Irish famines of 1817-1818, to the necessity of state relief—the first of a. long line of British statesmen brought unwillingly to paternalism by Irish troubles. The other "liberal" Tories, notably the Canningites and Robinson, who were held to the party largely by the name and tradition of Pitt, were ready enough for a change of policy. A parliamentary committee on the state of the poor in Ireland which reported in 1819, offered no general remedy for an admitted redundancy of population, and contented itself with suggesting public aid for drainage and roads;[49] but an

[48] *Annals of Congress*, 1817-18, p. 1053; the petition in *American State Papers, Miscellaneous*, II, 489-490; summarized in McMaster, *History of the people of the United States*, IV, 392-394. On its relation to land policy see Treat, *National land system*, p. 314.

[49] *Parl. Pap.* 1819, No. 409, p. 96.

English committee of the same year recommended the removal of all obstacles to emigration, and the encouragement of the movement to British colonies.[50] Even the High Tories were affected. Consuls Robertson at Philadelphia and Manners at Boston reported in 1818 and 1819 several cases of badly overloaded vessels fraudulently cleared from Ireland for British America while destined for the United States, and Manners suggested measures to check this rapidly growing practice.[51] His proposal was referred to Bathurst, who signified his disapproval of any effort to prevent the trade.[52] The fact that the offending vessels were necessarily British may have influenced his decision, but as its effect was to diminish the legal emigration to Canada in which he was deeply interested, his decision displays a considerable change of attitude. In 1820, when emigration was advocated by the *Quarterly Review,* there was little opposition left in any quarter.[53]

The question came before Parliament in three forms between 1820 and 1825. The more liberal commercial policy of Wallace and Huskisson was introduced in 1820 with petitions for a change in the timber duties, putting duties on Canadian timber and reducing them on Baltic. Joseph Marryat, Chairman of Lloyd's and champion of the Canadian shippers, fought the change partly on the ground that it would injure the emigrant trade, which was essential to build up a strong Canada against the United States.[54] But the day of that bogey was past, and

50 *Parl. Pap.* 1819, No. 529, p. 257.

51 Enclosures in Bagot to Castlereagh, June 2, Dec. 22, 1818; Manners to Castlereagh, Nov. 7, 1818, Feb. 14, 1819; Robertson to Planta, July 29, 1819; in F.O. 5/132-144.

52 Goulburn to Planta, Jan. 5, 1819; F.O. 5/147.

53 Vol. xxiii, pp. 373-400.

54 The underwriters' interest in the timber-emigrant trade requires some explanation. The leading opponents of changes in the timber duties and of

Marryat dropped the argument in later speeches. As a matter of fact, the new duties, which became effective in 1821, had no influence on emigration, though fear of them produced a great importation of timber in 1818 and 1819, and so glutted the market in succeeding years, that emigrant shipping was materially affected. By 1825 it had returned to normal, and Huskisson refused further changes at the expense of Canada, at the same time abolishing quarantine fees at home and all colonial fees on shipping—a minor boon to passenger ships. The abolition in 1820 of the requirement of bonds given in Britain not to exceed the passenger limit was also in their favor, but there is no evidence that any of these measures were taken with particular regard to emigration.[55]

Ministerial opinion is more clearly manifest in administration and new legislation for passengers. The old act against the emigration of artisans and seamen was the first to go. It was published at intervals in the Irish papers, but this was merely a form of indirect subsidy by the government, which paid handsomely for each inser-

more stringent passenger acts were successively Marryat, Alderman William Thompson, and G. R. Robinson—the three outstanding chairmen of Lloyd's board between 1815 and 1850. Possibly the insurance on the timber hulks was exceptionally profitable. Possibly also the practice of throwing together jerry-built vessels in New Brunswick for a single voyage with timber to England, where they were sold to the underwriters, means that the latter were taking a hand in the return trip with emigrants. But I can find no proof of this, and Marryat specifically denied the common accusation that these ships were rotten "C3s," stating that in 1819 the Quebec trade employed 183 first class, 249 second class, and only 2 third class vessels.—2 *Hansard*, I, 845-861; IV, 1503 ff.; V, 62. (June 5, 1820; March 29, April 5, 1821.) The first speech was printed as a pamphlet.

[55] Miss Cowan (p. 130) thinks this change was a step to facilitate emigration; but the measure was included in a blanket recommendation for the discontinuance of all bonds which did not give security to the revenue and impeded trade. *Parl. Pap.* 1820, No. 46; First-Sixth Reports of the Commissioners to inquire into the Departments of Customs and Excise, pp. 23, 31, 67.

tion. Peel stopped these proclamations in 1817.[56] The printed forms of the Irish Commissioners of Customs granting sailing permits to passenger ships still required an inspection to detain artificers, but this clause was habitually ignored. Vigilant consuls in America called attention to flagrant violations of the act, but government was not interested; and their abolition in 1824, utilized by Francis Place and Joseph Hume as a screen behind which they also repealed the combination laws, merely secured legal recognition of the existing practice of noninterference.

At first sight, the passenger acts of 1823 and 1825[57] appear to run counter to the tendency toward greater freedom. Both acts nominally restricted the legal number of transatlantic passengers to one for every five tons register, but by means of licenses regularly granted by the customs authorities this was extended in practice to one for every two tons. The effect was to cut the maximum on ships to British America by one-sixth, but to double it on ships to the United States, which now found their limits set by the American act of 1819. More serious for Irish shippers were the clauses requiring fifteen square feet of clear space per passenger, and the presence of a surgeon on all vessels carrying more than fifty people. These clauses arose out of genuine humanitarian sentiment, which had been shocked by the revelation of conditions on the passenger boats; but the new tonnage requirements reflect the changing commercial interests of the day. J. C. Herries, who as Financial Secretary to the Treasury piloted both bills through the House of Commons, had been in 1821 and 1822 an active member of the Irish Revenue Enquiry Commission, whose principal aim was the abolition of commercial barriers and the promotion of trade between Ireland and Great Britain. That

---

[56] Parker, *Peel*, I, 257.   [57] *4 Geo. IV*, c. 84 and *6 Geo. IV*, c. 116.

trade, since the introduction of the steamship, was rapidly concentrating Irish transatlantic shipments in passengers as well as in goods at the port of Liverpool. To the Irish merchant the timber-emigration trade was a principal source of livelihood; to the Liverpool merchant it was only one of many, and of less importance than the American cotton trade. The new acts, therefore, adhere to the practice of recognizing major commercial interests in revising the discriminatory policy of 1816 and in reducing the restrictions on passage to the United States. The Irish merchants received a concession necessary to their business in the exemption of passengers from the legal requirements for provisions, an exemption regularly practised under the act of 1823, though not specifically authorized until 1825.[58] This applied equally to vessels for British America and for the United States. Even the American passenger act, which still caused the poor to go to Canada, lost some of its effectiveness through the practice of remitting fines for overloading; and when Anthony Baker, British consul general at Washington, suggested in 1827 that measures be taken in the United Kingdom to limit vessels in accordance with the American law, the Board of Customs negatived the proposal.[59] In the main, the Liverpool and Canning ministries continued friendly to unrestricted emigration to the end, and its limitation by the acts of 1823 and 1825 was no part of their purpose.

The victory of *laissez-faire* commercial ideals in the

[58] Miss Cowan says (p. 163) that the Irish were exempted from the Act of 1825; that exemption extended only to the provisioning clause. In the *Letter book of the Collector of Limerick,* Vol. II (1827), is an answer to a circular letter from the Board of Customs, Apr. 21, 1826, inquiring how the exemptions had worked. The licenses at Limerick and Newry were all for passenger lists within the legal limit.

[59] Baker to Bidwell, June 23, 1827; F.O. 5/227; Frankland Lewis to J. Backhouse, Oct. 3, 1827, F.O. 5/234.

hands of liberal Tories, who had the whole hearted co-
operation of the Whig opposition, makes it somewhat
surprising to find in the same years the introduction of
a policy of assisting emigration quite at variance with
those ideals. Only an unusual combination of parties, individuals, and Irish difficulties made possible the expedi-
tions from north Cork to Canada under Peter Robinson
in 1823 and 1825. The accession of George IV in 1820
and the subsequent trial of the Queen drove Canning out
of the ministry, prevented Peel from entering it, and
nearly wrecked the Liverpool government. Caroline's
death in the spring of 1821 eased the situation at home;
and the gathering disturbances in Ireland, together
with the manifest incompetence of the Talbot-Grant regime, opened the way for a change. The Marquis Wellesley, a pro-Catholic and political associate of Canning,
had already been indicated as Talbot's successor. His
nomination, according to accepted policy, required an
anti-Catholic Chief Secretary, and at Peel's suggestion,
Henry Goulburn, formerly under-secretary for the Colonies, was appointed. Peel himself became Goulburn's
chief as Home Secretary, and the two, possibly with the
help of Lord Harrowby, united in filling Goulburn's old
place with Robert Wilmot, Peel's friend and neighbor
in Staffordshire.⁶⁰ This was the triumvirate which initiated state-aided emigration in Ireland. The idea was
Wilmot's, but the pressure for action came from the
harassed landlords of Munster.

The ministerial changes came at the end of 1821, and

---

⁶⁰ Wilmot, who in 1823 added the name of Horton, sat in Parliament for
Newcastle-under-Lyme, a borough long controlled by the Marquis of Stafford,
but at this time apparently shared by a number of the county gentry. The
Peel influence was strong there. On the new appointment see *Croker Papers*,
I, 173-174; and also Harrowby to Bathurst, Nov. 26, 1821, in *Bathurst Mss.*,
p. 523. Harrowby was also a neighbor of Wilmot.

for a year Ireland was comparatively quiet. Political agitators were inclined to see what the new Lord Lieutenant could do, especially as his views were strengthened by the advance of the Grenville faction in January, 1822, when C. W. Wynn, Lord Grenville's nephew, took cabinet office, and William Plunket became Irish Attorney General in place of the hated Orangeman, Saurin. With the succession of Canning to Castlereagh's place as Leader of the House of Commons, Catholic hopes had never looked brighter, though opposition in the House of Lords was as strong as ever. Agrarian disturbances, too, had died down, but for different reasons. The fearful spread of famine and typhus throughout the southern counties in 1822 killed all attempts at agitation; and it was not until 1823 and the reappearance of a normal food supply that the activities of the Whiteboys and Rockites again awakened the apprehensions of the gentry. Religious and agrarian issues were combined in an attack on the tithe system—an attack strengthened by some of the farmers for their own purposes. The religious champions of the peasants were as aristocratic as the High Tories and as determined to put down popular movement; and the usual measures of repression ensued. They proved quite inadequate, and for the first time since 1815 Irish troubles caught and held the attention of the ruling classes in parliament.

It was partly for financial reasons, and partly for strategical ones, that the actual motions for aid to emigration came from the Colonial rather than the Irish Office. The measure had been advocated for Irish relief in 1821, and though supported by Peel and Goulburn, was passed over in favor of other reforms. The tremendous pressure of business tied Goulburn's hands in 1823. Moreover, no Irish question could be brought forward without stirring up troubles which the government wished to avoid; and in the existing state of ministerial intrigue and lack of communication no reliance could be placed on full cabinet support. It was deemed wiser to leave the matter to the Colonial Office, which had had the experience of conducting military settlements, and was already in communication with Irish landlords. It could also supply the necessary funds without raising undue opposition. The plan as finally adopted was to take out and establish some five hundred Irish in Canada. It was put into operation in May without parliamentary sanction, under the charge of Peter Robinson, brother of the Chief Justice of Upper Canada.[61] Robinson's original orders came from Horton, but the final selection of emigrants from among the thousands of applicants was made by leading landlords with the single purpose of removing fiery and insubordinate spirits. Great care was taken not to assist anyone with capital of his own (though a few such were admitted in order to calm peasant suspicions); for the general antagonism to state aid except where indispensable was not abated. It was as a measure of Irish relief that the scheme was defended a month later in the House of Commons by Horton and Peel: a measure designed to encourage emigration in general, to show what government was prepared to do, and to pacify the most disturbed districts. On still broader grounds of Irish relief it received the support of Sir John Newport, and even of those twin *bêtes noirs* of Protestant Ascendancy—Thomas Spring Rice of Limerick and Christopher (Kit) Hely Hutchinson

[61] For Peel's share in the initiation of this policy, see Cowan, p. 151. His indifference as to whether the emigrants went to Canada or to South America is less a sign of colonial neglect than of the strong feeling at that time in favor of securing a hold in the Latin countries to offset the advance of the United States. Carrothers' statement (*Emigration from the British Isles*, p. 55) that but for the greater cheapness of the Canadian voyage paupers might equally well have been sent to the United States is true for the thirties, but not for the twenties.

of Cork. There was no opposition, and no consideration of the colonial aspects of the step.[62]

Horton and Peel hinted at larger schemes to follow if this experiment were successful, but their purpose was through government measures to encourage unassisted emigration, and not, as in the later colonization, to supplant private effort. A second committee on the employment of the Irish poor in 1823 approved the government steps and called the attention of landlords to the value of emigration. Prominent members of both parties—all of them, except Horton, Irish landlords—concurred in the report.[63] So long as agrarian agitation was rife, government was only too glad to let the restless spirits emigrate; and when an over-zealous magistrate detained some passengers at Cork on suspicion that they were rebels, he was promptly instructed to let them go— Wellesley, Gregory, and the Solicitor-General agreeing in the decision.[64]

Lord Bathurst was anxious to go ahead with further emigration in 1824, but the Irish authorities would not agree.[65] Peter Robinson reflected landlord attitude when he wrote that they needed more time in which to select the "most deserving"—i.e., the most unruly—emigrants. Horton, whose ideas on Ireland were derived from Peel and Goulburn, as theirs in turn came largely from Gregory, found Ireland "comparatively tranquil," and relief therefore unnecessary. This was a perfect illustration of the normal ministerial attitude. Horton's judgment was correct as far as it went; crops were better, and agrarian

[62] London *Morning Herald*, June 24, 1823. This debate does not appear in Hansard.

[63] *Parl. Pap.* 1823; No. 56, pp. 10-11.

[64] Henry Joy to Plunket, March 22, 1823; *Life, letters and speeches of Lord Plunket*, II, 136-137.

[65] Cowan, p. 107.

discontent at a minimum. Honest and efficient administration, with the elimination of some of the worst officials,
was beginning to win respect. A better magistracy, a new
police, and a thorough overhauling of the Irish bench
gave promise of more impartial justice. Subsidies to the
fishing and linen industries from funds collected for relief of the famine of 1822 were giving temporary stimulus
to prosperity. Above all, the Tithe Commutations Act of
1823, though merely permissive and limited in its operation, soothed some of the bitterest discontent. There were
those who grumbled about absentees and the lack of poor
laws, but they were in a minority.

The cloud which soon overspread the Irish horizon
came from another quarter. In 1823 O'Connell and Shiel
formed the Catholic Association, uniting Irish Catholics
from top to bottom for the single cause of Catholic Emancipation. It was an unnatural alliance, made possible by
the temporary lull in class conflict, but it contributed in
its turn to the quiescence of the country. To most Englishmen and to all High Tories it was a horrid monster,
capable of every evil—from rebellion in Ireland to
stamping out the Protestant religion. To the Whigs,
Canningites and Grenvillites it meant, what Lord Grenville had foreseen in 1822, the necessity of passing Catholic relief before it was forced from them by the democrats
and the priests. The English and Irish governments were
split asunder. Wellesley, living in oriental splendor and
isolation in the Viceregal Lodge, consulted only with
Plunket, and communicated with Goulburn and Gregory
by letter. By the beginning of 1825 everyone agreed that
the Association must be put down, but on nothing else;
and the last great effort for Emancipation prior to its
final victory in 1829, introduced in the House of Commons in February, raised excitement to fever pitch.

In the midst of this atmosphere of hysteria—a month

after the passage of the Act against the Catholic Association and four days before the second reading of the Catholic Relief Bill, when Peel had already tendered his resignation and Liverpool was threatening his—Horton brought up the vote for a second and larger emigration to Canada. The hour was late and the House nearly empty, but in the desultory debate which followed there was much criticism. Incorrect reports had come from Canada that the emigrants of 1823 had all decamped to the United States; correct reports described the management as grossly extravagant. Hume, the watchdog of economy, attacked the estimate, and was seconded by James Grattan, son of the orator. The Whigs, Hutchinson and Spring Rice, assailed the method and scale of assistance and alluded to better forms of relief. Horton's only Irish support came from Vesey Fitzgerald, former Irish Chancellor of the Exchequer, and his namesake, the Knight of Kerry. The ultimate consent to the vote in question was a foregone conclusion; but the general desire for more information before proceeding further had one unexpected result. The Chancellor of the Exchequer, Robinson, answering the request of two previous speakers, agreed that there should be a committee on emigration—an announcement greeted with cheers.[66] This was the pledge redeemed by Horton's two committees of 1826 and 1827, which acquainted the whole British Isles with the subject.

Long before the committees met, the Irish situation had entered upon a new phase. The defeat of Catholic Emancipation by the Lords in May, 1825, and still more, the open opposition to it by the King and the Duke of York, exhausted the patience of all but the aristocracy, and pleas sent out by Buckingham and the leading Irish

---

[66] *2 Hansard* xii, 1358-60; Apr. 15, 1825; and a better account in the London *Morning Herald*, Apr. 16, 1825.

pro-Catholic peers urging the people to be calm went unheeded. Canning refused to coöperate with them, and confined his efforts to thwarting an intrigue for early dissolution of parliament designed to secure votes by capitalizing the anti-Catholic mania in England. The Catholic Association, re-formed to comply with the Law of 1825, was drifting away from its aristocratic leaders both in the church and state. Power was apparently in the hands of the priests, and in 1826 landlords saw their tenants vote against them for the first time. The real power was Daniel O'Connell, and even he could not control the mass force he had evoked. He was landlord and aristocrat enough to agree to the disfranchisement of the forty shilling freeholders in 1825, and to aid Plunket in combating agrarian movements in 1826; but he had to disavow the former action, and the latter was quite ineffectual. Any chance of friendly concession which remained was blasted by the financial crash of December, 1825, which erased Irish questions from the English mind for almost a year.

The moment was by no means unfavorable to Horton's plans. The furtherance of emigration from Ireland had been throughout the work of the Protestant or reactionary party, while the advocates of reform looked on with, at the most, benevolent interest. Peel and Goulburn had ceased to concern themselves much with the subject; it was Horton's hobby, on which he staked his political future.[67] But the mounting distress throughout 1826, and the ease with which it could be demonstrated that Great Britain was suffering from effects of Irish misery, gave him a sympathetic audience in all but the most rigid "economist" circles. Goulburn also contributed indirectly to the cause. In the spring of 1826 he carried through an act

[67] See Goulburn's letter to Peel, Nov. 19, 1825, in Yonge, *Life of Lord Liverpool*, III, 351-354.

long advocated by Sir John Newport and others legaliz-
ing eviction of any tenant who sublet his holding without
the landlord's consent—a measure which soon proved
unenforceable without some means of removing the
ejected tenants and subtenants from the district. Five
days after the introduction of the act, Horton moved for
his emigration committee and secured it without opposition. Hume, it is true, voted for it as a means of proving
that assisted emigration was useless; but Hume's hostility was generally a favorable augury.[68]

The committee met for the first time on March 20th,
and in the two months before the dissolution of parliament accomplished a prodigious amount of work. It
included from among Horton's friends, Goulburn and
George Dawson, Peel's brother-in-law and under secretary at the Home Office; from the "Catholic" Tories,
Plunket, Vesey Fitzgerald, Lord Palmerston, Frankland
Lewis and Sturgis Bourne; and from the Opposition,
Lord John Russell and Lord Althorp. These members did
not sit regularly, and the Committee was really Horton's.
As chairman, he did practically all the questioning of
witnesses, and largely determined the findings.

When the committee began its sittings bad reports of
Robinson's management in 1825 were coming in. The
first witnesses called were Canadian officials, whose evidence it was hoped would counteract these reports. The
testimony was conflicting, and the support of Sir Peregrine Maitland, the enthusiastic Lieutenant Governor of
Upper Canada, was more than offset by the critical skep-
ticism of Colonel Alexander Cockburn, a non-partisan
engineer with experience of settlement, and a close friend
of Peel.[69]

68 2 *Hansard* XIV, 1364; Mar. 14, 1826.
69 *Parl. Pap.* 1826, No. 404, pp. 148-155. Horton later got Cockburn to

Since the "experiments" of 1823 and 1825 were frequently cited in ensuing debates, it may be as well to pass judgment upon them at this point. Peel's principal object, it will be remembered, was to stimulate voluntary emigration. If the removals under Horton's scheme had done any good in Ireland, except to ease the difficulties of a few influential landlords, it might have been by removing the fear of government aid in emigration, which was in many cases looked upon as a genteel form of penal transportation. But as the state did not again until long after this period give direct aid to emigration to America, the change in public opinion proved rather harmful than otherwise by raising delusive hopes. Not only was voluntary emigration checked, but government, realizing that fact, was the less inclined to raise the question in connection with the improvement of Ireland. The direct reason for the failure to follow up these attempts was financial, however. The management merited the observation of John Godley that "the whole thing was done as extravagantly as possible,"[70] and justified Gibbon Wakefield's later criticism:

Still less did Mr. Horton, notwithstanding his singular perseverance, excite a general interest in his plans of mere pauper emigration. Then as now the "shoveling out of paupers," as Charles Buller afterwards happily termed it, was a displeasing topic; and though Mr. Horton rode his hobby so as to induce parliament to try on a small scale a costly and deterring experiment of his well meant suggestions, he soon rode it to death.[71]

While the criticism is correct, Buller's phrase is unfair, for it was precisely because Horton was not willing sim-

withdraw some of his objections; *2 Hansard* XVI, 512. For Cockburn's intimacy with Peel, see the curious story in *Croker Papers*, I, 371.

[70] *Parl. Pap.* 1845, No. 657, p. 923.

[71] *A view of the art of colonisation*, p. 39.

ply "to shovel out paupers," but insisted on expensive plans of settlement, that his scheme was inacceptable to parliament.

The combined cost of the two experiments was more than £52,000 for less than 2,600 emigrants, and Ireland needed to lose two millions. No government would have dared to face the cost of a general removal at this rate, and the advocates of emigration admitted that partial removal would not be effective. The government attitude expressed again and again in ensuing years is summed up in the statement of Thomas Elliot, the agent general for emigration, in 1837:

In point of fact, in the case of a few settlements of people which have been made at the public charge by way of experiment, the result has been very gratifying as regarded the well being of the parties, but it has also demonstrated the great costliness of the operation. On the other hand, various examples in America and in Australia have shown at once the vexatiousness and the futility of trying to obtain repayment of large amounts of money advanced in small sums to poor emigrants.[72]

A comparison with the expenses of voluntary emigration shows that these were not fair experiments. Later advocates of colonization pointed out the fact, but the cost of the two ventures remained a reason as well as an excuse for government inactivity. Mismanagement in 1825 also provided material for an attack by Michael Sadler on humanitarian grounds;[73] and the emigrations under Peter Robinson, viewed from almost any angle, must be adjudged a failure.

It is clear that from the beginning Horton intended Ireland to be the chief beneficiary of his plans for gov-

[72] *Parl. Pap.* 1837-38, No. 338, p. 3.
[73] In his *Ireland: its evils and their remedies* (1828), and also in the House of Commons.

ernment aid.[74] Following the testimony of the colonial witnesses, he called a few English employers to prove that the influx of Irish to Great Britain lowered wages and caused unemployment, so as to impress his colleagues with the necessity of relieving Ireland for England's sake as well as her own. The importance of this evidence is emphasized in the third report of the committee in 1827, which says:

The question of emigration, as connected with Ireland, has already been decided by the population itself; and that which remains for the legislature to decide is to what points the emigration shall be directed, whether it shall be turned to the improvement of the North American colonies, or whether it shall be suffered and encouraged to take that which otherwise will be, and is, its inevitable course, to deluge Great Britain with poverty and wretchedness, and gradually but certainly to equalise the state of the English and Irish peasantry.[75]

Having made this point, Horton then devoted the bulk of the time to the examination of Irish landlords.

The Committee had before it not only plans for emigration, but various other suggestions for the relief of Ireland to which much testimony was devoted, particularly to the reclamation of waste land. This scheme was the chief competitor with emigration for the favor of the Irish members; but they disagreed heartily as to its practicability. The majority thought that while it might give local relief, it could not be carried out on a large enough scale to be an effective remedy, and would moreover be unprofitable. Horton's questions show that he was determined to deny the value of any alternative remedy, but he contented himself in the final report with the statement that emigration would be a better investment than

[74] Parl. Pap. 1826, No. 404: Report from the Select Committee on Emigration from the United Kingdom; and see Cowan, pp. 145-174.
[75] Parl. Pap. 1826-27, No. 550, p. 7.

reclamation.[76] For the success of his plan, Horton had to obtain the support of three parties, the government, the colonists, and the Irish proprietors. The colonial witnesses were on the whole favorable to a proposal which promised to develop their country, especially as two of them, A. C. Buchanan and W. B. Felton, had a pecuniary interest in emigration. They were also influenced by the argument that colonization was necessary to keep emigrants from going to the United States.[77] Government opposition did not develop until the report of the Committee was brought in, but its character may be judged from some of the points raised by Horton himself in the second committee of 1827. To combat the opinion held by many statesmen that there was no real redundancy of population in Ireland, and that in any case government should not interfere, he called Malthus and McCulloch to testify that the removal of some of the people was an absolute necessity, a necessity so pressing as to be a proper exception to the general rule of *laissez-faire*,[78] which was indeed already considerably modified so far as Ireland was concerned. The more difficult objection of expense was met by insisting that all government outlays should ultimately be repaid.[79]

The main difficulty in 1826 was with the landlords, who were to pay the initial expenses of the experiment. The

[76] *Parl. Pap.* 1826-27, No. 550, p. 41. Bog reclamation has been the favorite panacea of those who believe Ireland is capable of supporting unlimited population. There are dozens of tracts in its favor, and almost as many to prove its ineffectiveness. Most of the attempts during this period were unprofitable, and barely sustained a few people. The sanest discussion of the value of the bogs is in T. W. Grimshaw, *Notes on the statistics of waste lands in Ireland, in Journal of the Statistical and Social Inquiry Society of Ireland,* VIII, 522. Grimshaw was registrar-general of Irish lands.

[77] *Parl. Pap.* 1826, No. 404, p. 164. Evidence of Strachan.

[78] *Parl. Pap.* 1826-27, No. 550, pp. 312-326.

[79] *Ibid.,* p. 20.

report of that year, which was a preliminary announcement intended to prove the necessity of emigration, stated that government aid could be applied at once to Scotland and Ireland "provided that money was raised there for the purpose by local assessment, or that a specific tax was pledged for money lent for that purpose by the government."[80] The Irish members disagreed on the method of raising funds. Some of them wanted a tax on the ground that the poorer proprietors who most needed aid would be unable to act without financial assistance. Others said that the gentry in general would not stand for any tax, and the customary attitude toward government imposts gives weight to this testimony.[81] On the other hand, almost all the witnesses were willing to contribute toward the emigration of their own tenants. It was decided therefore to leave the manner of contribution unsettled.

Horton turned in the report of the first committee to an empty house at 1 a.m. on May 27, 1826, at the end of the last sitting before prorogation.[82] For three months it lay buried under the dust of a general election, but as the summer wore on and the specter of famine once more menaced Ireland interest revived. The danger passed, but ministerial anxiety was not immediately allayed. Lord William Russell wrote to his brother John, then in Italy: "Ireland cannot remain as she is, the Ministers feel it, and would gladly listen to any man who would point out the way to relieve her."[83] Horton, with Peel, Goulburn and Bathurst behind him, might well have appeared the man. In October the Duke of Wellington read

[80] *Parl. Pap.* 1826, No. 404, p. 5.
[81] *Parl. Pap.* 1826, No. 404. Evidence of Wm. Gabbett and Lord Limerick; 1826-27, No. 550, Evidence of Spring Rice and Wilson.
[82] *Morning Herald*, May 29, 1826.
[83] *Early correspondence of Lord John Russell*, I, 252-253.

the committee report and wrote to the Chancellor of the Exchequer approving its recommendations, although he did not accept the premises on which they were based.[84] The learned reviews devoted considerable attention to the subject, and the *Edinburgh,* which had been friendly to emigration since 1823, discussed the report in several articles.[85] The *Quarterly* did not comment specifically on Horton's work until 1828, when it was favorable, but in 1826 it expressed its approval of emigration by landlord aid. It was, however, torn between a desire to build up the colonies against the United States, and a strong distaste for the necessary expense.[86]

The same division of opinion existed among political leaders. The Canningites and some of the Whigs wanted free emigration as they wanted free trade in other things, but they were touchy on matters of economy. They disagreed also as to the extent to which emigration would relieve Ireland, and as to colonial policy, though the majority were for subordinating colonial to foreign trade interests. The old line Tories were equally divided. Wellington declared that emigration would relieve Ireland but be of practically no service to Canada;[87] Peel thought exactly the opposite.[88] Nevertheless, he and Bathurst, who were in close touch with Horton, sent out Colonel Cockburn in January, 1827 to survey lands preparatory to a large emigration scheme. A further proposal recommended by the committee was the suspension by Treasury Order of portions of the passenger acts, which were

[84] *Despatches, correspondence, etc. of Wellington* (last series), III, 432-437.

[85] In Vols. XLIII (*State of Ireland*), XLV, XLVII (*Horton's Report*), and XLVIIII (a caustic attack on Sadler's *Ireland*), 1826-1829.

[86] Vols. XXXIII, XXXVII, XXXVIII. The last is a strong puff for Sadler.

[87] *Wellington despatches,* III, 433.

[88] *2 Hansard* XIX, 1515-18; June 24, 1828.

totally repealed on May 28th.[89] This was accepted by all parties, though with reluctance by Horton himself, who saw in it a threat to his own scheme. In the long debate which attended the nomination of a second committee on February 15, 1827, it was generally agreed that expense was the one valid objection to assisting the Irish,[90] and if it could be shown—as it was later—that extensive relief would come from cheaper fares without government aid, only imperial considerations could justify the proposed settlement.

For the moment, colonial interests were receiving livelier consideration in the discussion. They induced the support of Peel,[91] and of Robert Torrens,[92] later a leader of the colonization movement, and the friendly interest of Alexander Baring,[93] who was, next to Horton, the most active member of the committee. It was beginning to be known that most voluntary emigration went eventually to the United States, just when fears of that country were revived by the growth of an enmity which caused many whispers of war from 1824 to 1829. The intense nationalism of Canning and of John Quincy Adams, and a diplomacy on both sides dictated largely by commercial considerations, created a keen rivalry in Spanish America and raised to a new pitch the bitterness of the West Indian trade dispute, which was at its worst in 1827. Added to that was Canning's personal inability to get on with any American except Clay; and a fresh aggravation of the Oregon dispute. So far as Canning and Huskisson were concerned, the jealousy was purely commercial, but it was seized upon as an argument by advocates of colonization.

One result was the construction of a number of military

---

[89] *7 and 8 Geo. IV*, c. 19.

[90] *2 Hansard* XVI, 475-512.

[91] *Ibid.*, p. 300; Dec. 7, 1826.

[92] *Ibid.*, p. 492.

[93] *Ibid.*, pp. 501-505.

canals and roads in Canada which gave employment to the flood of emigrants in 1827, and did much to prevent such suffering as occurred in the Maritime Provinces. A more important step from the point of view of emigration policy was the contract entered into in May, 1826, after two years of negotiation, between the government and the Canada Company. In the end, because of its control of crown lands, the company proved a stumbling block to emigration, but at this time it gave it a stimulus by providing employment, opening up new lands, and interesting British capital in Canada. John Galt, its organizer and manager, visited New York in the spring of 1827 to arrange for transporting emigrants to the company lands, and appointed J. C. Buchanan, son of the consul, as his agent.[94]

These factors played their part in arousing interest in emigration, and when Horton asked for his second committee there was no serious opposition. Peel, who replied to the insinuations of Baring that government was ". . . leaving the honorable gentleman who had opened the discussion in the lurch,'"[95] was frankly sceptical about the financial end of Horton's schemes, but he was willing that the committee should try to surmount the obstacle. If his attitude was on the whole less friendly than in 1826, it should be remembered that the ministry was on its last legs, and quarreling heatedly over foreign policy and corn laws. Two days later it was crippled beyond repair by the collapse of Lord Liverpool.

The two months of ministerial crisis which followed were as fateful for Mr. Horton as for greater men. His new committee, strengthened by Sir James Graham and the Honorable E. G. Stanley, two young men from the Canning-Whig combination, went quietly about its work,

94 R. K. Gordon, *John Galt*, pp. 43-82.
95 *2 Hansard* XVI, 506.

published the report of 1826, and put through the repeal of the passenger acts without trouble during the lull in more important business. But only political fatuity could have prompted them on February 26th to make a special report reversing the recommendations of 1826 for local and private contributions in favor of a grandiose national policy.[96] Horton had pledged himself in January to render every assistance to Huskisson and Herries in cleaning up the Colonial Office, which was a hotbed of extravagance. In his office he wrote economy; but in parliament he uttered prodigality, and Herries sent a savage letter on the subject in March.[97] Horton's choice of associates was unfortunate. Committed as he was to expensive governmental aid as against unassisted emigration, he had a better chance of over-coming the sluggishness of the "Pig-tail" Tories and the qualms of Peel than the indifference to colonial affairs and the devotion to public economy of his new friends, among whom only Huskisson was helpful. The more brilliant Canningites scoffed at the seriousness and clumsiness of Horton,[98] and so did young Mr. William Lamb, who succeeded Goulburn in the Irish secretaryship.[99] The control of Ireland was fast passing into the hands of politicians of the romantic school, like O'Connell, to whom economics was a bore, and Horton could hope for no assistance there. Yet he did not resign in April with his old allies. On May 23rd he was sworn of the Privy Council, and coöperated with Canning in deprecating parliamentary discussions on emigration.[100]

[96] *2 Hansard* XVI, 653.

[97] E. Herries, *Memoir of the public life of the Rt. Hon. J. C. Herries*, I, 145-147.

[98] Bagot, *George Canning and his friends*, II, 22.

[99] Torrens, *Melbourne*, II, 376.

[100] In reply to petitions for aid, Apr. 11, 12, May 21, 30, 1827; *Morning Herald*.

There were, it is true, some grounds for hope. The committee secured some excellent evidence for its proposals. In June it was supposed to have the ear of government; and its final recommendations were for a series of government loans to facilitate emigration, beginning in 1828-29 with a vote of £240,000. This money was to be used entirely for the settlement of emigrants in British America, and was to be fully repaid in the course of thirty years. On account of doubts of the effectiveness of repayments a vote was to be delayed until the results of some of the earlier Scottish settlements had proved their feasibility. The immediate costs of transportation to America were to be paid by local authorities—that is by the landlords in Ireland; and the first claim on government assistance was to be given to evicted Irish tenants or those about to be evicted.[101]

The report was a compromise, but it left Horton free to pursue his objects, and in July he went to Ireland. The ministerial changes of that month brought to the Home Office two Irish landlords, Lord Lansdowne and Thomas Spring Rice, the latter already won to his plans. Lord Palmerston, though not consulted, was himself promoting emigration from his Sligo estates. Even the death of Canning in August did not seem at first unfavorable. Huskisson succeeded the inactive Goderich at the Colonial Office, and for three months he and Horton were in frequent consultation. Horton, it is true, was officially supplanted by E. G. Stanley, and had gone to the Board of Trade as Vice President; but as Stanley was ill and the Board closely connected with colonial administration, it made no difference in his activities. These months were in fact critical for the whole policy. The daily press for the first time took an active—though usually ill-informed—interest in the committee reports, and the inevitable let-

101 *Parl. Pap.* 1826-27, No. 550, pp. 18-34.

ters from country gentlemen began to appear.[102] Huskisson, though never won to a large outlay, was convinced of the advantage of systematic over unregulated emigration, and conceded that Horton's scheme might even be economic.[103] Everything was propitious for a vote in 1828, when the Battle of Navarino put an end to all Huskisson's plans for colonial reform. Within another month the Huskisson-Herries-Lansdowne dispute had the best of Lord Goderich, and the ministry was practically dissolved.

The re-entry of Peel and Wellington into power was fatal to Horton's prospects. He had cut himself adrift from their faction without having gained any strong friends among his late colleagues, and in January, 1828, he found himself out in the cold.[104] He was superseded by Frankland Lewis at the Board of Trade, and his old place, now resigned by Stanley, was given to Lord Francis Leveson Gower, son of the Marquis of Stafford. Government was not against him, but neither was it for him; and it was in his capacity as chairman of the former emigration committees that he brought forward his motions to revive the passenger acts, to assist English pauper emigration, and to pledge the government to take up Irish emigration early in 1829.[105] The last was still his pet project, brought to the attention of the House almost every time that he rose to speak, and given in this one

[102] *Times* and *Morning Herald*. The latter gives full details of official movements, ministerial consultations, etc.

[103] *2 Hansard* XVIII, 1553-55; April 17, 1828.

[104] *Morning Herald*, though on January 10 he was talked of for a cabinet post. The *Dictionary of National Biography* erroneously dates his retirement from the preceding year.

[105] *2 Hansard* XVIII, 939, 1547; XIX, 1501; Mar. 4, Apr. 17, June 24, 1828. It was on this English plan that Hansard reported him as speaking "in the teeth of His Majesty's Government" (XVIII, 1549; quoted by Miss Cowan, p. 170), but the fuller report in the *Morning Herald* shows that he was denying that charge, made by his opponents.

session some genuine consideration. During March and April thirty-four members spoke for or against his ideas. The English country gentlemen were hostile, the Irish wholly friendly, with the exception of James Grattan, who had come forward as the champion of the new rival scheme of introducing poor laws into Ireland.[106] Cobbett, who had paid a flying visit to Ireland, raved against him;[107] Michael Sadler scribbled furiously for seven weeks to turn out his book on Ireland berating Horton,[108] and Nassau Senior lectured in his defense at Oxford.[109] The Catholic Association petitioned against his plans,[110] and newspaper controversy waxed hot. With any kind of ministerial support Horton's chances of some further experiment, at least, would have been excellent; but ministers were meeting only to quarrel and part without a policy, and no help came from them. Huskisson remained friendly but non-committal;[111] Peel secured him as large a hearing as possible, but showed openly his preference for capitalist emigration;[112] Lamb scoffed at "schemes of great and wild attempt."[113]

Before Horton's final full-dress motion came on in June, the Canningites were gone from the ministry, and he had himself refused the thankless job of Irish Secretary, which he would have welcomed six months before.[114]

[106] 2 *Hansard* XVIII, 953-64, 1208-19, 1350-55, 1417-22, 1552-56.

[107] In his *Register*, freely quoted in various journals.

[108] Sadler's statement in Parliament, May 7, 1829; 2 *Hansard* XXI, 1137-38.

[109] Senior, *Two lectures on population* (delivered in Easter Term, 1828, published 1829); especially pp. 80-89.

[110] Cited by Horton in debate, 2 *Hansard* XIX, 1507.

[111] 2 *Hansard* XVIII, 961, 1553; Mar. 4, Apr. 17, 1828.

[112] *Ibid.*, 1556, Apr. 17. Horton postponed his motion at Peel's suggestion, to get a better audience. *Morning Herald*, Mar. 28.

[113] *Morning Herald*, Apr. 2.

[114] Palmerston's Journal, Dec., 1828; Bulwer, *Palmerston*, I, 285-286.

But he was now listed as a reliable "liberal"[115]—a new name given to the Canningites and moderate Whigs— and had nothing to hope from his former associates. Peel gave him every courtesy and some support, but he refused to promise anything.[116]

From this time forward, Horton spoke and wrote mainly for effect outside Parliament, which now refused to give him serious attention. His speeches in 1829 were in the nature of duels with Sadler, in which he spoke more and more of great ultimate aims.[117] He was elected to the Political Economy Club, where he had the support of Malthus, Senior, McCulloch, Torrens, and John Abel Smith against the scepticism of Henry Warburton and young Poulett Thomson and the positive hostility of Henry Parnell.[118] The distress of 1830 gave him a better hearing for the moment, but ministers had a new and unanswerable objection to his schemes; namely, that emigration as heavy as the colonies could assimilate was already going on without any government aid.[119] His last speech on July 13, 1830 was a farewell to Parliament, in which he hoped that emigration would find a new champion.[120] He had already determined not to fight again in Newcastle-under-Lyme, which had cost him two expensive contests, and was subjected to the cross-fire of the powerful Stafford and Peel interests. His appointment by Goderich to the Governorship of Ceylon in 1831 removed

[115] In Palmerston's Journal, June 7, 1828; Bulwer, *Palmerston*, I, 278.

[116] *2 Hansard* XIX, 1515-18; June 24, 1828.

[117] *2 Hansard* XXI, 1131-39; 1720-29; May 7, June 4, 1829.

[118] *Political Economy Club*, List of Members and subjects for discussion. The latter are preserved only after 1832, but the opinions of all these men were either uttered or quoted in parliament.

[119] *2 Hansard* XXIII, 49; Speech of Sir George Murray, Secretary for the Colonies, Mar. 9, 1830. Miss Ramsay (*Peel*, p. 127) cites letters between Peel and Horton to show the former was still interested as late as Nov., 1830. By that time his help would have been worthless.

[120] *Ibid.*, 1168-69.

from the English scene a gentleman of singular zeal and pertinacity, but with little political acumen or influence.[121]

The direct results of pauper emigration agitation were slight, for at a time when every grant was under fire ministers naturally balked at plans involving tremendous expense with no real hope of reimbursement. The conception of expenditure as an imperial investment which would more than repay itself in the progress of British America was held by very few. Most educated opinion considered that Canada was destined to independence, which would be hastened by a rapid increase of population. But even had they been convinced of the soundness of the investment, statesmen then were much less ready than they are today to incur debts and mortgage the earnings of the future in order to meet an immediate need.

Control of the colonization movement, like that of other reforms, passed from the hands of a single agitator into an organized society, which owed to Horton far more than it was willing to acknowledge. Its work, however, had little effect on the Irish movement to America. The great value of Horton's committees lay in the fact that they stirred up greater interest in emigration, particularly in Ireland. Three hundred and sixty-four Irish petitions from 5393 persons representing every county were received during the committee sessions.[122] The hopes raised by Horton's motion for aid in 1826 acted as a slight check on voluntary emigration in that year,[123] but

121 Charles Greville noted as early as Feb., 1829, that "Wilmot is at a discount"; and Palmerston smiled at his zeal in December, when he found him in Paris ". . . indefatigably hammering at emigration, and writing his shorthand scribe down to a skeleton"—*Greville Memoirs*, I, 164; Bulwer, *Palmerston*, I, 355.

122 Summary of petitions in *Parl. Pap.* 1826-27, No. 550, pp. 484-499.

123 Horton feared this result; see his letter to an Irish Merchant, *Belfast News Letter*, April 11, 1828.

this was more than offset by the friendly attitude of the gentry, whose attention had been directed to emigration by the committee. The effect may be seen from a comparison of two editorials in the *Belfast News Letter*. In September 1827 it had quoted with approval MacDougal's very hostile judgment:

The power and riches of a nation depend upon the number and industry of its people. Its prosperity cannot by any means be so essentially augmented as by the increase of an active and useful population, on which these effects chiefly depend; and a greater evil cannot arise than the loss of it, or its being obliged by emigration to swell the power of other states.[124]

A few weeks later in discussing the last report of the Committee, the paper, while still critical of government schemes, had swung round to a full admission of the value of emigration as a remedy for Irish distress.[125] Indeed, the foes of government aid were as a rule friendly to unrestricted emigration. Hume and Grattan strongly supported the voluntary system which Horton opposed; and Huskisson during his tenure at the Colonial Office in 1828 gave his assent to A. C. Buchanan's tract in favor of free emigration,[126] which cited the last report of the Committee as evidence of its value.[127] All this publicity was good for the voluntary movement, and may account in part for the increased amount of aid from Irish landlords noted after 1826.

Some of the evidence was directed to show that emigration to the United States was bad for the emigrant.[128]

[124] Sept. 14, 1827.   [125] Sept. 21, Oct. 5, 1827.
[126] Buchanan to Aylmer, May 7, 1831; C.O. 42/223.
[127] *Emigration practically considered*, p. 2.
[128] *Parl. Pap.* 1826-27, No. 550, pp. 69-73; evidence of Thomas Moody especially question 401: ''Do you know whether the state of the Irish who are in the United States is not the most miserable, and whether they are not the most wretched part of the population?''

A. C. Buchanan's tract, like his brother James' (the consul) work on penitentiaries, was written partly with this purpose in view. James Buchanan finally got permission to publish his work in 1829.[129] The propaganda was almost wholly ineffective, and a new land policy initiated in the colonies proved far more important. The ingenious Lieutenant-Governor of New Brunswick, Sir Howard Douglas, inaugurated a system by which laborers could obtain small tracts in payment for work in opening roads and clearing other lands for sale.[130] This was applied after 1828 on an enlarged scale in Upper Canada. Beginning in that year the new Lieutenant-Governor, Sir John Colborne, an old military friend of the Colonial Secretary, Sir George Murray, was allowed to spend £5000 a year in locating settlers, and he used it primarily in this way. During the rush years he actually spent a great deal more than this amount. The aristocratic Goderich, who succeeded Murray at the end of 1830, disapproved in principle of a policy which turned laborers into landowners, but he did not object when Colborne continued the practice each year as an emergency measure. It was not, in Colborne's eyes, a land policy, but the only way of giving enough labor to the poor to keep them from going to the United States.[131] We have already noted the effect upon the Irish. Lt. Colonel Cockburn, who was sent out in 1827 to investigate the land situation found no good tracts of any size available for settlement except in New Brunswick, to which the Irish were now going in diminished numbers;[132] and when the Whigs sent an investiga-

---

129 Buchanan to Bidwell, Jan. 20, 1829; and notation thereon. F.O. 5/250.
130 Cowan, p. 140.
131 *Parl. Pap.* 1833, No. 141, p. 23; Colborne to Goderich, Jan. 10, 1833; 1834, No. 616, p. 18; Goderich to Colborne, Oct. 31, 1831; and see Cowan, pp. 230-231.
132 *Parl. Pap.* 1828, No. 109.

tor upon a similar mission in 1830 conditions had not changed.[133]

While land reforms originated in America, the commercial interest in emigration still secured primary consideration in the British Isles. The experiment of unrestricted emigration in 1827 proved beyond question the necessity of some regulation, and when Horton on March 4, 1828 introduced a new passenger act he had the support of every member of his committee, including such pronounced free traders as Stanley and Sir James Graham.[134] The new requirements as to space and provisions, and the limitation of passengers to three for every four tons, were mild enough, but the bill met with determined opposition from shipping interests, chiefly Irish. Sir Henry Parnell led the attack on behalf of the Dublin Chamber of Commerce, ably assisted by James Grattan and Sir John Newport for the Irish, and by Warburton and Poulett Thomson for the English timber merchants.[135] Good luck, and good management by the Colonial Office which had charge of the bill, got it through in time to affect the latter part of the 1828 emigrant season. Thomson discovered that his clients were not opposed to the measure, and reversed his opinion.[136] Huskisson consulted shippers, and promised that only the minimum of protection to emigrants consistent with health would be provided;[137] and the third reading was moved and carried by his under-secretary, Lord Francis Gower, one day

[133] *Parl. Pap.* 1831-32, No. 334. Report of Mr. Richards respecting waste lands in the Canadas, and emigration.

[134] *2 Hansard* XVIII, 939-964.

[135] *Morning Herald*, Mar. 21, 1828. This significant debate of March 20 is omitted from Hansard. Parnell's speech betrays an ignorance of the passenger acts and their history only equalled by Huskisson's medical lore in insisting that typhus was not brought on the vessels by emigrants, but generated there by bad conditions.

[136] *Morning Herald*, Mar. 21, 1828.   [137] *Ibid.*

ahead of schedule at the end of a dull session when the House was almost empty.[138] The episode illustrates the difficulty of laying restrictions on trade in 1828, even when advocated by Huskisson, the leader of trade reform.

Huskisson meant his act to be effective, and he sent Lieutenant Low to Liverpool and A. C. Buchanan to Quebec as emigration agents. The latter made it one of his chief duties to spread unfavorable reports about the United States,[139] a policy the more necessary as the timber ships were beginning to find a good profit in taking a cargo of emigrants direct from Ireland to the United States, and going thence to Quebec in ballast for their return load of timber. But the difference between the American and British passenger acts was enough to ensure the continuance of cheaper emigration by way of Canada, and in the tension which preceded the settlement of the West India trade dispute it caused one more diplomatic exchange.

One of Adams' last acts as Secretary of State in 1825 was to raise the question of duties on passenger vessels between British American ports and the United States, a trade by that time of considerable importance.[140] Huskisson, to whom the matter was referred, was quite prepared for reciprocal free trade,[141] but between a dilatory Board of Trade and an intransigent Senate, which refused to

138 *Ibid.*, Mar. 26, 27, 1828.

139 Regularly in his annual reports, which were printed and much copied in England; e.g., *Parl. Pap.* 1836, No. 76, p. 10.

140 H. V. Addington (Chargé d'affaires at Washington) to Canning, Mar. 1, 1825; F.O. 5/197. Rush also raised the question with Huskisson direct.

141 Thomas Lack (for Huskisson) to Planta, Oct. 5, 1825; F.O. 5/208; and Baker to Canning, Apr. 23, 1825; F.O. 5/203. Baker had told Addington to deny Adams' claims, and he appealed against Huskisson's decision. The American interest was principally in the steamer trade in Passamaquoddy Bay, from New Brunswick to the Maine shore.

pass an administration bill on the subject, the question dragged on for two years, when it was amicably settled in April 1827.[142] The settlement was the first step in a rapid improvement of Anglo-American commercial relations. In August the commercial convention of 1815 was renewed indefinitely. Three years later the old and bitter colonial trade controversy was put to rest forever by governments, each of which had thrown overboard its ablest commercial advisers; and emigration ceased to be a subject of diplomacy for more than a generation.

As if to clean the slate completely for their successors, Peel and Wellington stripped the mantle of Catholic disabilities from Irish shoulders in 1829, revealing even to the most unwilling observer the horrid sores of famine, poverty, and brutal class strife beneath. The removal itself inflicted new wounds. The disfranchisement of 200,000 forty shilling free holders led to a fresh crop of evictions and to some emigration. The stupid insults to O'Connell identified his grievances with those of the people and gave him, who was at heart an aristocrat, ten years more of leadership.

Four years of successful combination had created a peasant power such as no English government had ever seen before; and four years of fatal delay had given to the sword of democracy a religious as well as an agrarian edge which was not to be turned by any partial concession. Peel alone of the ministers had the political capacity to cope with the situation, and as Home Secretary it was his province. He was in a hopeless position, however. Distrusted by his old reliable, Gregory, and the whole of the Protestant Ascendancy, dependent on a "prodigious

---

[142] There are several letters on the subject in 1826-27, ending with Vaughan to Canning, Apr. 30, 1827, enclosing a Treasury Circular of Apr. 28; F.O. 5/224. The Senate tried to use the passenger traffic as a club to get concessions in the colonial trade dispute.

bore" of a Viceroy,[143] and a cold and cautious Chief Secretary—Lord Francis Leveson Gower, whom O'Connell called the "shave beggar" of the ministry[144] and whom Creevy termed "that offensive, inefficient sprig of nobility,'"[145]—he could at best order the continuance of Spring Rice's administrative reforms, and talk about a new police and a system of universal education. In 1830 he was too much occupied with strikes and riots and the first rumblings of reform at home to pay much attention to Ireland; and even before the fall of the Wellington ministry the conduct of Irish questions was slipping into Whig hands. From that fall no leader save Peel rose again. The old Toryism of Eldon, Wellington and Bathurst was on its deathbed.

During the eighteen months that Parliamentary Reform was in the making, when a patchwork ministry was only held together by the diplomacy of Grey and the urgency of the one great measure, Ireland drifted rapidly into chaos. Most of its representatives at Westminster no longer came from the class or spoke the language understood by English country gentlemen. They allied themselves naturally with the Radicals, frequently in opposition to the government, which in its turn did everything possible to increase their hostility.

The Irish appointments split Ireland into three factions under three heads: Lord Anglesey, again appointed Viceroy with full control of patronage at first, "hair brained and conceited,'"[146] an ardent and uncritical reformer, an aristocrat with the military man's conception of order; Mr. Stanley, Chief-Secretary, ablest of

---

[143] The Duke of Northumberland; Greville, I, 160.

[144] I.e., its barber's apprentice; *Mr. Gregory's letter box*, p. 266.

[145] *Creevy Papers*, II, 160.

[146] O'Connell's expression, but supported by many others. *Correspondence of O'Connell*, I, 268.

the young Reformers, but a Tory at heart, relying on coercion and a very moderate measure of tithe reform; and
O'Connell, wayward and fluctuating as the seasons,
pressing forward or withdrawing in his campaign for
tithe reform and repeal of the Union according as government appeared more or less friendly, acting too often
on personal grounds, but with the vast power of the peasantry behind him—nay, frequently in front of him as the
anti-tithe movement flamed into civil war through the bitter years of 1831-1835. With the ministry at home simi-
larly divided on all Irish questions, with its detailed administration in Ireland transferred from the bigoted and
efficient Mr. Gregory to the bigoted and inexperienced
Sir William Gossett, effectual reform was practically impossible. While government was arguing on religious
grounds the tithe question, which was pre-eminently economic, mere lack of policy was helping to drive thousands
and hundreds of thousands to emigration.

The long battle over relief for Ireland now entered on
a new phase. From 1830 it was waged mainly between the
proponents of poor laws—James Grattan, Sadler, and
Bishop Doyle (who converted Anglesey and nominally,
though not actually, O'Connell)—and their enemies, the
majority of the Irish gentry. Doyle secured a new inquiry
into the state of the poor in 1830, but Spring Rice packed
the committee with opponents of the poor laws.[147] It investigated both reclamation of waste and emigration, and
recommended both. Some of its questions indicate that
the members favored a plan of stopping part of the pay
of laborers on public works to build up a fund with which
they could emigrate,[148] but wages were not high enough
for such a scheme and the idea did not appear in the final

[147] So charged by Sadler, and not denied, June 3, 1830; *2 Hansard*
XXIII.
[148] *Parl. Pap.* 1830, No. 589, p. 76.

report, which recommended only that the government provide facilities for emigration, to be financed either by the landlords or the emigrants themselves.[149] Unless the appointment of emigration agents could be called providing facilities, nothing was done in response to this suggestion, and when in 1831 £50,000 was voted for public works it was purely as a relief measure, and no mention was made of emigration.

In 1831 Lord Howick, under-secretary for the Colonies, introduced a bill, which he acknowledged to be Horton's, for parish-aided emigration from England, and urged the desirability of a similar measure for Ireland.[150] The suggestion was not taken up, and a year later Viscount Goderich stated that voluntary emigration had made any such action unnecessary.[151] It had, in fact, required steps of a different character for the protection of emigrants. Several commissioners of emigration were appointed, whose main business it was to disseminate information about shipping conditions and opportunities in British America, but after a year their work was again absorbed in the regular Colonial Office routine.[152] During their term of office, due to the heavy emigration of 1831, Goderich recommended to all the British American provinces the imposition of a head tax on emigrants. This was passed in Lower Canada, New Brunswick and Nova Scotia early in 1832.[153] The later struggles over this tax between the governor and Assembly of Lower Canada, and between Lower Canada and Upper Canada, are not a part of this

[149] Parl. Pap. 1830, No. 667, p. 49.

[150] 3 Hansard II, 875-880; Feb. 22, 1831.

[151] 3 Hansard IX, 1147; Feb. 2, 1832.

[152] See Parl. Pap. 1831-32, No. 724; Reports from the Commissioners of Emigration; and Hitchins, The Colonial Land and Emigration Commissioners.

[153] Parl. Pap. 1831-32, No. 730; Copy of Acts passed in British North America by which a Tax is to be levied on Emigrants.

study, but they illustrate the difficulties of any attempt to regulate emigration through British-American authority.[154] The continuance of extensive emigration, especially during the cholera year of 1832, led to the appointment of more emigration agents at British and Irish ports, including Dublin, Belfast, Cork and Limerick, and later Sligo and Londonderry. The principal efforts of the agents were directed toward protecting emigrants and enforcing the passenger acts, but they also gave out reports about the colonies, and such discouraging information about the United States as they could gather.

American authorities had an even greater incentive to protect the community from the new deluge of paupers, but in the United States the principal menace was not from Ireland. New York began in 1830 by tightening up the administration of the Act of 1824, reducing the head tax or commutation money from $2.50 to $1.00 but refusing to accept the decrepit on any terms.[155] To relieve the distress, Mr. Buchanan once more sent some settlers to Canada, emigration societies assisted others, and many were returned to Europe. The next year brought forth a treasury circular demanding a more rigid enforcement of the federal passenger act with full penalties for infringements. The news was promptly sent to England, where the Board of Trade, as in 1827, refused to give it any special publicity. With the outbreak of cholera in 1832-33, quarantine regulations everywhere became more strict, and the first concerted movement against alien paupers commenced. Maryland joined New York and Massachusetts in legislation for immigrants, requiring the usual bond

---

[154] The quarrel in Lower Canada was over control of the purse, and was more concerned with the quarantine station at Quebec than the tax itself. Upper Canada's protests were a part of a general campaign against interference with its trade, which was at the mercy of Lower Canada.

[155] Buchanan to Aberdeen, Oct. 12, 1830; F.O. 5/261.

against pauperism or $1.50 commutation. The religious riots of 1833 and ensuing years brought the Irish into unpleasant notoriety, and in 1836 the Massachusetts Legislature resolved in favor of a federal law on pauperism. In 1837 it passed a new passenger act requiring a $2 head tax on all immigrants. Boston city council took up the cry for federal action, New York City ordered an investigation of alien paupers,[156] and the question of the exclusion of all pauper immigrants was brought before the constitutional convention of Pennsylvania.[157] In 1838, the House of Representatives asked for an investigation,[158] but the diminished immigration of that year weakened the anti-alien feeling for a time, and nothing more was done until the rise of Native Americanism in 1844. By that time the powers of states to tax immigrants for any purpose had been challenged, though not yet found unconstitutional, and the center of interest shifted to other aspects of the alien problem.

The influx of Irish had far more effect on struggles over the franchise than on legislation against paupers. After the first considerable rush of 1817-19, fear of their votes weakened the movement toward manhood suffrage, which had been making great headway in the preceding decade; and New York and Massachusetts were the only states to lower their electoral qualifications in the twenties. The heavy migration after 1827 almost killed electoral reform in the northern states, and from that year until 1844 only one state, the frontier community of Michigan, granted complete equality.[159] Disfranchisement was rarely fully effective in practice. Even where it was,

---

[156] All summarized in Garis, *Immigration restriction*, pp. 36-39. The text of the Maryland Act is in Abbot, *Immigration*, p. 108.

[157] On this and the attempt to prevent immigrant voting, see M. G. Bartlett, *Chief phases of Pennsylvania politics in the Jacksonian period.*

[158] Garis, *op. cit.*, p. 40.

[159] K. H. Porter, *History of suffrage in the United States*, pp. 58-102.

it proved no bar to immigration, but its existence and the reasons for it help to explain the anti-Irish attitude of many American politicians during the period.

The increase of emigrants which brought about regulation also produced a significant change in the shipping interests. No longer divided as to the Canada trade, they protested as one body when Althorp (at Poulett Thomson's instigation) attempted to reduce the preference on Canadian timber in the budget of 1831.[160] The importance of the timber trade to emigration was no longer as in 1821-22 a mere incidental argument. It was a vital factor both in the House of Commons and the press,[161] and if the figures given in debate are correct the profits on the westbound voyage must have been very close to those on the return trip with timber.[162] The damaging defeat of the government on these duties, while traceable in part to partisan tactics, arose also from the defection of Whig shipowners, who thereby secured a continuance of their privileges for another ten years.

Defections were the order of the hour, and when the one burning question of reform was settled, it was only a matter of months before the ministry began to disintegrate. The Irish Reform Act failed to restore the forty shilling freehold, and the character of Irish representation remained practically unaltered except for the elimination of a few pocket boroughs. It had been democratic

[160] 3 *Hansard* II, 414-465, 494-520; III, 456-465; Feb. 11, 14, Mar. 15, 1831. Alderman Thompson presented a petition of the London shipowners against the change, and Frederick Shaw another from Dublin.

[161] *Ibid.*, speeches of Thompson, Shaw, and Schonswar of Hull. *Morning Herald*, Feb. 17, 18, 1831.

[162] 3 *Hansard* III, 559. Poulett Thomson gave the rate on timber as 40/ per ton. Even with passage as low as £2, the fares would amount to 75% of the timber freight, exclusive of the numerous perquisites through sale of provisions, liquor, etc. The cost of handling was very slight on both voyages— *Vide infra*, Ch. VII.

since 1829, but the increased strength of O'Connell's
Radical allies in Great Britain widened the breach with
the ministry, to which the two groups were now the official opposition. Some change in Irish administration was
urgent, and in 1833 Lord Goderich was shelved with the
Earldom of Ripon, and his place given to Stanley, whose
continuance in Ireland was impossible. Mr. E. J. Little-
ton, an honest and liberal man, but without previous experience, was sent in his place. The change, accompanied
by the substitution of Lord Wellesley for Anglesey, won
the temporary support of O'Connell; but there was no
real alteration in policy and in any case the agrarian agitation was beyond O'Connell's control. The year did not
pass without one important step, however. The usual debates over a poor law brought together in opposition the
extraordinary combination of Stanley, O'Connell, Hume,
and Peel, but the continued pressure of its protagonists,
aided by the powerful voices of Lord John Russell and
Lord Lansdowne, secured the appointment of an extra-
parliamentary commission.[168] Its report, delivered in
1836 after exhaustive investigations, became the storm
center of Irish policy for the next two years.

Before that storm broke, ministerial offices had changed
hands three times. The tenure of the Melbourne and Peel
ministries from July, 1834, to April, 1835, was too fleeting
and too precarious to permit serious departures from
earlier policy. Ireland pursued her unhappy course while
government struggled vainly to solve the tithes question.
Discussion of poor relief was choked off until the commission should report. Meanwhile, Canada also was drifting
toward rebellion, while the eyes of the Colonial Office
were fixed upon the woes of the West Indies. The trans-

[168] Impromptu debates in February and on April 2, 1833; *Morning Herald*. Peel suggested the commission during the discussion in April. It was
generally considered as a means of shelving the subject.

portation of emigrants came in for a little attention, giving the young member from Liverpool, Mr. William E.
Gladstone, an early opportunity to display his capacity
for management. By consulting in advance with the London Shipowners Society and the consulate general in
America, he was able to bring in a new passenger regulation bill embodying a compromise between their views,
and to secure its passage practically without opposition.[164] The new act[165] cut the carrying capacity of emigrant ships by twenty per cent, reducing it to three passengers to five tons and increasing the provision requirement. Gladstone also suggested the need of tests for
seaworthiness, but the time was not yet ripe. The final
guidance of the measure after the resignation of the Peel
ministry was left to Sir George Grey, who followed Gladstone as Colonial under-secretary, but its ablest exponent
was Goulburn who was nominally in opposition. There
was indeed no real criticism except from the Radicals,
Hume and Warburton.[166] Two factors contributed to the
quiescence of the timber merchants. They were engaged
in a bitter fight over the timber duties against the combined efforts of Whig and Tory Presidents of the Board
of Trade, and they wanted the full support of public opinion. From 1835, when a Select Committee on the timber
trade was appointed, to 1842, when the merchants met
their first defeat, their cause was merged in the general
opposition to free trade, and the emigration argument
dropped into the background. At the same time, their interest in emigration was decreasing, partly because of the
growth of Liverpool-New York emigration in regular
packets, partly because of their interest in a new business
development by which timber was carried from the Baltic

---

[164] *3 Hansard* XXVI; Mar. 19, 1835. The bill had been requested by the
Quebec Emigrant Society.

[165] *5 and 6 William IV*, c. 56.   [166] *3 Hansard* XXVI, June 17, 1835.

to Canada and thence to the British Isles, leaving no room for passengers.[167]

The royal assent to the new act coincided closely in point of time with the first report of the Poor Inquiry Commission, which rang up the curtain on the last act of the relief-by-emigration drama. The political setting, though not altogether idyllic, was as favorable as it would ever be to Irish reforms. The solid Whig backdrop was perhaps a trifle insecure, as it had shown itself on commercial questions, but it was strengthened by the Radical and Irish wings, all neatly drawn together by the Lichfield House compact which had tripped up Sir Robert Peel in April 1835. The weakest part of the company upon the boards was the trio of aging Canningites who occupied the star positions—the indecisive Grant, Palmerston the irrepressible, and the Prime Minister himself. But the first two were not involved in Irish policies and Melbourne had learned eight years before that Ireland is best governed from Dublin and not from London. His Irish government was a tower of strength. Lord John Russell at the Home Office, Morpeth[168] the Chief Secretary, and Lord Mulgrave the Viceroy,[169] were all able and liberal men; and with three Irish colleagues, Lord Lansdowne, Duncannon,[170] and Spring Rice, in the cabinet, and two more, Henry Parnell and Sir John Newport, in office, they were well fortified on all Irish business. Duncannon, being closest to O'Connell, was especially useful, and for six years the agitator gave them violent and not always helpful support. Behind the scenes, and more effective perhaps than any of the figures on the stage,

[167] 3 *Hansard* XXVII, 214; XXXII, 139-155; Mar. 24, 1835; Feb. 25, 1836.

[168] George W. Howard became Earl of Carlisle, 1848; grandson of the Duke of Devonshire.

[169] Created Viscount Normanby in 1839.

[170] J. W. Ponsonby, who succeeded as fourth Earl of Bessborough in 1844.

was the brilliant young Scottish engineer, Thomas Drummond, who had obtained the position of under-secretary through his patron, Earl Spencer.[171] Drummond toiled at the relief of Ireland for five years, and died at his post.

These men for a period of six years gave to Ireland what it most craved—a sense of just dealing. Even agrarian turbulence, though it did not cease, was checked by opposition from among the peasants themselves.[172] Lady Morgan, who had been complaining in September 1835 that things were as bad as ever,[173] wrote a month later that the new crown officers (Drummond, Perrin, and O'Loghlen) were ". . . iron bound men, all their muscles rigid, like men who, living out of society, have lost the play and movement of gesture which men of the world exhibit from long practice; but what uncompromising minds and characters! What honest men! How much and how long they have been wanted!"[174] Six years later she could say, with more good feeling than judgment: "The days of sentimental and patriotic novels had passed away—Ireland had no serious wrongs to redress."[175] The triumphs of the government were primarily administrative, and included the revision of legal procedure and the organization of the Royal Irish Constabulary; but in the field of legislation it had three solid achievements to its credit. In order of importance these were the Municipal Reform Act of 1840, the settlement of the tithe question, and, for better or for worse, the Irish Poor Law of 1838.

[171] Viscount Althorp succeeded his father in 1834. The necessity of his leaving the Exchequer was the cause of the fall of the first Melbourne ministry. His recommendation of Drummond was a violation of his rule not to use influence, and was prompted by his experience of Drummond's unusual capacity in making all the preliminary surveys for the Reform Bill of 1832. See Le Marchant, *Memoir of John Charles Viscount Althorp*, p. 539.

[172] O'Brien, *Drummond*, pp. 249-250.

[173] *Memoirs*, II, 407.   [174] *Ibid.*, p. 409.

[175] *Ibid.*, p. 466.

The commission appointed under Melbourne as Home Secretary in 1833 reported in 1835 and 1836 to the government of which he was Prime Minister. It had been peculiarly Lansdowne's and Russell's appointment. Lansdowne applied to Spring Rice, who consulted his friend Nassau Senior, the ablest of the English Poor Law Commissioners. Senior suggested his intimate and successor in the chair of Political Economy at Oxford, Richard Whately, who had been made Archbishop of Dublin in 1831. Whately had already demonstrated his ability to coöperate with the Roman Catholic Archbishop, Daniel Murray, on the work of national education, and both men were put on the Poor Inquiry, with Whately as chairman.[176] The assistant commissioners included George Cornewall Lewis,[177] and Lansdowne later added J. E. Bicheno,[178] a man of considerable ability. Most of the commissioners were either inactive or colorless, however, and the conclusions and recommendations were generally believed to be the work of Whately and of the Irish Remembrancer, A. J. Blake.[179]

From the start, the dice were loaded in favor of some scheme of emigration. Whately had advocated it in the *Quarterly* as early as 1820,[180] and Horton had won most of the Irish landlords; but the Archbishop soon discovered that he had to meet a decided predilection at the Home Office for a system modeled on the new English law with

[176] They continued to coöperate in the new work. Torrens, *Melbourne*, I, 433. Murray was known to be friendly to the Whigs—*Correspondence of Daniel O'Connell*, I, 388.

[177] Later minister under Russell and Palmerston; son of T. Frankland Lewis.

[178] Torrens, *Melbourne*, II, 22.

[179] *Ibid.*, pp. 243-244. Blake was a survivor from the older administrations of Ireland, said to be particularly influential with Lords Wellesley and Plunket. Greville, *Memoirs*, I, 153; III, 31.

[180] *Quarterly Review*, XXIII, 373-400; and see his letters to Senior and Denman in 1832. Whately, *Life of Whately*, I, 150, 176.

workhouses and no outdoor relief—under which heading emigration fell.[181] In the face of the known opinion of Lord John Russell, the committee pointed out that the English Poor Law was inapplicable in Ireland, and that any general system of outdoor relief there was impossible. It said:

We consider it due to the whole community, and to the laboring class in particular, that such of the able bodied as may still be unable to find free and profitable employment in Ireland should be secured support only through emigration, or as a preliminary to it. In saying this, we mean that those who desire to emigrate should be furnished with the means of doing so in safety, and with intermediate support when they stand in need of it, at emigration depots. It is thus and thus only that the market of labour in Ireland can be relieved from the weight that is now upon it, or the labourer be raised from his present prostrate state.[182]

Aid to emigration was not, of course, their only proposal, and they later qualified these statements in the following sentence: "We must here observe that we do not look to emigration as an object to be permanently pursued on any extensive scale, nor by any means as the main relief for the evils of Ireland, but we do look to it for the present as an auxiliary essential to a commencing course of amelioration."[183] The committee definitely recommended that half the expense of emigration be met from imperial funds, and the other half be raised in part from Irish Poor Rates, in part from the landlords of emigrants, or their former landlords, if they had been evicted within the preceding twelve months. A new board of emigration commissioners to supervise the scheme was to have power to borrow from the imperial government and

---

[181] Whately, *Life of Whately*, I, 199; *Early correspondence of Lord John Russell*, II, 43. (His Memorandum on Ireland, Oct. 18, 1833.)

[182] *Parl. Pap.* 1836, No. 43, p. 8.   [183] *Parl. Pap.* 1835, No. 573, p. 17.

was to provide the transportation and look after the settlement of the emigrants. Emigration depots were to be formed to lodge those who could not support themselves before sailing. This was the relief proposed for all those capable of labor, for orphans, and for foundlings; only those physically incapacitated were to have workhouse support in Ireland. The amount which might be raised for other purposes was limited by the committee's bill, but that which could be spent on emigration was unlimited. Emigration was clearly the foundation stone of the committee's plan.[184]

Unable to carry even the whole commission with him,[185] Whately needed every ounce of parliamentary support he could get. A little preliminary skirmishing in the spring of 1836 under the leadership of Smith O'Brien and G. Poulett Scrope, Russell's fellow member for Stroud, and brother of the President of the Board of Trade, lined up a few supporters for the emigration plan, but there were dangerous signs of weakness in the party.[186] Whately's uncompromising stand on the tithe question and O'Connell's hostility weakened his influence. Senior suggested that he seek an English bishopric, but Whately refused to retreat.[187] The final report was well received in Ireland, but unfortunately Morpeth neither befriended nor opposed it,[188] and Drummond was busy on his own pet scheme of national railways. The old controversy between emigration and public works had cropped up again in 1835 in an ill-informed report of a committee on public

[184] *Parl. Pap.* 1836, No. 43, pp. 25-29.

[185] *Parl. Pap.* 1836, Commons No. 41.

[186] *3 Hansard* XXXI, 429; XXXIII, 590-607; Feb. 15, May 4, 1836.

[187] Whately, *Life of Whately*, I, 365.

[188] He told Lady Morgan that he was pursued by "another awful phantom, styled poor laws," in which he had little interest. Morgan, *Memoirs*, II, 414.

works,[189] and though the advocates of the two plans now
united in fighting English antipathy to any expensive
projects there was never real coöperation. The report ran
into unconquerable prejudices in high places. Melbourne
found it "impractical,"[190] Peel, "absurd."[191] Lord Holland was committed against any costly schemes.[192] Russell, having first postponed parliamentary consideration
of it,[193] sent it to Senior and Cornewall Lewis for criticisms. They made several practical objections, of which
the two most important were that paupers in the emigration depots could not be forced to emigrate, and that the
system would be extensively used by people able to pay
their own passage. Russell needed a clear-cut alternative
on which to base his opposition.[194] He had a minority report of the committee attacking some of its other proposals which could be used for undermining its authority
in general;[195] but the principal item in his strategy (sug-

[189] *Parl. Pap.* 1835, No. 573. It stated that emigration reduced the supply
of labor and injured the revenue, citing in proof the relative prosperity of
Down and Wexford as against Mayo, Clare and Galway, under the misap-
prehension that the latter were greater sources of emigration.

[190] Torrens, *Melbourne*, II, 243-244. Melbourne had a strong antipathy to
Whately, not unnatural between the man-about-town and the lecturer on
moral philosophy. See his letter to Russell, Sept. 19, 1837; *Early correspondence of Lord John Russell*, II, 203.

[191] Peel to Goulburn, Sept. 12, 1836; Parker, *Peel*, II, 326.

[192] Holland to Cloncurry, June 17, 1834; V. Lawless (Lord Cloncurry),
Personal recollections, pp. 389-390. Cloncurry, an eccentric patriot, usually
friendly with O'Connell, wanted poor laws to reduce the value of land and
so force the aristocracy to join in reform.

[193] *3 Hansard* XXXIII, 606; May 4, 1836.

[194] *Parl. Pap.* 1837, LI. *Letter from Nassau W. Senior on the Third Report from the Commissioners*, and *Remarks on the Third Report by George
Cornewall Lewis*. Russell later said he considered their arguments decisive—
3 Hansard LXXXV, 407; Apr. 1, 1846. Senior was really in favor of emigration; see his *Journals, conversations and essays relating to Ireland*, I,
xiii, 295.

[195] So used in Lynch, *Address to the electors of Galway on the poor law
bill for Ireland*, pp. 82-85.

gested by Cornewall Lewis)[196] was to send to Ireland one of the English Poor Law Commissioners, George Nicholls. The significance of this move was later stated by Lynch of Galway: "You will observe that the Poor Inquiry Commissioners proposed a general emigration and a national rate in aid of it. This was their compulsory relief for the destitute able bodied classes; and from this proposition arose the necessity of sending Mr. Nicholls to Ireland.'"[197]

Nicholls was to find reasons against the emigration scheme, and to propose an alternative plan. He worked on the principle of assimilating his proposals as closely as possible to the model of the English Poor Law, and recommended the usual workhouse system of relief with some aid to migratory labor in getting to and from employment, with assistance toward emigration only as a last resort.[198] In order to win Irish approval he dwelt on the evidence that conditions in Ireland were improving, and drew from it the unwarrantable conclusion that unemployment was only temporary. Landlords were offered a sop in the suggestion that government should repay one-half the amount recently spent by any of them in sending emigrants to America.[199]

While Nicholls was on his six-weeks tour collecting facts to bolster up his preconceived opinions, Spring Rice was at his home in Limerick consulting with his friends on means of carrying out the commission's recommendations; but fate, in the shape of the impending panic of 1837, intervened to send him scurrying back to his office at the Exchequer,[200] from which he emerged two years

[196] Erroneously attributed in the *Dictionary of National Biography* to Frankland Lewis; Torrens, *Melbourne*, II, 243, gives the correct account.

[197] *Address to the electors of Galway*, p. 30.

[198] *Parl. Pap.* 1837, LI; *Report of George Nicholls, Esq., on Poor Laws for Ireland*.

[199] *Ibid.*, p. 32.   [200] Torrens, *Melbourne*, II, 208.

later with a peerage[201] and his reputation as a statesman irretrievably damaged. Neither he nor Lansdowne took any active part in the poor law debates, probably because they disapproved of Russell's measures. Russell, having secured from Lewis an admirable and, as he later admitted, a decisive argument for the limited workhouse system based on Nicholl's report, used it with telling effect in introducing his bill on February 13, 1837. His best point, however, and one which was unanswerable, was that the Colonies, which were already suspicious of paupers,[202] would be in an uproar over emigration on such a scale and of such persons. Howick was anxious, also, to dissociate any idea of aid to emigration from the Poor Law, lest it give rise to false hopes.[203] All mention of emigration was, therefore, omitted from the bill, though Russell admitted that later on some measure might be desirable. The debates which followed cut across all party lines. Peel gave his support to Russell; O'Connell and his bitter enemy Frederick Shaw, the Recorder of Dublin, voted together.[204] In the Lords, Lansdowne and Fitzgerald, Peel's old colleague, agreed that wide-spread emigration was necessary.[205] Almost all the Irish members were in favor of emigration, and O'Connell represented their opinion more than his own when he said: "Why not take the waste lands of Canada? Why not dispose of them in such a way as to promote an effectual emigration? . . . It would enrich the Canadian people by sending out to them great numbers of healthy, able-bodied labourers. There would be something in that; but you do not talk

201 As Lord Monteagle.

202 3 *Hansard* XXXVI, 459-476; Feb. 13, 1837.

203 *Ibid.*, p. 496.

204 3 *Hansard* XXXVI, 476-518; XXXVIII, 360-441; Feb. 13, Apr. 28, 1837.

205 3 *Hansard* XXXVIII, 1444-47; June 13, 1837. Vesey Fitzgerald had been raised to the peerage as Lord Fitzgerald and Vesey (or Vesci).

of doing it.'"[206] He was using the arguments of Wakefield, which neither Russell nor any member of the Government chose to combat openly, though the time had passed when government could take the waste lands of Canada.

The death of William IV put an end to the session while the bill was still in committee and revived the opportunity for controversy; but except for Mr. Lynch's address at Galway and a speech of Thomas Wyse at Waterford it was passed over as an election issue in favor of the more exciting tithe question, or the personality of Mr. O'Connell. Agitation continued under the surface among the adherents of the ministry—Whately trying to get more cordial support from Senior,[207] Revans, secretary of the Commission, intriguing for a place in the good graces of Russell, who now ignored the Archbishop,[208] and Drummond accusing Spring Rice of protecting the landlords' pocketbook at the expense of the poor.[209] A more open campaign was carried on by the Wakefield colonization group under the leadership of Colonel Torrens.[210] Meanwhile, Mr. Nicholls visited Ireland for another six weeks and returned with an argument for an emigration provision copied from the English poor law. On this advice, and under the pressure of a House in which the Whig majority was now wholly Irish, Lord John Russell introduced a clause in his new bill of December 1, 1837, permitting the majority of rate-payers—votes being weighted according to the amount of rates

206 April 28, 1837, in *3 Hansard* XXXVIII, p. 370.

207 Whately, *Life of Whately*, I, 397-402.

208 *Ibid.*, pp. 398, 403.

209 Drummond to Spring Rice, Aug. 1, 1837; R. B. O'Brien, *Thomas Drummond*, pp. 257-259.

210 See Torrens, *Letter to Lord John Russell on Poor Laws in Ireland*. The Wakefield group, which had gone to pieces after its attack on Horton in 1831, was reorganized in this year. Wakefield was an old school-fellow of Spring Rice.

paid—in any electoral district to devote as much as one shilling in the pound of their assessment to assist emigration to British colonies.[211] This provision, so far from placating O'Connell, was denounced by him and others as ineffective for relief, and as giving a dangerous power to landlords to assist the emigration of their tenants at the expense of others,[212] and was one of several excuses for a general campaign against the bill. On the other hand, the clause had the support of two important Catholic leaders, Thomas Wyse and Smith O'Brien,[213] and the ministerial Irish were willing to accept it in default of anything better. When the clause came up in committee Russell moved to restrict still further the power of aiding emigration,[214] though he and Morpeth recognized that little use would be made of it. It was intended simply as a concession to Irish feeling, and, as Morpeth frankly avowed, the one item at all likely to be popular.[215] Its failure in that respect is shown by the final division on the bill, in which the Irish voted 35 to 22 against it—only nine county members and no Ulsterman supporting it. Many regular government supporters stayed away rather than vote for it.[216]

The bill was still in the Lords in June, 1838, when Spring Rice held an Irish dinner for the lately returned Governor of Ceylon, Sir Robert Wilmot Horton, to which he invited the Lord Lieutenant, Lord Palmerston, and other influential gentry,[217] but nothing came of it except a suggestion by Lord Fitzgerald that the administration should direct its particular attention to emigration.[218] So

211 *1 and 2 Victoria*, c. 56, section 51.
212 *3 Hansard* XL, 949; Feb. 9, 1838.
213 *Ibid.*, p. 979, and XLI, 378.
214 *3 Hansard* XLI, 378; Mar. 2, 1838.   215 *Ibid.*, p. 379.
216 *3 Hansard* XLII; Apr. 30, 1838. O'Connell was among the absent.
217 J. C. Hobhouse, Lord Broughton, *Recollections*, V, 136.
218 *3 Hansard* XLIII, 564; June 7, 1838.

much for Horton's grand schemes! Had the passage of
the bill been a little slower, or the Railway Commission a
little faster, emigration would have had the active support of Thomas Drummond and his colleague Sir John
Burgoyne, chairman of the Irish Board of Works. Their
report, delivered five days after the royal assent to the
Poor Law, strongly recommended emigration.[219] The
Railway Report has come to be recognized as one of the
ablest documents on Irish policy, but it is doubtful
whether Drummond's aid would have made much difference at the time, since he was already the focus of all the
Tory hatred of the new regime in Ireland.

The government's decision in preferring English
theory to Irish demands is open to criticism, but the ministry was in an awkward position. It had no stable majority, and was striving constantly to conciliate both
English and Irish opinion, which were on many points
decidedly antagonistic. The workhouse system proved
utterly inadequate to cope with the famine, but so would
any ordinary form of relief. It is a more serious charge
that the burden of poor rates helped to drag down all
classes, and gave only temporary relief in return. But the
Irish alternatives were impossible. Extensive uncon-
trolled emigration would have swamped the colonies, as
it very nearly did without government aid, and colonization could only be carried on by the provincial governments through the use of their lands, or by the imperial
government at an expense which no ministry would have
dared to incur. On the face of it, effective relief for Ireland seemed an insoluble problem, and the man who had
most power to unite the Irish and ministerial points of
view made no helpful suggestions. O'Connell was a
mighty champion of Irish liberties, but he was not an

[219] O'Brien, *Drummond*, pp. 289-311.

originator of new ideas. His genius was wholly political, and he was hampered by the traditional landlords' conception of Irish economic needs, so that in questions such as poor relief, the government was left perforce to work out its own salvation.[220]

The Irish poor bill was still in its first stages when news arrived from Canada that the long smouldering discontent had at length flamed up in open rebellion. One result was to stop the emigration of 1838, another was to emphasize the impossibility of relieving Ireland by taking the Crown Lands of Canada. But the most important outcome was the appointment in March of the Durham Commission to report on conditions in British America. Lord Durham took with him as commissioner of Crown Lands and Emigration, Charles Buller, whom Wakefield described as his *alter ego,* and Wakefield himself. These three were the joint authors of the Durham Report, presented in 1839.[221] In its attitude toward emigration, the Report is almost a colonization tract. Its conclusion after summing up existing conditions is as follows:

It is far from my purpose, in laying these facts before Your Majesty, to discourage emigration to Your North American colonies. On the contrary, I am satisfied that the chief value of these colonies to the mother country consists in their presenting a field where millions even, of those who are distressed at home might be established in plenty and happiness. All the gentlemen whose evidence I have last quoted, are warm advocates of systematic emigration. I object, along with them, only to such emigration as

220 O'Connell sometimes opposed reforms because they would delay Repeal, and the only defence of his policy rests on the superior importance of that measure to all other forms of relief. See Lecky's very fair and friendly essay in *Leaders of public opinion in Ireland,* especially p. 300 ff. on the Poor Laws.

221 James Collins' introduction to Wakefield's *A view of the art of colonization,* p. xiv.

now takes place—without forethought, preparation, method or system of any kind.[222]

The specific recommendation from this conclusion was the usual one for colonization to be supported by the sale of waste lands.

The Report made five principal charges in relation to emigration as it then existed. The first was that political troubles were putting a stop to it.[223] This was obviously true as it applied to 1838, but by taking the figures for 1832, 1837, and 1838, and ignoring the other years, the report gave an impression of continuous and lasting decline in numbers, which was altogether false. This decline, and the emigrants' antipathy to Canada deduced from it, were used as arguments for discouraging all voluntary emigration until the future government of Canada should be finally settled.[224] The second point, a sound and useful criticism, was that lack of political privileges, particularly in Upper Canada, was a deterrent to emigration, and a cause of reëmigration to the United States.[225] Here as elsewhere the Report was looking mainly to the retention of the better class of immigrant. We have seen that the Irish were not particularly deterred from coming to Canada, but they certainly did reëmigrate. The third statement, that an unsatisfactory land policy caused emigration to the United States, somewhat over-emphasized the importance of that cause, but was in itself a good point, and wisely directed attention to the evils of extensive grants to land companies and private individuals, which retarded the development of the country.[226]

---

[222] Lord Durham's *Report on the affairs of British North America* (Ed. C. P. Lucas), II, 259. Hereafter cited as Durham Report.

[223] II, 57.   [224] II, 330.

[225] II, 170-171; mainly exclusion from higher office. The suffrage was democratic.

[226] II, 216-218.

These charges were made in a discussion of other affairs, but the remaining two were directly concerned with emigration. The inadequacy and lax enforcement of the passenger acts was described in great detail, and reform advocated, though without definite suggestions.[227] One cannot escape the impression that the space given to the topic was in part designed to discourage voluntary emigration; and the same motive is apparent in the last point, of which the treatment is far less just. This was the insistence that emigrants after landing were entirely unregulated or unassisted, and were the cause of endless confusion, besides requiring support from charity every winter.[228] The Report states that Buchanan at Quebec had no instructions and no effective power,[229] and ignores in this section the agents in Upper Canada who provided labor for emigrants and looked after their transportation in that province. It also states that the main work of the Quebec and Montreal emigrant societies was to forward emigrants toward the United States, where they would get employment and proper attention.[230] The object of the evidence thus introduced and of the strictures on the voluntary system was to prove the necessity for settlement by colonization.

Quite apart from its merits or demerits, the Report was sure to encounter violent opposition. Durham and Buller were notorious Radicals; Wakefield something worse, in the eyes of Tory and Whig alike. Durham's conduct in Canada had laid him open to Brougham's bitterest invective. Wakefield was known to be careful of his

---

[227] II, 242-253.   [228] II, 253-259.

[229] A. C. Buchanan went to England in 1836 because of ill health, and was succeeded by his nephew, A. C. Buchanan, Jr., son of the consul at New York. The new agent was excusing himself for negligence in some matters. The annual reports show that he had considerable power.

[230] Obviously sending emigrants to Upper Canada was forwarding them toward the United States.

own interests, and was at this time the agent of an important Canadian land company.[231] So far as their main recommendation was concerned, it was already settled that the control of provincial lands belonged to the provincial government, and while British ministers were willing to adopt colonization if the Canadians wanted it, they would not take it up on any other terms. The issue was raised again in connection with Irish emigration by Smith O'Brien in 1840 and met the same objections.[232] The colonization group had to content itself with trying out its policies in Australia, where it was conducting some rather unsuccessful experiments at this time. These had practically no bearing on Irish emigration in our period, since only a few thousands were taken before 1845.

Minor points were assured of the same consideration they had been receiving all along. General dissatisfaction drove Lord Glenelg from the Colonial Office in 1839. He was succeeded in the shuffling of offices by Lord John Russell; but effective control of details remained with the permanent Under-secretary, Sir James Stephen, whom the Wakefield group hated. Stephen had been interested in 1837 in securing passage for emigrants at a fixed sum,[233] but neither he nor Elliot, the Agent General for emigration, wished for any considerable extension of government assistance. Russell had increased the funds for aid in Canada, but was set against help at an earlier stage. He also sanctioned the payment by the imperial government of the Canadian head-tax for such emigrants

[231] There is an extensive literature on the Report. Sir Charles Lucas' comments (*Durham Report*, I, Introduction; III, Notes) are still the most valuable. Wakefield's connection with the Beauharnois property (*infra* p. 325) seems to have escaped notice.

[232] *3 Hansard* LIV, 837-886; June 2, 1840.

[233] *The first Sir James Stephen*, p. 56; and see the defense of his policy by Knaplund, *Mr. Oversecretary Stephen*, in *Journal of Modern History*, I, 40-66.

as were approved by the emigration agents—a policy discontinued in 1842.[234] He was fortunate in having in Canada Sir John Colborne, who had long been aiding immigrant laborers in Upper Canada, and was now acting as Governor General until a new man could be sent out.[235] There was some talk of Wilmot Horton, but Melbourne dismissed him as "a particularly silly fellow,"[236] and the choice ultimately fell on the President of the Board of Trade, Poulett Thomson, now created Lord Sydenham— a gentleman with no previous interest in emigration. He sent an agent to London in 1841 to prove that colonial aid to emigration was impossible. The agent himself turned colonizer, but it did not alter the attitude of the provincial government.[237] Sydenham's appointment caused the resignation of Lord Howick, the only cabinet minister who had a personal acquaintance with emigration policy; but the loss was partly balanced by the creation in 1840 of a colonial Land and Emigration Board. This was one of the outcomes of the Durham Report, though the most active member of the new board, T. F. Elliot, the former Agent General for emigration, had been severely criticised in the report. The Board continued Elliot's policy of opposing aid to emigration,[238] but modified it to some extent in 1840 by asking for a grant of £50,000 to help pay the passages of poor emigrants,[239]—a request refused by Russell—and by trying to enlist the coöperation of the land companies. The answers of the companies

[234] *Parl. Pap.* 1841, No. 338, p. 36; Russell to Sydenham, May 3, 1841; *Parl. Pap.* 1842, No. 301, p. 267; Stanley to Bagot, Feb. 3, 1842.

[235] G. C. M. Smith, *Life of John Colborne*, pp. 262, 309.

[236] Torrens, *Melbourne*, II, 376.

[237] *Parl. Pap.* 1842, No. 301, pp. 241-245; especially T. W. C. Murdoch to Rolph (the agent), Apr. 3, 1841.

[238] *Parl. Pap.* 1840, No. 613; Correspondence relative to the Colonial Land and Emigration Board, p. 56.

[239] *Ibid.*, p. 65; Board to Stephen, Apr. 25, 1840.

showed the folly of attempting to aid emigration through any such scheme.[240] The Canada Land Company was quite willing that government should send emigrants to them, but refused to contribute. The British American Land Company offered aid in the form of a loan to the provincial government to be secured on its land and timber revenue. This plan guaranteed the company interest at full rate, the benefit of any new settlement which might be made, and the certainty that the government lands which might compete with its own would be sold, and not given to emigrants.[241] The third company, the North American Colonial Association of Ireland, interesting to us because of its avowed objects, was willing to use the proceeds of land sales to aid emigration; but in 1844, after it had been in existence ten years, it had not sent out a single emigrant. Like the others it was primarily a speculative concern, and Wakefield as its agent got a government canal put through the Beauharnois property which it had bought in 1839.[242]

Lord John Russell's colonial policy was one of the few strong features of the last days of the Melbourne ministry, and when he was replaced in 1841 by Lord Stanley there was no marked departure. Rumors of a government emigration scheme were afloat in the winter of 1841-42, but Stanley promptly scotched them at the opening of parliament in February.[243] The hard times of 1842-43 brought forth the usual appeal for aid, worked up by the indefatigable Buller and supported by Howick, but it was crushed under the combined weight of Stanley and Russell with the effective support of Sir Howard Doug-

---

[240] *Ibid.*, pp. 58-59.

[241] *Parl. Pap.* 1841, No. 49; *Correspondence relative to the memorial from the British American Land Company.*

[242] *Report of an extraordinary meeting of shareholders of the North American Colonial Association of Ireland* (1844).

[243] *3 Hansard* LX, 57, 76-91; Feb. 3 and 4, 1842.

las, M.P. for Liverpool and ex-governor of New Brunswick.[244] Colborne and Sydenham had done much for
emigrants by providing labor on public works, and Sir
Charles Bagot carried on the policy, but the tremendous
influx of 1841-42 caused him to appeal to Stanley to
discourage men of the laboring class.[245]

Bagot had been appointed partly because of his past
record at Washington. There was as much need of cautious and friendly policy to avoid war with America in
1841 as there had been in 1815. Among many more serious causes of irritation in the United States, was the
growing resentment at the dumping of paupers in American ports by British parishes. At the same time the Irish-
Americans, normally ready to join in any cry against England, were themselves antagonized by the strong anti-alien
and anti-Catholic movement. Both these passions played
into the hands of a colonial official less judicious than
Bagot, namely Sir John Colebrooke, the governor of New
Brunswick. An ardent enthusiast for the expansion of his
province, he wrote in August, 1841, to consuls Buchanan
at New York and Grattan at Boston, both of whom were
Irishmen, for as much unfavorable information about the
United States as they could give him, to be used as propaganda by the emigration agent and societies at St.
John.[246] They sent back replies which the governor forwarded to the emigration commissioners, and their information was included in a pamphlet for emigrants to

[244] *3 Hansard* LXVIII, 484-595; Apr. 6, 1843. Douglas showed that it
was too late for any settlement scheme in Canada. Stanley later applied to
Peel for help against Buller, and the Prime Minister suggested giving publicity to existing arrangements for emigration, while showing disapproval
of all costly plans. See Knaplund, *Some letters of Peel and Stanley on
Canadian problems,* in Canadian Historical Review, Mar., 1931, pp. 53-54.

[245] *Parl. Pap.* 1842, No. 373, p. 4; Bagot to Stanley, Feb. 17, 1842.

[246] *Parl. Pap.* 1842, No. 301, p. 313; Colebrooke to Grattan, Aug. 6, 1841.

British America.[247] Colebrooke also appointed agents at New York and Boston, who with the coöperation of emigrant societies shipped some British subjects to Jamaica, and some back to Ireland.[248] Thirty-four other Irishmen were settled on the road from St. John to St. Andrews, although it was then the middle of winter. This was a part of Colebrooke's more general plan for re-exportation of destitute emigrants from the United States to New Brunswick. When news of these doings reached London, Sir James Stephen pointed out the impropriety of the agents at United States ports, and opposed the re-export scheme;[249] but Stanley wrote Colebrooke that he did not object to that provided it were financed by the provincial government, and work secured there.[250] The plan was dangerous, as Planta had pointed out to Buchanan long before, and the decision was soon reversed. In 1842, Stanley and the commissioners of emigration came out definitely against the scheme and Colebrooke was forced to drop it.[251] He did however, secure a grant of £2,000 from the provincial legislature for the employment of emigrants, and he recommended to the Colonial Office a plan for settling the poor in villages near established centers, which was later taken up by Earl Grey.[252] The false hopes engendered by his activities, combined with really bad reports from the United States, caused a large number of the already too numerous emigrants of 1842 to stay in New Brunswick, where banks, farmers, and timber merchants were all in great distress. The re-

247 *Ibid.*, p. 229; for their letters in full, pp. 314-315.

248 *Ibid.*, p. 320; and *Parl. Pap.* 1843, No. 391, p. 188; Grattan to Aberdeen, Jan. 28, 1843.

249 *Parl. Pap.* 1842, No. 301, pp. 321, 315-316; Stephen to the Commissioners of Emigration, Oct. 8, 1841.

250 *Ibid.*, p. 319; Stanley to Colebrooke, Dec. 5, 1841.

251 *Ibid.*, pp. 324-325.

252 In 1845. Lord Howick succeeded his more celebrated father in 1844.

sult was that at the end of the season Stanley called the governor severely to account and gave these orders:

> I must for the future absolutely prohibit any inducement being held out on the part of the government to destitute persons to enter the province from any part of the United States. . . . The same prohibition of course applies equally to dissuading any persons from quitting the province as to inviting them to enter it. The summary of my advice to you is, to limit the intervention of government as much as possible to obtaining and diffusing correct information on all points which may be useful to enable the immigrant to decide upon his own courses; to carry this to as great an extent as the means within your reach will allow; but steadily to set your face against all artificial stimulus, by loans or otherwise, to the employment of labour, and to restrict within the narrowest possible limits all direct interference, and especially all pecuniary aid.[253]

Even after this Colebrooke remained active, and strong pressure from him obtained sanction for an experiment in land grants in 1845.[254] The results of this do not belong to our period, and the story of colonial policy ends, as it began, with the refusal to interfere actively in emigration.

The emigrant trade did not escape without one more parliamentary conflict before its conduct during the famine brought it unpleasantly to the notice of the whole world. It submitted without protest to the new and slightly more stringent passenger regulations in 1842,[255] but it could afford such changes. The invasion of the sacred timber duties, threatened by the Whigs in 1841, and carried triumphantly by Peel in 1842, was another

---

[253] *Parl. Pap.* 1843, No. 291, p. 139; Sept. 15, 1842.

[254] *Parl. Pap.* 1845, No. 617; p. 11; Fifth general report of the Colonial Land and Emigration Commissioners.

[255] *5 and 6 Victoria,* c. 107. *3 Hansard* LX-LXII, *passim;* Feb. 4-July 26, 1842.

matter. Full powers of negotiation were entrusted to Sir Howard Douglas, who could speak for merchants and colonists alike, and for lumbermen and emigrants, but every effort at compromise failed.[256] Down came the colonial timber duties, and down the Baltic duties still more, reducing but not eliminating the colonial preference. The Canada trade suffered for a time, as everyone had predicted, but in a few years Canadian shipping was as large as ever, and when the famine came it was in a position to take an important share of the exodus from Erin. It was not until the attainment of complete free trade and the rise of the steam packets that the timber-emigrant ship passed from the picture.

The Irish policy of a government which saw the revival of repeal agitation in its most virulent form, the passing of leadership from O'Connell into still more violent hands, and the coming of the great famine, is not easily judged after these events. The mere accession of the Tories to power was bound to cause trouble, and their Irish appointments did nothing to mitigate it. The Chief Secretary quarreled with both Viceroy and Undersecretary, and none could subdue the hydra of disaffection. Sir James Graham at the Home Office was hardly calculated to soothe Irish feelings; and he does not seem to have profited from Peel's advice that he play up against O'Connell such a loyal but reforming Irish landlord as Mr. Sharman Crawford.[257] Emigration, as in the days before 1835, was encouraged rather by the government's lack of policy than by any positive action.

T. F. Elliot, who was supervising emigration, had expected the Poor Law to increase the departures from Ireland, whether or not it was aided by government,[258] and we

[256] *3 Hansard* LXIII, 1282-1310; May 27, 1842.
[257] Parker, *Sir James Graham*, I, 350.
[258] Elliot to James Stephen, July 27, 1837. C.O. 384/42.

have seen that he was right. The provisions of the law were deemed insufficient, however, and in 1842 it was amended to permit the guardians of any union to send workhouse inmates of more than three months' standing to the colonies under rules laid down by the Poor Law Commissioners and the Colonial Secretary, provided not more than sixpence in the pound was spent in this way.[259] The party divisions on the subject were perfectly illustrated in the Commons, where the Irish Secretary (Lord Elliot) received the assistance of Smith O'Brien against the anti-emigration views of the Home Secretary and Mr. More O'Ferrall, a former Whig whip.[260] The total numbers aided under both provisions did not exceed a few hundred in any year up to 1845, and the clauses were generally considered too complicated to be effective.[261] Most of the emigrants were sent from Kilkenny or parts of Ulster where landlord assistance to emigration was an old practice, and the whole effect may be said to have been the transference of a part of the landlords' burden to the community, though a greater number were still sent by proprietors who did not resort to this machinery.

The one valuable service rendered to Ireland by the Peel ministry was the appointment in 1843 of a commission under the Earl of Devon to investigate the law of landlord and tenant in Ireland—the most prolific source of mischief. Its members were landed proprietors, but they took a very fair view of the whole situation, and their recommendations in 1845 included, in addition to land reforms, suggestions for the general improvement of Ireland. The section of their report dealing with emigration reads as follows:

[259] 6 and 7 *Victoria*, c. 92, section 18.
[260] *3 Hansard* LXVIII, 1322-35; LXXI, 234-235; May 5, Aug. 4, 1843.
[261] *Parl. Pap.* 1847, No. 255; *Return of the number of persons who have emigrated at the expense of the different Poor Law unions in Ireland in 1844, 1845, and 1846;* also Buchanan's annual reports at Quebec.

We should be sorry to see the system of emigration pushed beyond the extent to which it is called for by the population, or forced upon any persons who do not cheerfully look to its adoption as a means of providing for themselves or their families; but after considering the recommendations repeatedly made upon this subject and the evidence of Mr. Godley, in which the different views of the subject are well given, we desire to express our own conviction that a well organized system of emigration may be of very great service, as one amongst the measures which the situation of the occupiers of land in Ireland at present calls for. We cannot think that either emigration or the extension of public works, or the reclamation and improvement of land, can singly remove the existing evil. All these remedies must be provided concurrently, and applied according to the circumstances of each case. In this view, and to this extent only, we wish to direct attention to the subject of emigration.[262]

The Commission had nothing new to offer in the way of specific suggestions, merely recommending that colonial lands be granted at low or almost nominal prices, and that government find work for emigrants that they might earn the means of purchasing land.[263] In this as in previous reports, the Irish attitude that every man should have land came into conflict with the more aristocratic British theory which aimed to maintain a supply of labor dependent upon employers. Stanley soon showed that the ministry had no intention of taking up this aspect of the Devon Report, and the matter was dropped.[264]

A retrospect over the thirty years of Irish policy from 1815 to 1845 is not an inspiring one. The political chaos and groping of the period, the slow break-up of old forms of aristocratic control and the emergence of new mercantile and industrial interests are all reflected in the treatment of Irish questions. Great Britain was going through

262 *Parl. Pap.* 1845, No. 605, p. 28.
263 *Ibid.*, p. 29.
264 *3 Hansard* LXXXI, 212; June 9, 1845.

a period of readjustment and change more far-reaching
and profound than any in its history as a great power,
and the attention of statesmen and citizens alike was centered in its own problems. The kindred difficulties in Ireland attracted attention only when they became so clamorous as to menace the stability of government. Ireland
was at times a mysterious and annoying subject to be
avoided at all costs, at times a counter in the fierce game
of political supremacy. Great men gave it passing attention. The names of Peel, Wellington and Russell are all
associated with the Irish policy of the period. Small men
such as Horton used it as a ladder for personal advancement. But no really eminent leader, with the exception of
Daniel O'Connell, put Ireland in the forefront of his
activity; and O'Connell's own temperament and the folly
of government prevented much fruitful coöperation.
Drummond, the ablest of the British administrators,
worked himself to death four years before the crisis of
the famine with which he alone was competent to deal.

The truth was that no one had yet diagnosed the true
nature of Irish grievances. Neither Emancipation nor
Repeal was the answer, and the government's ventures
into the field of economic policy were too blind and timid
to touch the heart of the problem. While committees
weighed evidence and ministries wrangled, an increasing
number of the Irish people were taking their own way
out of the difficulty and leaving the country. Starting with
a few thousands in 1815 they had become an impressive
and eloquent total by 1845. It was a spectacle which could
not fail to attract attention, and to the baffled students of
Irish conditions it presented one possible remedy. Emigration came to be looked upon in many quarters as the
simplest and most immediate solution for the relief of
Ireland, and it was, as we have seen, made the basis of
several elaborate and costly schemes. British ministries

of both parties consistently rejected these schemes, and we must agree with the first historian of the emigration movement that from an imperial point of view they were right.[265] Neither Canada nor any other British colony was sufficiently developed to absorb the numbers contemplated in Horton's plans; and colonization by the use of waste lands was not advocated until 1829 when it was already too late to apply the policy to Canada. Whether anything useful on a smaller scale could have been done for Ireland is an open question. The lack of an educated class in touch with the people and willing to coöperate with the government created an almost insuperable obstacle to the administration of plans of relief, and prevented the formulation of such plans by men in close touch with Irish needs.

Considering the state of Ireland then and later, we must look upon any emigration as a blessing, and government approval of it as a wise policy. The situation justified the extreme unwillingness to strengthen the passenger acts enough to put up the cost of passage. The acts themselves might have been better administered without interfering with the emigrant trade, but, on the other hand, had the more stringent regulations called forth by the famine been put into effect twenty years earlier they would certainly have seriously decreased the emigration of this period. The least successful aspect of government policy was the attempt—as much in the mercantile interest as for imperial reasons—to turn emigration from the United States to British North America. The most conspicuous feature of the whole period is the ineffectiveness of measures for positive control of emigration, and the comparative success of the negative policy of noninterference.

[265] Duval, *Histoire de l'emigration*, p. 41.

CHAPTER VII

THE FRUITS OF EMIGRATION

What have ye brought to our Nation-building, Sons of the Gael?
What is your burden or guerdon from old Innisfail?

JOHN BOYLE O'REILLY.

FATE has not dealt kindly with the Irish Celt. It left him, after the Teutonic invasions of Britain, cut off by race and geographical barriers from the main currents of European life. For a brief period isolation had its advantages. Untroubled by the incursions of barbarians, Ireland in the sixth century developed a unique culture. Learning flourished, and the island sent forth its first great historic migration, a stream of missionaries and scholars second to none in Europe. But the blossoming period was brief, mists settled once more round the island, and the history of Ireland became a mere eddy on the outer shores of European life. Her problems were local, her leaders provincial, even her capacity for disturbing the rising British power did not bring her actively into continental or world affairs. Irish prelates, despite the unbroken tie with Rome, played little part in the development of the church. Occasionally a great Irishman, such as Berkeley or Swift, Burke or Sheridan, or Castlereagh, achieved European renown, but all save the philosopher abandoned their native land for a larger stage.

In 1931, the little island is politically more isolated than ever, but the Irish influence is felt as it has not been for eleven hundred years. In Glasgow and Manchester,

New York and San Francisco, Sydney, Melbourne and Montreal, Irish blood and Irish ideas permeate the life of the cities, and reach out into the state and nation. Through the person of Woodrow Wilson, Ireland has entered world history, and it is only a question of time until its leaders, absorbed for the moment in the reconstruction of a national ideal, seek a place in world polity. This is the work of the second great migration, which in a single century has transferred the majority of the Irish people to the North American continent, with enough left over to form the backbone of a dozen great industrial centers in other lands. What it may mean to Ireland, America, Australia, and to the world, no man can say; but what it meant in the days before 1845 when the movement was getting under way, and in the succeeding years of famine and civil war, may give some indication of the scope of its influence.

The significance of any great movement lies first of all in the aims and efforts of those who undertake it, and in its influence on their ways of life. A million Irish men and women crossed the seas between 1815 and 1845 to take up permanent residence in America. They were for the most part a home loving people, accustomed to no more travel than an occasional harvest migration to England, though a few harbored memories of Waterloo or the Peninsula. The majority had friends in America, but for all that it was a strange land—a land of danger as well as hope, separated from Ireland by 3000 miles of stormy ocean. The voyage involved from four to ten weeks of cooped-up wretchedness for the miserable land-lubbers making their first and usually their last sea voyage. They and the millions who followed them after the famine went not in ignorance of these facts but in spite of them.

Much pity has been expended on the "poor deluded emigrant" by reformers and writers—usually of the Anglo-Saxon race—who have not understood the business imagination of the Celt. The art of selling shoddy goods developed with astonishing rapidity in the emigrant trade, but it was nothing new to the Irishman. He knew that a horse was not half so good as its owner claimed, but he bought it, after much haggling, in the hope that he could make something out of it. He took his ticket for America in the same spirit. Later on, since this horse could not be resold, he might complain that he had been duped, and perhaps extract more than sympathy by the recital. It is in the light of these modest anticipations, and not of the glowing rhapsodies of political and religious propagandists, that the success of the emigrant must be measured.

First among motives leading the Irishman to emigrate we must put desire to escape from Ireland. The conviction that the country held no future existed as early as 1815 among some of the more prosperous farmers; after the Munster famine of 1822 it was much more widespread, and by the middle of the thirties had become fairly general among the lower classes except in Connaught. Steadily and inexorably the pressure of population extended unemployment, reduced wages, and raised rentals to a ruinous figure. Famine and disease swept over the country periodically, further endangering lives already precariously insecure. Civil war, coupled with political and religious dissensions and agrarian friction, completed the forces of expulsion. Foreign invasion, and transportation or exile, which have been important factors in other lands, played no part in Ireland during these years; and political disabilities even checked emigration in years when the agitation for their removal was hottest.

The emigrants did not, of course, wholly escape these evils by removing to America. Many of them died on the voyage. During cholera and typhus epidemics the mortality sometimes ran as high as ten per cent, but at no time was it worse than in the ports from which the ships sailed. The newcomers often brought disease with them into the American ports, where thousands more perished, mainly among the old and new emigrants. During the great famine it was said that one-third of the Irish died within three years of reaching America, and that the average longevity of the Boston Irish was fourteen years.[1] But this was an exceptional period, and the vast majority survived the chills and fevers of their first years in America to become sturdy citizens with the prospect of extending their span of life. In rural Ireland the average age at death was nineteen years, and not a fifth of the population lived beyond forty.[2] In the United States, the expectation of life at birth was approximately forty years, and for those who survived the first ten, it was extended to fifty-eight,[3] an age reached by less than five per cent of the Irish at home. The working life of a laborer in America was probably twice as long as that of a laborer in Ireland, and the burden of children therefore proportionately less. The difference did not lie in racial superiority; for the transplanted Irishmen, with a diet adequate to their needs, soon equaled in strength workmen of English descent.[4] Even in the city slums contagion was less widespread than in Ireland, and anything approaching famine was unknown. Deaths from starvation were sufficiently numerous to arouse comment in the winter of

[1] Ware, *Industrial worker*, p. 14.

[2] *Parl. Pap.* 1843, No. 504, Census of Ireland, 1841, pp. xlv, lxvi-lxvii.

[3] U.S. Census of 1850, p. 475. Only the returns from Massachusetts and Maryland are given. Of the other Irish communities, New York and Pennsylvania may have been somewhat worse; Ohio and Illinois were almost certainly better.

[4] *Parl. Pap.* 1836, No. 40, p. xii. G. C. Lewis found they retained their old diet, but gained strength by increasing the quantity.

1837,[5] but in the main, city charitable institutions and the well-known generosity of fellow-countrymen were adequate for relief.

During the early years it was easy to escape from the competition of numbers. In bad seasons such as 1816 and 1819 there was a temporary surplus of labor in the ports and some genuine suffering, but the whole body of immigrants was soon absorbed. After 1827, however, with the appearance of French Canadian competition and the tremendous increase in their own numbers, opportunities grew scarcer, and ten years later, after the panic of 1837, immigration practically ceased for a time. Cheap land in the west removed some of the American competition, but the immigrants, most of whom were unfitted for pioneer life, had to compete with the derelicts of American society for unskilled jobs. Wages of seventy-five cents a day in summer, and fifty cents or less in winter, were a fair average. At worst a man could work out his board and lodging through the cold weather on farm or canal, and earn an additional ten or fifteen dollars a month in summer. Some preferred to hide their few belongings and repose in the city almshouses from December to April. It was not an attractive life, even with the ample food and frequent rounds of whisky served in the construction camps, but it was healthier and more certain than the usual eightpence a day and unemployment for half the year in Ireland. Even the small farmer, though he often had less independence in the land of the free than under his landlord at home, found greater material security in America. Men of this class rarely stayed long in the poorest positions, and indeed most of the emigrants, up to the collapse of the public works in 1839, used them as stepping stones to other types of work, leaving the roughest jobs to the new arrivals.

[5] Buckingham, *America*, I, 160.

In spite of its hardships, life in the New World was a
more peaceful and orderly affair than it had been in Ireland. America had no replica of the burnings and the
shootings, the bludgeonings and hangings that marked
the bitter struggle for land at home, though something of
the same spirit cropped up in the labor disputes on canal
and railway work in the thirties. Unpopular contractors
or their agents took the place of the hated middlemen as
victims, and the same stubborn conspiracy of silence protected the perpetrators. "The worst vice of the Irish,"
wrote one astute observer in 1837, "is their ingrained
habit of taking what they consider justice into their own
hands.'"[6] Possibly the large rations of whisky served in
the camps had something to do with it; they certainly
helped to continue on American soil the familiar faction
brawls of Tipperary or Monaghan, but it is doubtful if
many of the emigrants really wanted to escape from
these. They were a normal part of social life. So too were
occasional political disturbances, which became on the
whole less destructive in America than in Ireland or even
in Great Britain. But when these were combined, as they
frequently were after 1830, with religious disputes, the
Irish Catholics discovered themselves in a new and unhappy situation. Instead of forming a vast majority of
the population, assured in every disturbance of public
sympathy if not of active coöperation, they had become
outcasts in a Protestant country, objects of positive antipathy among large groups of American workingmen
and of cold suspicion on the part of their masters. It
speaks well for the body of Protestant immigrants that
with everything in their favor they rarely sought to revive the old religious feuds, and the majority of anti-
Catholic riots show no evidence of Orange participation.
Most of the immigrants absorbed in time the American

6 Grund, *The Americans*, p. 97.

habit of tolerance, and the conflict which disrupted much of Ulster had no lasting influence in America.

By the measure of known evils, the escape from Ireland was more than justified. In the light of the unforeseen calamity which followed in 1845, it was a blessing beyond price. Nine-tenths of the emigrants were from classes which were helpless in 1846,—wholly dependent for food on a potato crop gone bad. They were saved from that cataclysm, and their earnings became the means of saving others. By the higher standard of American success, and their hopes and dreams of what Consul Grattan called ". . . the refuge of his race, the home of his kindred, the heritage of his children and their children . . . a sort of half-way stage to Heaven,'" they could hardly expect to do so well. Yet sentiment aside—and I have said that the majority were far less sentimental than the Consul—they did not do badly. The one outstanding attraction of America was high wages. Almost all the Irish immigrants began, and many ended, as unskilled laborers, in construction camps, in the building of factories, on the docks and the streets, or in the mills, wherever brawn was the primary need. While some earned only fifty cents a day, the majority made from seventy-five cents to $1.50 a day before 1830, and fifty cents to $1.00 afterward. The artisans, who formed an important group of emigrants during the early years, fared better and often earned $3.00 a day or more. They soon ran into strong native and British competition which cut their wages, but as long as the domestic textile manufacture remained an important one, Irish weavers, of whom there were several thousand in Philadelphia alone,[8] continued to earn double or triple

---

[7] *Civilized America*, II, 3, 5.

[8] F.O. 5/217; Consul Robertson to Bidwell, Jan. 31, 1826; saying that there were 5,000 looms in the city, mainly Irish. The consuls frequently gave wage statistics.

what they could in Ireland. With the rise of Lowell and
Paterson they drifted into the unskilled jobs, few going
over into skilled factory work. Only the miners, among all
the skilled immigrants, seem to have made little improvement in their condition. They lived in wretched shanties
among the Pennsylvania hills and toiled long hours for a
dollar a day or less.

An overwhelming proportion of the emigrants went
into the wage-earning groups. Shop-keeping, which has
long been a favored occupation in Irish opinion, absorbed
one or two out of every hundred immigrants. The majority were probably Ulstermen, who have done well in
American trade and commerce. They began usually by
catering to their own people, and a few rose to positions
of prominence in the business life of their cities.

Another group—ten per cent at most—went into agriculture.[9] It has often been a subject for speculation that
the Irish, a predominantly rural people, made so little
mark as farmers in America. Poverty, which kept many
of them on the eastern seaboard, was one reason; ignorance of improved or large scale agriculture was another,
while in the minds of most of them farming was associated with insecurity, turbulence, and unrest. Good
wages in a lively city offered far more attractions. The
gregariousness, which is so noticeable a feature of Irish
character, accords ill with pioneer life; and those who
took advantage of its opportunities lamented their isolation. One Irishman, who had worked for sixpence a day in
Ireland, became a farmer in Missouri (cursing the high
cost of labor); he rejoiced in land and stock, no rent, light
taxes, whisky without government inspection, free shoot-

[9] T. W. Page, in *Journal of Political Economy*, 1913, p. 35, gives a table
of occupations of the Irish-born and other immigrants from the Census of
1870, with some valuable comments. The farmers are given as 5%, but there
would have been more before 1845.

ing, and above all social equality, yet he looked back
regretfully to the days in Ireland, where after work "I
could then go to a fair, or a wake, or a dance, or I could
spend the winter nights in a neighbour's house cracking
the jokes by the turf fire. If I had there but a sore head I
would have a neighbour within every hundred yards of
me that would run to see me. But here everyone can get
so much land, and generally has so much, that they calls
them neighbours that lives two or three miles off—och!
the sorra take such neighbours, I would say. And then I
would sit down and cry and curse him that made me leave
home.'"[10] The same feeling finds expression in verses that
appeared occasionally in the newspapers and magazines.
In Canada, where the attractions of city life were less
conspicuous, a greater proportion of the emigrants took
up farming, and were on the whole successful. But in
Canada also, the mass of the immigrants became part of
the urban working class.

Measured in terms of standards of living, the increase
of wages was real and significant. There was better food
and more of it, and more drink also—on that all observers were agreed. Clothing was not noticeably better,
but the exigencies of climate demanded a little warmer ap-
parel than was customary in Ireland. Housing conditions
were generally more satisfactory. Families and even
strangers crowded together in the slums for warmth as
well as economy just as they did in Dublin, but the tenements were better constructed, and more comfortable,
though possibly less healthy than the turf huts of rural
Ireland to which most of them were accustomed. These
also made their appearance in America, as Hawthorne
found to his interest in the Maine woods and to his sor-

10 Letter in the *Belfast News Letter*, Apr. 17, 1821. T. A. Emmet warned
farmers that they would have to face loneliness; Dublin *Evening Post*, Sept.
17, 1818.

row on the shore of Walden Pond during construction of
the railway,[11] but this was only after the commencement
of the poorest emigration. The board-and-turf hut was a
transitory phenomenon of Irish-American settlement,
and disappeared as the immigrants formed permanent
communities. Beyond this improvement in his fundamental material needs the ordinary emigrant could rarely
rise. If he arrived in New York with capital, he ran the
gauntlet of the most highly organized and unscrupulous
combination of professional "runners," truckmen, boarding-house keepers and spurious transportation agents in
the city—all his own countrymen. Other ports harbored
similar parasites on a smaller scale. Their operations
helped to keep the new arrivals in the cities until it was
too late to go elsewhere. Then began the regular process
of demoralization inevitable in a society in which useful
goods were expensive and drink and rowdyism cheap.
The corner saloon and political club—usually one and the
same—became the center of existence for all but the most
energetic; and the curse of excessive spare time without
education in the use of it, long a problem in Ireland, continued to handicap her sons in the New World.

It is in the second generation that the success of emigration becomes apparent. Improvidence has been
charged as a national weakness of the Irish, and the one
most at odds with American character. There is some
truth in the charge. The upper classes, despite rigid land
laws designed to protect heirs, sank frequently into bankruptcy; the lower, their ambitions vitiated by long continued hopelessness, lived only for the day or the season.
In America they continued as they had begun, wasteful
and generous, aiding alike the distressed neighbor and
the parent or brother in the old country, with rarely a
thought of saving for themselves. The younger genera-

[11] *American Note-books*, pp. 53, 359.

tion, never wholly isolated as later slum children have been, came in contact with conflicting ideals: with the American gospel, natural to a young country but incomprehensible to European observers, of living mainly for the future; with the creed of material progress as the national goal; and with a pride in equality and in material self-development which ran counter on the one hand to deep rooted Irish prejudices and on the other to Catholic teaching. In the community, and above all in the schools, which thanks to Horace Mann multiplied rapidly after 1835, young Ireland-in-America imbibed eagerly the ideals of the new country. Worship of material success, which had been kept down in Ireland by the impossibility of attaining it, came easily, and Protestant and Catholic alike fell into line with the prevailing American tendency. No longer retarded by ignorance, and living in an age when opportunities in the west more than offset the pressure of growing competition for labor, they, like the children of other races, found their level in society in accordance with their capacities, and ceased for the most part to be distinguishable from the body of American citizenry. Irish memories and traditions kept them out of agriculture and sent them into brewing and distilling, local trade, and especially into the professions; but Ireland herself ceased to be a great factor in their lives. Pride triumphed over religious humility; a certain native individualism asserted itself; and comparative success and self-satisfaction undermined the spirit of caste, producing a deep though less vocal faith in the egalitarian doctrine. Only the failures joined the newly arrived in vociferating their equality with anyone in the republic, at the same time denouncing every concession to the negroes, the one class lower than themselves. On the whole, results fully justified the observation of an Irish traveller in America who wrote in 1845: "I learned upon enquiry that (although a large number continued in the lowest and most menial labour) a great proportion of the Irish rose in the scale very much in the same way as others; and all agreed that in the second generation they ranked in the class of respectable citizens.'"[12]

How strongly the emigrants desired social equality we cannot say. That desire is often listed as a major cause of emigration; but there is so little evidence of it in Ireland, and economic aims so far outweighed all other considerations, that it cannot have played any large part. It appears rather that America nurtured the ideal in Irish hearts until it became an accepted article of faith. Its expression took at times odd forms, as when the Irish Catholics of Philadelphia and New York proclaimed their right to select their own priests in defiance of the bishops and the whole ecclesiastical hierarchy. In the main, however, migration did not touch religious allegiance, and after the passing of this controversy over "trusteeism," the Irish submitted wholeheartedly to the dictation of their priests, always reserving, as in Ireland, the discretion to prefer political leadership when it promised more immediate and popular returns. The belief, once widespread, that large numbers left the Roman church after coming to America, is now discredited.[13] The Presbyterians have been somewhat more subject to the dissolving force of American scepticism, but in the period before 1845 there was no sign of religious or theological latitudinarianism on their part. In both groups the divorce between church and patriotism in America served in the end for the creation of a more genuinely religious attitude.

12 J. B. Tuke, *A visit to Connaught in the autumn of 1847*, p. 47.

13 Shaughnessy, *Has the immigrant kept the faith?* His argument is strengthened by the fact that he overestimates the proportion of Catholics among the early Irish immigrants.

The social characteristic which most affected Irish success in America was insobriety. America was not unusually temperate nor exacting in its demands, but Irish addiction to drunkenness and to its public display antagonized many groups beside the employers. During Father Matthew's crusade, the temperance of immigrants called forth general commendation, but in 1846 that influence ceased, and so long as contractors found it worth their while to get every last ounce out of their workmen by frequent doses of whisky, no serious modification of Irish habits in this respect could be expected. American opinion, however, would not tolerate the normal consequences of intoxication in so far as they took the shape of riots. American government, like Irish, rested largely in the hands of the wealthy classes, and it was equally determined to maintain the sanctity of property. The "low Irish" never recognized that sanctity, and in Ireland frequently invaded it with impunity, but American society with its greater solidarity was more effective in repression. Personal crimes aroused less reprobation in an age which still tolerated private vengeance, and American police were scarcely more effective than Irish. Brawling and petty disturbances aroused no more than a half-amused contempt. In any case, the decreased incentive to crime and the progress of the superior immigrants put a severe check upon this Irish propensity.

Of other social gains or losses to the immigrant it is impossible to speak in detail. An attempt to describe the effect upon the recreation and activities of the later generation would involve a comparison of modern Ireland and modern America. The original emigrants changed little. They sang in America the songs they had sung in Ireland, adding some new ones drawn from the emigration movement itself; they had the same sort of parties, dances and clubs. The change from rural hamlets to industrial and commercial centers was not as drastic as it seemed. Greenwich Village and Five Points—the Irish sections of New York—were as narrow and provincial as Burrisokane and Clonmacdermot. Pigs devoured garbage on the marble doorsteps of the finest New York residences; and street lights and sewers were slow to invade slum areas, which differed little save in extent from the villages of Ireland. Time has wrought great changes, driving the animals out of the city and banishing the open fields, until the majority of the Irish race are become city dwellers who think of the country as something pleasant to look at. It is a change which has come upon them long since 1845, not as Irishmen or immigrants, but as victims of a common misfortune of our age. It is, however, one of the characteristics which separates the Irish from the Irish-American today.

Freedom and democracy, or at least the semblance of democracy contained in political equality, have so long been catch-words of American patriotism that one hesitates to discount their influence. From 1830, when European visitors first began to assess our institutions with some show of judgment, to 1850, when slavery definitely overshadowed all other questions, travellers of every nationality sought to elucidate the American political system as something unique, and significant for the future of their own countries. They saw and judged America in the terms of Mrs. Trollope, Miss Martineau, Francis Lieber or Michel Chevalier, and believed that their emigrants were moved primarily by political considerations. For the most part they were mistaken. Few Irish read the propaganda of Birkbeck and Fearon, the aristocratic condemnations of Basil Hall, or even America's defense by Robert Walsh. They knew by heart the story of Ninety-eight and the subsequent careers of the United Irishmen in America, and during the first years

after 1815 Emmet, McNevin, Sampson and their associates in the Shamrock Society were a real force drawing
from Ireland the political malcontents. Even in these
years, however, republicanism and democracy were less
alluring than freedom from tithes and taxes. Not until
1848, when the last vain attempt at a united Irish revolt
betrayed the aspirations of Thomas Meagher, Gavan
Duffy, and Thomas Davis, did political exile again enrich
the American world. The myriads who poured forth in
the intervening decades asked little of their governments,
and most of it they obtained. Tithes existed only in British America, and there in a less obnoxious form than in
Ireland. County cess and spirit licenses plagued them no
more, and few were economists enough to protest against
the burden of indirect taxation laid upon them by a rising
tariff. If local government was oppressive and corrupt,
they got their share of the booty through Tammany or
the Boston Custom House party. Religious discrimination for office disappeared in the United States only just
before its abolition in Ireland. Property qualifications
for voting continued to exclude the majority of Irish in
many states until after 1845; yet the poor settled as
freely in Pennsylvania and Rhode Island where they
could not vote as in New York and Massachusetts where
they could. Political ambitions were clearly a minor cause
of their migration, and of these the desire for liberty was
more important than the belief in democracy.[14] Once established in America, however, the Irish immigrant could
no more resist the lure of politics than the sociability of
the dram shop, and the same ardor which made him the
willing slave of O'Connell sustained the ward leaders of
America.

[14] Page, *Causes of earlier immigration to the United States* (in *Journal
of Political Economy*, 1911, p. 682), overrates the political aims, which he
says were less frequently realized than the economic and social.

It would be foolhardy to suggest more than a rough comparison between the success of the Irish immigrants in these years and those of other races, or of their own countrymen in other periods. Crevecoeur ventured to state, largely on the basis of his own observation, that in the colonial period, out of twelve families of each race, nine Germans, seven Scots, and four Irish succeeded.[15] A century later we find the Irish outnumbering other immigrants in every unskilled occupation except agricultural labor, second to the British in textiles, iron and steel, and mining, and generally last in the higher employments. There is no reason to look for any different proportion between 1815 and 1845. British and Germans tended to settle at slightly higher levels than the Irish, whose only competitors for the meanest jobs were the French Canadians, and these only in New England in the last years of this period. But when the lower level from which the Irish started is taken into consideration—their arrival in America with less capital than the Germans, and less skill than the British—the measure of their success does not fall far short of other newcomers; and in succeeding generations the city-bred and educated Irish often progressed faster and further than the Teuton on his isolated western farm.

The comparison with other groups of Irish is easier to make, and bears out the theory that early emigration is as a rule more successful than late. Daniel Boone, the typical Scotch-Irish pioneer of the 18th century, moving with the frontier from the Appalachians to the Ohio valley and on across the Mississippi, presents a sorry picture of success by any other standard than that of adventure and personal freedom; but the number of famous Americans drawn from this stock, from Andrew Jackson to Woodrow Wilson, suggests that capacity and oppor-

[15] *Letters from an American farmer* (Ed. 1904), p. 82.

tunity were theirs in the long run. Those who came between the Revolution and 1815, many of them political
exiles of even better stock, arrived when immigration was
at its lowest ebb, and opportunity therefore greatest, and
they produced many able citizens. To this group belonged
T. A. Emmet, Attorney-General of New York, and Matthew Carey, the Philadelphia publisher and protectionist,
the first distinguished Catholic Irishman in America.
Between 1815 and 1819, the emigrants were men of the
same type, but thereafter both quality and opportunity
declined, with the results already described. In Canada
and New Brunswick, where immigration was just commencing, there was a somewhat higher level of success,
not among the original settlers, who were often of the
poorest class, but on the part of their descendants. Yet
when one compares the men and women of this period
with the hordes who came in the next fifteen years, or
with those who have arrived since the development of
Southern and Eastern European migration, it appears
that they escaped sooner from degradation and poverty.
If some remained among their successors in the slums
and poorhouses, a far greater number attained that state
of respectable mediocrity which is the foundation of
American society. There was criticism enough of the
poorer Irish after 1830. It was one cause of their segregation in both American and Canadian cities, but it required
the sight of post-famine destitution and squalor to bring
out the opinion of genteel New England expressed by
Edward Everett Hale:

The untaught and wretched Irish Celt of the pure blood could
no more stand the competition of the well compacted English social system, than could his progenitors or his kinsmen stand the
close knit discipline of Caesar's legions. If this view of the pure
Celtic race is correct, it is at this moment useless in the world, except, as Mr. Emerson has said, for the guano that is in it. There

its value cannot be counted. But for his active purposes the Almighty has done with it. What it may have been in the past, He knows, or what unseen good it has sought, He knows. We can only measure it by the lower standard of visible external success. And there we can see this—that in the epochs of written history the pure race has done nothing positive for mankind and been nothing but a monument of failure.[16]

Hale's verdict was echoed through the length and breadth of America during the fifties. Thenceforth, for seventy years, Irish questions and opinion entered too intimately into American life and politics to permit an unbiased estimate of the Irish influence in America. The World War and the creation of the Free State are at last modifying that situation, and Americans are beginning to assess the Irish contribution to their national development. There is no scale delicate enough to weigh such subtle and complex phenomena, but wherever statistics come to our aid the period between 1815 and 1860 is seen to be of primary importance. Earlier immigrants seem to have produced more distinguished heirs, later ones to have done more to affect American foreign policy; but the scope and magnitude of Irish settlement and its manifold consequences were determined in these years.

The Irish contributed not quite ten per cent to the increase of population between 1815 and 1845, and even in Upper Canada, which was almost a new land in 1815, they formed only twenty per cent of the increase, and fifteen per cent of the population by 1842.[17] Irish immigrants were one in twenty of the people of the United States, and one in thirteen in the northeastern states

16 *Letters on Irish emigration*, pp. 52-53.

17 Chickering, *Immigration into the United States*, p. 45; J. Lowe, *Population, immigration and pauperism in the Dominion of Canada* in Papers before the Economical Section, British Association for the Advancement of Science, 1884, pp. 194-224.

from Maine to Virginia, where four-fifths of them lived.[18] Their dispersion through this region was wider than has commonly been supposed, and they formed not more than twelve per cent of the population in any state. Yet they contributed to three distinct shifts in population. In 1790 more than half the Irish in the United States lived south of Pennsylvania; after that date they added only to the ever-increasing preponderance of the north. They swelled the ranks of the urban dwellers and helped to make New York the first city of the land, both by settling there and by digging the Erie Canal. They formed nearly as high a proportion of the total population (from fifteen to thirty per cent) in the counties along the Canadian border, as in the metropolitan area; and from ten to fifteen per cent on the route of the Erie Canal.[19] In Canada they did much to equalize the positions of the lower and upper provinces, paving the way for federation in 1867. No other immigrants could approach them in numbers. They formed forty-four per cent of the foreign born population of the United States in 1850, and more than half in every northeastern state except Maine, Vermont and Maryland. Ten years later, when they had brought over another million and more, and rescued Ireland from distress, their preponderance reached its height. Thereafter, the Irish race in America owed less to new importations than to the inheritance of this period.

It has been said that the impact of immigration on America was as great or greater in colonial times than in the recent age, and that the Scots-Irish, being essen-

[18] Census of 1850, p. 482. This was the first census to take account of the nativity of residents. The Irish-born then in the country were 961,000, or about 70,000 more than the immigration between 1815 and 1845; so the influx after 1845 exceeded the deaths of earlier immigrants by that amount. These later acquisitions increased the proportion of Irish in the west.

[19] New York State Census of 1845.

tially anti-British, were in some ways as alien as the Germans.[20] Had that still been true in 1815, the Ulster migration of the next thirty years, greater numerically as well as in proportion to American population, than it had ever been before or has been since, would have presented a problem in assimilation of the first magnitude. But it was not true. The older settlers had been fully absorbed by 1814, and their successors roused no antipathies, either political or social. It was the 400,000 or 450,000 Irish Catholics who first awakened public apprehension after 1831, and made America conscious of an immigration problem. The fears rested mainly on religious and social grounds, but behind them lurked the eternal economic conflict between the employers of cheap labor and the champions of a more orderly and slower national development. From 1831 to 1860 Irish labor was the storm center of that conflict.

Only a young country in the midst of rapid economic expansion can receive a rapid influx of labor without injury to its wage scale and to the chances for employment. The United States during most of the years before 1825 was in such a position. From 1825 to 1837, it absorbed the immigrants only by means of large public works and at reduced wages. After 1837 unemployment was added to the evils attributed to immigration, and the anti-alien movement gained real momentum for the first time. Canada, prior to 1845 was never able to take care of her immigrants, and suffered in much the same way, although the necessity of going on the land there proved in the end beneficial. Manufacturers, and theorists such as Hale, claimed that the Irish neither deprived Americans of work, nor lowered their wages, but filled a vacancy left by the departing pioneers bound for the west, and that reduction of wage or pauperism could affect only the

20 M. Farrand, in *New Republic*, 1916, pp. 147-149.

newcomers themselves. Hale elaborated this theory, en-
visioning a new race of Helots come to raise the status
of every freeborn American. The concept seems strangely
at variance with the ideals of healthy democracy, but it
was not unnatural in the mind of a Yankee defender of
slavery. Neither Hale nor Nathaniel Niles, spokesman of
the employers, were right, but they were less mistaken
than Samuel Morse, who predicted the ruin of America
from the "priest ridden slaves of Ireland."[21] The farmers' sons of New England, impoverished by the competition of western grain, had their choice between emigration to the west or to their own rising mill towns, and
those who went west owe a debt of gratitude to the Irish
who made the towns less attractive for them. But the
poorer and more indolent, who drifted in to rough city
labor, were under no illusion as to the intensity of Irish
competition, and they contributed no small element to the
unrest of these years. It was no longer true in Boston or
New York or Philadelphia that the Irish took jobs that
no one else would have. In those cities they were a distinct menace to the American workingman. In Canada,
Irish peasants, reproducing the conditions and standards
of life in the old country, undersold habitans in the market of Montreal.[22] Only in great constructive works on
canals and railways, which could never have been undertaken without the labor of the Irish, did they in a sense
create the jobs which they filled. For the time being they
even increased the amount of work available for others,
on the completed canals and in the west; but against that
must be set the evils which this too-rapid expansion produced after 1837.

[21] *Imminent dangers to the free institutions of the United States, through
foreign immigration*, in Abbott, *Historical aspects of the immigration problem*, p. 451.

[22] J. E. Alexander, *Transatlantic sketches* (1833), II, 213.

Their influence on the skilled trades was very much less marked. It was not until after 1845 that they drove the farmers' daughters out of the factories. In that year the Irish were only one in ten of the operatives at Lowell, but they had already initiated the shift from women to men employees which was possible because of the lower wages demanded by Irishmen, and their coming meant the end of paternalism, the disappearance of that model industrial town which so excited the admiration of European visitors in the thirties. The gulf between classes widened perceptibly, ushering in the modern age of acute class consciousness and the wage struggle. One result should have been a rapid growth of trades unions, but the immigrants themselves were a serious check to that. The first great era of labor organization in America, begun about 1828, was ended by the panic of 1837. Thereafter, the availability of former immigrants, now able to undertake skilled work, prevented an early revival of the unions. The Irish artisans, strongly organized at home, had their unions in New York and Philadelphia, but too large a percentage of the immigrants were men and women without any experience of combination and too desperately needy to hold their own against the employers. Their only previous associations had been temporary and turbulent, for the purpose of agrarian agitation, and they reproduced these features in America in numerous riots, two-thirds of which were unorganized and ineffectual strikes. The time was to come when Irishmen took a leading part in American labor unions, but not until they were themselves put on the defensive by the arrival of a newer and poorer immigration.

In some respects they contributed to difficulties of labor for which they were scarcely responsible. The importers of contract labor, operating in Baltimore from 1829 on, found a fruitful source of supply in Ireland, and a speedy development of that vicious system was only checked by the great unsolicited migration of the thirties. In all except very bad years, a high proportion of the remittances sent from America to pay passages was said to come from employers in the expectation of securing more workers. As there was no direct contract, however, the exact amount of these subsidies can never be ascertained. The immigrants were also more pliant than natives in accepting the truck system, living largely at the mercy of their employers in the construction camps, the mining villages, and the Canadian woods.[23] Indirectly their labor also injured the American factory hand to some extent; for the number of trained but impoverished Irish weavers, cobblers, and other artisans helped to preserve the domestic industry and to retard the introduction of machinery, which developed more slowly in America than in Great Britain.

In proportion to their numbers, the Irish immigrants of the first generation added surprisingly little to American economic life. Slight as was their contribution to agriculture, their influence in manufacturing was almost equally negligible. No new Matthew Carey rose to economic leadership. The only prominent capitalist immigrant was William Divine, who set up textile mills in Philadelphia. English rather than Irish artisans supplied the skill for new factories, training Americans to carry on their work. In the cotton and woollen mills from Massachusetts to Pennsylvania, and in the iron and steel mills of Pittsburgh, Irishmen took some part, but they were not indispensable to the industry. In mining they counted for more. Profits were too low to support native labor, and the necessary experience could only be secured

---

[23] On the truck system in Upper Canada, see Shirreff, *Tour through North America* (1835), p. 386.

cheaply from the Celtic miners of the British Isles.[24] The Welsh came first and the Irish second in the development of American mining. In the thirties we find them scattered through the coal areas of Pennsylvania, in the forties operating the lead mines of Illinois, Wisconsin and Missouri, and about to take a leading part in the development of California.

American mining could scarcely have developed without the immigrant; and transportation, which made even greater use of him, would certainly have developed very differently had he not come. In 1817 the steamship was just beginning to draw together the coastal districts of the United States. The back country found an outlet only by bad roads or worse trails, while the trans-Appalachian west looked north to the Great Lakes–St. Lawrence waterway or south along the Mississippi. Eight years later, when the Erie Canal was completed, the west turned half-face. Freight from Buffalo to New York, which had been at $100 a ton fell to $6 to $13, and New York definitely repelled the threat of New Orleans to become the commercial capital of America. From 1825 to 1839 canals multiplied in every northern state; and no sooner was the canal era ended than railway expansion began on a large scale. All this was the work of the Irish. Without their labor the canals would have extended more slowly, and many would never have been built at all. Cheap and abundant labor made possible the extravagant development of the thirties, and aided in producing the crisis of 1837. The most foolish state projects arose after 1830 under the joint stimulus of the treasury surplus and an extensive poor immigration. The more profitable earlier ventures did not need these stimuli and would have been made had there been no Irish to wield the pick and shovel; but the fact remains that it was the Irish who

[24] T. W. Page, in *Journal of Political Economy*, 1913, p. 45.

built them and contributed thereby to that major economic change which tied east and west together at the
expense of the south, producing the alignment of parties
which precipitated the Civil War, and added no small
amount to the advantages of the north during the struggle. One factor in the party shift was the decline of eastern opposition to preëmption of frontier lands by squatters, a right opposed on the ground that it encouraged
eastern workingmen to abandon their employers. The
fortress of opposition began to crumble as early as 1828,
but the final victory of the squatters was delayed until
1841, when the influx of Irish made many employers
indifferent to the ambitions of their laborers.

European observers have been prone to look upon emigration as a clear gain to America, transferring to it
working strength, knowledge, and other desirable qualities at no cost; but the economic historian may well question the gain from these great movements of the poor.
The cash value of the Irish immigrants on arrival was so
small as to constitute an insignificant addition to American economy, and their worth must rest upon their
personal contribution to American life. Against the services just recorded must be set certain intangible social
burdens on the whole community and some definite expenditures, of which poor relief through almshouses,
hospitals, and dispensaries was most costly. America had
almost no absolute destitution prior to 1831, and little,
according to European standards, in 1850. At that time
there were 68,000 foreign paupers, of whom 40,000 were
concentrated in New York. The majority of aliens and
usually from one- to two-thirds of the whole pauper
population were Irish. This was true in New York as
early as 1817; it became true in Quebec, St. John, Boston
and Philadelphia after 1830. Not only were the Irish the
most numerous, but the proportion of those receiving

relief to total Irish population was greater than that of other races.[25] Moreover, the Irish paid next to nothing into state and municipal taxes, although their labor undoubtedly aided others to do so. The excise and the tariff, through which like everyone else they contributed to the federal government, gave no recompense to the harassed local officials, who considered the Irish an expensive nuisance. Yet less than half the burden was borne officially. The majority lived at the expense of friends or relatives, on private charity, or the British Consuls, all of whom from Portland to Baltimore complained of the frequent calls on their assistance.

The direct burden of poverty was not heavy, and the most serious economic charge brought against the immigrants in these years is that they poured into the country in boom times, increasing the fever of speculation by their willingness to work at low wages, intensifying the crash which must come sooner or later; and that they continued to come in large numbers for a year or more after the crash when they could only swell the ranks of the destitute, and delay the reappearance of healthy business.[26] The unusual sensitiveness of the Irish to American conditions makes the latter part of the charge less applicable to them than to other later immigrants, but it is true that desperate conditions at home made thousands go to America even in the worst of seasons. The claim that they inflated still further the taut balloon of a fictitious prosperity seems amply proven by their share in the disastrous expansion before 1837.

On the basis of immediate results, the Irish immigration of 1815-45 might well be considered to have done

[25] E.g. The Irish were 16% of the population of rural Massachusetts, 28% in Boston, and 41% of the state paupers. Darling, *Political changes in Massachusetts*, p. 163, Note.

[26] On this whole question see Jerome, *Migration and business cycles*.

more harm than good to America. It is not until the subsequent history of the emigrants' descendants is added to it that the movement appears as a positive benefit. It is therefore correct to say that the gain to America from Irish immigration is in direct correlation with the success of the immigrants.

Had American labor been as powerful in 1820 as it was a century later, it might well have secured a decisive check on immigration. It was weak, however, and the most effective propaganda against the immigrant arose from groups alarmed over social rather than economic consequences. Only a few realized the most serious danger—the growth of filthy and overcrowded tenement districts with their thousands of potential plague-carriers and burdens on society. The Irish were the first slum dwellers of America. City authorities reacted almost automatically to their filth, commencing in the twenties and thirties some of those functions, such as street cleaning, which enlightened citizens like Franklin had advocated fifty years earlier. All but the largest centers had unsatisfactory water systems, where they possessed any at all, and improper disposal of waste. Sanitation was still largely a private concern, and not until later did slum conditions force public action. Officials took more notice of the rising cost of almshouses and hospitals, for which the slums were by no means wholly responsible, many hundreds drifting into them from the rural areas. In spite of worse effect upon health, the slums of the thirties and forties did less permanent damage than those of fifty years later, when segregation from the rest of the community was more pronounced, and the chance of assimilation of slum children proportionately decreased.

The rapid spread of popular education after 1835 came just in time to render invaluable aid to the rising generation of Irish Americans, and to forestall the development

of a non-English-speaking community among the more
ignorant immigrants of the forties. Here and there in
Canada or along the Maine–New Brunswick boundary
were little patches of a Gaelic world, but the great mass
of the city dwellers soon learned English, if they did not
already know it, and their children rarely used any other
tongue. Horace Mann and his associates were thinking
rather of native ignorance than of the aliens when they
started their drive for free schools, but the growth of an
immigrant problem lent weight to their propaganda.

The Catholic Irish presented an additional problem,
which was partially solved at New York and Lowell by
the creation of special Irish schools. The main issue in
their case was the use of the King James or the Douai
versions of the Bible, which was fought out in state
after state with the usual result of removing the Bible
altogether from state schools. The Roman church of
the forties was less satisfied with this result than it is
today. It would have preferred state aid for its own institutions, but was perforce content to secure its children
against Protestant instruction at the cost of an increasingly secular control of education.[27] Something of the
American idolatry of the state and the conviction of its
supremacy over all other forms of organization is due to
the appearance of a religious conflict instigated by Irish
priests and their congregations at the moment when the
American public school system was being formed. Mate-
rialistic ideals, independence of judgment, and a certain
basic scepticism (except where patriotism was involved)
have also been confirmed by the same cause. Time and
the growing influence of the church have somewhat modified the original and wholly unintended reaction against

[27] Maguire, *Irish in America*, pp. 433-437; a Catholic point of view. For
a Protestant reaction to Catholic demands see Lyell, *Travels in North
America*, I, 121.

its aims, but the force of that reaction still remains stronger than the subsequent counter-thrust.

By a similar indirection, the coming of the Irish also aided the development of white freedom. Indentured servitude was still common in Pennsylvania, Maryland and Virginia in 1815, though it was beginning to decline. A few redemptioners from Ireland and some hundreds from Germany arrived in the succeeding years, and the Pennsylvania legislature found it necessary to pass a new act in 1818 for the protection of these servants. But the arrivals of large numbers of free laborers, combined with the abolition of imprisonment for debt, rapidly wiped out a system which had proven uneconomic. In 1828 when Matthew Carey suggested a short-term indenture contract for the importation of harvest hands,[28] contractors were already beginning to bring in shiploads of Irishmen without legal ties, and his proposal was not followed up. Three years later the last servant appeared on the indenture register in Philadelphia, and the system had already disappeared elsewhere.[29]

These are results of immigration which time has disclosed, but to the American of the eighteen thirties they were passed by in favor of two controversial topics, drink and religion, which are still full of dynamite a century later. We have said that the difference between American and Irish intemperance was largely one of degree or of the manifestations to which it gave rise, but it was precisely those manifestations which gave the Irishman a bad name. "Drunken Irish" became a common epithet and one most useful to the rising temperance societies, which could point to the noise, the destruction of property, and other more serious crimes of intoxicated mobs.

[28] In his *Emigration from Ireland*, in Abbott, *Historical aspects of the immigration problem*, p. 255.
[29] Herrick, *White servitude in Pennsylvania*, pp. 263-266.

The Irish themselves, except during the brief years of Father Matthew's influence, belonged almost without exception to the "wet" party, and they followed Henshaw of Boston into battle against temperance in 1831 with the same enthusiasm with which their great-grandchildren followed Al Smith in 1928.[30] From the lofty distiller to the barkeeper and the consumer, they played a major part in the drink trade. The net result of their efforts, however, may have been an increase in the forces of abstinence as well as of drinking, a contributory factor to that sharp division of American opinion between rival schools of fanaticism.

The particular accompaniment of drink which aroused most antagonism was turbulence of the kind which distinguished Irish wakes and fairs. On Sundays and holidays in the camps along the advancing lines of canal or railway, and in cities just before an election, the Irish were always noisy, usually rough, and sometimes dangerous. The most celebrated example of their pugnacity was the Broad Street riot in Boston in 1837, caused by a fire company turning into an Irish funeral. Irish immigrants have been credited with introducing rioting in America, but the historian of colonial and revolutionary times cannot allow that claim. Popular prejudice in the thirties blamed them for most of the disturbances, and Grund, least biased of contemporary foreign observers, was inclined to believe that it might be true.[31] A large proportion of the riots were undoubtedly confined to the Irish, but the most serious outbreaks, which owed as much or more to economic friction and religious hatred as to drink, involved native Americans and others, and some at least were started by their enemies. The thirty years from the coming of the Irish Catholics to the Civil War

[30] Darling, *Political changes in Massachusetts*, p. 161.
[31] *The Americans*, I, 316.

saw many of these local wars. They tended to disappear as the position of the Irish became better established and new sources of friction arose, but the simpler type of brawl has continued, maintaining the Irish reputation for pugnacity without any serious effect upon American character or history. Belligerent self-assertion was a characteristic of Jacksonian democracy, in which the Irish were only one of several elements.

Irish participation in major crime was no greater than might be expected from the poorest section of the population, and much less in proportion than their share in poor relief. Rather less than half the inmates of New York City prison and penitentiary in 1844 were Irish, not more than one in five in Auburn, and fewer still in Pennsylvania. The Irish of this period did not fully maintain the lawless traditions either of their native land or of their predecessors on the Appalachian frontier, perhaps because adventurers found a richer field in Latin America. The slight Irish addition to the annals of crime was more than offset by their assumption from the beginning of the police duties of every city where they lived, a position recognized as theirs by 1840. Doubtless political organization accounted for their monopoly, but they were credited with providing the first effective check upon crime in a day when state protection of life and property was new and difficult.

Next to insobriety, the question which caused most trouble for the Irish immigrants was membership in the Roman Catholic Church. We have seen that not more than half the immigrants of our period were of that church, but the great body of Presbyterians and smaller groups of Anglicans, Methodists, Quakers, and Moravians[32] came to a country where their creeds were already

---

[32] From County Limerick. The descendants of the Huguenot refugees in Ireland also re-emigrated in large numbers, but in blood, speech and

well established, often under leaders of their own race, and where they added no new features or problems to American life. It was not so with the Roman Catholics, who emigrated in numbers for the first time after 1826.[33] Religious toleration was in theory a cardinal principle of American behavior. The quiet German Catholics who took up their farms in Ohio or Wisconsin were not molested for their religious views, but Irish belligerence, too often given free expression by editors trained in the scurrilous school of Dublin journalism, and the proximity of the poorest Catholic and Protestant tenements, caused Irish Catholicism endless difficulties. Troubles, however, were the last things that would separate the Irishman from his church, and the solid foundations of Roman Catholicism in the United States were laid by the Irish during these years. In 1820 there were approximately 150,000 Catholics in the country; by 1840 they had increased fourfold.[34] The gain was slow before 1830, and it was largely Irish. During these years Irish priests helped to organize practically every diocese from Boston to Charleston. After 1830 the growth was more rapid, and by no means all Irish. Against the 400,000 Irish Catholics who arrived before 1845 must be set an equal number of German immigrants, the majority of whom were also Catholics. Of the 1,112 Catholic churches in the United States in 1850, more than half were in the western states

even in name they had become almost indistinguishable from the native Irish.

[33] The latest semi-historical work on the Irish in America (Roberts, *Ireland in America*, pp. 24-27) magnifies the pre-revolutionary Catholic immigration. Church history, and the evident unfamiliarity of Catholic Ireland with America in 1815, clearly disprove the assumption.

[34] Shaughnessy, *Has the immigrant kept the faith?* pp. 72, 125. His estimates are 196,000 and 663,000 respectively. He overstates the proportion of Catholics among the Irish immigrants. I deduct less proportionately from the second figure, because it is based on the official American returns of immigration which are below the truth.

where the Germans greatly outnumbered the Irish, but in the east the Irish provided the membership of the church, and native Americans most of its wealth.

Irish influence was far more than a matter of numbers. The control of the American church by the hierarchy of Quebec, which was still dominant in 1815, was definitely broken except in British America; and the United States became under Bishops Carroll, England, Hughes, and Kenrick, the great missionary field of Irish Catholicism. The significance of that change extends beyond the limits of American history and touches the Vatican itself. Irish exuberance and Irish fundamentalism have more than once embarrassed the subtler Latin ecclesiastics, and Irish control of what is now one of the largest national bodies of Catholics in the world has created some delicate problems.

One such problem presented itself in a peculiar form between 1812 and 1832 in the battle over trusteeism. American Catholics, under the influence of democratic doctrines, claimed the right as trustees of their local churches to select their own priests, even when the bishop had chosen another. The ensuing bitter dispute between the hierarchy and the more independent laity aroused storms in all dioceses, but particularly in Philadelphia, where William Hogan of Limerick, the trustee's priest, for four years successfully defied Bishop Conwell and even excommunication. The Irish were on both sides of the question, though their press, with the notable exception of Carey's, largely condemned Hogan. The Protestant papers naturally applauded this demonstration of American independence, and Hogan was defended in court by Joseph Reed Ingersoll. The struggle was finally carried to the state legislature, where a measure to aid the trustees was defeated by Governor Hiester, and became an issue in the next election. Reference to a political body composed mainly of Protestants was bound to be fatal to the trustees' cause, and in the thirties they surrendered completely to Bishops Kenrick and Hughes. The attempt fostered by Irishmen, with American support, to infuse local self-government into the last and greatest of mediaeval monarchies had failed, and was not again revived.[35]

The opposite expectation and hope—that the growth of the church would prove a "salutary check" on the spirit of democracy[36]—was also disappointed. The apparent control of Irish elections by the priests after 1826 served to obscure the more powerful influence of O'Connell and the peasant movements, and Catholic emigrants to America carried with them the same mixture of religion and politics, in which political organization and leadership was dominant. They followed their priests readily enough on such questions as religious education, but took most of their orders from ward bosses whose connection with the church was at best formal. If the growth of the Catholic church did not retard the advance of democracy, neither did it do anything to check the growth of democracy's twin brother, nationalism, and for this too Irish influence may be in some degree responsible. In every Roman Catholic country in Europe with the exception of Ireland and perhaps Poland, there has been a tradition of opposition between church and state, and the church has perforce maintained actively what it always asserts in theory, namely, an insistence on standards of conduct and judgment transcending national or patriotic good. Ireland, however, thanks to a long period of alien and Protestant rule, so identifies religious enthusiasm and nationalism, that today the Irish Free State enforces a

[35] Shea, *Catholic church in the United States*, III, *passim;* and Finotti, *Bibliotheca Catholica Americana*, pp. 137-173.

[36] *Proposed new plan of a general emigration society* (1842), p. 18.

purely Catholic morality while the church tacitly approves the wildest ebullitions of national vainglory. The influence of the Irish hierarchy in America has undoubtedly aided in creating a similar attitude on the part of the Catholic church in this country, and in resolving the antagonism which might have arisen had control been in the hands of men with a background of resistance to the pretensions of national power. As it is, Italians, Spaniards, Poles, and Portuguese as well as Irish immigrants yield ready obedience to government and offer no opposition to the most blatant nationalism.

Irish Catholic influence on public opinion outside the church has been largely negative. Their church schools have not as a rule been so superior as to attract numbers of Protestant children. They have produced some able leaders in the field of teaching, but their institutions of higher learning have not attained the standards of the better European universities and seminaries, and many of the best church schools today owe their development to French and Spanish orders. They have therefore given no stimulus to the development of higher standards in secular education. In the press their efforts have been even less successful. Irish Catholic journals appeared in numbers during the thirties, from Boston to Cincinnati, and from New Orleans to Albany. Most of them died within a few years, though several, among them the Boston *Pilot* and the Philadelphia *Freemans Journal,* had long and distinguished careers. All the early papers were narrowly sectarian and over-fond of controversy, but their bibliographer found them preferable to the "money-making, sickly, riding-on-both-sides-of-the-fence efforts of more recent dates."[37] Their effect was naturally to inflame the latent religious bigotry of Protestant America, and in this Protestant papers gave them ample sup-

[37] Finotti, *Bibliotheca Catholica Americana,* p. 305.

port. The ability to arouse passions on both sides has continued to characterize Irish-American journalism to this day, and frequently neutralizes the effect of its propaganda.

A similar reaction has marked the purely religious influence of the Irish Catholic movement. To the believer in the creeds of the day, the growth of Catholicism in America was in itself an event of tremendous significance. The historian sees it rather as the transference of one portion of the Roman Catholic peoples from the old to the new world, where it might have somewhat greater influence in world affairs without materially altering the world religious equation. The United States became decidedly more Catholic but not predominantly so, and its experience of religious friction underwent a sharp revival. Some few Protestants and non-believers were converted to Catholicism; a somewhat larger number, though not nearly so many as the church once feared, were lost into agnosticism or indifference.[38] The most decisive effects between 1830 and 1845 were felt in New England. There a long period of comparative success and happiness had undermined the old hell-fire religious teaching and given birth to the Unitarian movement with its faith in human progress, as science and middle-class prosperity in England and France at the same period produced the Positivism of Comte and the humanitarian individualism of John Stuart Mill. The coming of the Irish was a disaster for Dr. Channing and his followers. "Prosperity" often gave way to seething discontent, and faith, especially fighting faith, became again a marketable commodity. While Massachusetts and Connecticut poured their emigrants into Iowa to save the West for Protestantism, Boston and New Haven were themselves the field of fundamentalist missionaries from Vermont

[38] Shaughnessy, *Has the immigrant kept the faith?*

and up-state New York, fighting simultaneously against
Catholic and latitudinarian doctrines. The older churches
closed their ranks against the Irish newcomers. Dr.
Beecher thundered at them from the pulpit, and the prestige and zeal of orthodox Protestantism reached new
heights. The fires have since cooled, though the back-
sliders are more often to be found in the new-New England of the West than in their ancestral homes, but the
spirit which roused Boston in 1831 is still alive and ready
to bring out tens of thousands who have long ceased to
call themselves Protestants, against the Roman Catholic
church. If to this reaction is added the effect of nearly
half a million Protestant Irish immigrants during the
years 1815-1845, the increase in the force of Protestantism, and especially of its more militant branches, is considerable.

From a people who lay claim to a high degree of sensi-
tivity, and from a church which makes greater use of
aesthetic appeal than most other Christian sects, some
positive contribution to American art might be expected.
The paucity of the church's work, at first sight disap-
pointing, is perhaps no more than a reflection of the
general backwardness of American production. The Irish
achievements in this field have also been pronounced unsatisfactory, largely perhaps because Irish boasting has
raised undue expectations; but the Irish names in the
history of American poetry, fiction, drama and music
suggest that the race has done its share—a very credit-
able share in the light of the general ignorance and tremendous economic pressure on most of the immigrants.
If they have not created any school or materially altered
American thought or expression, that is scarcely to be
expected in a country which is only now groping its way
toward some positive standard of its own.

The poverty of their contribution to the aesthetic development of America has been more than offset by their activity in the field of political action. It was natural that Irishmen, to whom politics were the salt of life, should take a lively interest in American affairs, and that they should disregard the warnings of emigrant societies to keep out of them. Political considerations did not bring many of them to America, but once settled in their new land they manifested an interest which gradually made itself felt as an important element in American politics. The emigrants were not welcomed by any considerable portion of the American people, and that fact had political consequences of the first order. From the beginning they had to face hostility to immigration which was not confined to one party. Their champions likewise came from different camps. The claim that Irish Democrats prevented restrictions on landing[39] is untrue. Two of the three states—New York, Massachusetts, and Maryland—which regulated immigration before 1845 were Irish strongholds. It was the demands of the employers rather than Irish activity that kept open the doors. But within the parties Irish influence was freely exercised. They had no use for Crawford, who opposed immigration, and gave undivided support to their favorite, Governor Clinton, until he allied himself with the Federalists. The normal ineffectiveness of the state passenger regulations is due in part, though not altogether, to the control of port cities by Irish politicians.

Political allegiance turned much more upon questions of naturalization than of immigrant regulation. Memories of the Alien and Sedition Acts were still green in 1815, and disputes over residence requirements in various states added fresh fuel to the flames. Local politics often made the five-year federal naturalization ineffectual, and

[39] Roberts, *Ireland in America*, p. 115.

Irishmen frequently voted within six months of landing at New York. Nevertheless, the campaign for easier naturalization was genuine, and unlike the agitation against restriction, it tended to follow party lines. The Federalists were already irretrievably damned in Irish eyes; Republicans, Whigs, and later smaller parties betrayed common desires to safeguard American institutions (as they saw them) from the alien. Only the Democrats opened their hearts and their jobs to the immigrant.

During the opening years of the nineteenth century the Irish had been Republicans. Between 1815 and 1830 their allegiance switched to the Democratic party, and there it has remained ever since. This major fact of American politics is attributable to a number of causes, no one of which was decisive. Hostility to England moved the earlier emigrants and influenced some of those who came after 1815. It made them implacable foes of the Federalists; yet they gave no aid to John Quincy Adams, whose foreign policy was far more irritating to Britain than was Andrew Jackson's; nor to the Whigs, though the latter raised the anti-British tariffs. The immigrants who came between 1825 and 1845 were in fact much less antagonistic to England, but they took their politics largely from their predecessors,—men like Emmet of New York and Andrew Dunlap of Boston, whose influence, like that of Daniel O'Connell, was immense, and who hated the name of Britain. This common Irish tendency to follow personalities rather than principles, commenced locally and cemented for the whole United States by the overwhelming popularity of Jackson, rendered the organization of the Irish vote peculiarly easy. Discipline and tradition made men good Catholics, Emancipationists, Repealers, and Democrats; for as A.E. wrote a century later, "Our (Irish) political movements, which required an army of drilled voters unanimous and thinking alike, destroyed national character and individuality.''[40] The shift from the Jeffersonian to the Jacksonian party was by no means confined to Irishmen, and one can detect beneath the personal issue a tradition which may have been more important than either personal or national loyalty. Both leaders were friends of the poor man and his champions against the ruling aristocracy of America, which included Adams and many of the Whigs. The Irish were certainly poor, and they had behind them a long history of opposition to the upper classes which transferred itself easily to the mercantile oligarchies of the American cities. The same attitude toward the mill owners influenced local politics in the rising factory towns, but had no effect on national policy, at least on the important matter of tariffs. The Irish did not understand the tariff as an economic issue and were on the whole indifferent to it. In more recent years their patriotism has made them easily susceptible to protectionist arguments and so helped to modify the earlier Democratic position. Their distrust of the ruling classes was not always to be counted on, and in the struggle between Van Buren and Calhoun for the leadership of the party, the majority arrayed themselves with the aristocratic planter. This was in part a result of their hatred of the negro, and it greatly facilitated the alliance between northern and southern Democrats.

The Irish tradition of being ''agin the government'' aided the growth of the Democratic machine in regular Whig states such as Massachusetts, and in such cities as Philadelphia and Boston, which only went Democratic once before 1845, but control of local government was most effective in bringing them into the Democratic fold. Tammany was largely Irish by 1820, and its management of city funds and charity was used then as it has been ever since to secure the immigrant vote. In Boston,

40 G. W. Russell, *Coöperation and nationality*, p. 58.

even without local power, Henshaw and his Custom House Party were able to use federal patronage for the same purpose. Well-drilled Irish voters existed in most of the larger cities, and drew in the new immigrants as fast as they arrived. These same bodies also protected the runners, sharpers and others who preyed upon the immigrants, and so nullified in practice the well-meant legislation of the states. They fed the wolf and the lamb, and got the votes of both! No national issue affected Irish interests as much as local questions, and none had so much effect on their party affiliation. The state equivalent of local charity was vast expenditures on public works, and the Irish of course supported them. Canal workers, however, found it less easy to get the vote than city laborers, and it is doubtful if the Irish were much interested in this phase of policy.

Outside the Democratic party Irish influence was neither concentrated nor very great. The Anti-Masons included in their program hostility to Catholicism and attracted few Irish. The Workingmen's party was in part anti-immigrant, and though its program included a number of points with which the Irish were in sympathy, they did not forsake their already established allegiance. Its strength was mainly rural, and as its followers were absorbed into Democracy they created a counter-weight to Irish city influence. By 1840 antipathy to the Irish both as aliens and Catholics had reached formidable proportions, and gave rise to Native Americanism, which attained its greatest strength in the fifties. Most of its recruits were drawn from the Whigs, thereby aiding the demolition of the Whig organization. The Irish were sorely perplexed by the adherence of many children of immigrants to the new group.[41] Their attitude was perfectly characteristic, however, of the established as

41 Maguire, *Irish in America*, p. 451.

against the latest-arrived immigrant family, and fore-shadowed the later support of restrictive immigration laws. It was confined to the Protestant Irish, and was in many respects a revival of Orange antipathies. The development of the slavery crisis broke up the Native American party; it also split the Democrats, and Irish partisanship was not fully reunited until after the Civil War.

The politics of the Protestant Irish were never unanimous. In New York they followed Emmet into the Democratic ranks, and in the west they joined the prevailing drift to the same party; yet the two Scotch Irish governors of Ohio between 1815 and 1845 were Whigs. Even in the Catholic ranks there were outstanding rebels. Matthew Carey, though he was never a party man, led his Philadelphia compatriots in the Whig cause of protection; and the Irish of the overwhelmingly Democratic Pittsburgh area turned down a Jackson man because he was against the tariff. Judge Gaston, the leading Irishman of North Carolina, was a Federalist. Against the assertions of the Whigs and the statements of historians as to the solidarity of the Irish vote may be set the judgment of Francis Grund in 1837 that their action was less unanimous than that of the Germans and comparatively unimportant in defeating the Whigs.[42] The influence of the minority who did join the Whig party was inconsiderable and their effect on it confined largely to providing issues which promoted its decay, and to swinging the precarious balance against Clay and Frelinghuysen in 1844.[43]

[42] Grund, *The Americans*, II, 39-40.

[43] Even then the Irish were beaten on local affairs in New York City by a Nativist coalition; the defection of Democratic workingmen from the agreement swung city, state and nation to Polk. See Scisco, *Political nativism in New York State*, pp. 46-49.

Even in British America, where their opportunities were on a par with those of other settlers, the Irish were not a major political force. Immigrants were rarely active in politics until they had been in the country for ten years, and the Irish, therefore, had little effect before 1840.[44] They were sympathetic with the assemblies in Upper Canada and New Brunswick in their struggles with the governors and with the ruling clique, but they supplied no leaders nor any prominent support in the rebellion of 1837. In Lower Canada the hostility of the French kept them loyal to the government. After 1840, when the issue of responsible government was crossed with an increasing number of factional questions, Irish politics reappeared in Canada in connection with long standing religious abuses, and Orangeism provoked riots and bloody affrays of the worst type. The connection between church and empire, which makes the Orangeman even more of an imperialist than he is a Protestant, has perpetuated the Orange influence in Canada long after it has ceased to be important in the United States, and it is still a pernicious influence in the politics of Ontario.

Fortunately for the United States, the more transitory character of the religious question permitted Irish influence to be exerted along saner lines. We have seen that the factors which attracted Irish voters were democracy for the poor, personal and organization appeal, and anti-English sentiment, and it was through these issues that they made themselves most strongly felt in American government. Their services to the cause of democracy are unquestionable. They fall into two distinct periods with an interval of reaction between them. The Irish of the older generation served their country well in procuring a tardy recognition by the states of the American principle of religious equality, and men of Irish descent such as

44 Durham, *Political unrest in Upper Canada*, 1815-1836, p. 10.

Governor Clinton and Judge Gaston led the way in abolishing religious qualifications for office. Fortunately, the
reform was effected, in every state where many Irish
settled, before 1830, when the coming of the Catholic
Irish stirred up religious animosities. Thenceforth the
fight was carried on strictly economic lines, though residence requirements for voting were a subsidiary issue.

American suffrage normally went through three stages,
from property qualifications through a small taxpaying
requirement to manhood suffrage. Most of the Irish were
excluded by the first, and a very large number by the
second. Hence they fought, with some success, under the
banners of Jeffersonian democracy, and between 1790
and 1815 three partly Irish states—Kentucky, New
Hampshire and Maryland—adopted manhood suffrage.
During the first ten years of the next period, while the
new western states were continuing the drift to pure
democracy, Massachusetts and Connecticut came down to
a small taxpaying qualification—the former without regard to the Irish, who were not yet important there, and
the latter in spite of them; for the dislike of the ''low
Irish and the niggers,'' expressed as early as 1803, was
becoming a political force. The greatest victory of the
period, the winning of New York to complete democracy,
only intensified that dislike. In 1820 the Irish captured
Tammany Hall and the New York City machine. In 1821
they secured the first step toward democracy in the state,
and five years later their triumph was complete. They
held the city, they made the state machine recognize their
candidates, and they could vote every immigrant almost
as soon as he landed.

The victory was a costly one for democracy. The ''horrible example'' of New York politics combined with a
rapid increase of pauper immigrants to check the advance of liberal ideas. This was no mere excuse advanced

to cover a policy of reaction, but a genuine fear in the minds of thousands of citizens, impelling them to reject further reform. From 1826 to 1844 only two states east of the Alleghanies made substantial modifications in their suffrage. The Pennsylvania Convention of 1837, evenly balanced between conservatives and democrats, compromised on a white taxpayers suffrage with residence qualifications, but only after an attempt to defeat the proposal by linking the Irish with the negro vote. In the very close popular vote on ratification which followed, the Irish helped to carry through the new constitution. Here as everywhere before 1845, they were a small fraction of the total democratic strength; but politicians, secure in the broad support of American rural and workingman's democracy, got just enough extra votes from the Irish to turn the scales in their favor. Wherever the Irish lacked that powerful background they were helpless. The Irish vote became important in Boston by 1828, but they only won the mayoralty once before 1845. They held the federal patronage in Massachusetts until 1838, thanks to support from Washington, only to lose it to George Bancroft and his rural cohorts. They never controlled Philadelphia, and though they were important very early in the rising city of Chicago, the estimate that they were fifty per cent of the voters in 1838 is certainly an exaggeration.[45] The one exception to Irish impotence seems to have been New York, and even there when Whigs and Native Americans could combine the cry for honest government with religious bigotry, they beat Tammany, as they did in 1837, 1841, and 1844. The states were more decidedly anti-Irish. Rural democrats in Maryland refused to redress the unjust under-representation of Baltimore in the legislature through fear of the city mob,

[45] Pease, *Frontier State,* p. 260. Local histories suggest that the Irish were not coming to Cook County in numbers before 1839.

swollen by immigrants; and Rhode Island, which made concessions in 1843 after Dorr's Rebellion had aroused nation-wide sympathy for democracy, retained a property qualification on all men of alien birth for the sole purpose of excluding the Irish.

Comparing the growth of democracy before and after 1826, there is no question that the coming of the "shanty Irish" delayed its progress for eighteen years. In 1844 the tide changed. Polk and Company needed every vote they could get, and for the first time the Irish became of importance in national politics. Enough immigrant voters appeared to offset nativist opposition in the central industrial states. New York was won against a divided enemy, and New Jersey followed its Democratic victory with sweeping changes in its electorate. A late survival of religious discrimination was abolished. Manhood suffrage was passed, and two anti-Irish amendments, one requiring a literacy test and the other longer residence, were defeated. Next year New Jersey was followed by Connecticut and Louisiana, the latter the only southern state with a distinct Irish element. Thereafter, the increasing hysteria of the Know-Nothing group is the mark of a losing battle. The place of the poor man and the immigrant in American politics was assured.[46]

The victory was not won without the growth of a new technique in politics, largely developed by Irish leaders. The cult of St. Tammany and his prototypes in other cities was not of Irish origin, but it was Irishmen who made it the ruling power of municipal government. They knew how to handle their own people, the first mass vot-

[46] On the general development of the franchise see Porter, *History of suffrage in the United States;* for the leading Irish states of Massachusetts, New York, and Pennsylvania, see the studies by Darling, Fox, Scisco, Mueller, and Bartlett.

ers of the slums, and as Latin and Slavic peoples came to dwell with them in later years, Irish wit and flexibility, unscrupulousness and experience of mass politics, made them the natural leaders of urban democracy. From gang leadership through ward bossdom to the control of great cities, Irishmen still outnumber all others. The breach between metropolitan and "up-state" areas is in part their work, but it was a breach bound to develop sooner or later. Their machines have been notoriously corrupt, but not more so than many of the "business men's governments" to which they were the alternative. The difference has been rather in kind than in degree; the Irish or Tammany type appealing through charity more directly to the lowest groups of citizens, debasing more people and at the same time rendering more genuine human service than the graft-by-contract or employers'-favoritism type—though this, of course, is also included in the Tammany program. The machine was defended in the early days as the sole source of political education for the immigrant, but it seems to have trained him only in indifference to public morality and in reliance on the manna of a beneficent bureaucracy, and so taken the first step toward the proletarian socialism now so loudly acclaimed as a cure for depression.

The machine developed in the cities a caste of politicians, separate from and superior to the ordinary citizen; but the creation of a similar caste in national politics through the spoils system was the work of Jacksonian democracy, for which the Irish have little responsibility. How far these groups have served to undermine the ancient bases of American democracy, preventing the application of talent to politics, and how far they have widened the breach between the city and the country or small town, where political leadership is still combined with some other source of livelihood, are questions beyond the scope of this summary.[47]

At one time democracy appeared to be scoring at the expense of the politician in the substitution of party nominating conventions for the caucus nomination of earlier days. The device resulted from the practical necessity of the Jacksonians in 1824, when they found their popular support almost wholly unrepresented in Congress. It was not unknown in Ireland, where O'Connell at this time was going behind the Irish M.P.s for his support, but it was the West rather than the Irish which was responsible for its development in America. The apparent gain for democracy proved illusory, and the later development of conventions, with all important decisions made by the bosses behind locked doors, has nullified the advantages once contained in the system.

Irish gangs were frequently accused not only of corruption but of introducing rioting and intimidation into American elections. The charge is impossible of proof. Intimidation was practised extensively during the Revolution by many others besides Irish; and the anti-Irish rioted fully as much between 1815 and 1845 as did their enemies. Impartial observers noted that there was much less real interference with voters in America, thanks to the ballot box, than there was in England at the same time. What the Irish did add was a picturesqueness and dramatic quality to city elections equivalent to the log cabin and hard cider campaigns of the west. All the ardor of their natures, suppressed in other things, burst forth in campaign song and oratory, and the familiar bombast and rhetoric of American declamation owed a good deal to the style of Grattan and O'Connell.

[47] Irish talent has suffered as much as any other by this exclusion. J. F. Maguire noted in 1868 that the best Irish never succeeded in politics; hence the race got a bad name. *Irish in America*, p. 306.

On just one point did his admirers disagree heartily with O'Connell. From north to south they had no use for the negro. Economic competition, anger at being classed by aristocratic Americans with an inferior race, the influence of such leaders as Bishop England, all conspired to turn the Irish against every effort to aid the slaves. They coöperated easily with southern Democrats, supported Calhoun against Van Buren until the latter hedged on slavery, and helped to bridge the gap between planters and workingmen until the fifties, when all efforts at compromise broke down. Their services to the North during the Civil War are no denial of this attitude. War has always attracted the Irish, and many fought with distinction on both sides. Lincoln's insistence in the early years that the war was solely to preserve the Union was essential to secure Irish loyalty, and it is significant that the only Irish opposition to the war—the New York draft riots of 1863—came after the Emancipation Proclamation. Yet the Irish, simply by adding to the population and the economic strength of the North, helped to settle the slavery conflict.

Irish participation in minor political issues before 1845 produced some political cleavages but little permanent result. The forces combined in New England Anti-Masonry—Congregationalism, abolition, and temperance—were all anti-Irish on different grounds. The later nativist movements were also anti-saloon, attacking the Irish in a vulnerable spot. In New York, politics were complicated by the school issue also. For four years Whig and Democratic nativists combined to keep all Catholics off the school boards and blocked any appropriation of state funds to Catholic schools, which had been sanctioned by law in 1841. The alliance broke down in 1845, and later party leaders were too anxious for the Irish vote to revive the issue.

The tendency of politicians to say more than they mean, and occasionally what they do not mean, throws a veil of obscurity over the extent of Irish influence in the field in which it is said to be most powerful, namely hostility toward Great Britain. How far American foreign policy has been affected by public feeling against England; how far public hostility has been genuine, and to what extent a mere vote-catching device; and how much the Irish nurtured that hostility, are questions incapable of exact solution. It is my belief that the Irish influence has been considerably overstressed. From the period of the Revolution to 1815 they were undoubtedly bitter against England, but no more so than thousands of men of other stocks. For some years after 1815 the older emigrants, exiles from the rebellions of 1782, 1798, and 1803, dominated Irish opinion. Carey's *Olive Branch,* a vicious attack on the Hartford Convention, emanated from a very dubious dove of peace. Thomas O'Conor, editor of the New York *Shamrock* and *Globe,* wrote an *Impartial and correct history of the war* [of 1812] which altogether belied its name.[48] The Shamrock Society and Tammany Hall were scenes of anti-British demonstrations, but a traveller records that he found no general abuse of Great Britain.[49] The fact is that from 1815 to 1829 the Irish had practically no influence on American opinion or policy, and took no interest in the long-drawn-out disputes over trade, fisheries, or the northern boundaries.

The rise of an Irish issue in Catholic Emancipation aroused a little comment. Matthew Carey pored over old texts to write his *Vindiciae Hibernicae* in 1817-18 in the hope that it would aid the cause of religious equality, but the book was hardly calculated to conciliate British opin-

[48] Finotti, *Bibliotheca Catholica Americana,* p. 209.
[49] J. M. Duncan, *Travels through part of the United States and Canada,* II, 273-274; Fearon, *Sketches of America,* p. 88.

ion. A committee from Ireland toured the United States in 1825 and was somewhat hysterically reported to be getting arms and talking of independence.[50] The next year Bishop England was sending inflammatory letters from Charleston, and British ministers feared his transfer to an Irish see.[51] This stir was confined to the Irish in America, and it is not until late in 1828, when Peel and Wellington were already determined on emancipation, that other Americans of standing and of all creeds joined in meetings of sympathy. The total collections at these meetings seem to have fallen short of a thousand dollars. By 1829 associations of Irishmen existed from New Orleans to Quebec, but as their *raison d'etre* disappeared most of them broke up.[52]

The bases of opinion began to change after 1829. The arrival of tens of thousands of starving Irish stirred many Americans to whom Ireland had been only an interesting source of trouble to England. The newcomers were, as Miss Martineau wrote, ". . . squalid paupers, looking as if they were going from shore to shore, to rouse the world to an outcry against the sins and sorrows of our economy."[53] S. G. Goodrich, the "Peter Parley" whose books were read to and by thousands of children, took up the cudgels for these "victims of tyranny."[54] All British accounts were systematically labeled "propaganda." The poorer emigrants, most of whom carried deep down the national grudge against England, though

[50] S. C. Whiting to H. V. Addington, Cincinnati, July 19, 1825, in Addington to Canning, Aug. 6, 1825; F.O. 5/198.

[51] Goulburn to Peel, July 25, 1826, in Parker, *Peel*, I, 418.

[52] Vaughan to Aberdeen, Oct. 20, 1828, and Buchanan to Aberdeen, Dec. 13, 1828; F.O. 5/238, 242.

[53] *Society in America*, I, 345.

[54] See an extract from his *Ireland and the Irish*, in Abbot, *Historical aspects of the immigration problem*, pp. 739-741.

as O'Connellites they were ready to coöperate with her, were nothing loath to profit by this new-born sympathy. Thus the tradition of poor, suffering Ireland passed into American consciousness, to emerge in the fifties as a deliberate belligerency which made a capital dispute of every light disagreement.

Meanwhile, the American government pursued a friendly course. The Andrew Jackson of 1829 was not the bellicose gentleman who had hanged Arbuthnot and Ambrister, and his Secretaries of State were clearly anxious for good relations with England. Upon the Maine–New Brunswick frontier American settlers, some few of them Irish, got into trouble, but the national government smoothed over the difficulty until the boundary could be determined. The Canadian rebellions of 1837, in which we found few Irish taking part, offered a golden opportunity to Anglomaniacs in the United States; but the men who conducted border raids into Canada in 1837 and 1838 were either Canadians or frontiersmen mainly of Yankee stock. At a pro-rebellion meeting in New York in December, 1837, Dr. E. B. O'Callaghan, editor of the Montreal *Vindicator* and the only prominent Irish rebel, was shouted down as an abolitionist, and mention of O'Connell's name was greeted in the same way.[55] The most the Anglophobes could do was to join in the outcry for repudiation of foreign debts, largely held in England, after 1840. Domestic politics and improvement in Ireland had reduced antipathy to England to its lowest point.

The revival of the repeal movement in 1840 reawakened the old feelings. Associations of "Friends of Ireland," first formed in Boston, spread rapidly through the United States and Canada, advocating a boycott on British goods and collecting a "rent" of twelve cents a

[55] Buckingham, *America*, I, 88-89.

month from members.[56] The amounts sent to O'Connell
were enormous; from Boston alone he was said to have
received $10,000.[57] City demagogues rode into office on
the repeal hobby. Yet when a national convention of the
Friends of Ireland was held in Philadelphia in 1842, it
wrangled for three days over slavery and then broke up
with mild resolutions of sympathy for repeal.[58] The next
year the fiasco of O'Connell's monster meeting at Clon-
tarf destroyed his influence, and the long attempt at independence without bloodshed came to an end. Irish leadership passed into the hands of hot-headed young men; men
with a splendid vision of a free Ireland without racial,
religious or class strife, but comparatively unknown in
America. Young Ireland got practically no support from
across the water, and the rebellion of 1848 was the last
which was not largely organized in the United States.
Before another attempt at revolution was made, famine
and the Encumbered Estates Act of 1849 had driven millions of embittered Irishmen to America, and civil war
had trained them to the use of arms. These evicted tenants, together with the United Irishmen of '98, formed
the Fenian army, but the emigrants of 1815-45 and their
children, trained in the spirit and methods of O'Connell,
were anti-Fenian,[59] as many of their descendants have
been anti-Sinn Fein. This division of Irish America into
moderate hostility and rabid Anglophobia, made possible
by the extensive emigrations of less restless years, has
probably produced a more effective propaganda against
England than either group alone could have done. The

[56] Grattan, *Civilized America*, pp. 44-49. The Boston movement was conducted from the Consul's basement by his cook.

[57] T. D. McGee, *History of the Irish settlers in North America*, p. 133.
The sum seems very large and may include ordinary emigrant remittances.

[58] *Report of proceedings, National Repeal Convention of the Friends of
Ireland, in the United States of America.*

[59] Maguire, *Irish in America*, pp. 607-612.

moderates have given the Irish cause some standing with thinking people, while the fire-eaters have roused the un-thinking and driven a spur into the sides of the pacific.

The year 1844 provided ample occasion for the use of spurs. The failure of repeal left the American Irish thoroughly aroused, with no outlet for their energies except Texas or Oregon. Texas offered pleasant opportunities for annoying England, but no such chance of war as did Oregon. The Democratic party, running a dark horse for president against a man of long experience and prestige, wanted a good jingo slogan, and found it in "Fifty-four forty or fight." It attracted westerners and Irishmen, neither of whom knew much about Oregon or the merits of the case. When Polk had been elected and the time came for negotiation, the slogan was a nuisance and, to the dismay of the belligerent Irish was dropped. Senator Hannegan of Indiana, an Ohio-born Irishman, led the opposition to the Oregon Treaty, but it was successfully negotiated by another Irishman, James Buchanan.[60]

The Oregon treaty, like scores of amicable adjustments, testifies to the falsity of the oft-repeated prediction that the Irish would embroil England and America in war. A considerable proportion of the Irish had no desire for such a war, and the majority of the American people have never wanted it. What the Irish wanted, and what for a number of years they secured, was a provocative attitude which would force England to make as many concessions as possible without themselves making any in return. Such a policy sometimes gains a point and more often prevents a valuable compromise, but it was a policy perfectly congenial to the leaders of a young and expanding country with an anti-English tradition, and it is impossible to say how much it owed to the Irish. The

---

[60] Howe, *The Mississippi Valley in the movement for 54-40 or fight*, in Miss. Valley Hist. Assoc. Proceedings, V, 99-116.

majority of Irishmen have looked upon it as a purely American policy, and the fact that they have not sought by threat or by war to use it for the liberation of Ireland, indicates how far their new patriotism has supplanted the old. Despite the continuance of republican propaganda in the United States, such points have sunk into insignificance since the world war and the creation of the Irish Free State, but they were important in determining the Irish attitude toward British trade restrictions as recently as 1916, or America's entrance into the war a year later. Whatever the Irish influence on these or other diplomatic questions, it has been the influence of American citizens of Irish descent, and not of Irishmen in America.

In assessing the work of the Irish in America, it has been impossible to differentiate clearly between the emigrants of different periods. The earlier emigrants obviously contributed to Irish influence after 1815, and both groups were so largely responsible for the post-famine emigration that they share credit for its results. At no time were they in numbers or position calculated to contribute to American life or character in the same degree that America contributed to their own, nor could that be expected. The exceptional plasticity of the Irish under new environment aided them in a rapid adjustment to American ways,[61] and perhaps their most notable achievement is that so many of them have, without losing any advantage of native character, ceased to differentiate themselves from other citizens. The result is of the greatest importance to Ireland, for it is gradually wiping out the distinction between Irish and Scotch-Irish. There are those who already deny the existence of such a distinction, but its prevalence in Ulster today is sufficient reason

[61] For evidence of this in the thirties and forties, see the report of Cornewall Lewis in *Parl. Pap.* 1836, No. 40, p. xii; and Tuke, *Visit to Connaught in the Autumn of 1847*, p. 49.

for its continued use. The Scotch-Irish are of necessity becoming increasingly Irish, and even in 1815 they were a mixed race, and the term Scotch-Irish was decidedly preferable to the older *Ulster Scot*. For the purpose of assaying their work in America the religious distinction is more valuable than the racial; for only on that basis can we say that one group contributed more to religious history, or followed a clearer political line. In all the main results of Irish immigration, economic, social, and political, Irish and Scotch-Irish are in the nineteenth century indistinguishable. We may balance the success of the one against the success of the other and get a common Americanism for the answer.

Rich and colorful as has been the contribution of Irish emigration to the development of America, its significance pales in comparison with the results of the movement for Ireland. We have spoken of the possibility of the Irish, through America, playing a greater rôle on the world's stage, and bringing Ireland herself more nearly within the main currents of human activity. That is still in the nursery of time. For Ireland during our period the bare physical fact of the removal of over a million people outweighed all others, and the principal importance of emigration lay in its consequences for those who remained at home. It was no small thing for a country, in which excess of labor amounted to fully one in three, to lose within thirty years one out of seven, and if we include emigration to Great Britain, one out of five of its inhabitants. Migration to America—the results of which were magnified by the simultaneous exodus to the British mines and factories—removed fourteen per cent of the Irish people, or nearly three times as many in proportion as it added to the American population. The majority of the emigrants were at the most fertile age, between fifteen and thirty; and the continued increase of Irish popu-

lation down to 1841 in spite of this drain throws a startling light on the fecundity of the people, and awakens
painful speculations on the state of Ireland in 1845 had
there been no emigration. This fecundity was not a new
development; it was a tendency evident in the alarming
increase of numbers between 1821 and 1831 when large
scale emigration started, and only partially checked by
the removals during the next decade. After 1841, a larger
exodus and the absence of many of those at the age of
parenthood further reduced growth, and there is reason
to believe that the population remained stationary from
1841 to the famine,[62] when decrease began. It follows that
the pressure of population, though not yet removed, had
been stabilized; and that there was hope of preventing
any further demoralization of the people until some
measure of redress could be devised.

To offset this gain must be set the possible loss of the
stronger and more enterprising workers, who are usually
among the first to emigrate. Experience has shown that
the Irish pick up rapidly under improved diet, and so far
as stamina is concerned, the increased vigor of those left
behind under a higher standard of living may be said to
have afforded some compensation. Initiative is a more
subtle quality and difficult to measure, and its exercise by
a peasant people bound by centuries of tradition is peculiarly limited. The superior development of the Irish in
America suggests either that opportunity brought out the
latent qualities of the race, or that America was getting
the best Irish. The comparative ill-success of the emigrants to Great Britain may also point either moral. The
transfer to America of leadership in the major political

[62] Older historians, assuming a continued increase of population after
1841, conjectured that deaths in the famine were far greater than any
records indicated. It is certainly more probable that the population had
ceased to advance.

movements of Ireland implies superior enterprise there, but the two most significant recent developments in Irish life—rural coöperation and the cultural revival—are wholly indigenous. It is fair to note, however, that the leaders of these movements have been drawn from the old aristocratic rulers of the country, whereas political chieftains have emerged from any and every class of emigrant.

Had the exodus continued on the scale and from among the groups sailing before 1845, the consequences to Irish ethnology might have been positively harmful. As it was, the flight of laborers after 1835 served to balance the preponderance of small farmers and artisans emigrating in earlier years, but the emigrants of all three types were among the more energetic of their class. The post-famine migrant was a very different sort of being, often the poorest and most wretched of his village, whose abandoned holding swelled the farm of a more substantial neighbor. In subsequent decades pioneer emigration became impossible, and weak and strong went out together under the close shepherding of shipping agents, and on money supplied as a rule from America, until today Irish population has decreased by a half since 1841 without any evident change in character or physique.

The growth of emigration between 1815 and 1845 not only made possible the flight after the famine; more than any other factor, it caused that flight. The stock view that the famine either killed or drove into exile some millions of people has been twice challenged. Spencer Walpole believed that the surplus population was drawn off by the coal measures of England;[63] Alison Phillips sees rather the attractive newly-opened lands of the Mississippi Valley as the prime cause.[64] The statistics of emigration,

[63] *History of England*, I, 67.
[64] *Edinburgh Review*, CCXXXVI, 123.

as this study has attempted to show, refute all three contentions, and prove that the thirty years before 1845 spread the emigrating spirit through three provinces and through all but the highest class, until it became the favorite remedy for hard times. It remained for the famine to bring in the fourth province, Connaught, and to introduce the excess relief shipping which carried the increased emigration. The tremendous rush of the next fifteen years could not have taken place without aid from earlier emigrants. Their remittances to Ireland rose steadily from £200,000 in 1847 to £1,439,000 in 1853, and by 1863 twenty million pounds, or much the larger part of the expenses of emigration had been paid in America.[65] Thereafter the removal of the Irish to America was almost as simple and much more usual than a similar transfer from Cork to Belfast.

The blessings to the individuals involved are incalculable. The million who left before 1845 could have done nothing to avert the famine; they would only have suffered in it, for they were members of the classes largely dependent on the potato by that time. The crying need during the famine was for merchants, shopkeepers and a machinery of distribution, and these classes did not emigrate, nor was their trade injured by emigration. Their absence was due to the wretched level of peasant selfsufficiency, which emigration had tended to break down. Hence direct aid by emigrant remittances, even when sent in the form of food, was of comparatively little value. Ireland was soon flooded with food, but the people had not the knowledge to use it, and there were not enough distribution centers to give it out ready-cooked. The best the American Irish could do was to rescue some hundreds of

[65] Hancock, *On the supposed progressive decline of Irish prosperity,* pp. 12-14; for a full account of relief and remittances see *Transactions of the Central Relief Committee of the Society of Friends.*

thousands by bringing them to America during the famine, and then to bring over millions more until a repetition of that catastrophe became impossible. Periodic local famines have continued, and will occur so long as more than a hundred thousand families exist on plots of less than an acre each, but the pressure of population was decreased in the fifties, and the standard of peasant living raised to a point from which it can not easily return to the old bad days.

By the standards of 1815, which are still held by some students of society, the wealth of nations is above all in their citizens, and any diminution by emigration sheer loss. Such a theory cannot apply to Ireland before 1850, when every third laborer was an extra mouth to feed, capable at best of producing just enough for his own sustenance, and often a burden on the community. In such a state every emigrant, unless he takes away productive goods more than equivalent to his own consumption, is a blessing; for the value of his labor is instantly replaced from the unproductive reserve. We have seen that the removal of mobile capital was infinitesimal, and except in the first few years after 1815, British and Irish statesmen, jealous of their countries' wealth, took no alarm. Most of it went to pay the expenses of transportation, of which a considerable part returned to Ireland and a still larger share was subscribed in America. If we set against this the sums sent to Ireland by emigrants, over and above what was remitted specifically to pay for emigration, the cash balance for Ireland before 1845 is not unfavorable. After the famine the advantage is more decided; emigrant remittances become a regular part of the income of thousands of farmers. Unlike the Italian of later days, the Irishman rarely carried back the savings of an American sojourn to bask in the admiring envy of his native village, but his contribution to its prosperity was no

less generous and effectual. Direct assistance was only
one of several aids to agriculture brought about by emigration. Even the critics of the movement have admitted
that in the case of Ireland, where necessary improvement
could not be made until some of the population was removed, it was beneficial.⁶⁶ We have seen evidences of this
before 1845 in the Ulster counties covered by the Ordnance Survey, and a comparison of its reports with the
records of the London Companies on their lands near
Derry substantiates the testimony.⁶⁷ After the famine all
Ireland shared in the gain. By 1853 employment was
steady and better times checked emigration; in succeeding years wages rose, and farms prospered. The change
meant more than immediate happiness; it enabled Ireland to return to its soundest economy, an economy based
on grazing rather than tillage, and so protected it in large
measure against the impact of American grain in the
mid-century, which proved so ruinous to British and continental farmers. The people as a whole continued poor
and sometimes distressed, for the resources under their
control were slight, and the bases of agrarian friction remained. But national destitution and insolvency no
longer threatened year after year.⁶⁸

Agricultural improvement meant better times for all
Ireland, though not in equal degree for all classes. Local
trade felt the stimulus first, and a system of distribution,

⁶⁶ E.g. Leroy-Beaulieu, *De la colonization chez les peuples modernes*, p.
687, though hostile to emigration, admits its value in this case.

⁶⁷ *Ordnance Survey*, Londonderry, county; and A. H. Johnson, *History of
the Worshipful Company of the Drapers of London*, III, 380-394.

⁶⁸ The best contemporary accounts of improvement are J. Locke, *Ireland's recovery* (1853) and W. N. Hancock, *On the supposed progressive
decline of Irish prosperity* (1863). The chief authority asserting a continuous decline is C. Booth, *Economic distribution of population in Ireland*,
which is based on the census figures of 1841, 1851, and 1861, although the
classifications used in those years differ so much as to invalidate compari-
sons.

so sadly lacking at the famine, struck root throughout the country. The change has not been wholly for the good; the village publican-shopkeeper-money lender (and often political boss) has tended to replace the landlord as the national vampire, and his treatment of debtors retains no trace of the paternalism. of the better landlords. It is something, however, to have money and a job on which to borrow. The larger merchants who dealt with the gentry secured a steadier trade, though swollen rentals sometimes fell with the declining competition for potato-ground. Export trade in beef and butter naturally improved, and the basis was laid for a valuable extension of the American market, which has always been a consumer of Irish linens in fair quantities. It would be impossible to say how much of Irish production has been bought by the Irish in America, but they have certainly aided in advertising Irish goods, as they are today carrying on the fight against Belgian and Czecho-Slovak competition. The export trade itself has been mainly in the hands of British and American merchants, and yielded less return to Ireland than the manufacture behind it. The linen industry profited by the expansion of market and lost nothing by the drain of labor, for the Belfast area was, like New York and Manchester, a goal of Irish migration. It is doubtful whether the factories advanced on account of decreased competition of domestic production brought about by emigration—that was doomed in any case. The only other large scale industry, ship-building, did not arise until the day of the iron ship, and owed little to the emigration movement. A more effective result is seen in the American demand for Irish liquor. As Irish demand also picked up with better times, the industry soon recovered from the injuries inflicted by Father Matthew's crusade.

Emigration had little effect on the social structure of

Ireland. The failure of emigrants to return minimized the influence of America on Irish customs, and today the Irish-American visiting Erin often feels himself in a strange land. The American cults of speed and hygiene make no headway there; standardization is imposed by government on an unwilling country; and the tree of democracy, though long the object of lip homage, remains an exotic on Irish soil. Emigration by drawing mainly from the lowest class, has tended to alter the balance of classes—a tendency counteracted, however, by long continued civil war. In one important respect only has the migration of 1815-1845 changed the Irish equation. It seems probable that it had far-reaching consequences on the balance of creeds in Ireland. A protestant exodus equal in numbers to the Roman Catholic, and drawn from a population at most one-third as large, completed the ruin begun in colonial times of the dreams of James I and Cromwell. Ulster continued to be a thorn in the flesh of statesmen, but it was wholly inadequate as a check upon Irish independence. After 1831 the higher proportion of Protestants going to America was offset by the almost wholly Catholic exodus to Great Britain and later to America and a balance was established. But within Protestant ranks change has continued, increasing the importance of the non-emigrant Church of Ireland, and decreasing that of the sectarians in general and of the Presbyterians in particular. The effect has been a closer association of Protestantism with property, with urban life, and with Unionism; for Presbyterians were frequently rebellious, whereas the Church of Ireland has been the most dogged defender of British power. The reverse of this picture is the increased Catholicism of rural Ulster, now taken for granted in all but two counties, but a subject of alarm a hundred years ago. Fierce religious-agrarian conflict accompanied the emigration from the border counties, and since prior to 1835 the emigrants were largely Presbyterian, Catholics were left in control of the field. Today these counties, Monaghan, Cavan, and Donegal, are almost wholly Catholic and owe to that fact their inclusion in the Irish Free State. The penetration into Armagh, Fermanagh and Tyrone was less notable, but it was sufficient to give them a distinct Nationalist tinge.[69]

The political implications of the religious change were not hidden from statesmen, and we have seen that some of them wished to prevent it. But if they expected, as the careers of the Volunteers and United Irishmen in America gave them cause to fear, that later emigrants would stir up Irish discords, they were destined to disappointment for more than two decades. An Irishman who started a weekly in New York in 1818 giving Irish news found the immigrants indifferent to events at home.[70] Ten years later when they had come into the Emancipation movement, they assured O'Connell that they did so "... without intending in any wise to interfere with the politics of Ireland";[71] and it is evident from the letters of the Catholic leader that he relied little on American support. Mr. Canning had played politics in 1825 in relaying an alarming communication on Irish-American plots to the King and the Home Office,[72] but later ministers took these missives more calmly. Throughout the thirties there was no attempt at interference, but with the revival of repeal in 1840 it became an important factor in the situation. O'Connell was able to make plans on the basis of American funds, and we have seen the sense of frustration

[69] *Supra*, Chap. II; and G. C. Lewis, *On local disturbances in Ireland*, p. 458.

[70] Letter of W. H. Creagh, in Bradsher, *Matthew Carey*, pp. 65-66.

[71] Letter of Philadelphia Irish to O'Connell, June 25, 1828, enclosed in Vaughan to Aberdeen, Oct. 20, 1828; F.O. 5/238.

[72] Notation on Addington to Canning, Aug. 6, 1825; F.O. 5/198.

among Irish-Americans at his failure. Money was the entering wedge of American influence, but as time and circumstance transferred the hot bloods of Ireland across the Atlantic, personal leadership also came from the United States. Whether Irish interest would have been better served by their parliamentary leaders without American revolutionary interference is a question which will now never be answered. The Act of 1914, had it not been killed in infancy by the Great War, might well have justified the parliamentary attitude; the settlement of 1922, unsatisfactory as it was, seemed to justify rebellion. Whatever the verdict on this point, the continued American support of a campaign of assassination and intrigue against a government recognized and supported by the main body of Irish citizens has been one unfortunate consequence of emigration.

Weighing social and economic gains against a dubious political influence, the advantage of emigration to Ireland seems clear. Some of the same effects are observable indirectly in England. The removal to America of one-seventh of the population saved England from an even greater influx of Irish labor than she received. Increased prosperity after the famine relieved the treasury of some extra burden and increased the market for British goods, and today the Irish buy more per capita than any other people except the New Zealanders. But it was in the field of politics that emigration had its deepest influence in Great Britain. Between 1815 and 1845 Irish distress was more clamorous and continuous than that of Great Britain, where displaced agricultural labor was being absorbed by an expanding industry. British humanitarianism, fresh from a victory over the slave trade and winning another over slavery itself in 1834, turned more and more to domestic concerns. British ills were before their eyes, but the remedies required delicate adjustments with powerful squires and millowners. Ireland, whose abuses were even more crying, offered a hopeful field for their intervention, and after 1831 the lords of the *status quo* had less influence with the government than the disciples of change. Even the landlord element of the Whig ministries acknowledged the need of reform. From this combination of forces came the first steps toward paternalism—admitting by the poor law an obligation of wealth already recognized in England, and sanctioning by the tithe settlements an invasion of property more drastic than any similar move across the Irish Sea. Emigration had no part in these measures, and when enthusiasts attempted to deal with it on the same humanitarian and paternalistic principles, they received a sharp rebuff. The rôle of emigration was, in fact, to postpone by almost fifty years the extension of state control in Irish and indirectly in British affairs. From 1830 to the famine the voluntary exodus stopped the advocates of colonization; and from the famine to 1880 it made possible the application to Ireland of Gladstonian Liberalism. The unshackling of trade and industry, begun under the stress of famine, progressed step by step with the advance of Irish prosperity. Men suffered in the process, as they do during every expansion of industry, but Ireland gained, and Great Britain gained still more. Ministers, set free from an ever-present horror at their door-step, were able to promote education and to disestablish the Irish church without setting the whole kingdom by the ears; and they could devote themselves to the liberation of English economy without being told at every turn, as they had been before 1845, that they were being unfair to Ireland. The soundness of imperial finance and economy from Gladstone to the World War, despite the fearful strain upon it in later years, owes something to the relief caused by Irish emigration.

The new policy came to an end in the eighties. The historic cycle swung from emphasis on production and the accumulation of wealth to emphasis on its distribution. Young Liberals paid more attention to the qualifications on J. S. Mill's individualism than to his main theme. Conservatives followed the bright star of Disraeli's new imperialism, with its concomitants of higher taxes, increased suffering, and the necessary palliative of social reform. Irish improvement from emigration had run its course, and the condition of its land laws after two unsuccessful attempts to settle them along liberal lines invited a renewal of paternalistic legislation. The new laws have been in effect, though not in intention, confiscatory—the landlords and the British people between them bearing the burden of transferring the soil of Ireland to the peasants. This somewhat dubious honor of expiating the sins of their ancestors has some justification in Irish history, but its effects have not stopped there. The official habit of interference in business, and the popular habit of looking to government for redress of evils, have both grown in England from its Irish policy, which has been since 1880 in advance of similar policy at home, and has helped to pave the way for socialism. Emigration has had no part in this last phase, which rather marks its failure to procure any fundamental change in political and social outlook.[73]

From modern industrial paternalism to the mercantile policy of a hundred years ago is a short step, and one which brings us to the last great field of emigration results—the rise of an emigrant trading interest. Britain's tenderness for her nurseries of seamen, newly aroused by the Napoleonic Wars, assured emigrant and timber carriers of the friendly concern of government, and preserved them for nearly thirty years after 1815 from any

[73] These conclusions, reached independently, are supported as to the three stages of Irish policy by C. Bastable in *Economic Journal*, XIX, 68-73.

drastic change in the system of mercantile privilege. It is impossible to estimate precisely the rewards of this policy to the shipper, but a selection of figures from two decades may give some idea of the profits of the emigrant trade. Well-built vessels in the last days of the eighteenth century cost about £25 a ton. The tremendous demands of the war period kept them at full value, but in the glut of shipping after the peace they fell fifty per cent in three years, and a vessel taking a full cargo of emigrants to British America at the fares prevailing between 1815 and 1818 could earn £3. 6. 4 a ton, or twenty-seven per cent on its capital value for the single westward voyage. The return trip with timber netted a somewhat smaller amount, but the gross income for the round trip totaled not quite a half the ship's valuation. That these are not purely speculative figures is proved by the case of the *Aurora*. By tonnage it should have been worth slightly over £2,000, and it was chartered by Hunt and Jeffcoat for the voyage from Cork to New Brunswick at £450, or twenty-two and a half per cent of its value.[74] Deducting from this two per cent for insurance,[75] approximately three per cent for wages, and a somewhat larger amount for port dues, fees, etc., there still remains a handsome margin of profit. Over and above this amount, the contractors or emigrant agents also made their own ample profit. Small wonder that after 1815 towering East Indiamen and the little pirate-dodging Mediterranean vessels both forsook their depressed trades to get into the timber-emigrant business. The inevitable oversupply soon cut returns, and the cessation of emigration after the panic of 1819, plus the glut of timber in Great Britain in anticipation of new duties in 1821, drove out much of the excess shipping. Profits on

[74] Copy of charter in Bagot to Castlereagh, December 22, 1818; F.O. 5/133.

[75] Wright and Fayle, *History of Lloyds*, p. 191.

timber fell to 5/4 a ton, and emigrant ships, though keeping up fares, sailed with less than half their complement of passengers.[76]

When the trade revived and assumed its regular form after 1830, it yielded smaller but steadier returns. A full passenger list at the minimum rate of 30/ meant an income of 22/6 a ton; or at the more usual rate of two pounds, brought in 30/ a ton. Timber rates averaged between 35/ and 40/, so that the entire voyage was worth between £3 and £4 a ton. The typical vessel making two trips with timber and one with emigrants each year made gross earnings of £5. 10. 0 per ton. As the cost of construction in the thirties was somewhat less than £20 per ton, this represented a year's income for a new ship of twenty-seven and a half per cent, and of fifteen to eighteen per cent for the voyage. Most of the ships were not new, however, or were thrown together in Canada at lower costs, so that the actual earnings were higher. When against these are set all the costs of maintenance and operation, the net gain is considerably less than that on many other enterprises, and it is not surprising to find the better ships forsaking the emigrant trade in years of brisk business activity.

The significance of the emigrant trade in British mercantile history lies not in its contribution to wealth, in which respect it never rivalled the great fields of commercial exploitation, but in its addition to the quantity

[76] Profits estimated on the basis of passage at £5, a low average for this period. For general statistics on cost of ships see Kirkaldy, *British shipping;* J. R. Smith, *The ocean carrier;* and Spears, *Story of the American merchant marine;* on timber rates, U.S. Doc. 590, No. 23; Isaac Andrews, *Special report on the trade and commerce of the British North American colonies.* All other facts from the speeches of Joseph Marryat on the timber duties in 1820-1821, in *2 Hansard,* I, 845-861; IV, 545, 1507; V, 50-63; and *Parl. Pap.* 1821, No. 186: First report of the Select Committee (Commons) on foreign trade.

and stability of British shipping. Timber and cotton were the only bulk commodities which repaid transoceanic shipment in the days before the steam vessel, and timber alone employed a third of British tonnage in the first half of the nineteenth century. Despite some fluctuations caused by fear of changes in duties, the Canada trade rose continuously from about 100,000 tons in 1815 to 800,000 in 1845, when it was employing over 2,000 ships, —no mean nursery of seamen. How much of this growth is due to emigration we cannot say. The trade got its start in war time without need of passengers, and it is evident in later years that the ships, or a large portion of them, made their voyages whether they got their passengers or no. Nevertheless, between 1815 and 1818 the profits on emigration exceeded those on timber, and after 1830 emigration yielded from one-third to one-half the total income of the trade. Furthermore, it was a useful argument for the maintenance of mercantilism, and so late as 1842 we find the timber duties defended for the sake of the emigrant trade. "This marvellous movement," wrote the North American Colonial Association to Sir Robert Peel, "which is there so fast replenishing the earth and subduing it, could not only never have so prospered as it has but for the timber trade, but could never have found its direction and seat within our dominions, nor even the means of opportunities of conveyance anywhere, but for that bridge across the Atlantic which has been formed by the timber ships.'"[77] The appeal was unsuccessful,— partly because the statement was ceasing to be true. By 1840 timber ships, though they were still useful in emigration, were no longer a necessity.

The value of the passenger traffic to other than timber

[77] *Memoir on the Colonial timber trade presented to the Rt. Hon. Sir Robert Peel, Bart., by the Committee on the North American Colonial Association*, p. 15.

vessels cannot be accurately ascertained. The early shippers obviously took passengers as an addition to their
cargo trade and counted on it only for a portion of their
profit on westbound voyages. When John Quincy Adams
stated that a serious check on emigration would stop all
Irish-American commerce,[78] he could not foresee the
practice of loading cargo in Great Britain and passengers
in Ireland. The later Liverpool trade undoubtedly created
some tidy fortunes, but they went largely to the great
agencies rather than to the actual shippers, whose profits
on the New York assorted cargoes westbound, and cotton
eastbound, far outweighed their income from emigrants.
Cabin passengers on the fast packets represented bigger
returns,[79] and when Cunard opened his steamship service
from Liverpool to Boston for freight and passengers,
there was little attempt to appeal to the emigrant. That
trade was still in the hands of a special group, and its
effect on shipping was indirect.

In their own day the emigrants played a definite but
not outstanding part in mercantile economy, but the shipping which carried them in the late thirties and early
forties determined with some additions the tonnage available after the famine. It has been said frequently that
this was of the worst possible description. The statement
was partially true; the ships of the post-war surplus,
many of them excellent vessels for their day, had largely
disappeared by 1845. The timber ships were none too
good, and one suspects some truth in the charge that the
trade kept afloat some hulks which might better have
been abandoned. Their easy convertibility for passengers was an attraction, however, and they were at least
cleaner at the beginning of a voyage than many cargo

---

[78] April 9, 1816; *Memoirs*, III, 330.
[79] Two thousand to five thousand dollars a voyage—Spears, *Story of the American merchant marine*, p. 224.

carriers. The Liverpool vessels were better and newer; they included a considerable proportion of American ships which were preferred partly on account of the ships themselves, but more for their superior crews. Everywhere there was an increase of size and speed. The one hundred and fifty and two hundred tons of 1815 was more than doubled, and the average time to America was cut to less than five weeks. Increased knowledge of British American coasts reduced the number of wrecks, though the voyage to Canada remained more dangerous than to Boston or New York. These changes owe little to emigration, which merely profited by them; but the fact that packets, general cargo boats, and timber ships were all familiar with emigration by 1845 aided enormously in the development of a true emigrant or passenger vessel. The construction of unconvertible vessels for passenger traffic only was in part dictated by the passenger acts of 1842, but it would never have been undertaken without the experience of thirty years profit in the emigrant trade.

The one incontestable advance in the passenger trade lay in the improvement of the machinery of regulation. It was neither adequate nor particularly efficient, but repeated failure prepared the way for more successful attempts when the famine emigration demonstrated their urgent necessity. The old prejudice against all control had died out in England in 1827, and it disappeared in the United States a decade later. In 1835 the use of regulation as an instrument of commercial politics practically ceased, and the way was opened for genuine humanitarian action. The principles of limitation of numbers in accordance with tonnage and space, of a minimum provision requirement, and of compulsory medical and surgical attendance, were recognized on both sides of the Atlantic, but the lessons of enforcement had been only half-learned. Great Britain had transferred control from the Customs Department to special agents under the Colonial Land and Emigration Commissioners, only to hamper their efficiency from motives of economy. The United States still relied on its customs officials, and the more effective state control was in 1845 found to be unconstitutional. Hence the failure on both sides to cope with the famine rush, but also the ability within a few years to create a reasonably effective system. The prevention of frauds was a more difficult problem. Experience was of little value against dishonest influence and ingenuity, but the evolution of passenger control was slowly removing the worst abuses. The change from the days when tickets were sold by the captain in person or in some corner of a Belfast or Dublin mercantile house, to the extensive offices of Fitzhugh and Grimshaw with their agents and sub-agents scattered up and down the length and breadth of Ireland, is in itself the greatest contribution of emigration to the commercial history of the time.

Control of emigrant traffic passed through three principal stages between 1815 and 1845. In 1815 the local merchant shipper was still dominant, sending back the ship in which he imported his flax-seed with such cargo and customers as he could find. As trade grew, a younger son or nephew devoted himself wholly to the passenger trade, sometimes opening a separate business, and hiring men to tour the inland towns during the season. They were soon forced to compete with a new type of agent, unconnected with the shipping business, who contracted either for a whole ship or for its passenger space. These men, unknown, and often completely unscrupulous, without prestige or attachable property, battened off the ignorance of the emigrants, and except in Ulster absorbed a large part of the trade. They secured by "charter party of affreightment'' many of the timber ships, and were still a power in the emigrant trade in 1845, though losing ground to Liverpool and New York firms. Lloyd's always championed their interests, probably for the sake of the insurance on so extensive a trade.

The future, in 1845, seemed to lie with the Liverpool and New York passenger brokers, especially the former. It has been said that long experience of the slave trade made Liverpool the center for emigration, but I can find no connection between the two. Twenty years elapsed between the abolition of English slaving and the rise of the passenger traffic; and of the slavers operating in 1807, only one, James Gregson, can be definitely identified with emigration.[80] Liverpool brokers had advantages enough without the lessons of the slave trade: an ample and dependable supply of shipping from the cotton and timber trades, frequent and rapid communication with America, whence came a constantly increasing proportion of the monies which financed emigration, cheap steamer communication with every Irish port and thence to their sub-agencies scattered throughout the land, and the ability to combine Irish with English, Scottish, Welsh and sometimes even continental business which was to make Liverpool the outport for all northern Europe. The volume of Liverpool traffic made regulation peculiarly difficult, and its brokers were fully as unscrupulous as their Irish rivals. They flooded Ireland with picturesque and highly misleading handbills, and sometimes shared in Liverpool the profits of questionable boarding houses and transfer agencies. The rapacity of the Liverpool agents passed into song in the popular ballads and chanteys of the day, and the complaint, "They steal your clothes and stores away," was not unjustified. Their

[80] From a list of slave-traders in G. Williams, *History of the Liverpool privateers*, p. 679.

numbers fortunately concentrated attention on their misdeeds and made them in the end more amenable to control than their Irish competitors, while the extensive business of the bigger firms lifted them above the temptation of petty pilfering. In 1845 there are signs that abuses at Liverpool were being checked. Conditions were worse again a few years later, but never so bad as at New York. The American brokers prospered chiefly through their connection with the sources of remittances, conducting their business in Ireland by means of agents and with the familiar types of misrepresentation, but they had no interest in any other sort of fraud.[81] The mulcting of immigrants on arrival was an entirely separate business carried on by their own countrymen and protected by local politicians. It was a thriving trade in 1845, and more remunerative than ever twenty years later.

The creation of powerful interests, honest and dishonest, in the promotion of emigration is the *chef d'oeuvre* of the Irish movement before 1845. Thousands of individuals had come to make their livelihood from the removal of Irish men and women to America, while hundreds of thousands on both sides of the water now considered it natural that the fruit of their toil should be the continuation of that movement. It is generally agreed today that the work of such interests, organizing and developing traffic for their own profit, is the greatest single cause of human migration. The Irish were not responsible for all that followed in the development of emigration, but they established the precedent. Theirs was the first mass movement, and it brought into being the first companies dealing solely in free human trans-

---

[81] For an example of handbill advertising see Abbott, *Historical aspects of the immigration problem*, p. 90. I have tried in vain to locate some early handbills, and I judge from the newspapers that they supplanted newspaper advertising about 1827, or at the rise of cheap emigration.

portation. In 1845 the metamorphosis of the passenger trade still lacked one stage of completion. Its nabobs were extraneous to the shipping interest proper; their business was in ships but not of them. But with the birth of the Cunard Line in 1838 the last stage was in sight. Rapid, regular and cheap steamship travel spelled the doom of the casual emigrant ship, and rendered inevitable the ultimate control of emigration by the shipping companies themselves. This absorption of the passenger trade by one of the four great British industries has been of immense value to emigrants of many nations, but its consequences lie beyond the sphere of our subject. It is enough here to note that the great transoceanic lines learned the value of the emigrant trade from the passenger brokers brought into being by Irish necessity in the years 1815-1845. From that knowledge have grown the leviathans of our own day, drawing together the corners of the earth and peopling four continents with men of European blood.

APPENDIX

STATISTICS OF IRISH EMIGRATION, 1815-1845

I. *Statistics of total migration.*

The statistics of Irish emigration to America after 1815 fall into three main groups: records kept at the Irish and English outports, available from 1825, records of arrivals at Quebec, which begin officially in 1828, and United States immigration statistics, commencing in October 1819.

Each of these groups presents special statistical problems. For the most important—the Irish records—we are dependent on printed materials, the original returns having been deposited in the Four Courts prior to its destruction in 1922. Until 1834 the control of emigration was in the hands of the customs officials, and their returns formed part of the papers of the Irish Commissioners of Customs. After 1834 there were emigration agents, who reported direct to the Emigration Commissioners in London in all the principal ports, except Waterford and Londonderry.[1] In 1838 agents were placed at these ports also. The two types of returns, by customs officers and by emigration agents, are the basis of the printed statistics of emigration by ports which appear in the Parliamentary Papers for every year since 1825. For the years before 1825 only one Irish return exists—a special report of the passengers for 1820.[2] There is also a statement in the Irish Census of 1841 of the number of *registered emigrants* from Ireland, 1821-1830, and an estimate of the probable emigration during those years, which is given as seventy thousand.[3] As the recorded emigration from Irish ports, 1825-30, was over eighty thousand, I discard these census figures as worthless.

---

[1] The first Emigration Commission ceased in 1836; thereafter reports went to the Agent General for Emigration (1837-39), and the Colonial Land and Emigration Commissioners (1840 ff.).

[2] *Parl. Pap.* 1822, No. 425.   [3] *Ibid.*, 1834, No. 504, p. x.

Criticisms of the returns before 1834, and of some after that date, all agree that the official figures are too low. To some extent this was inevitable from the nature of the returns. The customs figures give the number of *whole* passengers; but after 1817 children bound for British America were counted as one-half, one-third, or not at all, according to age. To judge from the Belfast emigration to Quebec in 1819—obviously a dangerously slender basis on which to construct a general estimate—one must add twenty per cent to the official totals on account of these children.[4] Another addition must be made for illegal vessels either failing to clear or presenting incomplete lists of passengers. Some extravagant conclusions have been reached concerning these, such as that of A. C. Buchanan, who calculated that 300,000 Irish had gone to America between 1815 and 1827.[5] I have found little evidence of large illegal traffic except in the years 1818-19, 1828-34, and after 1840; but I cannot quarrel with the Census of 1841, which adds ten per cent for it.[6] The Protestant Colonization Society of Ireland in 1832 estimated that on account of children and illegal trading, the official returns should be increased by twenty-five per cent[7]—a reasonable figure as regards. British American trade, but applicable to the United States only for the years 1823-26, when children going thither were also counted as fractions. For this reason I consider ten per cent a sufficient addition to the official returns of direct traffic from Ireland to the United States, while thirty per cent may be added to the returns to British America. These estimates may be under the true total during rush seasons and over them at other times, but any nearer approach to accuracy is impossible. A slight downward revision

---

[4] The total emigration from Belfast to Quebec, from January to July 5, 1819, was given in the *London Times* of July 20 as 2,579, and distinguished adults and children, counting each as one. The ships which left Belfast for Quebec during this period (as obtained from shipping news in the *Belfast News Letter*) arrived at Quebec with 2,141 whole passengers. (From the lists in the *Quebec Mercury*, which printed the official returns.) The difference is 456, or slightly more than twenty per cent of the official figure.

[5] Buchanan, *Emigration practically considered*, pp. 36-37.

[6] *Parl. Pap.* 1843, No. 504, p. xxviii.

[7] Transactions of the Society, p. 18. The Society's own figures are, however, hopelessly inaccurate and self-contradictory.

might be made for American citizens returning after visits to
their old homes in Ireland, since the Irish returns give the whole
number of passengers without regard to nationality; but this
would not be enough to affect the great bulk of emigration.[8]

The Irish statistics must be supplemented by figures from
Liverpool and other British ports. Statistics for these ports are
not available before 1825, and they are unnecessary before 1827,
when Irish emigration by way of Liverpool assumed some magnitude.[9] Henceforth, the Liverpool route to the United States grew
rapidly in importance. This very growth makes any judgment
concerning it hazardous. The Census authorities of 1841 estimated that two-thirds of the Liverpool emigrants during the past
decade had been Irish,[10] and for the succeeding ten years the estimate was increased to nine-tenths.[11] Though both calculations
seem to me a little high, there is no way of correcting them, and I
have adopted them for the years 1831-40 and 1841-45 respectively. Each will be most nearly correct for the end of the period.[12] A third estimate, made in 1852 without reference to the
Census of 1851, gives only one-half of the Liverpool emigrants as
Irish, adding one-tenth from other English ports and one-
twentieth from Scotland.[13] It is of slight value; for emigration
by way of other English ports, with the exception of a few from
Bristol, was almost unknown. A much higher proportion did sail
from Greenock and Glasgow, but I think they are balanced by

[8] In 1820 the only passengers on several ordinary trading vessels were
American citizens, and even on emigrant ships they sometimes constituted
one-fourth of the passengers.—U.S. Immigration Report, 1820, U.S. Doc.
45, No. 118. This was, however, a year of slack emigration.

[9] There was an extraordinary increase in emigration from Liverpool in
1827. The rapid advance of steam communication with Ireland during the
twenties made the Liverpool route possible; but Liverpool was never much
used as a starting point for British America before 1840.

[10] Parl. Pap. 1843, No. 504, p. xxviii.

[11] Parl. Pap. 1856, No. 2134, p. lv.

[12] The Liverpool route was used almost wholly for the United States, only
a few thousand going to Canada, but since this trade, however small, was
advertised in Ireland, I use the fraction for both destinations.

[13] C. L. Webb, *Suggestions on the present condition of Ireland*, p. 8.

the very large fractions assigned to Liverpool, and make no corrections on that account.[14]

In the following tables, and figures under A and D are the official returns of emigration from Irish ports to British North America and the United States respectively; under B and E are

TABLES OF IRISH EMIGRATION, FROM IRISH SOURCES,
1825-1845

	To British North America			To the United States		
	A	B	C	D	E	F
1825	6,841	8,893	8,893	4,387	4,826	4,826
1826	10,484	13,629	13,629	4,383	4,821	4,821
1827a	9,134	11,874	11,969	4,014	4,415	9,772
1828	6,695	8,703	8,824	2,877	3,165	7,861
1829	7,710	9,923	10,148	4,133	4,546	9,995
1830	19,340	25,142	25,679	2,981	3,279	12,765
1831	40,977	53,270	54,514	3,583	3,941	13,598
1832	37,068	58,188	50,305	4,172	4,589	15,092
1833	17,431	22,660	23,139	4,764	5,240	14,177
1834b	28,586	31,445	32,315	4,213	4,634	16,928
1835	9,458	10,404	10,764	2,684	2,952	13,307
1836c	21,000	22,300		4,000	4,400	

a This being a year of unrestricted emigration, the officials had no incentive to keep accurate accounts. I think the figures given are far below the truth.

b After 1833 only ten per cent is added to the official figures, as the emigration agents' returns presumably counted children as units.

c I have been unable to find an official return for this year. This estimate is based upon a statement of the average emigration, for the three years 1834-36, from the leading Irish ports; in *Parl. Pap.* 1837-38, No. 388, p. 15. As I have no figures for Liverpool, it is impossible to estimate the total emigration.

14 Some such fractional estimate must be the basis of the figures for English, Scottish and Irish emigration from 1815 to 1834, and from 1835 to 1850, in M. G. Mulhall, *Dictionary of statistics*, 4th edition, p. 248. He cites no authority, but refers to G. R. Porter's *Progress of the nation*, in which I failed to find a basis for such figures. He gives 420,000 Irish emigrants between 1815 and 1834; I estimate 383,000 Irish going to America, but not 37,000 to South Africa and Australia during these years. Mulhall's table is reprinted in I. Ferenczi, *International migrations*, I, 99.

	To British North America			To the United States		
	A	B	C	D	E	F
1837	22,463	24,709	26,102	3,871	4,258	22,089
1838	2,284	2,512	2,908	1,196	1,296	8,149
1839	8,989	9,888	10,943	2,943	3,127	20,790
1840	23,935	26,320	28,756	4,087	4,496	25,957
1841	24,089	26,498	30,923	3,893	4,282	36,428
1842	33,410	36,751	42,884	6,199	6,819	49,920
1843	10,898	11,988	14,668	1,617	1,779	23,597
1844	12,396	13,636	17,725	2,993	3,292	37,569
1845	19,947	21,942	26,708	3,708	4,079	50,578

the revised estimates for Ireland, while in Tables C and F the fractions from Liverpool are added to the revised figures to give the total Irish emigration.

The British American statistics present many of the same difficulties as the Irish, and are of little value as a check upon them. The only port possessing an emigration agent was Quebec, to which A. C. Buchanan went in 1828. His reports, which from 1829 distinguish Irish from other arrivals, are a valuable record of the Quebec trade. He does not state whether they give a full count of individuals, but a comparison of his figures with those kept by the Quebec Customs for 1829-30 suggests that he has counted children as units; for his totals are twenty-five to thirty per cent higher.[15] As in Ireland, an addition must be made for illegal trade or unreported cases. In 1831 Buchanan wrote: ''Mr. Fife the tide waiter who boards the ships assured me that in many cases vessels with emigrants from Ireland had no lists whatever, and frequently infants under five years had not been noticed by the vessels in general.''[16] Another practice reported was that of landing a number of the passengers below Quebec, bringing into port only the legal complement. Such references,

[15] The returns are:

	Customs	Buchanan
1829	11,796	15,945
1830	22,305	28,100

For earlier years Buchanan was dependent on official figures and the two returns are approximately the same. Buchanan to Aylmer, May 7, 1831, and Customs to Aylmer, May 2, 1831, C.O. 42/223.

[16] Buchanan to Aylmer, May 7, 1831: C.O. 42/223.

like similar ones in Ireland, are frequent only during rush years, and in fact usually concern the same vessels. For that reason I would add ten per cent to the Quebec statistics as to the Irish. The numbers going to the other ports (for which no figures are available) can only be approximated by subtracting the revised Quebec returns from the revised Irish totals to British America.[17]

TABLES OF EMIGRATION TO BRITISH AMERICA

	G Arrivals at Quebec and Montreal from Ireland; Buchanan's figures	H Revised total adding 10% for illegal entries and fractions of the Liverpool emigration (as in preceding tables)	J Estimated Emigration to the Maritime Provinces obtained by subtracting the figures in Table H from those in C on page 413
1829	9,614	10,575	
1830	17,796	19,476	6,103
1831	34,133	39,053	15,461
1832	28,204	32,502	17,803
1833	12,013	13,581	9,558
1834	19,208	21,836	10,479
1835	7,108	8,078	2,686
1836	12,596	16,335	a
1837	14,538	17,490	8,612
1838	1,456	1,847	1,061
1839	5,113	6,437	4,506
1840	16,291	20,125	8,631
1841	18,317	22,145	8,778
1842	25,532	31,867	10,917
1843	9,728	11,094	3,574b
1844	9,993	16,293c	1,432
1845	14,208	21,138c	5,570

a No estimate possible. See Note c., p. 413.

b Too large. The official total of all British emigrants to the Maritime Provinces in 1843 was 2,718; see I. Ferenczi, *International migrations*, I, 632.

c Estimated. The Liverpool figures for 1844 and 1845 were not reported.

[17] Direct comparison of the official Irish and Quebec figures before 1835 is impossible, as they treat children differently.

The United States reports are likewise useless for purposes of comparison, as they rest on an entirely different basis. They classify passengers by nationality (assumed to be that of nativity) regardless of the ports from which they came. They therefore include as Irish, emigrants coming from Liverpool or St. John, even though the passengers might have settled for some time in England or New Brunswick; while they exclude the British sailing from Irish ports. As a measure of the Irish exodus to the United States they might on that account be superior to the Irish figures, had they been at all carefully kept. It was the duty of the customs officials to keep the records of passengers arriving by sea, and from them Seybert got his analysis of the immigration of 1817.[18] Except for that year no report was made until a yearly summary was required by the Passenger Act of 1819, and beginning with October 1819, annual reports were made by the Secretary of State to Congress, exhibiting quarterly returns of immigration at all ports. From the first there was disagreement over the use of the term "Irish" as a designation; the officials at Charleston always included them as *British*, while others varied their practice, and their totals show "English," "Scotch," "Irish," "Welsh," and "British" all included. As time went on the tendency to group them under "British," unspecified, increased, so that the definitely *Irish* never exceeded ten thousand in any year before 1846. The problem of estimating the Irish proportion of the *British* classification was first studied by the New York Commissioners of Emigration, and their conclusions form the basis of a table of "Irish" by Edward Young, chief of the Bureau of Statistics, in his special report on immigration in 1871[19]—which has been accepted and reprinted without modification in all subsequent statistical works.[20] Yet Young's table of Irish immigration, estimated from the information available at the Bureau of Statistics, while it corrects the insufficient classifi-

[18] A. Seybert, *Statistical annals of the United States*, p. 29.

[19] *U.S. Doc.* 1470, No. 1, pp. xi *et seq.*

[20] The most authoritative compilation on American immigration is *U.S. Doc.* 5878, No. 756; Statistical review of immigration, 1820-1910 (Reports of the Immigration Commission, Vol. III). This table is reprinted in Ferenczi, *International migrations*, I, 380.

cation as accurately as is possible, suffers from two serious defects in the official returns, which he apparently overlooked. From 1822 to 1833 the customs officials were extremely lax in turning in their immigration accounts, and the most important quarterly returns from such ports as New York and Philadelphia are often missing from the annual reports to Congress, making their summaries valueless. Young's table of immigrants from the United Kingdom, the basis of his Irish table, is taken direct from these annual reports. Thus, for 1830 his estimate of 2,721 Irish is based upon a total of 3,874 from the United Kingdom, as given in the annual report to Congress, although in that year there was no report from New York, and no complete returns from any ports except Boston, Baltimore and New Orleans.[21] As a matter of fact, over 14,000 emigrants sailed to the United States from Liverpool alone.[22] Before 1827 the volume of immigration was not enough to throw Young's estimates far out, but from 1827 to 1834 his figures, like the annual reports, are worthless.

The other defect existed only prior to 1825, and was less important. Until that time the totals for nationalities were reached by adding the male and female arrivals from each country, but the sex of children was not stated. Thus in the return for 1824, Passamaquoddy district, we have: Irish; Male, 223; Female, 66; Total 289; no other nationality mentioned. Total immigration, 373. The other eighty-four were in fact the children of the 289, and should have been included in the Irish total. As these unspecified as to sex (and therefore as to nationality) amounted in some years to one-fourth of the whole immigration, they materially affect the results.[23]

21 *U.S. Doc.* 209, No. 127. The annual reports prior to 1833 run from Oct. 1 to Sept. 30, but the slack immigration of the last three months of the year makes it possible to speak of these reports as of single years, and to compare their figures with the British, which commence on January 4.

22 *Parl. Pap.* 1833, No. 696, p. 4.

23 A table of Irish immigration and of unspecified British from the official figures, as given in W. J. Bromwell, *History of immigration to the United States.* I have checked Bromwell's figures, which are taken direct from the annual reports, and they are accurate. Their only value is in showing the relative proportion of men and women in a section of the adult immigrants. The tables themselves are scarcely worth reproducing, but a

Inadequate or careless entries might call for a further increase. J. Chickering, the first American student of immigration, found that the New York health officers' returns for 1846-47 were eleven per cent above the customs figures, and he proposed to increase the official entries by fifty per cent.[24] Though his argument for the change was unsound, one may reasonably suppose the officials to have missed many passengers. However, it is not worth while attempting to make corrections in an estimate admittedly indefinite.

TABLE K

IRISH IMMIGRATION TO THE UNITED STATES

Young's Estimate

Year ending		*Year of*	
Sept. 30, 1820	3,614	1833	8,648
1821	1,518	1834	24,474
1822	2,267	1835	20,927
1823	1,908	1836	30,578
1824	2,345	1837	28,508
1825	4,888	1838	12,645a
1826	5,408	1839	23,963
1827	9,766	1840	39,430b
1828	12,488	1841	37,772
1829	7,415	1842	51,342
1830	2,721	1843	19,670
1831	5,772	1844	33,490
15 mo. to Dec. 31, 1832	12,436	1845	44,821

a This is too high. Emigration came almost to a standstill. See the British figures.

b Young's table gives 29,430, but this is a misprint, corrected in all later tabulations.

I give Young's table, for purposes of comparison with Table F, though with little faith in its value before 1834. It will be noticed that in most of the later years his figures are considerably above the others, as they should be; for his include Irish coming by way of New Brunswick, whereas the others do not—such emi-

comparison of them with Young's estimates has helped me to understand the basis of Young's revision.

[24] *Immigration into the United States*, pp. 3-4.

grants appearing as passengers to British America under Table
C.

The three sets of statistics, while they leave much to be desired
in the way of accuracy, give a fair view of the development of
emigration after 1825. Although the British statistics include all
passengers, and those of the United States all alien passengers,
no serious deduction need be made on that account. The proportion of travellers, merchants and other temporary visitors to
America, even among the cabin passengers, was too small to merit
consideration;[25] and few indeed were the bona fide settlers—at
least prior to 1842—who returned to the old country.[26] In this
respect the figures for the period 1815-1845 more truly represent
net immigration than do those for the later years of the century.
But for the years before 1825 we are less fortunate. In order to
form some judgment of the movement in the ten years preceding,
it is necessary to resort to many scattered sources of information.
Government publications supply figures for the total emigration
from the United Kingdom to the United States and to British
North America. Full tables of emigration, based upon customs
returns, were first published in the Colonization Circular of the
Colonial Land and Emigration Commissioners for 1853;[27] and
these tables have been accepted as the standard British figures
ever since.[28] Unfortunately, they differ materially so far as British America is concerned, from a Parliamentary return (also
from the Customs) made in 1830.[29] Furthermore, I have found
no evidence among the Commissioners' papers of the method of
compiling these figures, and the Customs Department denies all
knowledge of them. Under the circumstances, they merit only a

[25] Ferenczi, *International migrations*, I, 622.

[26] See T. W. Page, *Some economic aspects of immigration before 1870;*
in Journal of Political Economy, XXI, 54.

[27] Tables, commencing with 1825, had been published much earlier. This
was the first paper to contain the earlier years.

[28] They are printed in Table I of Johnson's statistical tables relating to
emigration, *Emigration from the United Kingdom to North America*, p.
344; and in Ferenczi, *International migrations*, I, 627-629.

[29] *Parl. Pap.* 1830, No. 650: *Return of the Number of Persons who have
Emigrated from the United Kingdom to any of the Colonies of Great Britain
etc.* (1821-29). The two tables agree perfectly from 1825, but not before.

qualified trust, and in any case are subject to the same additions for children and illegal sailings as the later statistics.

There are no Irish returns (except that for 1820 already mentioned), no estimates even, of the percentage of Irish, and the figures are useful mainly in suggesting a maximum of possible Irish emigration.

The only figures from Ireland are those of Belfast. Newspaper reports, drawn from official returns, give its total emigration for 1816-1818, and through the main season of 1819. The first report distinguishes individuals and families, but not destinations, for 1816-1818.[30] The last two give detailed information of destination,[31] and the last one distinguishes adults and children as well. These accounts have already been used in Chapters II and III, and I add here only the summaries:

TABLE L

EMIGRATION FROM BELFAST, 1816-1819

	Total	Quebec	Maritime Provinces	United States
1816	2,143	....	....	....
1817	2,811	....	....	....
1818	6,165	2,268	2,250	1,647
To July 5, 1819	5,881	2,597	2,833	451

The only other port for which there is definite information is Quebec. In 1831 the Colonial Office tried to collect information on emigration from all the British American possessions. A. C. Buchanan at Quebec was able to secure from the Harbor Master's register statistics of passengers arriving, from 1816.[32] Lord Aylmer, then Governor of Lower Canada, also examined the registers, and found Buchanan's returns "substantially correct."[33] These returns had been known in England earlier, for in 1826 Wilmot Horton gave to the Committee on Emigration figures for

[30] *Belfast News Letter*, Feb. 23, 1819.

[31] *Limerick General Advertiser*, Jan. 8, 1819 (for 1818). *London Times*, July 20, 1819 (for 1819).

[32] C.O. 42/223; Buchanan to Aylmer, May 7, 1831.

[33] C.O. 42/223; Aylmer to Goderich, May 18, 1831.

APPENDIX 421

1817-1823 practically the same as Buchanan's. Furthermore, Horton estimated that three-fifths of the emigrants were Irish.[34] Partly to check this estimate, I have examined the shipping arrivals in the *Quebec Mercury* for 1815-1824, which include the number of passengers arriving by each vessel. As the numbers, in every case open to comparison, coincide with the official number sailing from Ireland, they must also be official, and require the usual additions. The *Mercury* sometimes omitted shipping re-

TABLE M

IMMIGRATION TO QUEBEC, 1815-1824

	Buchanan's figures, 1831	Irish Horton's Estimate	Irish Quebec Mercury
1815		3,300a	25
1816	1,250	3,300	238
1817	6,796	4,186	2,218
1818	8,400b	4,933	4,599
1819	12,809	7,744	5,971
1820	11,239	6,743	5,580
1821	8,050c	4,834	4,041
1822	10,468	6,282	8,374
1823	10,258	6,155	8,413
1824	6,515	3,909	5,168

a Horton's estimate of 5,500 emigrants each year for 1815 and 1816 was obviously founded on ignorance.

b This figure is too low. On Sept. 9, the *Quebec Mercury* noted 8,422 arrivals to date; there were at least 119 after that. In all other years the *Mercury* and the official returns are in substantial agreement.

c On Oct. 30, the *Mercury* had "9591 arrivals to date"; on Nov. 23, it gave 8,050 for the year; on Nov. 22, 1822, it referred again to the 1821 immigration, putting it at 9,159, possibly a mistake for 9,591. I rather favor this last figure.

ports, and its summaries are not complete, but it soon improved in this respect, and the reports for 1818 and 1819 are nearly perfect. A comparison of the *Mercury's* reports with Horton's figures shows that he, like many others, overestimated the early Irish emigration, being ignorant of the strength of the Scottish movement.

[34] *Parl. Pap.* 1826, No. 404, p. 324.

The Nova Scotian Customs officials were also able to report figures for arrivals, distinguishing Irish and Scottish from 1810, but the number of Irish is too small to be worth recording.[35] St. Andrews sent in a beautifully complete return, by vessels, of passengers arriving in 1823-30; but before 1823 it was an outport of St. John, and had no records of its own.[36] The St. John report is the one essential, and there is none at all reliable before 1823. In many earlier cases no notice was taken of passengers, and the records were destroyed before 1831. There remain the return of the visiting physician for 1819-30, and an official return of arrivals at the outbays for the same years. The doctor's figures, which count children as one, should always exceed those of the officials, yet in three years they are less. The St. John records are evidently highly untrustworthy, and I am inclined to think they are much too low.[37]

TABLE N

EMIGRATION TO NEW BRUNSWICK, 1819-1824

	Arrivals at St. John Dr. Boyd's return	Arrivals at outbays	St. Andrews	Total
1819	2,380	264a	....	2,644
1820	2,592	433	....	3,025
1821	1,985	82	....	2,067
1822	4,684	542	....	5,226
1823	3,224	442	1,095	4,761
1824	1,175	599	275	1,049

a If these include St. Andrews, as they should before 1823, they are absurdly low. Belfast alone sent over 2,500 emigrants to St. Andrews in 1819.

The deficiencies in the United States statistics having already been pointed out, we are faced with the necessity of arriving at an estimate of Irish emigration from other sources. For this pur-

[35] C.O. 217/152. Report of T. N. Jeffery, Collector of Customs, in Sir P. Maitland to Goderich, May 11, 1831.

[36] C.O. 188/41. Customs, St. Andrews to W. F. Odell, May 18, 1831.

[37] C.O. 188/41. Customs, St. John, to W. F. Odell. Miss Cowan (*British emigration to British North America*, p. 117) has compiled from these various returns a total of 65,704 emigrants for six of the years 1815-25. My own computation makes the number somewhat larger exclusive of these omissions in the St. John return and other deficiencies.

pose I have made a close examination of shipping records from the Irish newspapers. The entries at Belfast and Waterford are practically perfect, at Londonderry and Limerick nearly so, but at Dublin they are defective after 1817.[38] Table O shows the amount of shipping from these ports to America in each year, 1815-1819.

TABLE O

TABLE OF SHIPPING, IRELAND TO AMERICA, 1815-1819

Number of Ships from Irish Emigrant Ports to the United States and British North America[a]

	1815	1816	1817	1818	1819
Londonderry to					
New York	6	21	3	5	3
Philadelphia	..	7	3	4	3
Baltimore	..	1	..	1	..
U.S. total	6	29	6	10	6
Quebec	..	..	..	1	3
Nova Scotia	..	1	3	3	..
New Brunswick	..	..	7	19	25
B. N. A. total	..	1	10	23	28
Belfast to					
New York	9	28	13	14	8
Philadelphia	1	9	6	11	4
Baltimore	..	6	7	7	7
Norfolk	..	1	4	..	..
Charleston	2	6	7	5	8
New Orleans	2	..	3	2	4
Boston	..	..	..	1	..
U.S. total	14	50	40	40	31

[a] From the *Londonderry Journal, Belfast News Letter, Dublin Evening Post, Saunders News Letter, Dublin Correspondent, Waterford Chronicle,* and *Limerick General Advertiser.*

[38] The Dublin shipping news from 1816 is from the *Correspondent,* for 1817 from *Saunders News Letter.* After 1817 the paper only gave a list of outvoices and invoices, so there is no check on those sailing in ballast. Fortunately, emigrant advertisements became much more common in 1818.

TABLE O (Continued)

	1815	*1816*	*1817*	*1818*	*1819*
Quebec	2	4	10	13	18
Nova Scotia	1	1	1	3	2
New Brunswick	1	1	5	17	20
B. N. A. total	4	6	16	33	40
Dublin to					
New York	15	19	22	18	8
Philadelphia	..	2	5	4	2
Baltimore	..	..	2	..	1
Norfolk	..	..	..	..	1
Charleston	..	..	..	1	1
New Orleans	..	..	1	1	1
Boston	..	3	4	4	3
Portland	..	..	1	..	..
U.S. total	15	24	35	28	17
Quebec	..	4	8	18	17
Nova Scotia	..	..	6	5	..
New Brunswick	..	1	5	3	9
B. N. A. total	..	5	19	26	26
Waterford to					
New York	..	2	1	b	..
Philadelphia	b	..	1	..	..
Baltimore	..	..	..	..	1
Charleston	..	..	1	..	1
Boston	..	1	..	..	3
U.S. total	..	3	3	..	5
Quebec	..	2	3	..	12
Nova Scotia	..	2	3	..	5
New Brunswick	..	2	3	..	8
B. N. A. total	..	6	9	..	25
Limerick to					
New York	..	2	1	1	3
Quebec	..	..	4	..	2
Nova Scotia	..	1	3	2	5
New Brunswick	..	1	..	4	1
B. N. A. total	..	2	7	6	11

b Files of the *Waterford Chronicle* for these years are lacking.

TABLE O (Continued)

	1815	1816	1817	1818	1819
Total to					
New York	30	72	40	38	22
Philadelphia	1	18	15	19	9
Baltimore	..	7	9	8	9
Norfolk	..	1	4	..	1
Charleston	2	6	8	6	10
New Orleans	2	..	4	3	5
Boston	..	4	4	5	6
Portland	..	..	1	..	..
U.S. total	35	108	85	79	62
Quebec	2	10	25	32	52
Nova Scotia	1	7	16	13	12
New Brunswick	1	3	20	43	63
	4	20	61	88	127

The average size of vessels from the Ulster ports was about 250 tons in 1818, and about 200 tons from the South.[39] Outside the emigrant season, tonnage is no indication of the number of passengers; but during the season, from 1816 to 1818, voyages without a full legal complement were extremely rare. The point is important; for it gives us the chief basis for estimating total emigration, and I have verified it from over a hundred cases; in the ship news of the Belfast, Dublin, and Waterford papers, where the numbers of passengers were sometimes noted; in the notices of arrivals in *Niles' Weekly Register;* and above all in the entries of vessels in the British Consular returns from American ports.[40] The tonnage of every incoming British vessel is there entered; the number of passengers was only occasionally mentioned before 1818, but in that year a new form required it. Had we similar reports of American ships, there would be no need of estimating totals. As it is, the entries are our best guide. They show for 1817-18 a normal passenger list of thirty to fifty (exclusive of

[39] From tonnages in Consular Reports, B.T. 6/23-27; and a list of the vessels registered at Belfast, *Belfast News Letter*, July 10, 1827. A general average of tonnages between Irish ports and America agrees with this. *Parl. Pap.* 1822, No. 523.

[40] B.T. 6/23-26.

illegal vessels); whereas in the unrestricted year of 1816 the average from Dublin was forty to fifty,[41] from Waterford and Limerick sixty, from Belfast eighty-five, and from Londonderry and Newry over one hundred.[42] The small number of ships from each port, and the relatively high margin of error in such a system of averages, make it unwise to apply them to arrive at estimates of emigration from the ports, though they do help to substantiate the accepted statement of the time that the four leading ones were Belfast, Dublin, Londonderry and Newry. When applied to all Ireland, however, with its hundred ships a year to the United States, and another hundred to British America, the estimate according to legal capacity no longer seems an unsafe guide. It is, therefore, by allowing to every ship sailing during the emigrant season its full quota of passengers, and adding for out of season emigration according to the demand shown in the advertisements, that the following rough table of Irish emigration in 1815-1818 is devised:

TABLE P
IRISH EMIGRATION TO NORTH AMERICA, 1815-1818

	United States	British North America[a]
1815[b]	1,000	Negligible
1816	6,000	500
1817[c]	2,500	5,000
1818[c]	6,500	13,500

[a] The numbers for Newfoundland are not included. After 1815 they are negligible.

[b] The basis is useless for this year, when ships even in season, made little bid for the passenger trade.

[c] Considerable addition necessary for late season sailings. Seybert's table of arrivals in 1817 (*Statistical annals of the United States*, p. 29) shows 11,977 from the United Kingdom. My estimate, adding 2,800 from New Brunswick to the 2,500 direct to the United States, would be 5,300 Irish, or less than half the British total. This is not unreasonable, as there was a very large movement from England and Scotland.

[41] Dublin was a bad harbor. Also, a large number of packet sailings out of season keep down its average.

[42] These ports have few besides seasonal emigrant vessels.

It is not worth while carrying on estimates, necessarily very rough, into succeeding years, when emigration was less than in 1818, and on the whole, unimportant. The chief value of the above table is to show how in a few years emigration to the United States became, so far as shipping was concerned, emigration to North America.

II. *Statistics of age, sex, and occupation.*

The recent publication[43] in convenient form of all the available statistical information concerning the character of British and Irish migration to America renders unnecessary the reproduction of such material here, but requires a word of caution as to its use. In general, the information available as to Ireland refers to such a small fraction of the total Irish movement, or is so confused with that for the whole United Kingdom, that no safe deductions may be drawn from it. Thus the British American returns beginning in 1843 which indicate the age (over or under 14 years of age), and sex of immigrants, give only the annual totals from the United Kingdom;[44] it is probable that the Irish would show a higher proportion of women. For the United States, age[45] (under 15, 15-40, and over 40) and occupation,[46] statistics exist only for the whole body of immigrants, among whom Irish are wholly indistinguishable. Sex differentiation by nationalities does appear from the beginning,[47] but the fact that this differentiation exists only in the original returns, where the vast majority of Irish men and women are concealed under the heading "British, unspecified," vitiates much of its value. The definitely "Irish" figures are too small to yield more than an uncertain indication of sex proportions, and the "unspecified"

43 In I. Ferenczi, *International migrations*, I, Statistics.

44 *Op. cit.*, p. 633; from Colonial Land and Emigration Commissioners, *Colonial Circular*, No. 34.

45 *Op. cit.*, p. 397, from U.S. Bureau of Statistics, Arrivals of Alien Passengers and Immigrants, 1820-1892, p. 51.

46 *Op. cit.*, p. 399; from *ibid.*, pp. 59-62. Ferenczi gives only the main headings.

47 *Op. cit.*, pp. 401-412; from W. J. Bromwell, *History of immigration to the United States.*

include too many English, Welsh, and Scottish artisans and farmers to be a safe guide. The one exception to this rule is the return of 1820,[48] which prints in full the age, sex, and occupation of each immigrant; but this is for a year of minor importance in the history of immigration. Such inferences as may be drawn from these unsatisfactory sources have been included in the text of this work; they have no place in a purely statistical analysis.

[48] *U.S. Doc.* 45, No. 118.

BIBLIOGRAPHICAL NOTE

The sources for this study of social evolution in three lands are necessarily widely scattered, the most important single collection lying neither in Ireland nor in North America, but in London. The records of the British government, published and unpublished, contain a wealth of material on free emigration, on the movement to the United States as well as on imperial migration. Emigration fell within the province of the Colonial Office, and after 1831 was handled by a special commission, whose papers are grouped under C.O. 384: *Emigration.* Earlier papers, commencing in 1816, are found in this file, but the official reports and most of the correspondence begin in 1831. They deal primarily with plans of colonization. The more important papers after 1831 have been printed in the Parliamentary Papers. Of greater value for unassisted emigration is C.O. 42: *Original correspondence of the Secretary of State, Canada,* containing most information for the period up to 1830, and of constantly increasing importance for the character and effects of the movement. It should be supplemented, for 1830-31, by C.O. 387: *Aylmer Papers,* Aylmer being Governor-General at the time of the first great Irish influx. The corresponding series for New Brunswick, C.O. 188, and for Nova Scotia, C.O. 217, contain little of interest on the Irish.

The other field of governmental interest in emigration lay principally in the carrying trade, and caused considerable correspondence with the United States government and with consular offices in America. This is scattered through F.O. 5: *America,* which also gives incidental information on the results of emigration. Detailed statistics of British trade to the United States, including full accounts of passengers arriving in British vessels, were transmitted from the Foreign Office to the Board of Trade, and appear in B.T. 6: *Consular Returns, America.* These cover the years up to 1821 only; thereafter the returns will be found in F.O. 5. Some additional glimpses of Irish trade have been gathered from Customs 1: *Minute Books of the Irish Commissioners of Customs,* but they are useless for emigration, although the Commissioners had supervision of the Passenger Acts. The above are all in the Public Record Office, Chancery Lane. A better source for the detailed study of Irish trade, including the operation of the passenger traffic, is the *Letter Books of the Irish Port Collectors,* in the London Custom House. Unfortunately only Newry, Limerick and other minor ports are there represented for the period before 1845.

Of the above sources, only selections from the Colonial Office papers have been printed by command, but for Irish materials we are dependent almost wholly on the Parliamentary Papers. The destruction of the Dublin Custom House and of the Four Courts in 1922 left only the Castle Library with any large collection of records, and these are of little value for the study of emigration. Happily, parliamentary inquiries into Irish affairs between 1815 and 1845 were frequent and sometimes thorough, and the printed reports of the committees of 1819, 1823, 1825, 1830, 1833, and 1843 on Irish conditions, are economic documents of the first importance, as are the reports of Horton's emigration committees in 1826-27, and of Drummond's railway commissioners in 1837-38. Despite the inaccuracy of all Irish governmental statistics prior to 1835, they form the principal source of information as to causes and conditions of emigration, as well as for the bases of government policy. The latter also requires frequent reference to Hansard, which reproduces the common errors of statesmen in their speeches, and on such minor subjects as emigration adds some errors of its own, giving shorter and less accurate reports than the newspapers.

Probably the most valuable single source used in this study, and the most illuminating picture of Irish conditions in the period before the famine, is the Ordnance Survey of Ireland, compiled under the supervision of Jeremiah O'Donovan for the Irish government between 1833 and 1840. The survey was abandoned, except in its technical and military aspects, after only two counties, Antrim and Londonderry, had been completed, but there are returns from scattered parishes in other counties. The whole comprises fifty boxes of manuscript now in the Royal Irish Academy, Dublin, and describes every phase of social and economic life, with detailed information on emigration. Some additional material of the same character has been gleaned from the papers of Charles O'Conor, librarian at Stowe, the Irish antiquarian and religious controversialist who wrote under the name of Columbanus. These papers include letters, a brief MS. history of his own time, and some accounts of the Irish estates of the Duke of Buckingham. They are in the Huntington Library at San Marino, California.

American records are less important, though occasional items of interest are scattered through them. Canadian official interest in immigration was considerably greater than that of the United States; its results have already been described in the Colonial Office papers. Census figures begin to be useful only at the end of the period. The Irish census of 1841 and the Canadian censuses of 1842 and 1844 are all printed in the Parliamentary Papers. The United States census of 1850 is the only one of importance to this work. The annual reports of the Secretary of the Treasury, giving quarterly summaries of immigration, commence in 1820, but except for the first year they are inaccurate and incomplete. State documents of New York and Massachusetts dealing with population and immigration appear to be of interest largely for the period after 1845; no attempt has been made to search them in detail.

Newspapers are of special importance for the years before 1825, when other sources are scanty. Of those used, the London *Times* and *Morning Herald* throw some light on government policy, but give no reliable news on emigration; *Niles' Weekly Register* is useful for American opinion. Irish papers valuable for their discussions of emigration are the *Belfast News Letter* (Tory), Dublin *Evening Post* (Irish), and *Londonderry Journal* (Tory, later Whig). The Belfast and Londonderry papers have excellent and reliable shipping news, and the same is true of *Ramsay's Waterford Chronicle* and the *Quebec Mercury*. All these papers, and others listed below, published frequent advertisements to emigrants, which are more illuminating than their

432   IRELAND AND IRISH EMIGRATION

news. As files of the Irish papers are rare, I give the location and the years covered. Unless otherwise mentioned they are in the British Museum repository at Hendon:

Belfast News Letter, 1815-1832. (In Linen Hall Library, Belfast.)

Cork: Southern Reporter, 1823-1827. (Earlier years in Library of Trinity College, Dublin.)

Dublin: The Correspondent, 1816, 1817. (Of slight value.)
Evening Post, 1815-1825.
Saunders News Letter, 1815, 1817-1819.

Limerick General Advertiser, 1815-1824.

Londonderry Journal, 1815-1825, 1828-1836. (In Library of Macrae-Magee College, Londonderry.)

Newry Examiner, 1830, 1831.

Ramsay's Waterford Chronicle, 1816, 1817, 1819-1823.

Other contemporary materials are of uneven value. The controversial literature on Ireland is enormous, the Halliday Bequest alone yielding thousands of pamphlets on the period between 1815 and 1845. They deal primarily with political and religious affairs, but throw considerable light on emigration. They are arranged chronologically in boxes at the Royal Irish Academy, Dublin, and an index is now being made. Of the many more pretentious accounts of Ireland during this period, the following have either proven most helpful or deserve special mention for other reasons: W. S. Mason, Statistical account or parochial survey of Ireland, 3 vols., 1814-19, the first attempt at an exact account of Irish conditions, never completed; S. Lewis, Topographical dictionary of Ireland, 2 Vols. and an atlas, 1837, an invaluable compendium, but often out of date, as based largely on county surveys made between 1800 and 1832; Digest of Evidence taken before Her Majesty's Commissioners of Inquiry into the state of the law and practice in respect to the occupation of land in Ireland, 2 Vols., 1847, practically a government document, edited by J. P. Kennedy, secretary of the commission, not without some bias in the selection of material, but excellent for its summaries. It needs checking against the full evidence and reports in the Parliamentary Papers.

The above are primarily statistical; the most important general accounts are: E. Wakefield, *An account of Ireland, statistical and political,* 2 Vols., 1812, the starting point for every study of Irish economy in the next period; W. Graydon, *Reflections on the state of Ireland in the nineteenth century,* 1825; J. E. Bicheno, *Ireland and its economy,* 1830, by an English economist and later poor-law commissioner, an expert on land and agriculture, but prone to snap judgments on other phases of Irish life; H. D. Inglis, *Journey throughout Ireland in 1834,* 2 Vols., 1834, in which the author seeks and gives answers to the questions propounded by the Poor Inquiry Commissioners, the best book since Wakefield's; G. C. Lewis, *On local disturbances in Ireland,* 1836, a penetrating analysis by the future Whig statesman, then just making his reputation; G. Beaumont, *L'Irlande,* 2 Vols., 1839, a much cited authority by the French traveller, who was assisted by Drummond and O'Connell, and biassed on the relation of classes (Beaumont came to Ireland to find proof of certain preconceptions—see O'Brien, *Thomas Drummond*); S. Nicholson, *Report on the general state of agriculture in the district of country adjoining the middle Shannon,* 1841; J. G. Kohl, *Ireland,* 1843, a judicious answer to Beaumont by an experienced German traveller, the last good authority on pre-famine Ireland; R. M. Martin, *Ireland before and after the Union with Great Britain,* 1843, a defense of British policy by a wholly unfair collection of statistics—a man of straw to be knocked down by every Irish propagandist. Four later authorities are of such importance as to deserve inclusion here: J. Pim, *Conditions and prospects of Ireland,* 1848, by a Quaker banker of first-rate knowledge and judgment; W. S. Crawford, *Depopulation not necessary,* 1849, an anti-emigration tract by the most influential Irish M.P. during the Peel ministry; W. N. Hancock, various works between 1848 and 1866, a Dublin professor with access to official sources, working partly for propaganda, but critically, for Thomas Larcom, the first great Irish statistician; and William Temple, first Marquis of Dufferin and Ava, *Irish emigration and the tenure of land in Ireland,* 1867, an able defense of his class by the imperial statesman and excellent Irish landlord.

The quantity of similar materials, other than travel books, for America is considerably less. Statistical works from the publication of Seybert's *Annals* to the census of 1850 are very unsatisfactory. Most of the pamphlets are political or religious in character, and shed little light on immigration. Even the controversy over immigration in the thirties does little more than illumine American public opinion. For less passionate appraisals one must turn to the European travellers who set themselves, especially after 1830, to depict American life in all its phases. As the description and quality of these works is now well known, it is enough to note here that the more famous accounts of Basil Hall, Harriet Martineau, Mrs. Trollope, and Captain Marryat are almost valueless for this work, which has profited most from the publications of the forties, when the Irish had achieved a recognized place in American life. The best of these are: F. Grund, *The Americans,* by a German traveller, which is in part an answer to Francis Lieber; J. S. Buckingham, *America;* and T. C. Grattan, *Civilized America,* by the British consul at Boston, the only important contribution by an Irishman. All of these include Canada as well as the United States, but the sections dealing with the British possessions are less satisfactory. Two other books deserve comment for their sapient comments and the high reputations of their authors: Michel Chevalier's *Lettres sur l'Amerique du Nord,* 1836, and Charles Lyell's *Travels in North America,* 1845.

There are few works dealing specifically with Irish success in America. The dozens of guides to emigrants published in England and Scotland after 1815 had not many counterparts in Ireland. The two most useful have been the anonymous *Emigrants Guide,* Westport, 1832, with seventy pages of letters from America, and P. B. O'Kelly, *Advice and guide to emigrants going to the United States of America,* 1834.

Not until after the famine did special studies of the Irish in America begin to appear, and all of them were colored with the feelings inspired by that catastrophe. The earlier ones are source material for the preceding years. These are J. H. Tuke, *A visit to Connaught in the Autumn of 1847,* which includes valuable observations on the Irish in the United States, from which the author had just returned; T. Mooney, *Nine years in America,* 1850, by an emigrant agent, and warped accordingly; and T. D. McGee, *History of the Irish settlers in North America,* 1852, a panegyric on the Irish race and the Catholic church, but containing useful information, by a violent Anglophobe who later became a builder of Canada and patriotic British subject. Among later contributions to this theme the most noteworthy are J. F. Maguire, *The Irish in America,* 1868, still the fullest and most valuable compilation, but ill-organized and repetitious, by an Irish M.P.; N. F. Davin, *The Irishman in Canada,* 1877, also diffuse but less encomiastic than the others; and E. Roberts, *Ireland in America,* 1931, a journalist's estimate of Irish contributions to the United States, seeking with some degree of success to be scrupulously fair, but too slight and, for the period before 1845, too little informed to give weight to its conclusions. A similar but less judicious effort is H. J. Ford, *The Scotch Irish in America,* 1915, a patriotic sketch devoted primarily to the colonial period of United States history.

A survey of more scientific historical studies touching upon the effects of Irish migration in America discloses one of the gaps which it is hoped this study will help to fill. The best general history of the period 1815-1845 in its social and economic aspects is still that of J. B. MacMaster, who gave to the subject more interest than Channing and more space than Beard. The same interest, with the results of more recent scholarship, appears in J. T. Adams, *New England in the Republic* and in the *Commonwealth History of Massachusetts,* but outside New England these phases of Irish influence must be unearthed from among the genealogical accumulations of local histories. Of the more specialized studies, it may be said that the standard histories of American immigration pay scant attention to the years before 1870, relying for that period on J. Chickering, *Immigration into the United States,* 1848, a pioneer effort, inaccurate, but suggestive; on W. J. Bromwell, *History of immigration to the United States,* 1856; and on the more careful studies of Friedrich Kapp covering the years after the famine. Economic and industrial histories seem almost unconscious of the existence of laborers or their place in economic life, excepting such recent studies as A. C. Cole's *American wool manufacture*. Even the great works on labor of J. R. Commons and others neglect the immigrant influence. It is only in religious and political fields that the results of Irish migration are adequately discussed. J. G. Shea's *History of the Catholic Church in the United States* necessarily deals extensively with the Irish, and the same is true of G. Shaughnessy, *Has the immigrant kept the faith?* Presbyterian histories are less satisfactory; they deal more with schisms and growth, and do not distinguish the Irish. In the field of politics, the works of Darling, Fox, Scisco, Mueller, Olbrich and Bartlett referred to in the last chapter, cover the activities of the Irish in their three major settlements.

The same limitations apply to the history of the Irish in Canada. Canadian political history has been or is being written, but the detailed results of immigration of any one people appear only fragmentarily in reviews and transactions of local societies. Fortunately, the fashion for studying colonial policy has drawn students into the wider ramifications of the emigration movement. Thus S. C. Johnson's *History of emigration from the United Kingdom to North America, 1763-1912*, which is merely an outline of the subject drawn from official sources, gives a most useful bibliography for further study. H. J. Cowan, *British emigration to British North America, 1783-1837*, is a much more thorough piece of work, based largely on government documents and emigration tracts, and concerned primarily with official policy, but throwing some light on free emigration. W. A. Carrothers, *Emigration from the British Isles*, is a useful short study with a broader basis of judgment than the preceding, but it adds no new material for this study.

Other works dealing with government and indirectly with emigration are increasing; the most valuable being the articles of P. Knapland on Sir James Stephen, and F. Hitchins, *The Colonial Land and Emigration Commissioners*, which appeared as this work was being completed. The propagandist works of A. C. Buchanan, R. W. Horton and the Wakefield group are of course sources for government policy rather than accurate descriptions, and the books about these men partake of the same controversial flavor. Sir Charles Lucas' edition of the Durham Report is a notable exception. Special studies on colonial affairs have generally failed in correlating emigration policy with the broader interests of the time, for which the standard biographies and printed papers of British statesmen have been most helpful. At best, however, these leave serious gaps in tracing the formation of policy, which may never be filled. No final history of the period before 1827 can be written until the colonial papers of Lord Bathurst at Cirencester, as yet untouched, have been examined.

Emigration trade policy, as a phase of British mercantilism, has received no attention, but its setting can be better appreciated after a study of such standard histories as Cunningham's *Growth of English industry and commerce;* A. E. Murray, *History of the commercial and financial relations between England and Ireland from the period of the Restoration;* and D. G. Barnes, *History of the English Corn Laws.* Diplomatic histories also throw some light on the commercial conflict of England and the United States, the most profitable for this study being H. W. V. Temperley, *Foreign policy of Canning.* The trade itself, with all its interests, still lacks a historian. It is passed over in maritime and commercial chronicles, but invaluable material is preserved in Porter's *Progress of the nation* (1837 edition for all years preceding 1835). F. Morehouse, *The Irish migration of the forties,* in the American Historical Review, XXXIII, contributes a lively picture of estate migration.

Irish studies illustrating the causes and development of emigration suffer more than any others from partisan bias. For general political background Lecky's *History of Ireland in the 18th century,* Vol. V, still remains a masterpiece from the Anglo-Irish point of view. S. Gwynn, *History of Ireland,* gives the patriotic side as well as any. J. O'Connor, *History of Ireland, 1798-1924,* is the best recent history, giving more attention to economic affairs, from the standpoint of a Catholic landlord. The inescapable starting point for any economic study is G. O'Brien, *Economic history of Ireland from the Union to the famine,* a piece of protectionist propaganda containing a mass of information drawn uncritically from controversial sources, but providing an invaluable key to the materials of Irish economic development. In perspective and judgment it is exceeded by D. A. Chart, *Ireland from the Union to Catholic Emancipation,* a brief but comprehensive study. Four special studies display the wealth, while their number exposes the poverty, of Irish economic scholarship: A. Marmion, *Ancient and modern history of the maritime ports of Ireland,* 4th edition, 1860, containing a quantity of useful information, wholly undigested; M. Dillon, *History and development of banking in Ireland,* 1889, a sound treatise; A. Redford, *Labour migration in England, 1800-50,* 1926, which deals with the habits of Irish laborers; and C. Gill, *Rise of the Irish linen industry,* an admirable and scientific analysis of that great industry. There is also an excellent chapter on Ireland in G. T. Griffith, *Population problems of the age of Malthus.*

INDEX

444   IRELAND AND IRISH EMIGRATION

Wexford, 120.

Whately, Richard, 311, 313, 317.

Whitworth, Lord, 249.

Wilmot, *see* Horton.

Woolen industry, 57, 136.

Wynn, C. W., 244, 275.

Young, Arthur, 39.